18436

THE SELECTED WRITINGS OF
WILLIAM LYON MACKENZIE

UPPER

CANADA

THE SEAL OF UPPER CANADA

PARLIAMENT BUILDINGS, FRONT STREET, YORK, AS THEY APPEARED WHEN FIRST ERECTED IN 1832

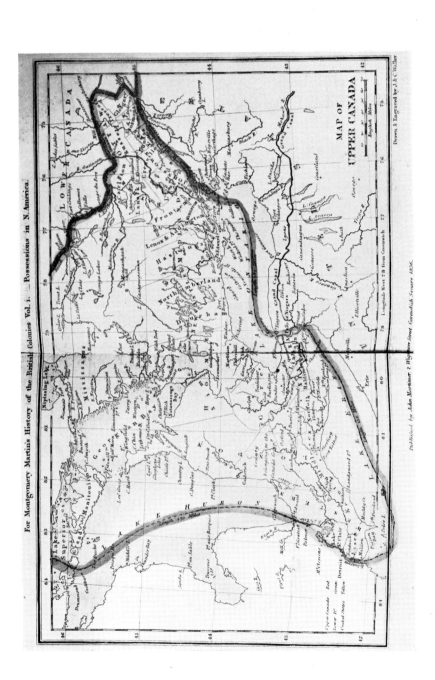

For Montgomery Martin's History of the British Colonies Vol. i. — Possessions in N. America.

MAP OF
UPPER CANADA

English Miles

Drawn & Engraved by J. & C. Walker.

Longitude West 78 from Greenwich

Published by John Mortimer, 2 Wigmore Street, Cavendish Square, 1836.

THE SELECTED WRITINGS OF
WILLIAM LYON MACKENZIE

1824-1837

EDITED BY MARGARET FAIRLEY

Toronto
OXFORD UNIVERSITY PRESS
1960

PRINTED IN SCOTLAND BY
GILMOUR & DEAN LTD., GLASGOW

CONTENTS

1. THE CANADIAN SCENE

CONTENTS

2. EDUCATION

3. BOOKS AND NEWSPAPERS

CONTENTS

4. THE SCENE ABROAD

5. APPEALS TO THE PEOPLE

CONTENTS

6. ADDRESSES TO GOVERNMENT

CONTENTS

CONTENTS

9. CURRENT COMMENT 1834-1837

PREFACE

This selection of the writings of William Lyon Mackenzie covers the period from the first number of his paper, the Colonial Advocate, *on 18 May 1824, to the outbreak of the Rebellion in December 1837. The material is divided into nine chapters, and is chronologically arranged in each chapter. By this arrangement it is hoped that the character and activity of Mackenzie, as well as the life and political ferment of the time, will emerge more clearly than if an overall chronological order had been followed. Biographical and other background material will be found at the beginning of the first six chapters.*

The printed sources quoted are: the Colonial Advocate, *1824-1834, the* Correspondent and Advocate, *1835-1836, the* Constitution, *1836-1837 (all in the Ontario Archives);* A Catechism of Education, *1830,* Poor Richard, or the Yorkshire Almanack for 1831, Sketches of Canada and the United States, *1833,* A New Almanack for the Canadian True Blues, *1834, the* Seventh Report of the Select Committee on Grievances, *1835 (all in the Toronto Public Library); and* The Life and Times of William Lyon Mackenzie *by Charles Lindsey (1862).*

Valuable manuscript material was found in the National Archives in Ottawa, and, thanks to the kindness of Colonel Charles Lindsey, in the Lindsey Papers *in the Ontario Archives.*

Most of the contents of this book have not been reprinted until now. Exceptions are the Independence *broadside of November 1837 and a few short passages in Lindsey's* Life; *the letter to John Neilson of November 27, 1828, included (with several mis-transcriptions) in Doughty and Story's* Documents *Relating to the Constitutional History of Canada, 1819-1828; and short quotations in various histories of the period. There are copies of the* Sketches *and the* Seventh Report *in many libraries, and of the* Catechism *and the two* Almanacks *in the University of Toronto Library and the Toronto Public Library. The rest of the material is inaccessible except in the Archives. The cuts at the head of each chapter are reproduced from the* Colonial Advocate.

Readers will notice certain omissions for which an explanation is necessary. Mackenzie was the victim, during these years, of attacks upon his person, his character, and his property, as well as of repeated expulsions from the Legislative Assembly. And from time to time he hit back. The details of all this are to be found, from different points

of view, in Lindsey's Life, and in J. C. Dent's Story of the Upper
Canada Rebellion *(1885). Mackenzie's answers to his opponents in his
own defence and his counterattacks have not been included here,
because it would have been necessary to add a great deal of material
which would fall outside the scope of this book. Throughout the years
Mackenzie kept his mind fixed on the needs and grievances of his
countrymen, and did not allow himself to be diverted for long into
personal disputes.*

*The publication of these writings establishes him as a man with an
immense respect for factual evidence. His judgement was based on
detailed knowledge, so that he came to be recognized as the authority
on banks, canals, roads, post-office, etc. at home, and could be relied
on to give his readers first-hand news from abroad. Egerton Ryerson,
even when disagreeing most sharply with Mackenzie's conclusions,
paid tribute to his "great strength and merits . . . in eliciting
facts". (C. B. Sissons,* Egerton Ryerson, *vol. i, p. 205.) In later
appraisals he has been presented more often .. a man of prejudice
and passion than as a patient and methodical collector of evidence.
Recently, however, Lillian F. Gates,* (Canadian Historical Review,
XL.3.) *and S. D. Clark* (Movements of Political Protest in Canada,
University of Toronto Press, 1959) *have done much to set the record
straight.*

*These writings establish him too as a man of wide interests and
sympathies. He rightly saw the Reform movement in Upper and Lower
Canada as part of a long and widespread process, and was at pains to
remind his readers of similar movements in different parts of the world.
He saw the connection too between political reform and general education,
and his concern for a more popular government went hand in hand with
concern for a well-educated electorate. His writings on education have
never been given their due, even by the most sympathetic of biographers
and historians, and it is time that they took their rightful place, not
only in the assessment of Mackenzie's importance, but also in the
history of educational theory in this country.*

*When Mackenzie was escaping to the border after the Rebellion, a
reward of £1000 was offered for his apprehension. This reward was
not claimed, although he was at the mercy of many to whom he was
personally unknown. The reason may be found in the chapters "The
Canadian Scene" and "Appeals to the People". Mackenzie was, during
the ten years before the Rebellion, in close touch with the settlers in
Upper Canada. He was their representative in the Legislative Assembly,
re-elected four times after expulsion. There is no doubt that among the
farmers he was regarded more as a spokesman than as an agitator.*

PREFACE

In preparing the text it was found after much deliberation that it was better to follow, with minor concessions to common sense, Mackenzie's punctuation and use of capitals and italics. He seems to use all three for the sake of emphasis, and any attempt at modernization would lead to the risk of misinterpretation. His commas and dashes and capitals often seem to mean "Note this!", and a comma often indicates a pause which brings out the full meaning of the sentence. It is of course also difficult to decide how far the printer was to blame for irregularities. But in spite of all this I do not think the reader today will have much difficulty in following his arguments.

Archaisms of spelling, such as "burthen" and "controul", have been kept; obvious typographical errors have been corrected; the wavering between -or and -our has been sacrificed, and -our used throughout. Over-long paragraphs have occasionally been broken up.

I would like to thank the many who have helped me in the various libraries, particularly Colonel Charles Lindsey and Miss Jessie Jackson in the Ontario Archives. Robert Kenny and Dorise Godefroy gave me valuable help in preparing the selection, and various members of my family came to the rescue in the process of proof-reading. For the rest the credit all goes to William Lyon Mackenzie.

MARGARET FAIRLEY

Toronto,
January 1960.

13

Chapter One

THE CANADIAN SCENE

EDITOR'S PREFACE   *Mackenzie knew the Canadas of his day at first hand and also through books and journals.*

He travelled, by coach, on horseback, on foot, and by steamship, west to St Thomas, north to Lake Simcoe, and east through Kingston, Cornwall, and Montreal to Cap Rouge ("Carouge", as he called it) below Quebec. When collecting signatures for the petition to the Crown in 1831, he attended meetings in almost every township in Upper Canada, going as far east as Merrickville. Along the muddiest of roads he set out for Quebec in the spring of 1831, encountered ice in the St Lawrence, was shipwrecked, but carried on with his intention. In 1835 he again visited Quebec, one of a deputation of Reformers to consult with Papineau and the patriotes *of Lower Canada. In 1837 he travelled through Upper Canada, attending public meetings in many places, this time called to organize support for Papineau.*

He read parliamentary reports of all the Colonies, and studied their law records and journals; he knew Robert Gourlay's Statistics of Upper Canada, *and he kept abreast of the times with the* Christian Guardian, *the* Vindicator, La Minerve, *the two Hamilton papers, the* Quebec Gazette, *the* Novascotian, *the* Acadian Recorder, *and many other papers. He was familiar with current books about Canada. He quoted, for example,* Observations on Professions, Literature, etc. in the United States and Canada *(1833), by Rev. Isaac Fidler, a clergyman from England who lived for a few months at Thornhill, near York* (Sketches, *p. 404). He published a favourable review of* Canadiana *(1837), an informative book on Canadian institutions for English readers by W. B. Wells, a fellow member of the Assembly* (The Constitution, *26 July 1837). He recommended* The Geography and Geology of Lake Huron *(1824) by J. J. Bigsby, naturalist to the United States - Canada Boundary Commission, who was in Canada from 1818 to 1827* (Colonial Advocate, *30 March 1826). For one chapter heading in his* Sketches (*p. 179*) *he used a quotation from* Basil Hall's *Travels in North America (1828).*

Developing his early experience in the office of a canal company in England, and on the Lachine when he first arrived in Canada, he became an expert on canals, and knew everything connected with the planning, building, and financing of the Welland and the Rideau. Number 6 of the Colonial Advocate (*27 September 1824*) *consists entirely of an "Essay on Canals and Inland Navigation and the Reports to the President and Directors of the Welland Canal Company".*

He had at his finger-tips facts and figures about the public revenue and expenditure of the Province.

And he knew the people. Through conversation with many settlers, from one end of the Province to the other, he learned the circumstances of their lives, the value of their lands and crops, the condition of their roads, and the distances they had to travel to school or voting-place or market or church.

He was of course especially well informed about his own constituency, the County of York. His loyalty to Scotland never stood in the way of his growing feeling for Canada, and before he had been here a dozen years he wrote of the countryside and people north of York with pride and affection. He seldom makes us aware that he is a newcomer, so completely does he identify himself with his new surroundings.

SMUGGLING IN 1822

As I happened to be a witness of the following proceedings at Fort George, during the time the Niagara River was frozen over to its mouth, in the winter of 1821-2, I am induced to publish them for the purpose of showing his majesty's government that arbitrary regulations, intended to advance the private interest of certain persons on this side the water at the expense of the lawful gains of the North American colonists, will, when carried to a certain extent, become null and void by the operation of public opinion. In 1821-2, tea was, as at present, prohibited from being imported into Canada from the Republic; but the East India Company had overreached themselves—their anxiety for gain drove the colonists to the Union for nearly every pound they consumed. Canada thus paid a tax to the United States of many hundred thousand dollars, as import duties on tea alone, the tax on hyson then being about two shillings sterling per lb.

It was late one evening when I arrived at Lewiston (United States). I proceeded to Youngstown, opposite Fort George, having business to do with a forwarder of goods; went down to his store on the bank of the river immediately opposite the British fortress, and perceived that he was busy loading a couple of two-horse sleighs with barrels at bottom, and with large white boxes of the size of two chests of tea, at top; about fifteen or eighteen hundred weight was placed on each sleigh; they were then roped; the drivers mounted and drove across the only path cut through the rough masses of ice that led to the Canada shore, where a party of the regular soldiers were placed as sentinels to watch the coast *and prevent smuggling*, with a large blazing fire before them. The troops had enlisted in his majesty's service for the purpose of defending their king and country, and not as excisemen, police, or common informers; and although they could have cleared a good many hundred dollars by seizing the tea (if it was tea), they were pleased neither to see nor hear. There was no bribe given them, for I afterwards inquired particularly as to that fact.

"A witness of the highest authority in this matter," says Sir Henry Parnell, "stated, in his evidence before the Committee of Finance, that the duty of soldiers in the West Indies was that of a police." Englishmen toil and sweat to pay soldiers to go to the West Indies and guard the oppressor from the vengeance of his slave! I suppose Sir Henry Hardinge must have had in view the unfitness of the Canadian militia for acting as a police, or as excisemen over their fathers and brothers, when he denounced them as inefficient in the debate upon the War Defences of the Colonies.

After I had done my business in Youngstown, I also crossed over and went to take supper at Mrs. Rogers's, where I had left my horse. The two sleighs had driven right into the heart of the town, and I passed them in the yard of the same hotel. After the drivers had supped they left Fort George, and I have no doubt but that in two days' time they had supplied a dozen of merchants (who were probably postmasters, justices, coroners, bank directors, &c. &c.) on their route by land, travelling day and night through the thick-settled country around the head of Lake Ontario, a hundred miles to York, where I have been credibly informed the shop-keeping establishment of the then custom-house officer did not lack a supply of the scarce and valuable commodity any more than the others, although, of course, that officer did not conduct that domestic department himself in person.

I would here remark, that not less than 1500 persons must have seen these sleighs—none who saw them could doubt much what their loading was—(although, of course, they did not know any more than myself, not having opened the packages)—everybody was aware that by giving an information to any of the custom-house officers or their deputies, a large reward would probably be secured, yet no one interfered. Why was this? It was because the people of Upper Canada, in 1822, were of opinion that their country ought not to be made a tributary state, and as such, turned over to the East India Company by way of compensation for the tea they lost in the old colonies prior to the revolution. The East India Company lay down a rule, they allow free trade in their own dominions, and the people of Upper Canada, in such cases as the above, content themselves with rendering the prohibitory ordinances of the aristocracy as ineffectual as possible.

While I admit the illegality of the proceedings of the smugglers, I am of opinion that, if these tea prohibitions had been agreed to in a legislature in which the landowners were represented, they would have been morally bound to have conformed to measures intended for the general good;—but why the British parliament renewed a prohibitory charter to the Company, including the colonies, and thus taxed them without their consent, in the teeth of a solemn obligation not to do so, while they allowed the Company to pocket the profits, I am unable to explain. SKETCHES, p. 81.

A JOURNEY TO THE BUSH

In Chinguacousy . . . not one tenth of the settlers have got deeds. It is really bad policy to deprive those industrious settlers, who have left their homes in Britain, to seek an asylum in the woods of North America, of their birthright, because they cannot pay £5, £10, or £20 of fees; yet such is the case. Not one of these people who have done settlement duty, and built houses on their farms, can obtain deeds, without first paying as much for one deed, as would furnish parchment, printing, sealing-wax, and slender clerks, to fill up blanks to half a township. The new parliament will feel less delicate about this matter; and I hope they will lay before the King of England a memorial, stating the ill consequences which result from the system pursued in this case by his representative. Many families in the woods have fared very hard this season for want of the necessaries of life. The opinion of several farmers in the New survey is, that the present crop in the ground will scarcely be an average one, on account of the cold in the early part of the year, the ground retaining the water in many places being new.

There is only one Justice of the Peace in the six townships of Esquesing, Chinguacousy, Erin, Aramosse, Nassagawa and Trafalgar; consequently *no courts can be held*, the magistrate, Mr. John Scott, lives in Chinguacousy. There is another magistrate in Caledon, but he is far distant from Mr. Scott. Nineteen or twenty men have to go from Esquesing township, each year, to be sworn into office, a distance of twenty miles, to the nearest district magistrate; others, in other townships, greater distances,—this is a great inconvenience, but it will perhaps be remedied in time—there is surely no lack of J.P.'s throughout Canada in general, and the selection, as far as it has been made by the present administration, is *worthy of all acceptation*, the late Col. Nichol's philippic to the contrary notwithstanding.

The poverty of the people in this back country may be inferred from the following statement, which may be relied on:—"that not one fifth of all the people in the new townships, settled from two to five years, raise their own provisions."

Mr. Thomas Fyfe, a very intelligent and industrious man, was the first settler in the town of Esquesing—he is from Dundee, in Scotland, and took a considerable sum of money with him into the Bush four years ago—he encountered many difficulties, and has now cleared above 60 acres of his farm. A frame barn, 54 by 54, and 18 feet high, cost in framing and erecting only $30, and the victuals and drink given to 40 or 50 men, who turned out for one day to aid him to rear it—he shingled it himself with the aid of his son; he is in good circumstances, and perhaps the most independent settler in the township, having expended about $1800 on his farm.

There is very little *training* imposed upon the new townships on account of their poverty and miserable roads. If the English government should order settlers to receive their deeds free, it would enable them to use their judgment in selecting proper assemblymen; but it might be proper in lieu of fees, to oblige each settler to do the repairs of some part of the road, near to his residence, to the amount of his fees, or at a stated equal amount; a general benefit would then be conferred, and the Canadians, like the ancient Romans, might shew their wisdom, by early attention to the formation of good highways. COLONIAL ADVOCATE, 29 July 1824.

CANDIDATES AND
VOTERS, 1824

For upwards of sixty miles, the road, as we passed upwards to the ground where the election was to take place, was well travelled by people interested for some one or other of the candidates. I saw a Methodist church near St. Thomas; about fifty miles below there is another, which was erected at Waterford, chiefly by the liberal aid afforded by Mr. Loder. On Monday morning we arrived at St. Thomas, the place appointed for holding the election for the county of Middlesex, of which I will now give a brief account.

The hustings were placed near the church, on a high and well-chosen spot of ground. The village was crowded with people, and the result of a contested election, not yet begun, was joyfully anticipated by the friends of all three of the candidates, though, of course, only two could succeed. Groups stood in every direction, some wearing an oak-tree leaf in their hats, which signified "Mathews and Liberty;" others, ribbons as favours. On one man's hat was tied a broad orange ribbon: the inscription, "Rolph and Mathews," showed his party: three-fourths of the people had no party emblems about them at all.

A little after ten o'clock, Mr. Warren, the returning officer, Colonel Talbot, Mr. Rolph, Colonel Burwell, Captain Mathews, and Mr. Bostwick, mounted the hustings. Mr. Warren was dressed in blue, had his sword appended to his side, and cut a fine figure as returning officer. He read the writ, and five or six hundred persons, who were bystanders, were hushed, when the tall figure of Colonel Burwell was extended to its full length, as he arose to address the multitude. He commenced pleading in justification of his past conduct, and parried admirably the thrusts of some teasing electors who were perpetually demanding why he had acted so and so, why he did this, and said that? He spoke of the milk of human kindness, of location tickets, of flogging bills, of asking no votes, and read part of the Upper Canada Gazette for the edification of those present—this was all well; and had I not known his votes in the house, I confess all I yet saw had served to prepossess me in his favour; but towards the end of his speech he unfortunately stumbled on some political squib or cracker, that he had understood to have been written by an old acquaintance. He spoke of this performance in harsh terms. Some one desired him to read it, which he did; and his passion having obtained the mastery of his better judgment, he burst at once into such a strain of personal invective against the author—a jolly good-looking farmer—who was present, that I felt for both parties. This ebullition of resentment, in so inappropriate a place, lost him many friends; and a poor man of the name of Gardiner, with whom he had had a law-suit concerning the value of an old house, and who complained of foul play, lost him a good many more.

I addressed the electors from my waggon at considerable length in favour of the popular candidates, and electioneered for several days with great activity, but it was unnecessary; the Talbot settlement would have elected the opposition candidates, if twice the influence the local government and Colonel Talbot possessed had been exercised against them; and I am proud to acknowledge that they made a noble choice.

The next speaker, after Colonel Burwell, was Captain Mathews, of the half-pay (or rather retired allowance) royal artillery; he met a joyful, kind reception. His manly, athletic form and courteous demeanour, added to the independent English principles he professed to espouse, secured to him a distinguished place in the good graces of many a worthy yeoman. He resided at Queenston when he first came to Canada; and his departure for "the west" is thus announced in an old number of the Argus:—

"We are informed that Captain Mathews of the Royal Artillery, with his family and servants, consisting of nearly thirty persons, passed through Ancaster, about four weeks ago, on his way to the Bush in Lobo, with six waggons, one cart, twenty-four horses, a flock of sheep, and some cows." This wealthy, intelligent, and patriotic Englishman made an excellent speech, remarkable for its brevity, considering the variety of subjects he embraced; as he concluded the people rent the air with their acclamations—and well they might; they never had a more sincere friend than the gallant officer they have sent to parliament. His well-wishers have only one fear, namely, that he will act *too independent* a part.

Mr. Rolph (who spoke last) promised to act with independence, and to defend the people's rights; spoke with considerable animation of the fine country in which he that day had the honour to be a candidate; expressed a warm interest in its prosperity and that of the province at large; adverted to the time when it was a desert; reminded them of what had been effected in twenty-one years, and augured well of the future fate of the country, its agriculture, and its infant manufactures. Getting warm, he forgot that he was at a county election, and commenced a sentence in his professional way, "Gentlemen of the Jury." He, however, quickly recollected himself, but indeed the expression was not ill-timed—

> " For lawyers, like women, however well bred,
> Will aye talk of that which runs most in their head."

Colonel Talbot, to whose care the settlement of Middlesex was originally confided, was born in Malahide, near Dublin, in Ireland, and has given that name to one of his townships in Middlesex. He is, without doubt, a man of eccentric habits; but many of the stories that are current in the country respecting his manner of living have no foundation in truth. He was, when I saw him, dressed in a plain blue surtout coat and trousers; there was nothing fanciful about his dress or horse furniture, save an Indian blanket, which was wrapped up like a horseman's cloak and fastened behind his saddle; his air is that of a military officer. In youth he must have possessed a handsome person and well-formed features; for even now, and he is nearly sixty years of age, his features have nothing harsh, and his appearance is rather prepossessing.

The ardent desire for rational freedom which obtains in this district was to me very pleasing. I saw it in many instances made abundantly manifest. Long Point is fifty miles from St. Thomas, yet more than a hundred rode that distance to vote against Burwell for the independent candidates. Those who had no horses were furnished by those who had—those who had no money were cheerfully supplied by their more affluent neighbours; and in a few instances, men who declared their willingness to join the good cause, but lamented their slender circumstances, were paid as much as they could otherwise have earned, or else young farmers who had no votes in Middlesex worked their oxen in their absence. It was a cheering spectacle to a friend of Canada to see the happy groups of horsemen from every quarter ride up to the hustings, shouting blithely "Rolph and Mathews!"—"Mathews and Liberty!" Even the newly-elected members of Oxford came with their bands of yeomen to vote for the men of the people's choice.

Mr. Burwell had represented the county for twelve years, and his votes and conduct had so incensed the farmers that they determined to put him out. That precious political selection, the local magistracy, supported him almost to a man.

There is a Scotch settlement in the neighbourhood, but they would not on any account give him their votes.

Mr. Rolph is a native of England, a barrister of the Inner Temple, and graduate of Cambridge University. COLONIAL ADVOCATE, 2 September 1824; SKETCHES, p. 110.

PLAY-ACTORS

A company of play-actors have been wiling the villagers of Niagara out of their money and time—we hope they may not come here [*Queenston*], and wish them no good luck, if they do come. COLONIAL ADVOCATE, 7 October 1824.

THE THEATRE

Last Friday evening, we freed ourself from the toils and vexations of a provincial newspaper, and, for the first time in America, essayed to drive dull care away in a Theatre, this too in despite of the praiseworthy writings of our respected brother journalist, Mr. Andrew Heron against the Drama, in despite of Dr. Wotherspoon —nay—(worse and worse) contrary even to our own consistent declaration against players in general as expressed in last year's *Advocate*.

We think we hear our friend Mr. Andrew, in his satirical dry way, exclaim—"Consistency and the Colonial Advocate have no great affinity," which is a postulate that we would willingly contend against if we had room or time.

To the play-house we went, and, as in the elegant theatre in the gude town where we were born, "VELUTI IN SPECULUM," in fair letters, painted over the vaulted dome, served to remind us that there our follies would be reflected as thro' a mirror, so here the mottoless device above the green curtain, and the confined space in which the votaries of Thespis, the son of Erechtheus were likely to be compelled to occupy, convinced us that the follies of the town creep slowly among us, for, as we have no stage in this country, they cannot, as in Hardcastle's neighbourhood, approach us "in the basket."

The house was truly a thin one, consisting of a few barristers' clerks, attorneys' apprentices, shopkeepers, with an editor or two; even the pit (which answers to the one shilling gallery, occupied by the gods, in Old Drury) was well-nigh desolate. Mr. Heron would have given a silver dollar to have seen the triumph obtained by puritanism over "jollity, mirth and frivolity," in the pious town of York.

On Monday night we found the scene had changed in more

23

respects than one, the house was literally crammed: Gentlemen and Ladies of rank and fashion, peers, parliament men, placemen, cabinet ministers, *and other ministers*: all had agreed to save the reputation of the capital from the stigma of sending a meritorious company of comedians "empty away."

Among the gentlemen present we observed the Hon. Mr. Allan, the Hon. Mr. Macaulay, Colonels Adamson and Ingersol, Major Heward, Messrs. Matthews, Hamilton, Clark, Fothergill, Lefferty, Gordon, Morris, D. Jones and Wilkinson, M.P's—also Messrs. Campbell, Richardson, Washburn, Boulton, G. Monro, Gamble and Rogers.

We had written from our notes a critical dissertation on the merits and demerits of the respective actors, but our foreman tells us (11 P.M. Wednesday) that it is too late for this week.

Yesternight they had a full house to see the Miller and his Men; and, as His Excellency's eldest son was there, we think they ought to assume the title "Theatre Royal". Messrs. C. Jones, Proudfoot, Lee, J. Jones, Lyons, and others of our fashionable people this night honoured the play with their presence.

We have often seen Kean in his favourite character of Richard,— and, if it is considered that Drury Lane affords to a player many peculiar advantages; that the reverberation of its lofty arched roof marvellously aids the actor's voice; that its internal splendour and magnificence, added to the power given the player of choosing his distance, heightens the effect produced on the spectators by his acting, we would say that Davis was at home in the hump-backed Gloster. At times, 'tis true, his voice was *loud* where Kean's is deep, and any approaches to rant in playing such a character should be carefully guarded against; but Davis's person and voice had a resemblance to Kean's, the height of the two is about the same— and in the scene where the usurper tells Lady Anne how cordially he hates her, his acting was really beyond our praise. Upon the whole, we were highly gratified with the performance.

Mr. Gilbert's person, his voice, and his lofty bearing, well fits him for the part of a noble, generous character, and Mr. Smith is quite at home in the droll parts of low comedy. The comic powers of this latter actor would command approbation even in a more fastidious audience; and whether as the Lord Mayor, Sancho, or Sharp, his performing was honoured by the boxes and pit with loud and continued peals of laughter.

As to the ladies, we must postpone our criticism, but cannot help remarking, that if the manager would choose his loving maidens from among the females beyond eight years of age, and give Mrs. Gilbert the hint to bestow on her pretty face certain appropriate streaks, and on her hair a little hair-powder, when she condescends to appear as the representative of wintry three-score, it would, we think, be well enough. The chief beauty of an opera is its close resemblance to scenes in real life; and the strength of a company is shewn to great disadvantage when young women won't grow old, and babies play the parts usually allotted to their mothers. COLONIAL ADVOCATE, 29 December 1825 (2nd edition) and 5 January 1826.

RETIRED COLONELS NEAR ST. THOMAS

To George Frederick Russell, Esq.
Strand, London.

WALSINGHAM, JULY 29, 1825.

Dear Brother,

My last letter was forwarded to you from Port Talbot, through Messrs. Collins & Co. I now continue my narrative.

Colonel Burwell, of whom I have given you some anecdotes already, lives in a large log house, by the side of the road, at the head of Talbot Street; a beautiful orchard and garden surround his dwelling, and his lot is the farthest west on that road. He is building a handsome brick house a little higher up. To the north and north-west of this place there is a succession of little hills and knolls, which, were the country settled and the woods cleared, would add greatly to the many natural beauties now visible in this fertile township. From Col. Burwell's to St. Thomas, going down the Talbot Road, is 10 miles; the country is almost a dead level, and the soil very productive. I rested a day at St. Thomas. Although it is the only village in the county of Middlesex, it increases but slowly. I visited the newly built academy, in company with Mr. B. I. Shaw; it is a house of two stories; the lower part is very neatly fitted up with black walnut tables, desks, and seats, and the upper story is to be divided into seven students' rooms. For this seminary, the Hon. and Rev. Dr. Stewart, who was here this summer, has promised to provide a master. The church is a brick edifice; it has a spire covered with tin, having an elevation of 70 or 80 feet. The pulpit is ill-contrived and badly furnished; they speak of pulling it down again. St. Thomas is a post town 150 miles from York. It is intended to build a harbour at the mouth of Kettle Creek 8 miles below this, on Lake Erie.

I left St. Thomas in the afternoon and that same evening rode 26 miles,—14 on Talbot road, and the rest in the woods—There is very little danger of Robbers or Murderers in this infant Country, but suspicious circumstances do sometimes occur, and are treated with a culpable neglect.

I was informed that a Mr. Benjamin Hardison had walked out into the woods in Yarmouth, Middlesex on a day not long ago, was found dead within three miles of Kettle Creek. This person was going a trading to Sandwich, and was often known to carry sums of money about with him. No inquest was held over his body, nor did any investigation take place; other cases not very dissimilar are said to have occurred in that township,—and tho' the Coroner or the Inhabitants or both are to blame, yet the evil will only be remedied by an increased population.

I had a two-fold motive for leaving the road for the woods, I wished to call on Colonel Backhouse at Silver Creek, and to see Lake Erie. It was night when I left the main road, and I trusted to the moon on my right to guide me to the lake, thro' ten miles of a thick wood, my path being at right angles with the street. No correct idea of an American forest can be gained by riding in an English or Scottish wood—nor can the Duke of Athol's plantations, or Lord Breadalbin's fine parks, extensive as they are, convey to the mind the faithful picture of a country covered with trees, as it were all over, from Dan even to Beersheba. Once or twice I missed my path, and having no compass, dismounted and led my horse towards the moon's shadow until I regained the concession line. During the first seven miles I saw only two or three log huts, and they were deserted. A few acres had been chopped down and sown around each hut, and on making enquiry at Silver Creek, I learnt that the inhabitants had gone out to work on their neighbours' farms to earn a little towards their subsistence during the long winter. If some of our English mechanics, and labourers, grumblers, could but take a peep at these mansions of independence possessed by the poorer sorts of Canadian Lords of the soil, it would neutralize all their useless discontents.— They would see that the enjoyment of the multiplied blessings attendant on an Englishman's fireside, and moderate wages, cannot be bartered for a den in the forest, without a loss so great as scarcely to be appreciated by any who have not made the exchange.

It was within an hour and a half of midnight when I arrived at Colonel Backhouse's residence, and having had a warm invitation a year before, I met with a cordial welcome. The Colonel is a jolly old Yorkshireman, and emigrated to Canada thirty years ago, he is senior magistrate and chairman of the quarter sessions for the London District.—His principal seat is at Walsingham near Vittoria, but he has been here occasionally for a year or two, superintending improvements on the Silver Creek estate, which have already cost him upwards of $12,000. He has built a Grist and Saw Mill, and at much expense erected a large mill-dam on the sand banks, and cleared 150 acres of forest. Mrs. B. and his youngest son, Mr. Jacob, were at Silver Creek when I arrived.

The next morning we had a choice breakfast, but by way of anticipation the Colonel helped himself to his morning cup of new milk two parts, whisky one part, no stinting. I pledged him, but used the latter liquid in greater moderation.—During our *dejeune* a green bottle filled with excellent aquavitae was placed in the centre of the board, and mine host qualified each cup of Mr. B's hyson with about an equal proportion of the clear liquid from the aforesaid bottle. I attempted in my last cup to follow his example—but it was not pleasant to my taste.—I am strongly inclined to believe that the worthy Colonel could lay the Dean and the whole of the chapter of C——— under the table, for, notwithstanding that he indulged himself thus freely, I perceived not the least alteration in his conversation during the day.

His mansion is situate on Lake Erie, a few rods back from the edge of the bank; I was very much delighted with the view I had of the Lake and coast from this place. The shores of Erie are very high and abrupt, as far as the eye could reach either way, I judged the elevation above the surface of the water of the Lake, to be from fifty to seventy and even eighty feet.

A very remarkable though not uncommon occurrence happened here lately. The Colonel was enjoying himself taking his morning walk near the margin of the high bank in front of his house, when he felt the ground giving way, he had scarce enough of time left to remove nearer his house, when an immense body of the bank loosened itself from the rest of the field and gave way, to the length of ten chains or more, and of various widths, sliding slowly and magnificently down into the bosom of the Lake. I saw the trees and shrubs growing below on the beach with their tops and foliage on the level of the earthy precipice on which I stood. No stone is found on the coast in a distance of many miles.—Mr. Backhouse told me that a harbour could be constructed here by building out a few rods into the Lake with fifteen feet water.

On taking my leave of the family, the Colonel gave me a letter of introduction to his son at Walsingham, and I pursued the Lake road to Vittoria,—distant 42 miles, on this road for the first 18 miles I noted many large clearings, a few orchards and some frame houses, the people appeared to be comfortable and contented. I saw one school house, but there is neither post office, church, nor minister, within many miles. I crossed many small rivulets. The big Otter Creek runs through a very deep hollow, has a good bridge, a store house and potashery; a frame dwelling house, and clearing are close by. Nature has greatly embellished this spot. The creek, the farm, the bridge, the buildings, the hilly and broken ground, relieve the eye, oppressed with the dull monotony of miles of unbroken forest. The little Otter Creek is below the big Otter, where they enter the Lake, the distance between them is said to be half a mile only.

I dined on my way down at the house of a Mr. Wilson, an Englishman; he has a choice library, this was the most valuable selection of books I met with since I left Capt. Crooks's at Ancaster, except at Capt. Mathews's. I obtained the following items of information while I staid at Mr. W's.—Property like life, is here held by a very uncertain tenure;—the half of a cleared field of ten acres adjoining Mr. W's farm in Bayham disappeared lately and sunk down into the Lake. The inhabitants of this Township offered to defray the expense of a new post route, from Vittoria to St. Thomas, *via* Otter Creek, by the Lake Road—but Mr. Sutherland the P.M.G. at Quebec did not vouchsafe them an answer to their letter, which was forwarded about a year ago.—Perhaps when the Townships of Bayham and Malahide are thicker settled, a new application will be more graciously received.

Col. Burwell who resides fifty miles off is collector of the customs at Otter Creek; his deputy with whom he divides the profits, is a Mr. Draper who was a sailor under Lord Cochrane formerly in South America—he had just completed a seizure of contraband salt from the U.S. when I passed down.

Big Otter is said to be navigable within the bar for vessels drawing 10, 14 or even 16 feet water. The bar of sand at the mouth of the Creek has sometimes only one foot of water, and seldom more than three feet upon it. If a harbour were constructed to protect the creek from the S.W. winds, it would render this spot very important as a trading depot, and place of shelter for vessels navigating Erie. I made particular enquiry as to who was the proprietor of the lands on each side of the mouth of Otter Creek, and learnt that during Colonel Burwell's Parliamentary career, his loyalty had got him both sides of the bank granted *free* by the Provincial Government,—a valuable present truly.—How much more correct it would have been if this spot had been laid out in lots reserved as the site of a future town; or granted only on condition that the grantee built a harbour for the protection of trade. I am ready to admit however, that under the system hitherto pursued, such sacrifices were indispensable, and that none were found more avaricious after such gifts than those men who were deputed to the Provincial assemblies by the ignorant and deluded yeomanry. "Should some of our present members veer about" said my informant, "it might be well to enquire whether another Otter Creek had not been the back-slider's reward."

Four miles below the big Otter you enter the township of Houghton which is a school reserve; the Hon. Thomas Talbot is empowered to effect sales of 100 acre lots at $2½ an acre, one fourth paid down, and the rest in annual instalments. There are also wild lands reserved in Southwold, Yarmouth and Westminster, for building and endowing an university in Upper Canada, the terms are the same as in Houghton, the lands are good and have been long surveyed, but there are very few buyers. Col. T. is empowered by the board at York to sell at these prices only. (For his own wild lands he asks $6 an acre. But I am told that the population in Dunwich and Alborough, two of his townships, has not increased during the last three years.) How much better would it have been to have divided these townships into farms of 80 acres each, and sold them by vendue, payable in ten years, a payment every year after the first three, and 10 per cent down. I am willing to grant that the price at which wild lands are sold in the United States by government, $1¼, is too low to prevent speculation, but there is a wide difference between that sum and the charge made by the board of education.

I stopt to rest at the house of Mr. Thomas Burger, being the only house in that part of the township. It seems that Houghton has been on sale these six years. Burger told me that six years ago he bought 100 acres by auction at 10s 3d. currency per acre. Other four lots were sold at same time and then the sale was stopt. Col. Talbot also sold six lots last summer at 10s or 12s 6d per acre. Now it would be satisfactory to know why the sale was stopt after five lots were sold six years ago? Where is the proceeds of what was sold? Is it at interest?—Is it at the disposal of the Provincial Legislature? —While these lands remain in their primeval state, being many thousand acres, the people of the province are in many places sunk in ignorance and unfit to exercise the elective franchise, or act as jurors, for want of teachers, and it would surely be a wise policy to sell these lands cheap, settle them and then tax the settlers for an university, [rather] than to sell a few lots and induce four families (the number now in Houghton) to establish themselves in a permanent desart. " If " said Burger, "I had known that the township was not to be settled I would have purchased else-where, but now I and my family are here, we must do as well as we can." An acquaintance of mine in Walsingham said that these Townships ought to be placed at the disposal of Parliament, as the Governor could exercise his prerogative and prevent abuses in grants or sales, and the house could check the close secret system now in use,—but I think different; I would much rather that England would so far unite us to herself as to allow our counties to send representatives to the home Parliament and that our accounts should be audited in Britain entirely.

The soil of this township is in one part sandy and in another part all clay. The lake road has the lake in view now and then, and the forest is intersected with prairies or evergreens on which there are no trees. The front of the township is sand mixed with a blackish loam and would yield excellent summer crops. At a greater distance from the lake the soil is marshy, and very rich iron bog ore is abundant.

In answer to subsequent enquiries respecting the ore in Houghton, I obtained a confirmation of the fact that it is rich and would well pay the working. But what good is it that there is ore when the university or school board keep the township as a block in the way of population and improvement.

Colonel Burwell owns 1500 acres being his quota as surveyor. One of his lots is finely chosen—it is a prairie facing the lake, and here is the only place in several miles where cattle can go down to the lake without difficulty. I met a man with a basket of sloes which he called wild cherries; he had with him three dogs and a gun, and caught a large wild turkey and a racoon. On the poplar trees in the prairies I saw hundreds of insects much resembling the locust, the country people call them sun bugs. The winds and storms have created large hills of sand facing the beach of the lake, I had no instrument with me but judge these hills to be from 80 to 140 feet higher than the lake, and from 20 to 70 feet above the level of the surrounding land. I tied my horse to a tree and contemplated for a time in silence the heavenly prospect around me, Lake Erie on one side reflected a golden lustre in the beams of a July sun, the beach was far below; the rich and luxuriant clusters of wild grape vines, the mountain balm, the stunted sloe, and many other trees and shrubs grew in abundance around me. On one side was a large prairie extending to the very edge of the lofty banks of Erie, and beautiful as the regent's Park: here and there were clumps of trees covered with verdure, the grass was green and velvety, for the heat of the warmest summer in the memory of man had not impaired its native hue; behind me was the vast and extensive forest, rich in metallic treasures, but full of marshes and quagmires, engendering agues, remittants, intermittants. These marshes might be drained with ease thought I if we had a population adequate to the task,— but it cannot be while a few irresponsible individuals have the management of the lands. Did Great Britain but know the value of these colonies, were Englishmen awake to a true sense of their best interests, England and Canada would soon become one people, represented in and controlled by one Legislature. As I proceeded I met several labourers with their dogs and guns enjoying the pleasures of the chase. Here is plenty of game and no game laws. But even if we had game laws—a high-minded resident nobility and gentry such as are in England would be worth making the concession to.— A gentleman in Bayham told me that if I would wait over Sunday he would start a deer and run her into the lake with his hounds— but I could not tarry.

Burger said that within the last four years the lake had risen three or four feet, and further, that a Mr. S—— an old resident in the District remembers having rode from Long Point to Colonel Talbot's on the lake beach—a distance of fifty or sixty miles; I doubt the truth of the latter assertion. In the road through Houghton, a prairie is succeeded by a thicket, then scattered trees and shrubs, then a sand bank on your right; in an instant the path leads by the very brink of a precipice of sand, almost perpendicular, and some 70 or 80 feet above the waters of Erie; still farther and the evidence before you of chasms made by the ever and anon mouldering soil, induce a belief that horse and rider may sink in the vast abyss below. The margin of the lake is discoloured with the mud and sand washed from the banks; on which Erie daily gains. I beheld many beautiful springs issue from the bank below at the beach every two or three rods. Water is easily got throughout by digging. There is a fine creek in the eastern part of the township. There are no snakes here, but rattlesnakes are seen at Long Point. I never saw but one rattlesnake in America, and that was stuffed in the New-York museum.

I have been this particular in describing Houghton because it is devoted to the classics, because it is a town abounding in beauties, valuable as stretching many miles on the shore of Erie although as yet a howling wilderness!

Walsingham, from whence I write, succeeds Houghton, and by virtue of the letter of introduction to Mr. Backhouse from his Father, I have received every attention which a traveller could desire from a highly respectable, and amiable family. At Mr. Backhouse's dairy there is manufactured the finest cheese I ever tasted in the province. The Hon. Robert Hamilton of Queenston once sent a ton of it to Quebec and it brought half a dollar a lb. Adam Wragg's of Seend near Devizes was green curd compared to it, and you know I used to think Adam no indifferent dairyman. The Long Point county is an old settlement, and has been greatly improved of late years. I took some notes as I passed downwards and they will afford materials for another letter.

PETER RUSSELL [*pseud. for W.L.M.*]

P.S.—One circumstance I had like to have forgot; Burger of Houghton already mentioned, had a child very sick when I arrived there. No Surgeon was near, nor had they any medicine of any kind, not so much as a dose of salts. Poor emigrants at a distance, in the bush, are often very badly off for medical aid. A Scotsman's wife of the name of Hardy lost two children, the one after the other, caused by the distance they lived from the Doctor; and except in thickly settled neighbourhoods, you only find a few ignorant itinerant quacks, practising, contrary to law, upon the lives of his majesty's subjects *Secundum Artem.* P.R.

COLONIAL ADVOCATE, 9 February 1826.

A QUAKER SCHOOL

A few miles from Lake Erie, in the township of Bertie, in a quiet and retired spot, near by a concession road, stands the plain and unadorned place of worship of the society of friends; and at a little distance beyond, their school.

On entering the latter, I recognized in the teacher my old friend Mr. William Wilson. He had from twenty to thirty boys and girls round him, the children of the neighbouring quaker families. The healthy, happy, cheerful, and placid countenances of these young innocents it was delightful to look upon. How happy is youth when placed at a distance from the snares of vice, and far away from the cotton or lace factory!—here is the native abode of innocence and peace. These children never see their parents contending and quarrelling about dogmatical points in religion or politics, for their parents refuse to adopt creeds, and are loyal and true to the government which protects them; willingly obedient to the law, enemies of oppression, the friends of all mankind, charitable and humane. This is the character of a true professor of the religion of Fox, Barclay and Penn.

Opposite the school-house, and fastened to the boughs of the lofty beech and maple trees which surround the area, are placed two swings, made of the bark of the elm and bass-wood, prepared in an ashery—one is for the boys, the other for the girls. I took a turn in one of these machines, was sent aloft in the air, and thought for a few minutes that I had gone back to the halcyon days of youth. Mr. Wilson then took us to see the burying-ground of the society, where these children of peace rest in quiet, awaiting their eternal morning. We retired to dine at Mr. Thomas Moore's, much pleased that we had not missed the quaker meeting-house. Mr. Moore, in 1813, planted in the fall ninety-nine apple trees on an acre of ground, on an acclivity—they now form an excellent and valuable bearing orchard; this is worthy of imitation.

COLONIAL ADVOCATE, 22 February 1827; SKETCHES, p. 234.

NEGROES IN UPPER CANADA

One day last summer a poor black girl, who had escaped from the whip-lash to this side the water, was seized on a Sunday, near Queenston, in broad daylight, between eleven and noon, by two hired scoundrels, who hauled and pulled her through that village; she screaming and crying in the most piteous and heart-rending manner, and her ruffian cream-coloured tormentors laughing at her distress, and amusing the villagers with the cock-and-bull story that she had stolen five hundred dollars, and that the money had been found in her bundle. To the everlasting disgrace of the inhabitants of Queenston, they stood by, many of them, and allowed the poor African lass to be placed by main force on board the ferry-boat which was to carry her back into slavery of a far worse nature than she had formerly experienced. Her lot would now be, 1st, exemplary punishment, and 2d, a slow murder (for so it may be called) in the unhealthy climate of the rice or sugar plantations. Is it not time that kidnapping of this sort, in Upper Canada, were put an end to by the strong arm of the law?

The above case was related to me by a friend on whose accuracy I can fully depend. The following case of *James Smith* was published in the newspapers. I am acquainted with Smith, who (April, 1828) was a young man of about twenty-three or twenty-four years of age. I had from him the whole of his early history, and it was a horrible tale indeed. That slavery must have been galling indeed which could tempt a human being to trust himself to the broad and deep waters of the Niagara rather than return under it.

"A black man, by the name of James Smith, in the employ of Mr. R. M. Long, of Clinton, was seized a few nights ago in his bed, by a band of slave-holding ruffians from the south, and conveyed across the Niagara river gagged and pinioned. He was kept concealed near Lewiston in some old barrack, while his Virginia master, whom he recognized, was making arrangements for proceeding onwards with his captive; but very fortunately Cuffee made his escape, and, after lying concealed for forty-eight hours without fire or food, actually swam the Niagara river in the night, and thus secured his retreat. The poor fellow landed at the fishing-ground on this shore, and was first discovered by a party of fishermen, buffeting the chilly element nearly exhausted. He states that some of the party who seized him were disguised; they are supposed to be Canadian spies bribed for the disgraceful purpose. It is a pity that the law could not seek them out for punishment as an example to others." SKETCHES, p. 21.

STATE OF THE TOWN
OF YORK

The tragical death of Nowlan[1], with the circumstances which led to it, are well worthy of our most serious consideration; and there are

[1][Charles French, printer until two weeks earlier in the office of the *Colonial Advocate*, was charged with the murder (on 4 June) of Nowlan outside the York theatre during the performance of "Tom and Jerry, or Life in London" which they had both attended. Nowlan was a notorious brawler and bully, and had threatened French with violence a few days earlier. His repeated threats on the night of 4 June led to the murder, which was believed by many to have been in self-defence. It was hinted that Nowlan was made use of by those anxious to take vengeance on French for the part he had played in 1826 as an eye-witness of the wrecking of Mackenzie's press and as one of the chief agents in bringing the vandals to justice. In spite of Mackenzie's efforts to win mercy for French, and in spite of a petition for clemency signed by 1100, French was executed on 23 October.]

other matters of importance to our townspeople which we shall take the liberty of mentioning at the same time.

1st. The company of theatrical performers now in York profess to open their house at seven in the night, but seldom or never begin until 9 or 10—thereby introducing irregular habits among our youth, encouraging midnight depredators to make the playhouse their rendezvous, and alluring the hardworking tradesman from his peaceful home and regular hours of rest to the midnight company of persons dangerous to the public peace. We warned the manager early in the season of the bad results likely to attend such a deviation from the usage of other theatres, but it was not attended to.

2nd. There is neither town-constables nor soldiers set as a watch about the theatre, and in it, to guard the lives and properties of his majesty's subjects—nor is this place of public entertainment required to be shut up at 10 or 11 at night.

3rd. Altho' the official return of the population of York is under 2000 souls, there are about sixty stores, houses of entertainment or taverns, in some of which strong beer or spirituous liquors are either sold or permitted to be drank at all hours of the day and night and on all days and nights of the week—many of these stores and taverns are creditably kept by respectable persons, but there are other houses, either of ill-fame, or the resort of the idle, the dissipated, the worthless, and the profligate, which are known to the magistrates, and in some cases *owned by them*, but which they permit to exist and to multiply, as hotbeds of vice and infamy, and allurements to draw youth [along] the swift road that leadeth to destruction.

4th. Instead of the people being allowed the management of their police and the periodical election of a police judge, as is the case in Glasgow, Birmingham, Newcastle, and many other police towns of Great Britain, magistrates burthened with other avocations profess to attend daily in turn at a police office, and are so remiss in the performance of their duty, and often so difficult to be obtained in cases of emergency; that the York police, acting by no known rule or system, is in fact little better than a burlesque on regularity and good order.

5th. There is no ordinary town-watch or night police, to see the streets cleared of strumpets, drunkards, thieves, and vagabonds. If a man calls out MURDER in the night, as it appears French did when assaulted by Nowlan, he can only be aided, if in real danger, by individuals unarmed, and that at the risque of their own lives. No watchmen being near, the man of rank and the labourer may alike chance to bite the dust, the victims of brutality, passion, or inebriety.

6th. In front or in rear of the houses of many of the inhabitants of this town, and even on the public streets, individuals are permitted to collect, or to throw out and exhibit all sorts of filth and nastiness—puddles of stinking water and offals, noisome and pestiferous, are allowed to exist without complaint—and even at the old jail, on the glebe lands of the church, in view of the principal street of the town is a pestilent stenchhole permitted to set, in aid of the marsh, spreading the elements of disease among our citizens.

7th. Ponds of stagnant water, in which decayed vegetable substances are rotting, may be seen under the houses of many of the townspeople. But although this occasions disease to pass up through the boards of the floor to the ignorant or careless inmates, nothing has been done to compel the owners or occupiers of such houses to clear away the contagious puddles—which are to be found outside of houses as well as below them.

8th. A large sum is annually collected by the magistrates or some one for them for the leased lots in the Market square block, but so little respect do they manifest for public opinion, that they have hitherto appropriated this public fund, privately; and that too in defiance of Mr. Peterson's act respecting district funds; for York is no incorporation, further than as to its £100 police.

9th. The public press, the earliest means of giving public notoriety to such circumstances, is not only silent, but even endeavours to stifle the truth, and render obnoxious to the vengeance of the drunkard, those who would dare to state facts with impartiality.

10th. The populace (some of them) are deeply impressed with the idea that government would not consider it a very capital crime if some desperate villain, however set on, were to waylay and kill or render helpless for life, such an individual as the writer of this article, this idea they imbibe from the conduct of persons in high authority under recent circumstances.

11th. The population of the town and county consists of persons of many sects and denominations in respect to religious belief—and who are either natives of Canada, or emigrants from other parts of North America, or from Europe, Asia, and Africa—a mixed race, neither amalgamated in manners, customs nor habits—doubtless containing many enlightened and well informed men, as well as others of a very different character.

Such being the present state of York, it is not surprising that the death of Nowlan has caused some excitement.

COLONIAL ADVOCATE, 12 June 1828.

THE CHILDREN OF PEACE

Among the many sects which have taken root in the soil of Upper Canada, a new order of Christians has, within a few years, arisen and become conspicuous (even to our legislature) less by the peculiarity of their doctrines (for they have no written creed) than for the outward form of their worship, which is very splendid; whereas the Quakers or Friends, from among whom they chiefly took their rise, have made plainness and simplicity their distinguishing characteristic, even so far as the very cut and colour of their garments.

The Children of Peace consist, at present, of thirty or forty families, residing in or near the village of Hope, in the township of East Gwillimbury, about thirty-five miles from York, and four and a half from Newmarket. The situation is healthy and salubrious, the country open and well cleared; and I noted down the names of tanners, weavers, hatters, blacksmiths, tinsmiths, coopers, joiners, shoemakers, cabinetmakers, carpenters, tailors, harnessmakers, storekeepers, and wheelwrights, who already follow their vocations in the village of Hope. In its neighbourhood I stayed two nights, in the house of Mr. Enos Dennis, an old settler from Pennsylvania, a part of whose family belong to the Children of Peace. Mr. Dennis is at once a millwright, wheelwright, blacksmith, cabinetmaker, and cart and plough maker, and displays considerable ingenuity as a workman. The Society of Friends had once a meeting-house in Hope, not a vestige of which remains; but, on the same ground, Mr. David Wilson is now erecting an elegant and fanciful building, on two sides of which are the representation of a setting-sun, below which is inscribed the word "Armageddon,"—the historical meaning of which may be found in the Old Testament.

There are two schools in Hope; one for the ordinary branches of education, and the other, on a far larger scale, for the instruction of young females in knitting, sewing, spinning, making chip and straw hats and bonnets, spinning wool, and other useful accomplishments of a like description. There is a male and a female superintendent resident in this latter school; the pupils cook, make their own clothes, keep the garden in order, receive lessons in reading, &c., and work at their various avocations. I counted nearly a dozen of large wool-wheels in one of the rooms. Among the pupils I saw either one or two young girls from York, and they all seemed happy and contented.

37

The new church or chapel of the Children of Peace is certainly calculated to inspire the beholder with astonishment; its dimensions —its architecture—its situation—are all so extraordinary. On a level plain, inclosed first with a fence, and afterwards by a row of maple trees, on every side, stands the chapel or temple of Hope. It is a regular square, each of the four sides measuring sixty feet at the base. The main body of the chapel is twenty-four feet high, and is lighted by twenty-four windows, with seventy-two panes each; having also one door in each front. Surmounting a pavilion roof, so near a level as to permit me to walk upon it without danger, adding only six feet to the height of the main building, rises a square tower, hall, or gallery, measuring twenty-seven and a half feet on each side, and sixteen feet in height. Inside, this place is one blaze of light, containing twelve windows of sixty panes each: it is to be used as an orchestra or music room, being open within as a part of the chapel below. Here will be placed, as in a gallery, the musicians and organist, at least thirty feet above the congregation. And when the large full-toned and soft-set organ, built by Mr. Coates, of York, shall be set up in this room, together with the players on the flutes, violins, bass-viols, bassoons, clarionets, and flageolets, used by the society in their worship, the effect will remind a visiter of "the music of the spheres," about which bards of old have sung, and poets, in "lofty lays," recorded fancy's fictions. This tower or gallery is supported inside by sixteen pillars, and, like the former building, has a pavilion roof, rising so gently, however, as to permit us to walk on it with ease. Beautifully placed on the centre of this roof, and supported inside by four pillars, is a third tower, in exact accordance with the architectural taste displayed throughout the work. It is twelve feet high; square, each side being nine and a half feet, with four double windows of fifty-four lights each. At the corners of each roof, and also on the four corners of the highest tower, are placed large ornamented lanterns, which add to the beauty of the temple, and are lighted up at the annual grand festival, which commences on the morning of the first Saturday of September, and continues till the Monday following.

The highest tower is surmounted by a gilded ball, on each side of which is inscribed "Peace." The temple is painted white; and when finished inside, will be the most surprising and original fabric allotted for divine worship in the colony. Being seated on a rising ground, it has a fine effect when viewed from the surrounding country, towering above its mother earth, unequalled and alone, in all the sublimity and majesty of castellated grandeur. The elevation of the new chapel is from seventy to eighty feet, measuring from the ground to the tops of the four highest lanterns.

The religious services of the society are performed as yet in the old chapel, a plain building outside, but finished within in very handsome style. The number of members and hearers is about 200, and the utmost regularity is said to prevail at their meetings. As I remarked before, the Children of Peace, like the Quakers, have no written creed; the church discipline being altered and amended, if need be, on motion, by a vote of the majority of the congregation. As yet, however, every alteration of church government has been carried without opposition.

On Saturday, at noon, there is a relaxation from labour—the children give over their work or tasks, amuse themselves, and take their recreation in the fields. In the evening there is a meeting in the chapel for religious exercises: besides, I was informed that the sabbath is strictly kept.

In the old chapel, I observed several paintings by Coates,— Peace, represented by an elegant female figure with an infant on each arm, and Eve trampling the serpent under foot; there is also a third painting of Peace by the same artist. On one side of the organ is a picture of King David's harp; on the other, his spear, bow, and shield. Four black flags, used at funerals, with a star in the centre, and gilt at the top of the staff, wave from the organ-loft.

Early on the morning after I arrived, I found some of the singers in the chapel practising their hymns and tunes. A number of young females sang a hymn, composed, as is all their poetry, by members of the society. Two young men had bass-viols, and the full-toned organ aided the music, which, I will venture to say, is unequalled in any part of the Upper, and scarcely surpassed even by the Catholics in the Lower province.

I should like to have heard their minister preach a sermon, as it would better have enabled me to understand their mode of worship, but another opportunity will doubtless offer, which I can embrace. It is a question with many, whether the society will increase and spread over other parts of the colony, or confine itself to the original meeting. By some of the neighbouring sectarians, the Children of Peace are reviled with great bitterness, while others have been equally strong in their commendation. One thing is evident, they afford ample proofs, both in their village and in their chapels, that, comparatively, great achievements may be accomplished by a few when united in their efforts and persevering in their habits and systems. Such of the members of the parliament of this colony, as have visited the society, speak of it with approbation; and a few more years will probably determine, beyond a reasonable doubt, the tendency of its doctrines and peculiar mode of worship.

.   .   .

The children of peace itinerate; I therefore had another opportunity of beholding their mode of worshipping on the 2nd September, 1829, at nine in the morning of a Sunday, eight miles from York.

I found seated in the temporary chapel, around a table, at the upper end of the apartment, the musicians, from fifteen to twenty men, and six or eight young women, altogether presenting a band of vocal and instrumental performers, such as are seldom to be met with, unless in choirs, or perhaps at the grand festivals for sacred music, which now and then occur in England. The first tune played was Darlington; J. Willson and Tebbitts each performed on the violincello; Jesse Doan and Benjamin Dunham on the first and second clarionets; Charles Doan on the bassoon; Richard Coates and Hugh Willson on concert horns; Job Hughes on the violin; Ira Doan on the flageolet; Charles Haines and Joshua Harris played on the German flute, and Judah Lundy and Enos Doan performed on octave flutes. It may be easily conceived that the effect was very pleasant and delightful.—Westminster was the next tune; after which the females sang a psalm to the music of Cornish; they sang it beautifully in trio. Their preparatory services were concluded by performing a solemn Scottish air.

At eleven in the forenoon, the congregation had assembled, perhaps 200 or 300 persons in all, attentive, decorous, and well dressed; some came in carriages of various descriptions, many on horseback, and not a few on foot. The service began with sacred music, first instrumental, and afterwards both vocal and instrumental. A pause ensued, after which Mr. David Wilson, their principal minister, gave out a hymn or rather paraphrase of part of St. John's gospel, from which also he afterwards took his text. The women singers, who have very fine voices, and are all dressed in white garments, sang this hymn, accompanied by such of the members of the society as chose to join them, the lines being given out two at a time for the benefit of the congregation. Their style of singing would here have been pronounced faultless by the best judges of the art. They compose all their own hymns and psalms to suit the occasions on which they are sung, have a large organ in their chapel at Hope, and assemble regularly once a quarter both here and at Markham, on certain stated sabbaths.

After another pause their preacher rose up and began his discourse, which lasted, perhaps, over an hour.

JULY, 1830

Hope, the village of the Children of Peace, is fast improving. Their new and spacious temple, intended chiefly, I believe, for vocal and instrumental sacred music, will soon be finished. The materials for a third church or place of worship are collecting, and a structure of the dimensions of 50 by 100 feet of brick, with elegant workmanship, will soon be commenced.

In the house of Samuel Hughes, a member of this new society, I found an undoubted evidence of practical Christianity. Three years ago, an old decrepit Negro, who had up to that time begged for a subsistence, was struck with the palsy in his body and one of his sides, and lost the use of his limbs and one arm. Mr. Hughes took him in—had a chair with wheels made for him—and continues to wait upon him and assist the helpless object, who can do nothing for himself. Whether he and his family do this altogether at their own expense, or whether they get some help from the society, I know not; but their conduct might put to the blush many who make extraordinary professions of that meek faith, of the effects of which their proud lives afford but a faint specimen. COLONIAL ADVOCATE, 18 and 25 September 1828, 29 July 1830; SKETCHES, p. 118.

STANDING ARMIES

The Montreal Herald very justly remarks that the present distribution of the British Army presents *facts not destitute of instruction.* It appears that in *Ireland* there are stationed five cavalry and twenty-three foot regiments, besides seventy-six companies as depots, these are to keep down the Catholic Irish, of course. In all Scotland there are *but two regiments* and in England sixteen horse regiments, thirteen foot ditto, fifty-two depots of four companies each. In the North American Colonies (one million of people) there are nine regiments and one battalion: being stationed—two at Quebec, one at Montreal, two in Upper Canada, two at Halifax, one in New Brunswick, and one in Bermuda—these regular troops are intended of course to keep down *sedition* and preserve us from becoming republicans. In the thirteen old colonies (upwards of two millions of people) immediately before the commencement of the revolution, there were but four foot regiments of British troops stationed. In Jamaica alone there are five regiments; four at Ceylon; at Bombay, Bengal and Madras, eighteen regiments; three in New South Wales; three and a half at Malta; six at Gibraltar; two at Barbadoes; *none in Wales*; ninety-seven marching regiments are abroad. The British military force consists in all of a hundred and thirty regiments.

We perceive that the militia bill failed in the Lower Canada Assembly, as did Sir John Colborne's recommendation in our legislature, and it appears that the extraordinary punishment of Mr. Barry by the legislature of Nova Scotia arose out of militia complaints in that colony. Let governments learn to be just to the people, and they will find freemen both willing and able to protect their rights; but at present they would only be called upon to support and maintain an administration of justice they have deprecated, a church establishment they detest, and a host of pampered placemen who swallow up their means and ungratefully entreat the land that maintains them. COLONIAL ADVOCATE, 16 April 1829.

CANALS

BURLINGTON CANAL—RIDEAU CANAL—WELLAND (OTHER-
WISE ERIE AND ONTARIO) CANAL—DESJARDINS' CANAL—
ST. LAWRENCE CANALS.

Up to 1824, the year in which I commenced the publication of this periodical, not one practical effort had been made in the Province of Upper Canada, to improve its vast inland navigation, either by canals or rail-roads, and in the month of September in that year, when I published my second essay "on canals and inland navigation", wheat was at half a dollar a bushel, and the Burlington cut had just been commenced under the superintendence of Mr. Hall, now of Nova Scotia. Very different however is the present state of the Province, and greatly improved are its prospects—The Burlington Canal has been so far completed as to admit schooners and steamboats, drawing nine feet water, into the bosom of the Lake in its rear; the Desjardins' Canal is in steady progress; the Rideau Canal, a vast chain of inland navigation, carried through 160 miles of new country, between Kingston on Lake Ontario and the great

River Ottawa above Montreal, will be completed next year; and the Erie and Ontario junction Canal, otherwise named the Welland, is now nearly ready to be opened permanently to the commerce of the vast countries on both sides of the valley of the St. Lawrence. This is assuredly a cheering prospect to the Canadian. Instead of 1s. 10½d. to 2s. 6d. per bushel for the superior wheat of this fertile Province, paid too often to the farmer in goods at double their value, we now find the miller and the merchant eagerly purchasing grain at 5s. and (in some places) even at 6s. currency, per 60 lbs.

In 1824 there was to be found but one solitary steamboat, the Frontenac, on the British side of the Lake, which made sometimes two, oftener three and rarely four trips in the month between Kingston and Fort George—now there are some eight or ten tight steamers, plying in every direction in quest of freight and passengers at moderate rates, and a considerable steamboat proprietor is so much encouraged by the present aspect of affairs, that he has now on the stocks a steamship on a new and elegant model, the estimated cost of which is £15,000.

I had been favoured with a variety of very contradictory opinions concerning the condition of that important undertaking usually known as the Welland Canal, and to the best of my judgment had expressed such sentiments concerning its utility, stability, progress, and prospects, as I considered warranted by the facts elicited during my enquiries. I had, in the Legislature, moved the appointment of a select Committee to enquire into the management and expenditure of its officers, directors, and servants, and had patiently and carefully endeavoured as a member of that committee to acquire a correct knowledge of its affairs—but had been less successful than I could have wished. In April last, I received an invitation from my friend the commissioner appointed by Act of Parliament, fully to investigate and report upon its condition, to accompany him and another of the members of the House of Assembly on a tour of inspection. Sickness prevented me from going at the time appointed, but last week I had the pleasure of examining the whole line of canal, as well as the feeder, up to the dam at its western extremity on the Grand River.

Having overtaken the commissioner on his second excursion, near its western extremity, I accompanied him and three or four other gentlemen from various parts of the Province, on a visit to the several bays and inlets in Lake Erie, which had been named as presenting a choice for the termination of the ship canal, whenever Parliament shall authorize the completion of the sections west of the

River Welland. We examined Kinnaird's Bay, Grabiel's Bay, Savage's Bay, Steel's, better known as Gravelly Bay, and several others, and returned from our excursion highly gratified, and very agreeably disappointed.

I took notes on the journey, of every thing which to me appeared worthy of recollection, which I mean hereafter to transcribe and publish, and I returned to York far better satisfied concerning the utility of the canal, and the stability of the excavation, locks, aqueducts, harbour, etc. than when I had left it—and hesitate not to confess myself convinced by personal observation, that in point of permanence and utility, it appears destined greatly to exceed my previous expectations. The whole of these observations on the condition of the Welland Canal, and the pleasing results I met with, have greatly heightened my desires in favour of the improvement of the River St. Lawrence. So soon as the Rideau Canal is completed, it will take away the forwarding business from the river, because the rates on the canal, lockage up and down included, will, on the whole, be cheapest, and the transportation safer—But the river navigation, if improved, would be the most permanent, and infinitely more useful.

In canalling, we should not attempt to do too many things at once, it is highly injudicious; but if we could obtain the aid and assistance of the sister colony, it would be the interest of both Canadas that the 38 miles of artificial navigation which are required in the valley of the St. Lawrence should be excavated, so that European ships might be able to reach the great lakes, and that the schooners and steamers of Lake Ontario might have a safe and uninterrupted passage to Montreal and Quebec. If some plan could be determined on combining prudence and judgment in the expenditure, I would cheerfully consent to involve the Province in debt, in conjunction with Lower Canada, in order to improve the St. Lawrence to the ocean.

It may be said that the national debt of England ought to deter these Provinces from speculations of this sort, but I know that the cases do not apply.—England borrowed money and accumulated debt in order to carry on war with France, America, Spain, and other foreign countries, leaving her subjects to complete canals and establish railways out of their private fortunes—a very different object indeed from borrowing at interest to improve her resources, and add to the national wealth. Were the St. Lawrence canals, a distance of $37\frac{1}{2}$ miles completed, the navigation from Quebec, inland in nearly a straight line to the gulph of Mexico and New Orleans would be unbroken, save 110 miles of canal along the valleys of the Wabash and Maumee Rivers, for which Legislative provision has been made by the state of Indiana. The liberality with which the Parliament of Lower Canada have come forward of late years, in favour of objects of public utility, leaves it without a doubt that their vote of last session for a survey of the St. Lawrence above Montreal, will be followed up in due time by the requisite appropriations for the improvement of that noble river, on a scale commensurate with the growing trade of the country. COLONIAL ADVOCATE, 13 May 1830.

THE CREDIT INDIANS

At the mouth of the river Credit, on lake Ontario, the government has a purchase or grant of six acres from the Indians, with a tavern upon it, the rent of which is paid to the receiver-general, who accounts for it, neither to the British nor to the provincial Parliament, but to the "Lords of the Treasury."

We reached the Indian village about two o'clock in the afternoon of the 24th December, 1830; it is situated on a high ground on the west bank of the river, perhaps two miles above lake Ontario.

About half-way between lake Ontario and Dundas-street, in the middle of 3800 acres of their reserved land, is situated the village of the Credit Indians. It is built upon the table land overlooking the high banks of the river, on each side of which are fertile meadows in a state of cultivation. A number of the houses were built with the proceeds of the sale by government to the Rev. Mr. M'Grath, of part of the Indians' land, sold as they say against their consent. In the rear of each dwelling is a garden, and the chief, Mr. Sawyer, and several other Indians reside in frame houses, for they now have an excellent saw-mill, which, to their honour be it spoken, was built without a drop of spirits. The Methodist mission-house, in which resides Elder Youmans, is a commodious two-story frame building, well finished; and nearly opposite is the Methodist episcopal chapel, a neat, clean and commodious place of worship. Close by is the flag staff, on which the British ensign is hoisted on great occasions, such as a visit from his Excellency, (who has been once at this place).

Although the reserve is a military territory, where the chief marries the Indians, and the woodlands are undivided, yet each family has its own town lot. The Indians are sober, comfortable and

45

orderly; they make sleighs for sale, also many other articles, but no shoes. In their school are taught about fifty Indian children; the girls by Miss Rolph, a sister of the late member for Middlesex; the boys by Mr. Edway Ryerson, a brother of the late editor of the Christian Guardian.

The school-room is a large and commodious apartment, with tiers of raised benches in the rear; on one division of which sit the girls, and the boys on the other. There are also desks and slates for ciphering, and copy-books and copperplate lines for those who write. The Bibles and Testaments are chiefly those of the London Society for Promoting Christian Knowledge; some of the other books are English printed, and some American: no sectarian intolerance prevails in that way. Among the school-furniture, are a handsome map of the world; the Arithmeticon; attractive alphabets on pasteboard; regular figures illustrative of geometry, some of them cut out of wood, and some of them made of pasteboard; the picture of Elijah fed by ravens; figures of birds, fishes, and quadrupeds, on pasteboard, coloured, accompanied with the history of each animal; the figure of a clock, in pasteboard, by which to explain the principles of the time-piece. The walls of the school are adorned with good moral maxims; and I perceived that one of the rules was rather novel, though doubtless in place here.—It was, "No blankets to be worn in school." We should have been much gratified by seeing the progress of the scholars while at their lessons, but Mr. Jones told us that the master had gone to York for the day.

The translating-office is occupied by Mr. Peter Jones, the Indian minister. He has a very select library, and is now employed in translating St. John's Gospel into the Mississagua [*Missisauga*] language. His translation of St. Matthew is already published.

In the Dorcas Society-room there are a variety of books, Indian baskets, and other articles of ornament and use. This association of Indian females have set apart every Thursday on which to work for the support of their missions. Last year, they made fancy work, such as gloves, moccasins, purses, and the like, to the value in money of one hundred dollars; and have not this season relaxed their laudable exertions. To those who, with me, remember the state of the Indians ten or twelve years ago, their pleasant, happy, and comfortable condition will afford much pleasure. Divine Providence has wisely reserved to itself the government and direction of the seasons; and man, to whom has been awarded the power of forming a temporary government for his species during their mortal pilgrimage here below, seems even in this to have received too great a task, of which the conduct of the Europeans to the Indians, generally, is a proof. Right glad, therefore, am I to be able to record one instance in which the native tribes have really profited by their acquaintance with the Europeans.

The Indians are regular subscribers for the *Colonial Advocate* newspaper, and very punctual payers.

They presented the following very interesting petition to General Colborne, in 1829; he referred it to the Assembly, which complied with their requests:—

"The petition of the Mississagua Indians, settled at the River Credit, to our Great Father, Sir John Colborne, K.C.B., Lieutenant-Governor of Upper Canada, &c. &c. &c.

"Father!—Your children, who now petition to you, are a remnant of the great nations who owned and inhabited the country in which you now live and make laws;—the ground on which you and your children stand covers the bones of our fathers, of many generations. When your fathers came over the great waters, we received them as friends, and gave them land to live upon. We have always been friends to our great father the King and his white children. When the white men came they made us sick and drunken; and as they increased, we grew less and less, till we are now very small. We sold a great deal of land to our great father the King for very little, and we became poorer and poorer. We reserved all the hunting and fishing, but the white men soon grew so many that they took all: when all the rest was gone, we kept the ten-mile creek, the twelve-mile creek, and the river Credit. The two first are gone from us, but we are wishing to keep the Credit. We reserved one mile on each side of the Credit, where we now live. About four years ago, the Great Spirit sent to us good men with the great word the Gospel of our Saviour Jesus Christ, and we became a new people; we have thrown away our sins; we live in houses, in a village where we worship the Great Spirit, and learn his word, and keep his sabbaths; our children and young men learn to read; and many of our people from a distance have joined us. We now want the fish in our river, that we may keep our children at home to go to school, and not go many miles back to hunt for provisions. We also catch salmon, and sell them very cheap to industrious white men who bring us flour, and other provisions, and cattle; and they say it is much better than to fish themselves. But now, Father, we will tell you how wicked white men have used us.—They come in the fall and spring, and encamp for many weeks close by our village. They burn and destroy our fences and boards in the night; they watch the salmon and take them as fast as they come up; they swear and get drunk and give a very bad example to our young people, and try to persuade them to be wicked like themselves, and particularly on the Sabbath;—their wicked ways give us much trouble and make our hearts sorry. Others go to the mouth of the river and catch all the salmon; they put the offals of salmon in the mouth of the river to keep the fish from passing up, that they may take them with a seine near the mouth of the river in the lake; and often in the dark they set gill nets in the river and stop all the fish. By those means we are much injured and our children are deprived of bread.

"Now, father, once all the fish in these rivers and these lakes, and all the deer in these woods, were ours; but your red children only ask you to cause laws to be made to keep these bad men away from our fishery at the River Credit, from Mr. Racey's line to the mouth of the river, and along the lake shore one mile on each side of the river as far as our land extends, and to punish those who attempt to fish here. We will not fish on Saturday night, Sunday night, and Sunday, but will let the fish pass up to our white brothers up the river.

"And your petitioners, &c.

(*Signed*) "JAMES ADJITANCE,
"PETER JONES,
"JOSEPH SAWYER,
And fifty-one others.
"*River Credit, Jan.* 31, 1829."

Near Dundas Street, we met an Indian sleigh with eight deer in it, all which the owner had shot in the woods within the space of two days. There are fortunately very mild and judicious game-laws in North America. SKETCHES, p. 130.

TOWN MEETINGS

On Monday last, the representatives for the county attended the town meeting of Toronto, pursuant to their promise to be present at one of the town meetings each new year. The meeting was held at Cook's Tavern, and was the largest ever held in that populous township. The kind and friendly manner in which the yeomanry welcomed their members, received and merited their most grateful acknow-
ledgements. The business of the town meeting was conducted

quietly and peaceably, and the utmost good humour and goodwill were manifested by the people to one another. After the order of the day had been gone through with, the subject of the roads was taken up, and the general sentiment was evidently opposed to any system of statute labour, or commutation thereof, which would appropriate the work or money in any other way than by officers appointed by the people at their town meetings. Toll gates were evidently unpopular. None of the Lt. Governor's propositions were formally brought under review by the magistrates. We looked in at the Etobicoke town meeting, where his Excellency's proposals were severally put by Squire Gamble. We learn that they were all negatived, with scarcely a show of support. We hear that they met the same fate at Scarboro'. A gentleman who was at the York town meeting has stated to us that His Excellency's plan was rejected in that township also.

In Toronto meeting, there were a variety of topics brought under review, such as the militia system, voting by ballot, education, land granting, road systems, and the application of the sales of wild lands and reserves to improve the roads, the navigation of the St. Lawrence, law-fees, the revenue, the mode of appointing the magistracy, the judiciary, and the unfairness of allowing 10 or 15 members in parliament for a population scarcely equal to that of this county which sends two.

The more we see of the farmers of Upper Canada, the more are we convinced that they *will have* "equal laws and free institutions." As to Toronto, it is now the second township in the Home District, in point of numbers, and possesses a fertile soil and a generous and intelligent population. The river Credit and other beautiful streams water the township; and the villages of Streetsville, McNab'sville, Springfield and the Indian Reserve, are among the evidences of its future wealth and greatness.

After passing one of the most pleasant days of our life in Toronto, we found ourself turning the corner of Yonge and Dundas-Streets at a quarter past ten o'clock. COLONIAL ADVOCATE, 6 January 1831.

CHURCHES

MONTREAL, APRIL 10TH, 1831.
The Scots Presbyterian church is shut up at present, owing to a difference between the ministers. I went this forenoon to the American Presbyterian church, the clergyman of which is greatly

celebrated here as a preacher. The house is a large and commodious stone building, handsomely finished both inside and outside. The pulpit is of the most costly mahogany, with crimson cushion, very splendid. The windows are all made double to keep out the cold. The congregation sit while singing, as in Scotland, but the organist and band of musicians alone join in the melody; at least I did not observe that any others of the congregation opened their lips to sing. The music is very pleasing; some of the choristers, male and female, having fine, powerful voices. The congregation is numerous, and the people generally very well dressed, forming evidently an important and influential part of the citizens of Montreal. Yet the minister, because he was born in the United States, is forbidden to marry even the members of his own congregation. . . .

The Catholic cathedral may be justly termed an ornament to the world. I like the outside, however, rather better than the interior arrangements. The spires or towers, it seems, are to be carried to a great height. Perhaps it is owing to early associations, but I confess I see more beauty in the bluish grey freestone of the church of Montreal than in the costly marble of the New York city hall. Strangers visiting this place should by no means omit going to see the foundling hospital, and that of the Hôtel Dieu. . . .

Never did a church establishment in any country present fewer objectionable points than that of Lower Canada.* The Catholic religion is professed by a majority of the people, and the clergy of that faith are maintained, not by a tithe, but by a twenty-sixth part of the produce of the land of those persons only who are members of that church. No man is forced to be a Catholic, consequently no man is forced to pay or maintain a Catholic minister. . . .

The Canadian pays tithe of wheat only. There are no other tithes demanded. COLONIAL ADVOCATE, 28 April 1831; SKETCHES, p. 147.

*Early in this session of the legislature [1832] I introduced my annual motion, declaratory against a government-appointed chaplain in assembly, and against an established church. The question was left to a committee, which reported that "in England there is a church established by law, which the king at his coronation is solemnly sworn to maintain," but "Your committee do not admit that the church of England is the established church of this province, and are therefore of opinion that the executive, if possessed of the right, might appoint a minister of any sect of Christians to officiate as chaplain of this House. Constituted as the House of Assembly of this province now is, and must always continue to be, of persons of various religious denominations, the appointment of any chaplain will, in all probability, be unsatisfactory to a majority of the House." The House adopted the report by a large majority, and the chaplain and his kneeling-stool were dismissed soon after. [*Footnote in* SKETCHES *only.*]

LATE WINTER IN QUEBEC

MAILHOT'S HOTEL, QUEBEC, APRIL 21, 1831.
What a variety of climates and temperatures are to be found in Canada! At York the ice had left the streets and open country more than a month ago; at Montreal, the scavengers were clearing it out of St. Paul Street, its last resort within the city, a week ago. But here, in the ancient capital of the Canadas, there are as yet left abundant memorials of turbulent winter. In defiance of sun and rain, and "gentle April breezes," vast quantities of snow and ice are accumulated even in the most open and exposed parts of the country round Quebec; I came down from Cape Rouge the greater part of the road in a sleigh, and in many places the ice and snow lay two, three, four, say even six feet deep on the highway. In the harbour here there is a great deal of ice; and on crossing hither from Mackenzie's Hotel at Point Levi there is much difficulty experienced in making the shore. The Canadians who ferried me across skipped like supple-jacks from island to island of floating frost, with their moccasins on, and in utter defiance of cold and wet. Now and then they held on by the boat and pushed it towards land with astonishing celerity.

I like Quebec; I always admired its bold and romantic scenery. Nature here exhibits her handy-work on a grand and magnificent scale; and Art has done much to second her efforts. Steep as are the streets and heavy the ascents, yet nevertheless would my Scottish taste prefer this rock to the most level plains in Canada. The environs of Quebec in every direction appear to be well and thickly settled, and the style of cultivation in which the farms are kept is highly creditable to the Canadian farmers. They labour under one great disadvantage, as compared with the Upper Canada grain growers, not being able to sow fall wheat and depend on the crop. On the other hand, they are nearer the market.

COLONIAL ADVOCATE, 12 May 1831; SKETCHES, p. 181.

A QUEBEC THEATRE

We of the Canadas surely require much keeping and are a very valuable race of people. I saw as many military and naval officers at the Amateur Theatre, assembled to witness the representation of General Bombastes Furioso, as would have swallowed up any other

51

nation than Great Britain for their maintenance in idleness. They were generally good-looking men, and if placed on farms, like Cincinnatus after the Roman war, would have raised wheat, Indian corn, pigs, poultry, and Johnny cake, to the benefit of our common country. General Bombastes sat immediately opposite General Aylmer, and supported his assumed character, style, and dignity, much to my satisfaction. General Aylmer is a hale, good-looking, elderly gentleman, above the middle-size, and if he does not live very comfortable, it must be his own fault, for he has a castle in the clouds—a court studded round with fighting cavaliers and fair damsels—a baroness who (I am told) speaks French like a native, and does the honours of his venerable chateau with the grace and dignity of a Maintenon or a Josephine—a crimson throne and chair of state—and last, but not least, about 10,000 pounds a year of spending money!

COLONIAL ADVOCATE, 12 May 1831; SKETCHES, p. 180.

NOTES ON THE GROWTH OF YORK

The people both in town and country were opposed to the law vesting in the magistrates power over the town's funds, but their opposition was altogether futile. The county members voted against the measure, but it was of no avail. Now TWENTY SIX THOUS-AND DOLLARS are at once to be expended on a court-house, and the money must be raised hereafter, principal and interest, by a direct tax to be levied on the inhabitants. Yet, they will have no more control in the expenditure, nor over the building after it is erected, than the Great Mogul or Grand Turk. We do not like to complain of our townsmen, but it must be owned they have not thus far been greatly distinguished for independence or public spirit. Perhaps they reserve their courage for grand occasions; and if so, they can by a requisition to Mr. Van Allen the town-clerk, clap an extinguisher upon the bill, the tax, and the $26,000; for daring as the faction have shewn themselves, they will be in no hurry to contract in the face of a petition from York to His Majesty to exercise his prerogative by repealing the act.

.   .   .

The Executive Government propose to assemble the provincial legislature in October next. They are alarmed at the example of the

Lower Canada Parliament which will meet at that period, and fearful lest we of this colony (our sages) should have the benefit of their earlier deliberations.

Instead of expending 25,000 dollars on a Court House and bringing on a direct taxation on the people of York, would it not be better to build respectable and efficient wharves for the accommodation of the shipping? The office of the Surveyor General has been removed to the brick building west of the new parliament house. The Surveyor General, a Mr. Hurd from Nova Scotia or New Brunswick, has been enjoying the revenues of office for some time but has not yet appeared among us. There are a host of surveyor generals now—1st, this Mr. Hurd; 2nd, Mr. Peter Robinson; third, Mr. Chewitt, 4th, Dr. Dunlop. These four receive at least three thousand sterling pounds a year of the money of the people of Upper Canada. Two of them might be dispensed with.

.   .   .

Whenever it shall be determined to improve the means of conveyance, between this town and lake Simcoe to their fullest extent, we are of opinion that a rail road will be projected and made. But for that improvement the time has not yet come.

.   .   .

The college and surrounding buildings are now nearly finished; the parliament house is far advanced; and the Lawyers' Hall will be completed soon enough for their clients. The Scots Kirk and baptist chapel have got the seats in and the plaster work almost done; and the building for the public offices begins to be occupied.

.   .   .

Seasoned Lumber is in great demand in this place, and cannot be had for love or money. Frame houses and brick houses are in progress in every direction. We hope and trust that room will be left for public promenades, they are too often neglected in planning towns.

.   .   .

When the merchants puff the York Bank monopoly to the farmers and tell them how much more its loans enable them to pay for the bushel of wheat, it would be well if they were made aware that such a monopoly is very dangerous to civil liberty, always siding with the few against the many. The London declaration against reform was got up by a set of persons connected with or dependant on the Bank of England and East India Company, and written by the Rev. Sir Harcourt Lees. The interests of the English banking monopoly are represented in parliament by saleable or pot-walloping boroughs

—Lord Grey wishes to do these boroughs away—and therefore the monopolists complain.

.   .   .

We visited the apartments of Stevens the portrait painter, in the Ontario House, the other day, where were displayed several specimens of his art. We immediately recognized the countenance of persons of our acquaintance, or with whose faces we are familiar, faithfully portrayed by the pencil of the limner on the inanimate canvas before us. Mr. Stevens deserves, and doubtless receives a large share of public patronage. COLONIAL ADVOCATE, 19 May 1831.

THE YORK MUSEUM

We paid a visit to the Museum [*advertised as the British Museum, York*] in the Market Square of this town on Thursday last, and feel a pleasure in recommending its enterprising proprietor [*William Wood*] as well deserving of a continuation of public patronage. The stock of birds and beasts, reptiles and insects, is greatly enlarged, and a collection of the most rare and curious fishes is in preparation. An assortment of Indian Curiosities, coins and medals have been lately added to the Museum; and to them who go in the evening the phantasmagoria presents many attractions. It says a great deal in favour of the good taste of the capital of Upper Canada, that while miserable obscene strolling players have been unable to winter in it, the proprietor of the Museum has found support in exhibiting his collection of the wonderful works of nature and art. COLONIAL ADVOCATE, 9 June 1831.

IMMIGRANTS

QUEBEC, April 22nd to 25th, 1831. One forenoon I went on board the ship *Airthy Castle*, from Bristol, immediately after her arrival. The passengers were in number 254, all in the hold or steerage; all English, from about Bristol, Bath, Frome, Warminster, Maiden Bradley, &c. I went below, and truly it was a curious sight. About 200 human beings, male and female, young, old, and middle-aged; talking, singing, laughing, crying, eating, drinking, shaving, washing; some naked in bed, and others dressing to go ashore; handsome young women (perhaps some) and ugly old men, married and single; religious and irreligious. Here a grave matron chaunting selections from the last edition of the last new hymn book; there, a brawny plough-boy "pouring forth the sweet melody of Robin Adair." These settlers were poor, but in general they were fine-looking people, and such as I was glad to see come to America. They had had a fine passage of about a month, and they told me that no more ship loads of settlers would come from the same quarter this year. I found that it was the intention of many of them to come to Upper Canada. Fortune may smile on some, and frown on others; but it is my opinion that few among them will forget being cooped up below deck for four weeks in a moveable bed-room, with 250 such fellow-lodgers as I have endeavoured to describe. COLONIAL ADVOCATE, 20 May and 9 June 1831; SKETCHES, p. 179.

YORKSHIRE SETTLERS

On Saturday last, the Steamboat *Great Britain* arrived with about 200 emigrants, chiefly English, from Yorkshire; and last Tuesday the *Queenston* brought about 400 more settlers, two-thirds from England (chiefly Yorkshire) and the remainder, one Scots family excepted, Irish.—These emigrants are, on the average, possessed of means to enable them to choose their location—they are a hardy, wholesome, good-looking people—a people of whom Canada may well be proud, for their active industry will powerfully aid in changing her forests into fruitful fields.—We were at much pains to ascertain from the well-informed and experienced among these strangers, the actual condition of England. Agriculture, they say, is at a low ebb; the farmers in general are so enraged at the avarice and flint-heartedness of their landlords that many are putting their farms out of order, wearing them out, and crossing or preparing to cross the Atlantic. Hundreds of Yorkshire farmers will be out next year, both to Canada and the United States—they say it is the best thing they can do—hundreds of farms are to let in the hands of their owners. Nothing less than an idle armed well-fed and well-paid standing army could have kept the people from rising last winter and crushing the borough-mongering oligarchy who have so long dictated to King and Country. My Lord Brougham is a great favourite with these settlers—as he has long been with the farmers and peasantry of Westmorland.

.   .   .

Several intelligent English settlers who left Yorkshire last month assure us that lands in England are in many places very much wore out by continual cropping, and will not produce half as much as formerly. Wheat is sown in England in the fall, and we are assured that in addition to the indifferent crops of past years, the prospects are by no means favourable. Had it not been for American Wheat and Flour, they say, England last winter would have been in a dreadful state, and they think the demand for grain from this side of the Atlantic will be likely to be increasing and permanent. If this reasoning is good, emigrants should endeavour above all things to get good deeds of fertile lots of land, fit for wheat, and confine their attention as much as possible to its production. But we merely state the facts that have been stated to us, leaving our numerous and highly intelligent readers to draw their own inferences.

In conclusion—we would request such of our friends and acquaintances as may become neighbours of these English and Irish settlers, to endeavour to impress strongly on their minds that the best way to avoid in Canada the evils they have left in England is to be industrious and prudent, and to love their country, always seeking its peace and prosperity, and keeping in mind the divine command to love their neighbours as themselves.

.   .   .

By the latest authentic accounts from England and Scotland, obtained from a quarter well entitled to credit, we are happy in being enabled to state that although agriculture is greatly depressed, trade and commerce are in a flourishing condition. In Glasgow, Paisley, Manchester, Sheffield, and other manufacturing towns, there were very heavy foreign orders on hand unfulfilled, and all hands employed. True, the labourer and mechanic would not receive a liberal price for his labour, prices being low. But it is a great satisfaction to be enabled to inform those who think yet of their ancient home and its pleasures, that *hope* tells us things may mend. COLONIAL ADVOCATE, 9 June 1831.

YORK AND SIMCOE PETITIONERS

Travel thro' these counties, as we have done, gentle reader, and you will perchance find various opinions with regard to public men; but with reference to the great questions involved in the address to His Majesty adopted in this town on the 16th July last, one opinion prevails, and that opinion is decisive in its favour. In Etobicoke, in Scarboro', in Pickering, in Whitby, in Uxbridge, in Markham, in Whitchurch, in East Gwillimbury, in Brock, in North Gwillimbury, in Tecumseth, in West Gwillimbury, in King, in Albion, in Caledon, in Chinguacousy, in Vaughan and in Toronto, in nineteen public meetings regularly convened, and attended by between two and three thousand of the landowners, householders and others, heads of families and influential inhabitants, at the farmer's throngest season of the year, one sentiment prevailed, and one voice was heard with regard to the measures to be pursued for the maintenance and advancement of the prosperity and happiness of Upper Canada.

The petitions to the King and Parliament will be signed by all classes, and ample means will be put into the hands of the General Committee in this town to enable them to fulfil the important duties which devolve on them. Lawyers and doctors, priests and placemen, merchants and mechanics, have had their societies and associations, and committees and corporations, their private and partial schemes and designs for their own benefit, and the people have suffered by them all—but now the people will have their associations also; they will go regularly and steadily to work, and we will see whether complete success will fail to attend their honest and united efforts. THE FEW may continue to cry out, that wisdom remains with them, but THE MANY will cease to regard the voice of the charmer.

Are there those who begin to ask themselves—Will the other counties and towns of Upper Canada unite with the Home District in this matter?—We will reply by another question: Do you believe that the townships who have expressed an unanimous opinion and prepared to follow it up by decisive measures in favour of the address to the king, have different interests from the other counties, or that the people inhabiting these townships think so? If so, get up a petition in favour of African slavery, church and state exclusive establishments, clergy reserves, sinecures, pensioners, perquisites, district funds squanderers, extravagant law fees, unequal representation, the primogeniture laws, the Canada Company monopoly, the tea monopoly, the bank monopoly, Strachan's College, the opening our ports to American produce while theirs are shut to the produce of the Canadas, taxation and application of the farmers' money without their consent, and other like matters opposed to the principles laid down in that address. Get up such a petition and try it in Stormont and Glengarry those abodes of ignorance, as Speaker

McLean informed the Legislature—try it in Stormont and Glengarry you that doubt, and be not surprised if the inhabitants call upon you to render a reason why you should not pay a visit to Bedlam. COLONIAL ADVOCATE, 11 August 1831.

WHITCHURCH

Unquestionably the country north of the Ridges far surpasses the south in beauty. Whitchurch, the east or settled part of King, near Yonge Street, East Gwillimbury and North Gwillimbury, form one continued settlement; and such might have now been all the *good land* in this fertile colony, but for the narrow-minded policy of the government, who have been a dead weight upon the energies of the country, and the protectors and preservers of wolves and bears, and forests and swamps, and fevers and agues, and bad roads—the gaolers of the people—penning them up here and there, and squeezing from their industry a miserable tribute. Where is there in America a lovelier spot of earth than the country north of Lake Ontario?

Mr. John Bogart, sen., with whom I breakfasted one morning at his house, situated on one of the highest pieces of table land in Whitchurch, county of York, probably 700 feet above Ontario's margin, was one of the first settlers, and now owns, with his sons and family, a valuable and improving estate. Bogart's mills are built on a never-failing stream falling into Lake Simcoe, and a village has been laid out close by. The new mill is a large and extensive flouring establishment, and must have consumed a great capital. Mr. Bogart's son called the town meeting, and the father presided; Mr. Eck, who has a farm and tannery in the next concession, acting as secretary. If those persons in office in England could but enter into the feelings of the farmers here, and properly understand the effects of their exclusive system, it would be altered. *And it will be altered.*

The meeting in East Gwillimbury, to petition the king for a redress of grievances, was followed in the evening by many demonstrations of joy; and the spirited young men of the volunteer amateur musicians, composing the powerful band of the militia regiment, marched up and down the streets of Hope, playing cheerful and enlivening airs. I had the curiosity to count their instruments, and there were three or four clarionets, two French horns, two bassoons, besides German and octave flutes, flageolets, &c. They have also violins and violoncellos, and are masters of their delightful art.

WHITCHURCH

While riding through the Georgiana woods, we lost our way about half an hour before sunset; there were many forest tracks, but we could not tell the true one. As we journeyed on, guessing our way, jumping over fallen trees, and wading the creeks as carefully as possible, lest our horses should sink in the mire, a young woman came up, with silver brooch, plaid, bare legs, shoes and stockings in hand, and dressed very plain, Highland Scottish fashion. She spoke very little English, and Mr. M'Leod and I had forgot what little Gaelic we once possessed; but we ascertained that she had come from (I think) Breadalbane, and was on her way to a relative in Thorah, thirty miles farther back in these woods. It would, indeed, be hard, if the distress brought on by the cruel and unfeeling monopolizers of power in Britain and Ireland, which could drive a lass like this 4000 miles off to wander in these deserts to seek an independent home, could be made to reach the emigrants permanently in America. But it will not—Canada is not lashed alongside of Great Britain like Ireland, to be scourged and oppressed for ages in the name of Jesus Christ, Christianity, and the Protestant religion! And perhaps, too, there is some reality in the Reform Bill. COLONIAL ADVOCATE, 18 August 1831; SKETCHES, p. 242.

KEMPTVILLE TOWN MEETING

I passed through some very agreeable and wealthy settlements in my journeyings in Leeds and Grenville. Elizabethtown and Yonge appear to be settled with able and independent farmers; many of their houses are large and commodious, some in the European and some in the Lower Canada fashion. Stone is a very common building material in this section of the country. I had been led to believe that the soil near the line of the Rideau Canal was indifferent but so far as my observation extended this is not the case. The farmer, taking one farm with another and one season with another, raises about fifteen bushels of wheat per acre. This is less than the average near York. But on the other hand, the spring crops on the Rideau are very abundant. In Gower and Oxford there is a great deal of good land, but the export of wheat is quite inconsiderable.

We arrived at Kemptville, (a thriving village thus named in honour of Sir James Kempt), on the morning of the meeting, about eleven.—Kemptville, like Merrickville, has considerable water power; it is situated on the south branch of the Rideau. There is a post-office, also stores, an English Chapel, and several public houses. The meeting was held in front of Mr. Adams's Inn, which it seems is the residence of Mr. Patton, the English Clergyman. The principal or largest room upstairs we intended for the meeting, but the reverend gentleman and his friends were, it seems, holding a caucus in that room, in order to defeat our objects and introduce resolutions of a contrary tendency. The people of the Gore District will stare with astonishment when I tell them, that among the reverend gentleman's chamber counsel when the caucus broke up, appeared on the battle ground no less a personage than Mr. Daniel O'Reilly of the twelve mile creek, a freeholder, as he afterwards told the people, of four several Districts; and, as it appears, an inhabitant of Merrickville, where he had bought a lot, made improvements, and resided six weeks. Knowing nothing of this change of domicile, I imagined that Messrs. Simon Washburn (the *friend* of Willis!), Colonel Fitzgibbon, Doctor Strachan, John Willson, and Doctor Lee would follow suit, but they did not appear.

The meeting opened, and the assemblage was very numerous and respectable; many freeholders, and not a few magistrates and militia officers being also present. Mr. O'Reilly and the priest's party commenced their opposition the moment Mr. Beach took the chair, and named Squire Burritt in his stead, but the meeting amply sustained their first choice. The priest threw every possible difficulty in our way, objected strongly against the proposal for a sale of the clergy reserves or applying them to educate the youth of the colony; and after the petitions had been adopted by a glorious majority, tapped people on the shoulder and advised them not to sign when he saw them about to do so. Mr. Patton is a very good looking young man, the son of Major Patton, but he is a fair specimen of what may be expected from Colborne College as now constituted.

Mr. O'Reilly, McKay, and a few other persons were for some time very riotous and quite abusive. They would interrupt the speaker or reader as the case was, with "that's a lie", and such other charming expressions, but the good sense of the people eventually kept them in order. The Irish and Scotch behaved nobly during the day, and were well backed by the other settlers. It was remarked that at the very moment the Secretary was reading the resolution of the thanks to Mr. Hume the Steam Boat arrived in the river from Bytown and fired her gun.

I have never missed an opportunity, from the 16th of July last down to the present day, to address the people at their several meetings, generally for one, two, and not seldom two hours and a half, upon the state of public affairs, the conduct of the government, the amount and sources of the revenue, the wasteful expenditure of the public money, the course taken by the governor and the causes why he takes that course, the public debt, the York Bank, the character of the British Ministry and the excellent example shewn by the King, the miserable pittance granted to Common Schools, Colborne College, the Law Monopoly, Church Monopoly, Land Granting Monopoly, Representation Monopoly, District Funds and Magistrate appointing Monopoly, Legislative and Executive Council Monopoly, Education Monopoly, Office holding Monopoly, the Reign of Terror, the Tea Monopoly, the Canada Company Monopoly, the Law of Primogeniture, the Trade with the United States, the Militia appointment system, and the utter inefficiency of the popular branch of the legislature unless the means of bribery and corruption be taken out of the hands of the vindictive family faction, and the people granted that constitutional control over the public revenue and property which is so essential to good government.

So attentively have these *lengthy* political discourses been listened to, and so utterly ineffectual has been the opposition of those who have offered sophistry in answer to *stubborn facts*, that altho' the unusually early opening of the session will cause me to return to York in a few days, I now respectfully announce my intention, if it please providence to spare me in health and strength, to continue my tour over Upper Canada at the close of the legislative sitting. I am indeed highly gratified with the kind, cordial, and even affectionate reception I have met with everywhere from the people. A representative of Upper Canada and resident freeholder can nowhere be considered an intruder. I have sometimes puzzled an angry opponent with such a hard question as this—What measure did I ever support in the Assembly, what vote did I ever give, that was at variance with the best interests of Upper Canada? Perseverance in a good cause is the surest road to success; and the friends of education and equal rights through patience and vigilance, will assuredly win the day. We are now only beginning to find out our strength, and learning to organize in a glorious cause. As for Lord Grey he will take good care that there be no gagging bills in operation in Upper Canada during his ministry, and with regard to political libel prosecutions they are altogether out of fashion. The people are the same in sentiment throughout the colony (so far as I have been)—they may differ a little, perhaps, as to men, but they perfectly agree as to what they wish to have done for their own good. On the other hand "the family faction" rule them with a sway as absolute nearly as the perpetual dictatorship of Paraguay. Petitions and remonstrances have been thus far alike ineffectual.

To return to my narrative—

Mr. O'Reilly spoke "on behalf of the government," as he had the modest assurance to tell us. He would recommend it to the people to consider the subject for a fortnight and then come back to Kemptville and determine. For as to the "harangue" he had heard he would not pretend to reply to the whole of it. Whatever else Mr. O'Reilly said or whatever he meant to have said, or could or would or might or should have said, he is to say hereafter through the press for the edification of the learned. As the organ of the priest's party, he was of infinite service to us, for his statement being added up was less than nothing.

So the people voted for the petitions and subscribed them, and voted against adjournments equivalent to parliamentary readings that day six months. As a general rule, I have found that opposition to the petitions enlisted the people more anxiously in their own cause. COLONIAL ADVOCATE, 3 November 1831.

THE METHODISTS

The "Christian Guardian" of the 29th of August, 1832, gives a statement of the Methodist body in Canada, from which it appears that within the bounds of the Upper Province there are 14,901 members of the church, of whom 1090 are Indians; that the increase of members in society since last year is 3553; that the Rev. James Richardson is to be the editor of the "Conference" paper for 1832-3; and that the Rev. Egerton Ryerson is delegated by the Canada Conference to come to England next May with propositions for a union with the general Wesleyan Conference in England, which also has three or four missionaries itinerating in Upper Canada.

It is estimated that there are about four or five regular hearers to one member, consequently the regular attendants upon the Methodist church in the colony may be reckoned at from 60,000 to 70,000.

Many of the ministers of this connexion are men of excellent ability as preachers of the gospel. They have done great good in the colony, and are held in deserved estimation by the people for their zeal and faithfulness in the performance of their high duties; but from the government and its officers they have suffered many wrongs.

THE METHODISTS

Although I have heard a great deal about camp-meetings I never was at any time a spectator of the proceedings at these rural assemblies for public worship; and, having never seen them, cannot describe them. I should, however, incline to the opinion that the accounts of extravagance in action which are circulated concerning them, by Mrs. Trollope and others, are mere caricatures. The Methodists are a highly respectable and intelligent body, and their ministers often men of talent and great knowledge of mankind, who labour unceasingly to promote the interests of morality and religion, receiving an income scarcely sufficient to support themselves and families. SKETCHES, p. 105.

WOMEN VOTERS

When my friend Colonel Baby, of Sandwich, contested the county of Kent with Messrs. Lyttle and Wilkinson, no less than thirty-five ladies came forward to the hustings and gave their votes,—maids and widows,—one of them gave Wilkinson a plumper. This was almost equal to a declaration in form. Only one married lady voted. But in Lower Canada there have been numerous instances of women exercising the freehold right of voting in person for a favourite candidate. Sometimes the wife votes on one freehold and the husband on another.

There was a contested election at Montreal, in May, 1832, which lasted about a month; during its continuance two hundred and twenty-five women came forward to vote. One of the candidates, Dr. Tracy, was an Irishman, and for him ninety-five ladies recorded their votes. The other gentleman was Mr. Stanley Bagg, a citizen of the United States, naturalized in Canada. For him there were one hundred and four female voters. The other twenty-six did not vote. Several ladies voted one way, and, it is said, their husbands took the other side. One married lady voted in her own right. Her husband was found to have no vote. The Irishman won the day, but by a very small majority. The Quebec Act, under which the ladies vote, was passed in the British parliament forty years ago.

It is in my recollection that when Canning was standing for Liverpool, he told the ladies in a jocular way, that if ever he advocated the doctrine of universal suffrage, he would not fail to include them. What is it that may not become fashionable? SKETCHES, p. 20.

Chapter Two

EDUCATION

EDITOR'S PREFACE I. EDUCATION IN UPPER CANADA *In 1830, when* A Catechism of Education *was published, there were various types of school in Upper Canada. Before the end of the eighteenth century schools had been started here and there by the initiative of the settlers. Such were the schools at Matilda, in Dundas County, built by "a few of the neighbours" in 1788, and at Moraviantown, in Kent County, opened in 1794, and taught by "Brother Senseman", a local farmer. In the London District "schools were opened by the persons themselves as a private enterprise, without Government or municipal aid." (See* Pioneer Schools of Upper Canada, *by Frank Eames, Ontario Historical Society, vol. 18, pp. 91-103.)*

In 1807 the District Public School Act provided for the establishment of a grammar (high) school in each of the eight Districts: Western, London, Niagara, Home, Newcastle, Midland, Johnstown, and Eastern. In 1816 the Common School Act made provision for the inhabitants of any community to set up an elementary school, to be financed partly by a government grant and partly by voluntary subscription. (See Eighty Years of Progress of British North America, *by H. Y. Hind, etc., Toronto, 1863.)*

But though these various schools existed, there were too few of them, the teachers were in most cases inadequate and their equipment and efficiency were poor, as testified by witnesses before the Committee of the Assembly on Grievances, 1835. In 1820 the reduction of government grants and the poverty of the settlers had led to the closing of many country schools. And, as for the District Schools, they were only available for children living in the chief towns and for those whose parents could afford to pay the cost of board.

The Report on the Midland District School at Kingston, published in the Colonial Advocate *for 6 January 1831, and sent by the Trustees to Sir John Colborne, reveals that there were in attendance thirty-one boys; that in the examinations the boys showed a pleasing proficiency in Latin, Greek, English, and Mathematics; that of the six leaving school from the top class, two were going on to study Divinity, three*

Law, and one Medicine. The Trustees considered it urgently necessary to increase the grants for teachers' salaries; they found the school building "decayed and inconvenient"; the cost of tuition and board was too high; and they deplored the fact that, though provision was made in the Act for the free education of ten children, none were as yet receiving this education because of the expense of paying board. The Trustees end by asking the Government to go on to "supply the means of education to thousands, who aim not to follow the learned professions, but whose adequate instruction is quite as important to the well being of the community as that perhaps of any other class."

In 1823 Archdeacon Strachan became head of the central Board of Education for the Province. In a letter to Wilmot Horton of the Colonial Office, 16 May 1827, he made it clear that he envisaged a network of Church of England schools throughout the Province. He advised the appointment of additional clergy, sent from England, to make up the number of two or three hundred, to "infuse into the inhabitants a tone and feeling entirely English; and acquiring by degrees the direction of education which the Clergy of England have always possessed." In the same year a charter for King's College was granted, with the Bishop as visitor, Strachan as first President, and seven members of the Church of England making up the Corporation. There were, however, to be no religious tests for students. In 1828 the Common School at York was transformed into a Church of England National School. In 1829 the District School at York was superseded by Upper Canada College, under Church of England patronage and control. Against these developments there was determined opposition by Presbyterians, Methodists, and Reformers. (See Doughty and Story, Constitutional Documents, *vol. 3, pp. 371ff.; the* Colonial Advocate, *11 October 1827; 31 July 1828, etc.)*

Both boys and girls attended the Common Schools and some privately organized schools. (See the Colonial Advocate, *22 February, 26 July 1827.) For girls there were in addition, in York at least, private seminaries. (See the* Colonial Advocate, *6 January, 4 August 1831, etc.)*

*Mackenzie refers several times to Lancasterian schools (*Colonial Advocate, *19 May, 1 September 1831;* Catechism, *Qu. 85, Note). These schools followed the monitorial system, whereby older scholars helped in the teaching of beginners. Unlike the Church of England National Schools (sometimes called "Madras" after experiments made by Bell in India), which followed a similar system, they were undenominational. Joseph Lancaster (1778-1838), who opened his first school in London in 1798, aimed at teaching as many children as*

c

possible to read and write in the shortest possible time, and thousands of English children became literate through his system before public elementary education was established. At one time the system was *widespread in France* (Colonial Advocate, *1 September 1831); Gottfried Keller mentions it in Switzerland; and from 1818 to 1836 it was followed in the public schools of Philadelphia, and in some of the schools of Baltimore, Boston, and Washington.*

In Canada the first Lancasterian school was founded in Quebec in 1814. Others followed in Montreal, Kingston, and Three Rivers. In 1829 Lancaster came to Canada en route from the United States to England. He was detained by family ill-health, and remained four years, during which time he won the interest of Papineau, who was instrumental in obtaining government grants for Lancaster in 1830-2. Sir James Kempt, Lord Aylmer, and Papineau all contributed personally. After 1832 government support was withheld, and Lancaster himself turned his main energies towards the relief of his "suffering dying neighbours" during the cholera epidemic. The school languished, and Lancaster withdrew to the United States, where he died in 1838. (See a Report *published by Lancaster in Montreal, 1833,* Toronto Public Library; *and* Development of Education in Canada *by C. E. Phillips, 1957.) The similar Bell system is described in detail in the* Colonial Advocate, *21 August 1828.*

Advertisements in the Colonial Advocate *show that there was considerable activity in the field of adult education. Evening classes were given in York in various subjects, including Chemistry, English, Penmanship ("the very worst writers" taught in three short easy lessons), Mathematics, Accounting. The York Mechanics' Institute was founded at the end of 1830. Its plans* (Colonial Advocate, *9 December 1830) included a reference and circulating library, lectures on useful scientific subjects, and "suitable accommodation for the ladies". The Natural History Society offered essay prizes (9 September 1830), and four months later the Literary and Philosophical Society of Upper Canada was founded* (Colonial Advocate, *3 February 1831). The Home District Agricultural Society began its meetings in March 1830. The following year the York Young Men's Society was organized "to promote the moral and intellectual improvement of young men".*

Such was the background of education in Upper Canada when A Catechism of Education *came off the press.*

2. MACKENZIE'S EDUCATION   *When he arrived in Canada in 1820, Mackenzie was already a man of considerable learning.*

As a little boy at home, before he went to school, he became familiar with the Bible. During his schooldays he often sat up well into the night reading, and when, at the age of fifteen, he went to work in a counting-house in Dundee, he regularly spent his evenings in the public reading-room.

By 1819 he had read nearly a thousand books, and from many of them he copied out passage after passage into the note-books which he brought with him to Canada. His reading included histories of Scotland, England, Greece, Rome, modern Europe, and America; travels in Africa, Arabia, India, Europe, and America; Scottish and English poetry; popular and critical journals; books on agriculture, natural history, medicine, mathematics, mechanics, and chemistry; diaries, letters, and biographies of the leading men of the eighteenth century; theology and sermons; novels and plays. In translation he had read something at least of Molière, Cervantes, Le Sage, Mirabeau, Voltaire, Montesquieu, Homer, Virgil, Plutarch, and Josephus. And he knew "song books ad infinitum". A full list of his early reading is given in Lindsey's Life *(1862) Appendix A. By 1830, as we learn from the notes to* A Catechism of Education, *he had added many philosophers, economists, and educationists.*

Mackenzie acquired, probably through observation, an understanding of the printer's craft, and a down-to-earth sense of the need for good paper, ink, type, printers, binders, and readers. He "did much, in spite of many difficulties, to improve the technique of printing in Upper Canada" (J. J. Talman, Canadian Historical Review, *vol. xviii, p. 414).*

3. NOTES ON THE TEXT OF A CATECHISM OF EDUCATION   The Catechism, *of which only Part I is known to exist, is here reprinted without abridgement. But only a few of Mackenzie's Notes are included. These Notes are very voluminous, taking up a good deal more space than the text. They are for the most part quotations from many sources without comment from Mackenzie. Besides the authors mentioned by him in his Preface* (q.v.), *sources include:* Washington, Burns, the Edinburgh Scotsman, the Spectator, the Edinburgh Review, the London Magazine, the Philadelphia Journal of Health, Bell's Weekly Messenger, the Encyclopedia Britannica, the Nova Scotia Parliamentary Debates, the Edinburgh Journal of Science, the Mechanics' Journal, the Library of Entertaining Knowledge, the Canadian Miscellany, the American Quarterly Review, the Westminster Review, the Philadelphian.

4. NOTE ON THE OCCASIONAL PAPERS   *There are many more references to education scattered throughout Mackenzie's editorials in his newspapers than those given here. He never failed to put education high*

up on his list of needed reforms, and he repeatedly emphasized the need for an informed electorate and an entirely literate population. His remarks on education thus overlap with those on books and newspapers.

CATECHISM OF EDUCATION

To David Thorburn, of Queenston, the Following Catechism is Respectfully Inscribed by His Most Obedient Servant
W. L. MACKENZIE

PREFACE

To Mr. Joseph Hume (whose active benevolence, and unwearied exertions, to promote the happiness of his fellow creatures, are known and appreciated both in Europe and America) the compiler is indebted for an Essay on Education, which lays down and explains principles of vital importance to the best interests of the Canadas; the perusal of which first suggested the design of this Catechism.

In the part now published, reference has been had to the works of Dugald Stewart, Adam Smith, Reid, Milton, Locke, Addison, Watts, Boyle, Simpson, Gillies, Paley, Bacon, Burnet, Pope, Milner, Hume, Bolingbroke, Priestley, Hartley, Mill, Adams, Newton, Jones, Cudworth, Burke, Humboldt, Cochrane, Crichton, Fairbanks, Blair, Johnson, Thomson, King, Jefferson, Clinton, Penn, Phillips, Mitchell, Gray, Lavater, Thomas Smith, Brougham, Jeffrey, Brewster, Campbell, Gregory, Chace, Cooper, Wolf, Beattie, &c.; and the sacred Scriptures have been frequently quoted as evidence in favour of a more general diffusion of the blessings of education among mankind.

In the first part, under the heads, Domestic, Technical, Social, and Political Instruction, it has been attempted to shew chiefly what the means are by which the human mind may be endowed with those qualities on which the generation of happiness depends. In the three remaining numbers [*probably never published*], it is intended to describe, and prove by analysis, the exercises which would be most conducive in forming those virtues, which are included under the name of Intelligence, and to consider more fully those branches of moral education which operate upon the whole

period of human life, but more directly and powerfully after the youth is launched into the world under his own control.
York, March 12th, 1830.

INTRODUCTION

1. *What is Education?*

The best employment of all the means which can be made use of by man, for rendering the *human mind* to the greatest possible degree the cause of human happiness.

2. *On what does Happiness depend?*

Happiness depends upon the condition of the body, either immediately, as where the bodily powers are exerted for the attainment of some good; or mediately, through the mind, as where the condition of the body affects the qualities of the mind.

3. *What is required as the foundation of a good Education?*

Good practice; *which can, in no case, have any solid foundation but in sound theory.*

4. *What is theory?*

The *whole* of the knowledge which we possess upon any subject, put into that order and form in which it is most easy to draw from it good practical rules.

5. *In what does the character of the human mind consist?*

In the sequences of its ideas.

6. *What are the grand instruments or powers, by the use of which the purposes of education are to be attained?*

Custom; and Pain, and Pleasure.

7. *To what points is Custom to be directed?*

First, to form those sequences which make the component parts of a good train of ideas; and secondly, to join those sequences together, so as to constitute the trains.

8. *Does every operation of the senses imply* judgment *or* belief, *as well as simple apprehension, notion or imagination?*

Yes.

9. *Whence are all our trains of ideas?*

They start from a sensation, or some impression upon the external or internal nerves.

10. *Which are those sensations, or aggregates of sensations, which are of the most frequent occurrence?*
Those which occur in the ordinary business of life.

11. *Is it not of the greatest importance that beneficial trains of ideas should commence from those sensations?*
It surely is.

12. *Which are the aggregates of sensations of the most frequent occurrence?*
Rising up in the morning, and going to bed at night; also, the commencement and termination of meals.

13. *Did not the practical sagacity of priests, even in the rudest ages of the world, perceive the importance, for giving religious trains an ascendancy in the mind, of uniting them, by early and steady custom, with those perpetually recurring sensations?*
It did. The morning and evening prayers, and the grace before and after meals, have something correspondent to them in the religion of, perhaps, all nations.

14. *What effect will be produced by skilfully selecting the trains of ideas which lead most surely to the happiness, first of the individual himself, and next of his fellow creatures, and effectually uniting with them by custom the sensations which are most apt to give commencement to trains of ideas?*
A provision of unspeakable importance will be made for the happiness of the human race.

15. *What is appetite?*
It is the feeling towards pleasure or pain in prospect, and has great power over the mental trains of ideas.

16. *What are the best means of applying the prospect of pleasure and pain to render beneficent trains of ideas perpetual in the mind?*
We must first ascertain, what are the really ultimate objects of human desire; Next, what are the most beneficent means of attaining these objects; and lastly, accustom the mind to fill up the intermediate space between the present sensation and the ultimate object, with nothing but the ideas of those beneficent means.

17. *As a train commences in some present sensation, and may be conceived as terminating in the idea of some future pleasure or pain, what description of ideas intervene between the commencement and the end?*
Either beneficent or hurtful.

70

Qualities of Mind, to the Production of which the Business of Education should be directed

18. *What are the qualities with which it is of most importance that the mind of the individual should be endowed?*
Intelligence, Temperance, Justice, and Generosity.

19. *What are the ingredients of Intelligence?*
Knowledge and Sagacity.

20. *What effects are produced by an union of these qualities?*
The one affords the materials upon which the other is to be exerted; knowledge, shewing what exists; sagacity, converting it to the greatest use; knowledge, bringing within our ken what is capable, and what is not capable of being used as means; sagacity, seizing and combining, at the proper moment, whatever is fittest as means to each particular end.

21. *What is Temperance?*
A perfect command over a man's appetites and desires; the power of restraining them whenever they lead in a hurtful direction; that possession of himself which insures his judgement against the illusions of the passions, and enables him to pursue constantly what he deliberately approves.

22. *Is Temperance indispensably requisite to enable mankind to produce the greatest possible quantity of Happiness?*
It is.

23. *What is Fortitude?*
The power of resisting Pain.

24. *In how far are these two qualities, the* intelligence *which can always choose the best possible means, and the* strength *which overcomes the misguiding propensities, sufficient for the happiness of the human race?*
They appear to be sufficient for the happiness only of the individual who possesses them.

25. *What, then, are the qualities with which an individual ought to be endowed, to make him produce the greatest possible quantity of Happiness to others?*
A man can affect the happiness of others, either by abstaining

from doing them harm, or by doing them positive good: To abstain from doing them harm, receives the name of Justice; to do positive good receives that of Generosity.

26. *Do the four cardinal virtues of the ancients, Intelligence, Temperance, Justice, and Generosity, include all the qualities, to the possession of which the human mind should be trained?*
The description is far too general. What is wanting is, that the incidents of human life should be skilfully classified; both those on the occasion of which they who are the objects of the good acts are pointed out for the receipt of them, and those on the occasion of which they who are to be the instruments are called upon for the performance. The science of Ethics, as well as the science of Intellectuals, must be carried to perfection, before the best foundation is obtained for the science of Education.

SECTION III

Happiness, the End to which Education is devoted.—
Wherein it consists, not yet determined

27. *Wherein does human happiness consist?*
Although happiness has been often defined by the general terms, Blessedness, Content, and Good Fortune, and although it is the grand central point to which all other enquiries converge, it yet remains a controverted undetermined question, implying that the simple ideas included under the term are not clearly and precisely known, and that this branch of philosophy is far from its highest point of perfection.

28. *What are the speculations on this subject?*
They may be divided into *two great classes;* that of those who trace up all the elements of happiness, as they do all those of intellect, to the simple sensations which, by their transformation into ideas, and afterwards into various combinations, compose, they think, all the intellectual and moral phenomena of our nature; another, that of those who affirm that there is something in human happiness, and in the human intellect, which soars high above this corporeal level; that there are intellectual as well as moral forms, the resplendent objects of human desire. These philosophers speak of eternal and immutable truths; truths which are altogether independent of our limited experience; which are truly universal;

which the mind recognizes without the aid of the senses; and which are the objects of pure intellect. They affirm, also, that there is a notion of right and of wrong wholly underived from human experience, and independent of the laws which regulate, in this world, the happiness and misery of human life.

29. *Are they agreed as to the means whereby the distinction between this "right and wrong" is discovered?*

It is perceived, according to some, by a peculiar sense; according to others, by the faculty which discerns pure truth; according to others by Common Sense; it is the same, according to some, with the notion of the fitness and unfitness of things; according to others, with the law of nature; according to others, with truth; and there is one eminent philosopher who makes it depend upon sympathy, without determining very clearly whether sympathy depends upon the senses or not.

30. *Is it not of great importance that this enquiry should be perfected?*

It is; for while there is any vagueness and uncertainty with respect to the real object to which Education is pointed, it is utterly impossible that there should be the greatest precision and certainty in combining the means.

31. *Do the actions, called moral by all men, agree in the quality of conducing to the general happiness?*

They do.

32. *Is there any habitual disposition towards virtuous actions, which it is not conducive to the happiness of an individual to entertain in such a degree as to render it impossible for him to prefer an act of vice for its separate advantage?*

No philosopher has ever yet ventured to point out such a disposition.

SECTION IV

Instruments, and practical Expedients of Education

33. *What are the means at the disposal of mankind for endowing the human mind with the qualities on which the generation of happiness depends?*

They are attempted to be enumerated in this work, under the heads Domestic, Technical, Social, and Political Instruction; to which Dr. Reid correctly adds, that "*Reason* and *Reflection* must superadd

73

their tutory, in order to produce a *Rousseau,* a *Bacon,* or a *Newton."*

34. *In what degree are the useful qualities of human nature under the powers of Education?*

This is the subject of a famous controversy, with names of the highest authority on both sides of the question. M. Helvetius says, that if you take men who bring into the world with them the original constituents of their nature, their mental and bodily frame in that ordinary state of goodness which is common to the great mass of mankind, you may regard the whole as equally susceptible of mental excellence, and may trace the causes which make them to differ. He showed at how early an age indelible characters may be impressed; nay, that some of the circumstances over which man has a controul (for he speaks not of others), circumstances on which effects of the greatest importance depend, may be traced beyond the birth.

35. *What are the opinions of those who controvert the doctrine of Helvetius?*

They have contented themselves rather with rejecting than disproving; and, at best, have supported their rejection only by some incidental reflection, or the indication of a discrepancy between his conclusions and theirs. Some persons include in the term Education little more than what is expressed by the term schooling; commencing about six or seven years of age, and ending at latest with the arrival of manhood.

36. *Has it not then been proved that any difference exists between large bodies or nations, but that which Education creates?*

It is rather assumed than proved. Large bodies or numbers of men are raised to a high degree of mental excellence, and might, without doubt, be raised still higher. Other large bodies, or whole nations, have been found in so very low a mental state, as to be little above the brutes. All this vast difference or distance is undeniably the effect of Education. (6)* Enough is ascertained to prove that if Education does not perform every thing, there is hardly any thing which it does not perform.

Circumstances of the Physical kind which operate upon the mind in the way of Education

37. *What are the Physical circumstances which operate upon the human mind?*

They are either, 1. inherent in the body; or, 2. external to the

* See note on page 87.

body. Those which are external to the body operate upon the mind, by first operating upon the body.

38. *Which of the first kind seem to be the more remarkable?*
Healthiness or sickness, strength or weakness, beauty or deformity, the temperament, the age, the sex.

39. *Of the second sort which seem to be the more remarkable?*
The aliment, the labour, the air, temperature, action, rest.

40. *Is health favourable to Intelligence?*
It is partly favourable, and partly unfavourable; it is favourable, by allowing that time to be given to study, which many kinds of sickness withdraw, and by admitting a more vigorous attention, which the pain and langour of sickness often impairs. It is unfavourable, by introducing that flow of pleasurable ideas which is called high spirits, adverse to a certain pitch to the application of attention; and by leading to that passionate pursuit of pleasure, which diminishes, if it does not destroy, the time for study. (8)

41. *Has the mode in which disease operates upon the mental sequences been clearly ascertained?*
It is a subject of great complexity, and in which little has been done to mark distinctly the events, and ascertain the order of their succession. When the connection between particular states of body, and particular trains of ideas has been carefully watched and recorded, and the events, one by one, accurately distinguished and made easy to be recognized; and when the order in which they follow one another is known, our power over the trains of those events, power to prevent such as are unfavourable, and to produce such as are favourable, to human happiness, will then be at its height; *and how to take care of his health will be one of the leading parts of the moral and intellectual education of man.*

42. *In what way does muscular Strength (or Weakness) operate upon the human mind?*
Muscular strength is apt to withdraw the owner from mental pursuits, and engage him in such as are more of the animal kind; the acquisition and display of physical powers. Few men of great bodily powers have been much distinguished for great mental (9) excellence; some of the greatest ornaments of human nature have been remarkable for great bodily weakness. Muscular strength is apt to operate unfavourably upon the moral as well as the intellectual trains of thought. It diminishes that respect for other men, which is

so necessary to resist the impulses of passion; it presents innumerable occasions for playing the tyrant with impunity; and fosters, therefore, all that train of ideas in which the tyrannical vices are engendered.

43. *In what way do* Beauty *and* Deformity *affect the happiness of the human race?*

Illustrations will occur to every body, to prove that their power is not inconsiderable; so little, however, has been done to ascertain the facts, and record them in the best possible manner, that any thing which deserves the name of knowledge on the subject hardly exists.

44. *What are the trains of ideas and permanent tendencies impressed upon the human mind by means of Food?*

Aliment is good or evil, by quality and quantity. Bad quality, however, is seldom resorted to, except in consequence of deficient quantity, which latter operates unfavourably in many ways upon the *moral* temper of the mind. As people are ready to sacrifice every thing for a sufficient quantity of food, the want of it implies the most dreadful poverty; that state in which there is scarcely any source of pleasure, and in which almost every moment is subject to pain. A human being, almost constantly in pain, hardly visited by a single pleasure, and almost shut out from hope, loses by degrees, all sympathy with his fellow creatures; contracts even a jealousy of their pleasures, and at last a hatred; and would like to see all mankind as wretched as himself. The evil of insufficient food acts with an influence not less malignant upon the intellectual, than upon the moral part of the human mind. Food is the most important of all the stimulants applied to the living organs. If applied in less than a sufficient degree, the irritability is diminished in proportion. One of the first and best means of introducing intellectual and moral excellence into the minds of the principal portion of a people, is by providing for them a generous and animating diet. Nature herself forbids that you shall make a wise and virtuous people out of a starving one. A great part of our intellectual pleasures are ultimately deducible from those of taste. The social pleasures seem in a particular manner to be derived from this source, since it has been customary in all ages and nations, that we should enjoy the pleasures of taste in conjunction with our relations, friends, and neighbours. Nauseous tastes and painful impressions upon the alimentary duct give rise and strength to mental pains. The most common of these painful impressions arises from excess in eating and drinking. This excites and supports those uneasy states, which attend upon melancholy, fear, and sorrow. These states are introduced in a great degree during sleep, during the frightful dreams, agitations, and oppressions, that excess of diet occasions in the night. There ought to be a great reciprocal influence between the mind and alimentary duct, agreeably to common observation.

45. *Under what circumstances are unfavourable effects produced upon the mind of man by labour?*

Labour may be injurious either by its *quantity* or by its *quality*, or by both. The labour in which the great body of the people of a country are employed, has a tendency to grow less and less favourable as civilization and the arts proceed.

46. *In what manner is the progress of the arts injurious to labour?*

The division and subdivision of labour confines the attention of the labourer to so small a number of objects, and so narrow a circle of ideas, that the mind receives not that varied exercise, and that portion of aliment, on which almost every degree of mental excellence depends. Disuse destroys, in a certain degree, the faculties of the mind.

47. *Is there any risque of the arts reaching that dangerous point of subdivision and degeneracy in Canada at an early day?*

Not much; not, at least, from the causes which operate in Great Britain.

48. *Under what circumstances is the* quantity *of labour injurious?*

Labour may be to such a degree severe as to operate upon the mind with nearly the same effects as an habitual deficiency of food; obliterating sympathy, inspiring cruelty, and intemperance, rendering impossible the reception of ideas, and paralyzing the organs of the mind. Without the bodily labour of the great bulk of mankind the well-being of the species cannot be obtained; but if that bodily labour is carried beyond a certain extent, neither intellect, virtue, nor happiness, can flourish upon the earth.

49. *What then is the middle point, at which the greatest good is obtained with the smallest quantity of evil?*

This question contains a problem not yet solved; but enquiry may lead men to a juster estimate of the physical circumstances which concur in fashioning the human mind.

50. *What are the usual effects produced upon the mind of man by exercise?*

77

A Moderate degree of exercise, is necessary for the preservation of health and strength; and is most beneficial to the sedentary and the studious, when the mind can be brought to take pleasure in the species of action in which the body is engaged. Exercise, like labour, becomes injurious when taken in excess; and fatigues both mind and body when it is all of one sort.

51. *In what manner is the human mind affected by rest and sleep?*
Those operations of the human mind which depend on our volition are suspended during sleep; the vital and involuntary functions suffer no interruption; and, on awaking from our slumbers, if in health, we perceive that the mental and bodily powers are renovated and refreshed.

Circumstances of the Moral Kind which operate upon the Mind in the way of Education

52. *What are those moral circumstances which operate to the formation of the human mind, and determine the character of the actions of mankind?*
We have divided them into four classes, under the terms, Domestic, Technical, Social, and Political Education.

Domestic Education

53. *What is denoted by Domestic Education?*
All that the child hears and sees, more especially all that it is made to suffer or enjoy at the hand of others, and all that it is allowed to do in the house of its parents, or in which it is bred.

54. *What sensations produce the greatest effects?*
The first experienced; more especially, the earliest repetitions of one sensation after another produce the deepest habit; the strongest propensity to pass immediately from the idea of the one to the idea of the other. Hence the sympathies between brothers and sisters— hence love of country—hence that passionate attachment to the soil, the people, the manners, the woods, the rivers, the hills, with which our infant eyes were familiar, which fed our youthful imaginations, and with the presence of which the pleasures of our early years were habitually conjoined.

55. *What are the means by which children acquire a knowledge of the meaning of those words which are applicable only to the operations or*

78

affections of the mind, and cannot therefore be referred to the things they are intended to signify; such as, for instance, the words which denote the faculty of memory or of imagination? The meaning of many words, of which it is impossible to exhibit any sensible prototypes, is gradually collected by a species of *induction.* The connexion in which an unknown term stands in relation to the other words combined with it in the same sentence, often affords a key for its explanation in that particular instance; and, in proportion as such instances are multiplied in the writings and conversation of men well acquainted with propriety of speech, the means are afforded of a progressive approximation towards its precise import.

56. *When ought Education to commence?*

As much as possible, with the period of sensation itself. *For the early sequences with which we are accustomed form the primary habits; and the primary habits are the fundamental character of the man. As soon as the infant, or rather the embryo, begins to feel, the character begins to be formed, and the habits which are then contracted are the most pervading and operative through life.*

57. *How can those early sequences be made to take place in the minds of infants, on which habits, conducive to intelligence, temperance, and benevolence, are founded?*

The pains and pleasures of the infant, the deepest impressions which he receives, ought, from the first moment of sensation, to be made as much as possible to correspond to the real order of nature. Children ought to be made to see, and hear, and feel, and taste, in the order of the most invariable and comprehensive sequences, in order that the ideas which correspond to their impressions, and follow the same order of succession, may be an exact transcript from nature, and always lead to just anticipations of events.

58. *What is the moral procedure of parents?*

In general it is directly the reverse; they strive to defeat the order of nature, in accumulating pleasures for their children, and preventing the arrival of pains, when the children's own conduct would have had very different effects.

59. *Are not very injudicious impressions often made upon the minds of infants, by the imprudent conduct of nurses, grandmothers, and other weak-minded or foolish people, to whom their destiny is confided?*

Yes. The impressions from which ideas are copied are made to follow an order *very different from the natural one;* wrong trains of

79

ideas are introduced. When those who are about children express by
their words, or indicate by other signs, that terrific trains of ideas
are passing in their minds when they go into the dark; terrific trains,
which have nothing to do with the natural order of events, come up
also in the minds of the children in the dark, and often exercise over
them an uncontroulable sway during the whole of their lives.—This
is the grand source of wrong education; to this may be traced the
greater proportion of all the evil biasses of the human mind.

60. *What is the most common foundation of a servile character?*

If the expressions, and other signs of the ideas of those who are
about children, indicate that trains, accompanied with desire and
admiration, pass in their minds when *the rich and powerful* are
named, trains accompanied with aversion and contempt when *the
weak and poor* are spoken of, the foundation is laid of a character
stained with servility and meanness to those above, and tyranny to
those below them.

61. *What is the most common foundation of bigotry, and those inveterate antipathies to persons of particular political or polemical
creeds, which infuse so much bitterness into the cup of human life?*

If indication is given to children that ideas of disgust, of hatred,
and detestation, are passing in the minds of those about them, when
particular descriptions of men are thought of, as men of different
religions, countries, or parties in the same country; a similar train
soon becomes habitual in the minds of the children.

62. *What is the grand object of human desire?*
A command over the wills of other men.

63. *How is this command to be obtained?*
Either by acts and qualities which excite their love and admiration,
or by those which excite their *terror*.

64. *By what means is a man fitted to become an instrument of the
greatest good to his fellow men?*

By conducting his education so as to make the train of his ideas
run habitually from the conception of the good end to the conception of the good means; and, as often, too, as the good means
are conceived, viz: the useful and beneficial qualities, to make the
train run on to the conception of the great reward, viz: the wills of
other men—*the power of doing good.*

65. *What is the grand source of all wickedness, of all the evil which
war brings upon man?*

A command over the wills of other men, pursued by the instrumentality of *pain*.

66. *How is the foundation laid of the maleficent character?*

When the education is so deplorably bad as to allow an association to be formed in the mind of the child between the grand object of desire, the command over the wills of other men, and the fears and pains of other men, as the means; the foundation is laid of the bad character,—the bad son, the bad brother, the bad husband, the bad father, the bad neighbour, the bad magistrate, the bad citizen,—to sum up all in one word, *the bad man*.

67. *By what means is the maleficent character established and confirmed?*

Besides the impressions just recounted, if the trains of ideas which pass in the minds of those by whom the child is surrounded, and which he is made to conceive by means of their words, and other signs, lead constantly from the idea of command over the wills of other men, as the grand object of desire, to the ideas of pain and terror as the means, *the repetition of the copied trains increases the effect of the native impressions*, and establishes and confirms the maleficent character.

Technical Education

68. *What is denoted by Technical Education?*

Technical Education chiefly consists in the communication of Intelligence.

69. *Is* Intelligence *equally attainable by all?*

No. It is absolutely necessary for the existence of the human race, that labour should be performed, that food should be produced, and other things provided, which human welfare requires. A large proportion of mankind is required for this labour. In regard to all this portion of mankind, that labours, only such a portion of time can by them be given to the acquisition of intelligence, as can be abstracted from labour. Time must be exclusively devoted to the acquisition of intelligence; and there are degrees of command over knowledge to which the whole period of human life is not more than sufficient. There are degrees, therefore, of intelligence, which must be reserved to those who are not obliged to labour.

70. *Is* Intelligence *a desirable quality in the great body of the people?*

Until lately, it was denied, that *intelligence* was a desirable quality in the great body of the people (34); and as *Intelligence* is power, such is an unavoidable opinion (35) in the breasts of those who think that the human race ought to consist of two classes,—one that of the *oppressors*, another that of the *oppressed*. But, if Education be to communicate the art of happiness; and if Intelligence consists of knowledge and sagacity; (36) the question whether the people should be Educated, is the same with the question whether they should be happy or miserable.

71. *Have not the most beneficial effects often resulted, to individuals as well as to society, from the establishment of public libraries for apprentices, mechanics, labourers, and others, who were not able out of their own means to acquire a select assortment of useful books; as also from parochial and Sabbath-school libraries?*

The establishment of institutions of this sort have, in general, been attended with the happiest consequences; the minds of the people have been enlightened, and their manners improved, by study and reflection.

72. *Is the scheme of libraries for the community practicable and likely to be successful if attempted in the townships and villages of Canada?*

Experience, both in Britain and the United States, as well as in several places in these colonies, has fully demonstrated its practicability.

73. *Have not the most profound scholars; the greatest philosophers; the most eminent statesmen and divines, been self-taught?*

Instances abound in the history of the latter ages, of individuals who, after receiving instruction, only in the elements of reading and writing, and without the aid of teachers, have overcome innumerable difficulties, and attained an enviable eminence in the walks of science and literature. These men studied books, studied nature, and studied the arts, without the help of a schoolmaster; and persevered in their labours, though often under the most unfavourable circumstances; nevertheless, most true it is, that every thing that is actually known has been found out and learned by some person or other, without an instructor. (40)

74. *What is the degree of* Intelligence *attainable by the most numerous class of mankind, namely those who labour?*

There is an actual loss, even, in productive powers, even in good economy, and in the way of health and strength, if the young of the human species are bound close to labour before they are fifteen or sixteen years of age. But if those years are *skilfully employed* in the acquisition of knowledge, in rendering all those trains habitual on which intelligence depends, it may be easily shewn that a very high degree of intellectual acquirements may be gained (43); that a firm foundation may be laid for a life of mental action, a life of wisdom and reflection, and ingenuity, *even in those by whom the most ordinary labour will not fail to be performed.*

75. *Is it essential, in the constitution of any establishment, university, school or college, for the education of that class of society, who have wealth and time for the acquisition of the highest measure of intelligence, that there should be a provision for perpetual improvement; a provision to make the institution keep pace with the human mind?*

Such a provision is essentially necessary.

76. *Are not many of the old and opulent establishments for Education in Europe, rendered far less useful than they otherwise would be, by reason of their aversion to all improvement upon old practices?*

Yes.

77. *What are the effects produced on universities, colleges, or other associated seminaries of Education, by their union with an ecclesiastical establishment?*

The evil tendencies, which are to be guarded against, are apt to be indefinitely increased when they are united with an ecclesiastical establishment, because, whatever the vices of the ecclesiastical system, the universities have in that case an interest to bend the whole of their force to the support of those vices, and to that end to vitiate the human mind, which can only be rendered the friend of abuses in proportion as it is vitiated intellectually or morally, or both; it must, notwithstanding, be confessed, that there are *great advantages* in putting it in the power of the youth to obtain all the branches of their education in one place.

78. *Have the governments of Europe acted wisely in selecting the clerical body, almost exclusively, to conduct the technical Education of their youth?*

They have not. Clergymen are, or ought to be, the fittest persons to instruct mankind in the science of theology; and such of them as are acquainted with Latin and Greek, may be allowed to teach Latin and Greek, when and where these languages are shewn to be the proper objects of Education; but until they prove themselves the most competent to teach politics, and law, and economy, and sciences, and arts; all that society wants and is about to demand; they ought not to be entrusted with the civil education of youth.

79. *What effects may be reasonably expected, from the operation of a judicious system of* National Free Schools, *on the government and general interests of a people among whom intelligence is already widely diffused; and who have, for many years, enjoyed the blessings of the representative system of government, in their fullest extent?*

The beneficial effects attending such a system are incalculable. Additional stability would be given to free institutions; the sum of public and private happiness would be greatly increased; the power of the people extended; crime diminished; an inviolable respect for the laws maintained; and a constitutional vigilance more increasingly exercised, against all encroachments upon national or individual rights.

80. *What is the common consequence of entrusting the education (schooling) of the youth of a colony to its government, or to persons patronized by such colony government?*

They are trained generally to habits of servility and toleration of arbitrary power, in as far as precept and example can influence their minds; but fortunately obtain those keys of useful knowledge, the faculties of reading and writing, by means of which, "the liberty of the press," and the intelligence of the age, they are prevented from becoming instruments of evil, and enabled to form a just and correct estimate of their own situation, and of the conduct and character of the government under which they live.

Social Education

81. *What is the object of Social Education?*

To ascertain the extent of the influence that the society in which an individual moves produces upon his mode of thinking and acting; the mode in which that influence is brought about; and hence, the means of making it operate in a *good*, rather than in an *evil* direction.

82. *Whence springs the force of this influence?*

From two sources; the principle of imitation, and the power of the society over our happiness or misery.

83. *By what motives are we influenced in the society in which we move?*

By the intense desire which we feel of the *favourable regards* of mankind; Whatever are the trains of thought, whatever is the course of action, which most strongly recommends us to the favourable regards of those among whom we live, these we feel the strongest motive to cultivate and display; and whatever trains of thought and course of action expose us to their unfavourable regards, these we feel the strongest motives to avoid.

84. *What are the ordinary pursuits of wealth and of power, which kindle to such a height the ardour of mankind?*
Not the mere love of eating and of drinking, nor all the physical objects put together, which wealth can purchase or power command. With these every man is in the long run satisfied. It is the easy command, which those advantages procure over the favourable regards of society,—*it is this which renders the desire of wealth unbounded, and gives it that irresistible influence which it possesses in directing the human mind.*

85. *To what extent will the habits and character which the social influences tend to produce, engross the man?*
That will no doubt depend, to a certain degree, upon the powers of the domestic and technical education which he has undergone. We may conceive that certain trains might, by the skilful employment of the early years, be rendered so habitual as to be uncontrollable by any habits which the subsequent period of life could induce, and that these trains might be the decisive ones on which intelligent and moral conduct depends. The influence of a vicious and ignorant society would in this case be greatly reduced; but still, the actual rewards and punishments which society has to bestow, upon those who please, and those who displease it; the good and evil, which it gives, or withholds, are so great, that to adopt the opinions which it approves, to perform the acts which it admires, to acquire the character, in short, which it "delighteth to honour," can seldom fail to be the leading object of those of whom it is composed. And as this potent influence operates upon those who conduct both the domestic education and the technical, it is next to impossible that the trains which are generated, even during the time of their operation, should not fall in with, instead of counteracting, the trains which the social education produces; it is next to impossible, therefore, that the whole man should not take the shape which that influence is calculated to impress upon him.

86. *Is not that intimate acquaintance with the manners and customs of other nations, which may be obtained by travel, essentially necessary to complete the Education of that class of society who have wealth and time for the acquisition of the highest measure of intelligence?*
The effects of travelling, in enlarging and in enlightening the

85

mind, are obvious to our daily experience. The observation of men and manners, in various countries, is surely not the least useful part of education.

Political Education

87. *What is denoted by Political Education?*

Political Education consists in a right understanding of the science of Government, the business of which is to increase to the utmost the pleasures, and diminish to the utmost the pains, which men derive from one another; it is an agent employed in forming the character of man, and is like the key-stone of the arch; the strength of the whole depends upon it.

88. *By what means is the direction given to the desires and passions of men?*

By those means through which the grand objects of desire may be attained.

89. *On what do the means by which the grand objects of desire may be attained, depend?*

Almost wholly upon the political machine; and such as is the direction given to the desires and passions of men, such is the character of the men.

90. *What then are the natural effects of a beneficent system of government?*

When the political machine is such, that the grand objects of desire are seen to be the natural prizes of great and virtuous conduct—of high services to mankind, and of the generous and amiable sentiments from which great endeavours in the service of mankind naturally proceed—it is natural to see diffused among mankind a generous ardour in the acquisition of all those admirable qualities which prepare them for admirable actions; great intelligence, perfect self-command, and over-ruling benevolence.

91. *What effects are produced upon mankind by the operations of a government in which the interests of the subject many are but a secondary object?*

When the political machine is such that the grand objects of desire are seen to be the reward, not of virtue, not of talent, but of subservience to the will, and command over the affections of the ruling few; interest with the *man above* to be the only sure means to the next step in wealth, or power, or consideration, and so on; the means of pleasing the *man above* become, in that case, the great object of pursuit. And as the favours of the *man above* are necessarily limited—as some, therefore, of the candidates for his favour can only obtain the objects of their desire by disappointing others— *the arts of supplanting rise into importance; and the whole of that tribe of faculties denoted by the words intrigue, flattery, backbiting, treachery, &c. are the fruitful offspring of that political education which government, where the interests of the subject many are but a secondary object, cannot fail to produce.*

MACKENZIE'S NOTES TO

A Catechism of Education

A SELECTION

Qu. 36, Note 6 In countries where a proper value is placed on education, the schoolmasters are always exemplary men, and respected next to the parson of the parish or preachers of the Gospel. But here (in Nova Scotia) *any thing does for a schoolmaster*, and so little preference is given to men of correct habits and proper qualifications, that there are but few of this description, but what can employ themselves in more advantageous pursuits. These illiterate people are so void of discernment and so careless who they entrust with the tuition of their children, that they suppose any depraved wretch who calls himself a schoolmaster will answer the purpose. And it is no uncommon thing in our country towns to see a poor vagrant, who has taught a school or pretended to do so, perhaps for two or three months in the winter, go to the public houses and there wallow and riot in drunkenness until he has spent the few shillings he has earned by teaching, and then travel on to the next village to seek further employ. What can be more injurious to the morals of youth than a dissipated schoolmaster? When children see the man who they ought to look up to for example, associating himself with the lowest company, tippling in grog shops, and staggering in a state of inebriation from the tavern to the school house, there perhaps sleeping through the school hours, it must be destructive to their morals, and as their schoolmaster considers it no crime to go to the tavern and get intoxicated, so they, as they grow up, accustom themselves to the same vices. This is a great source of moral depravity and wretchedness, and in every point of view has an evil tendency, and ought to be suppressed.—*Nova Scotia Parliamentary Debates.*

Qu. 40, Note 8 It is not by any means intended, by the answer in

87

the text, to deny the general application of the sacred proverbs which inform us, that "a merry heart doeth good like a medicine; but a broken spirit drieth up the bones." And that "a merry heart maketh a cheerful countenance; but by sorrow of the heart the spirit is broken."

Qu. 42, Note 9   Upon looking over a long list of men of learning and genius, I felt a strong disposition to erase this sentence. The number of hale, stout, robust, laughter-loving philosophers and jolly statesmen, who furnish in their own persons a practical argument against the all but exclusive claim to mental excellence on the part of the feeble and infirm, is so great as to weaken my belief in an assertion, which has become almost proverbial.

Qu. 70, Note 34   Even Milton and Locke, though both men of great benevolence towards the larger family of mankind, and both men, whose sentiments were Democratical, yet seem, in their writings on education, to have had in view no education but that of the *gentleman*.

Qu. 70, Note 35   This doctrine has long been exploded in the United States of America; and the concern which is now felt in Great Britain and Ireland for the education of the working classes, shews that the English have made a great step in knowledge, and in that genuine morality which ever attends it.

Qu. 70, Note 36   In every hamlet, hole, and corner of the States, there stands a public school, and these are supported, not by the miserable dolings of eleemosynary aid, but the people are taxed that the tree of knowledge may be every where planted. There is no country in the known world where the elementary branches of education are so much attended to. Well, then, what naturally follows is, every man gains a knowledge of the Constitution under which he lives—every man is a politician. It thus follows that almost every village has its Public Press; the meanest farmer takes his newspapers, for which payment in cash is totally out of the question. The printer requires provisions, and he obtains all sorts in abundance—thus the light materials of the brain are exchanged for the more substantial ones of the belly, and information from all quarters of the world comes home to every man's door. Whatever is important to the Union is as well known in the cottage as in the capital. Thus there is no other community on earth where each man feels his *individual strength* and *consequence* as in the American States.—*Nova Scotia Parliamentary Debates.*

Qu. 73, Note 40   To the unassisted efforts of Arkwright, a barber, England owes the improvements in cotton machinery, which has secured to her the cotton trade. "Who was Ferguson? A simple peasant; a man who, wrapped in his own plaid, passed the winter nights in contemplating the heavens, and who, by arranging his beads upon the cold heath, at length completed a map of the stars. Who was Doctor Herschel, the discoverer of so many important astronomical facts? A boy who played the pipe and tabor in a foreign regimental band. Who was Watt, the inventor of the steam engine? A mathematical instrument maker."

Qu. 74, Note 43 Mr. Boyle acknowledged that he had learned more by frequenting the shops of tradesmen than from all the volumes he had read; and Dugald Stewart exclaims—"How many beautiful exemplifications of the most sublime mechanical truths are every day exhibited by the most *illiterate* of the people."

Are not these powerful inducements in favour of General Education, in order that these illiterate persons may be enabled to profit by the knowledge of those sublime truths of which, in their several trades, and professions, they afford so many beautiful exemplifications, and also benefit mankind by treasuring up carefully, whatever inventions or discoveries they may make or find out, or whatever general rules or methods may have occurred to them while following their several occupations, as materials to be afterwards collected, classed and arranged by others?

THE NEED FOR A UNIVERSITY

We coincide with Mr. Strachan, in opinion respecting the very urgent necessity which exists in Canada, for the establishment of a university, and transcribe from his tour a few remarks on the subject.

"The liberal professions now demand the establishment of a university. The church requires a long course of study, which cannot at present be obtained.—Young men designed for the bar, have not the necessary opportunities for preparing themselves for that important profession. The students of medicine, the sons of liberal merchants and of the more opulent landholders, would certainly attend a seminary on an extensive scale; and it is very certain that, in a few years after its establishment, more than one hundred students would be found at the university of Upper Canada."

The number of students found at the university, if it be established, will very much depend upon circumstances. If it is to be an arm of our hierarchy; if students are to be tied down by tests and oaths, to support particular dogmas, as is the case in Oxford, the institution will answer here no good purpose.

Arts and sciences, manufactures and commerce, have greatly progressed thro'out Europe and America during the last fifty years. The invention of the steam engine, and the useful application of steam pressure, has placed us centuries in advance of even the last generation, in point of power. The whole world is indebted to Great Britain, for many a banquet rich with mental luxury. Let us, therefore, lose no time, but free from party spirit and narrow sectarian motives in our institutions, endeavour to benefit by this general diffusion of knowledge. Let us remember Lord Bacon's wise and laconic saying, "Knowledge is power."

We ought to enrich the minds of our youth, by giving them such instruction and conformation of character as may enable them to serve their country, by the practical application of a systematic education, and like William Pitt, to blend the wisdom of age, with the complexion of youth.

We very much want men in Canada, who have received a liberal education; men untainted by the enjoyment of power and place, who, if called on, would not hesitate to sacrifice their personal interests for the good of their country; and who, if elected to our house of assembly, would return to their homes at the end of a fourth or fifth session, as free from the enthralments of patronage and place, of honours and pensions, as when they were first placed in the honourable situation of guardians of their country's rights.

We want barristers who would at all times prefer, on principle, to plead the cause of a poor man oppressed, rather than of a rich oppressor; who would rather *physic pomp* than pamper it—rather *despise* arrogance, clothed with a little brief authority, than cringe to and flatter it.

It even occurred to us when we were in the Gore District, at the last Assizes, that we wanted a Sir Matthew Hale in his miller's dress. Perhaps this was a fancy of our own—we wonder whether the thought struck any one else. It is not to be denied, however, but that Mr. Justice Boulton was very edifying in his way, and we doubt not decided with as profound professional wisdom as would have Sir Matthew; though perhaps it would have been as well if he had paid *less* attention to the town clerk of Ephesus's adage, "Do nothing rashly." But to return.

We want churchmen who would come up to, or nearly to, the

picture of a gospel minister, as we have copied it; lovers more of the flock, than of the fleece.

If we are, indeed, to be blessed with such pastors, counsellors, and politicians,—if we are to lessen our importations of the first and last classes; and if we hope to feel no inconvenience at having laid an embargo on the second,—if we really love to encourage *native talent*,—if we desire to see in the pulpits and in the ranks, at the bar and on the bench, in the senate and in the field, in the counting-house and in the navy, *our Canadian* Blairs and Fenelons; our Erskines and Romillys; our Pitts, Foxes, Cannings, and Clintons; our Moores and Washingtons; our Nelsons and Duncans; our Burkes and Sheridans, and Broughams and Barings; if we desire, hope or expect British America to produce men eminent both at home and abroad; if, in fact, we entertain a single wish for the welfare of our country, we must encourage—*liberally encourage*—competent professors of science and literature to emigrate hither.

The education which a boy now receives at any of the district schools is very costly. Not less, if the youth's board is included, than from seventy to ninety pounds, provincial currency, a year. Far more—aye, *more than double* what would be required in Scotland to send a student to Edinburgh, or any other Scots University, and keep him there for the same space.

Knowing this, we opine that the honourable and reverend Doct. John Strachan, D.D., &c. &c., or his brother, or whoever wrote *Strachan's Tour*, must have been half asleep, or nodding, when he or they stated that children can be instructed cheaper in Canada, and as well as at home (Britain). We wonder what part of Canada, and what part of Britain are meant to be spoken of. COLONIAL ADVOCATE (vol. I, no. I), 18 May 1824.

There are only two alternatives which present themselves to our mind—an University at home, or an University abroad. Our youth, many of them are now receiving the rudiments of their education in the colleges of the Union, and those few children whom their parents can afford to send to our district schools, are, from want of proper libraries, and other necessary aids, much cramped in their studies. For what is one of our district schools other than the counterpart of a Scottish parish school or an English classical or *demi*-classical academy? We have often repeated that we want more legislators who are able to sign their own names, and write three words following each other without misspelling, and we must allow them to get an education somewhere. COLONIAL ADVOCATE, 27 May 1824.

SOCIETY FOR DIFFUSING
USEFUL KNOWLEDGE

"The Messrs. Carvills, booksellers of Broadway, have been appointed agents for the sale and distribution of the publications of this Society, in the United States. . . ."

Greatly do we desire that scientific information may be widely diffused over this colony. It is a means whereby man approaches nearer and nearer to the infinite creator of the universe, and has his soul filled with more just and extended views of the supreme architect of worlds. The design of the society in London of whose labours the excellent and patriotic writer in the New York Commercial Advertiser (above quoted) makes honourable mention, is fraught with important benefits to mankind. And shall their enlightened researches not come into the wilderness of Canada, even when offered to us at a York shilling a number? Let it not be so said. What is within the reach of every American is also surely within the reach of Canadians, and we earnestly and sincerely recommend the objects of this institution to the notice of all who have the means and disposition to promote its views; in particular we call upon those in authority, that they employ some part of their salaries in disseminating useful knowledge; knowledge which can interfere with no man's political opinions. We recommend to mechanics and farmers to give each a half dollar to some common friend in their respective villages, who should remit the same to us at York, with the names of the parties. Half a dollar will purchase *four* numbers of the English edition in New York, and we will cheerfully undertake the agency of forwarding their monies to Messrs. Carvills, will pay the cost of carriage of the packages as they arrive from New York, and charge nothing for our trouble. And if Messrs. Carvills are authorised to allow agents an abatement on taking a quantity, we will purchase with the surplus *extra numbers*, and send them round the country among the post-masters and agents for this paper, as specimens.

What a pity it is that a mechanics' and agricultural society is not established in this colony on liberal and extended principles!—In the promotion of designs like these, more than in governing an ignorant and bigoted mob at the point of the bayonet, consists true patriotism. For a lover of his country will always desire to better its condition; and to know that it grows in useful knowledge, and that he has been a means in the hand of providence of contributing to the spread of science among the humblest and most despised of his people will gratify and cheer his declining years far more than a recollection that he triumphed in battle or won laurels in the senate chamber.

We anticipate much from the scientific treatises of the London society, and are glad in being able to direct public attention to such rich and valuable intellectual banquets offered at a price too which every man can afford to pay. COLONIAL ADVOCATE, 12 July 1827.

THE CHARTER FOR KING'S COLLEGE

Archdeacon Strachan has obtained a charter for an *University* in this town upon the following principles:—

1. The Lieutenant Governors are to be *perpetual* chancellors!

2. The Archdeacons of York are to be *perpetual* presidents!

3. *All* the professors, whether of divinity, physic, or mathematics, must sign the 39 articles of the established church and become members thereof—no Scotch presbyterian or British dissenter can be a professor, even altho' he may have been one of the greatest ornaments of the university for learning and skill!

4. The (king or his) lieutenant governors are to have the sole appointment of all the professors!

5. Doctor Strachan, Sir P. Maitland, and the seven professors are to form the college council!

6. To this college council is left the sole and entire control of the university; it is empowered to make laws, statutes and ordinances, which will be binding on all the scholars and members of the incorporation—and in these laws the scholars and graduates have no voice!

7. Even the council dare not propose or enact any rule or statute, unless it is first *prepared for them* by the lieutenant governor of the colony, as chancellor!

8. Divinity Students must swallow all the test-oaths, and go through all the ceremonies so well described by Vicesimus Knox in his essays, as being in use in the Tory university of Oxford!

9. Students other than in divinity, if they can submit to the above arbitrary enactments, and such others as may be expected from such a source, are not obliged to swear any oaths on taking a degree.

Anticipating such a charter as this, Doctor Strachan procured a clause to be inserted in a former act of the provincial parliament, authorising an university *to send a member* to sit in the assembly, and, my lord, if the people will submit quietly and without a murmur to be priest-ridden in this fashion, if they will peaceably admit another tool of Doctor Strachan, they deserve to have the dungeons of the inquisition set up among them, priests, familiars, racks and all for the next half century. . . .

In a former number of the Advocate [*27 Sept. 1827*] which has been sent to your lordship, I pointed out many glaring *errors* in the chart offered for the *information* of Lord Goderich—the names of a number of presbyterian ministers and their locations are omitted or forgotten, the increase of the church of England is swelled up infinitely beyond the bound of truth or probability—and assertions as to the temper and feelings of the people in regard to the established creed hazarded, which are not only at variance with the votes of the assembly (30 to 3) but also contrary to the doctor's own personal knowledge. . . .

My Lord—this and similar charts have procured for Upper Canada one of the most obnoxious chartered institutions on earth, namely a bigotted seminary of learning, probably possessing a voice in the provincial councils;—but it is hoped from the well known liberality of your lordship's religious and political sentiments, that your powerful influence will be added to that of the colony, recommending its immediate revocation. (*From a letter to Lord Dalhousie, 8 October* 1827.) COLONIAL ADVOCATE, 11 October 1827.

COLLEGES AT QUEBEC AND YORK

While in Quebec I visited the college or seminary of education founded and endowed many years ago [1663] by the French Government. It is situated in the heart of the upper town, in a pleasant and commanding situation, overlooking many miles of the surrounding country. The centre building of the college is one hundred and eighty feet long, and four or five stories high; and there are two wings of proportionate dimensions. The massy walls are of stone, of very substantial workmanship; and there is a chapel attached, as also spacious gardens and offices. The system of education has become liberal. Those who desire instruction in theology receive it; and those who do not are under no obligations to adhere to the doctrines of the church of Rome. Messire Parent, the superior of the institution, was so very kind as to accompany me through the apartments devoted to the studies of the several classes; at the same time affording me such explanations of the system pursued as I required. Upwards of two hundred students are now receiving their education at Quebec College, under eight professors, who instruct them in the mathematics, philosophy, the Greek, Latin, French, and English languages, history, arithmetic, geography, and attendant sciences. There is also a teacher of Latin upon the Lancasterian system. Theology is taught to those who require it. There is a museum and valuable library, with a philosophical apparatus for experiments; air-pumps, an orrery, a galvanic battery, electrical apparatus, a camera-obscura, &c. &c.

About seventy scholars are lodged and boarded in the seminary; the others reside with their parents and friends in the city. Students who do not board in the college pay £1 a year in full of fees, and find their own elementary books. Boarders, for education, lodging, washing and board, pay £20 a year; and if absent at vacation time, only £17. 10s. currency.

It was evening when I visited the college. The supper-room had plates for seventy or eighty. The table-cloths were of Lower Canada manufacture; and each youth's napkin or towel was carefully wrapped round his knife and fork. Their drink is water. Spirituous liquors are never permitted; and wine only at such seasons as Christmas, Epiphany, Easter, Ascension, Whit-Sunday, and the anniversary of the superior's birth-day. The health of the students is watched over with paternal attention; and an hospital, with cold and warm baths, is attached to the seminary.

The Superior showed me, from the garden, some of the lands from the rents of which the establishment is supported. They are situated below the city, beyond the falls of Montmorenci, and are valuable. The college holds them in its corporate capacity. Messire Parent is a mild, amiable man; very affable and unassuming in his manners. Such, indeed, is the general character of those catholic clergymen in Lower Canada with whom I am acquainted; and to this, added to a sincere desire constantly manifested to promote the happiness of the people, they owe an influence over the community, which legal enactments and the persecution or proscription of all other denominations could never have bestowed.

As to the exercises of the students, I made but small inquiry. I presume they differ some little from the usages of Edinburgh and St. Andrew's, in which venerable establishments boys of fifteen or sixteen may be seen attending the class of logic; and, "without having formed a single idea, writing essays to refute Hume, Locke, Aristotle, and Des Cartes!"

The chapel of the college contains a choice collection of beautiful paintings, as does also the cathedral church, which latter is very tastefully ornamented within, although plain on the outside.

Let me now direct the attention of the reader to York College [*Upper Canada College, opened in January 1830*], and the monetary system of the executive in Upper Canada.

Instead of £1 a year of college fees, the charge is £8, besides extra charges for fire-wood and other contingencies; instead of £17. 10s for board, lodging, washing, mending, and college dues, the demand is from £35 to £42. 10s., with £3. 10s. of entrance money to buy bedding.

The college here at York in Upper Canada is most extravagantly endowed with from two to three hundred thousand acres of the very best picked lands of the colony; £1000 a year is allowed it from the Canada Company's payments; and thousands of pounds are realized at will by its self-constituted managers from the sale of school lots and school lands, and the proceeds applied as if they were the private property of the government officers. Splendid incomes are given to masters culled at Oxford by the vice-chancellor, and dwellings furnished to the professors (we may truly say) by the sweat of the brow of the Canadian labourer. All these advantages, and others not now necessary to be mentioned, are insufficient to gratify the rapacious appetites of the "established church" managers, who, in order to accumulate wealth and live in opulence, charge the children of his majesty's subjects ten times as high fees as are required by the less amply endowed seminary at Quebec. They have another reason for so doing. The college (already a monopoly) becomes almost an exclusive school for the families of the government officers, and the few who through their means have in York already attained a pecuniary independence out of the public treasury. The college never was intended for the people, nor did the executive endow it thus amply that all classes might apply to the fountain of knowledge. No! the same spirit which induced the present chief justice and venerable archdeacon to trample in the dust Mr. Clark's modest bill for bestowing on the infant Grantham Academy [*later St. Catharines Collegiate*] £125 a year for four years, out of the public taxes, for the promotion of learning, never did, never could intend to model the college at York upon liberal principles towards the Canadian people. COLONIAL ADVOCATE, 19 May 1831; SKETCHES, p. 187.

EDUCATION IN LOWER CANADA

Government Grants

In the last received number of Neilson's Gazette [*Quebec* Gazette, *ed. Samuel Neilson*] we have an account of many thousands of pounds granted this year by the legislature of the sister province to encourage education: among the appropriations are £50 to the Natural History Society of Montreal; £100 each to the Quebec and Montreal Mechanics' Institutes, and Literary and Historical Society; £350 to qualify Ronald McDonald to conduct an institution for the instruction of the deaf and dumb; £4000 to aid in building schoolhouses; £500 each, to the colleges at Chambly, St. Anne de la Pocatière, and St. Hyacinthe; £854 to the Society of Education at Quebec; £2000 to the schools of the Royal institution; £200 to the Education Society of Three Rivers, &c. &c. COLONIAL ADVOCATE, 26 May 1831.

Divine Right

Just before leaving this place for the Gore District, we received our copy of *La Minerve* [*a semi-weekly published in Montreal by Duvernay*] of the 15th. inst. in the correspondence of which we find an able and interesting article upon Education. Interesting not only for the talent developed in its composition, but because it clearly proves that Lower Canada has begun to find out what even England had but lately discovered, namely, that colleges of priests can and will only teach that which they know, and that if British America is to keep pace with the adjoining republic in useful learning, many very essential improvements must take place in the system of education with which their youth are introduced into the busy world.

The writer of the letter in *La Minerve* (a translation of which we may hereafter publish) animadverts upon the course pursued with students in the catholic college of Montreal; the time consumed in poring over the ponderous tomes of antiquity, and the great neglect of more useful modern authorities; the lost labour in copying what is printed elsewhere; the late period at which the mathematics are taught; the ignorance of some youths at the period of leaving college; and the evident tendency of the instructions of

D

the priesthood to impress upon the minds of their pupils doctrines favourable to arbitrary power and the divine right of kings to govern wrong. The evident tendency of incorporated priesthoods of many denominations to seek for support in the *jure divino* of princes, and to cling to it rather than trust in their religion and the people for whom they officiate is truly unfortunate as regards the liberties of the human race, and proves the great necessity there is of watching and checking the silent inroads of the clergy upon civil rights and the freedom of opinion. The ministers of the independent presbyterian order, as our readers will have seen in this province, were to the full as ready to trumpet forth to the Duke of Wellington's government, in memorials, their absolute fitness to receive pensions from absolute power, as the kirk priests from Aberdeen and St. Andrews, or their very venerable brethren of the ancient creeds of Pius 7th and Henry 8th.—Doubtless, had they succeeded in being freed from an *irksome* dependence on their congregations, they would have soon chanted the song *de la puissance absolue des rois,* passive obedience and non-resistance, and that too with as good a grace as ever did a doctor of *Aberdeen*, Oxford, Dublin, Salamanca, or the Sorbonne. We honour religion and admire patriotism, but denounce selfishness under whatever cloak. COLONIAL ADVOCATE, 25 August 1831.

ILL-EDUCATED FRANCE

France, with its multitudes of men of science and *littérateurs*, is one of the worst-educated countries in Christendom. The Governments, Royal and Imperial, found millions of money to lavish on wars, on military roads, on museums, monuments and public buildings, but what did they give towards expelling ignorance from its strongholds ? —mere words—decrees, which were left to execute themselves! They have actually done less than nothing, for they have prevented the people from supplying their own wants. Dupin informs us, that of 900 Lancasterian schools existing in 1821, the Frères Chrétiens, a zealous Catholic sect, had contrived to get 600 shut up in five years. Why was this done and suffered ? Partly because the government considered knowledge as a *hostile power*; but chiefly because the Ministers of the established religion think they have a patrimonial right of controul over the opinions of the people. To dispense knowledge was, in their opinion to sap their authority.—Ignorance perhaps answers their ends best; but next in value to ignorance is knowledge *spiced* with the doctrines of their Church. Instruction in a shape that would suit both Catholic and Protestant, is a thing they hold in abhorrence, and having power on their side, their opposition is too formidable to be resisted. COLONIAL ADVOCATE, 1 September 1831.

EDUCATION IN YORK AND QUEBEC

One of the unsuccessful petitioners to Chancellor Colborne for an alteration in the system of his public college, brought us, some time ago, the manuscript correspondence which had then terminated just where it might have been expected to end—*in nothing*. As the Universities of Oxford and Cambridge have set their faces against reform and the putting down of abuse and insult to the people of England, it would be too much to look for good manners and decent behaviour in the catalogue of courtier-like qualities taught by the professors imported from these schools by Sir John and the Archdeacon to cultivate the understandings of the sons and grandsons of pensioners, placemen and gentle-beggars at £1000 per annum here. Accordingly, we find among the collegians of sheriffs, judges and custom house officers in embryo, a race of impudent youths who insult and ridicule the farmers from the country, apply the knockers of the citizens' doors and are off, and use provoking and insolent epithets to our fellow citizens both men and women on their way to and from the 114,000 acres ground. We are rather suspicious that although parents and teachers may not have formed a distinct class for the propagation of these curious proceedings, *they do less than nothing* to hinder the development of such hopeful characteristics in "the young gentlemen blackguards" for whose *education* the Canadian public pays in fifty shapes and ways; and who were doubtless born to rule over the country clowns and vulgar tradesmen of the Home District, whose bread their fathers unblushingly eat.

We have been informed that in the most populous country township in the Home District there is not *at this time of the year* more than one school of ten scholars, altho' the number of persons between six and sixteen is over 600!!! This is the best practical commentary upon Doctor Strachan's system of education for keeping the great

99

mass of a people in ignorance and educating and instructing a few sons of pensioners and placemen to hold them in the chains of mental bondage.

.   .   .

In the *Minerve* of Monday the 12th. inst. under the head of Editorial Correspondence, we find a reply to the exposition of the system of Education pursued in Montreal College and other principal seminaries of education in the sister colony, which appeared in a late number of that interesting journal, as noticed by us some weeks ago [Col. Adv. *25 Aug. 1831*]. The answer is couched in less temperate language than the charges, but the defence is nevertheless a tolerable good one—the best, perhaps, that could be given in such a case. We are glad to perceive that the Lower Canada liberal Journals are open to the discussion of such delicate questions, in the French language—the result will be to the advantage of the cause of education in general, a subject in which the Canadians now take the deepest interest. In those nations where a few individuals, comparatively speaking, possess nearly the whole of the landed property, and the law of inheritance gives all the estate to the eldest son, large masses of military men are required to be hired to protect the unjust division. But in countries where general education flourishes, and one son is held to be as dear to his father as another in the eye of the law, standing armies are not wanted, the great mass of the people having a direct interest in the preservation of the rights of property. COLONIAL ADVOCATE, 22 September 1831.

ENVOYS OF GOOD WILL

A writer in the Montreal Courant says that as the vast possessions of the Jesuits in Canada were granted for education before the conquest from France, Upper Canada is entitled to a share of the benefits that may accrue from them. There is certainly some reason in this; and perhaps the sister colony will establish and endow a liberal university from this new and plentiful source, making at same time a permanent provision that one third of the scholars may be from Upper Canada, and that their board and education shall be defrayed out of the produce of these estates. In that case it would be well to provide that the townships in this colony should select these scholars, one each, successively, in proportion to their population; the most populous townships to choose first, and so on in order. Such a system as this would serve to unite Upper and Lower Canada together by a much more permanent ligament than Robinson's Union Bill and the rotten boroughs therein provided. These scholars would, on their return, be the best possible evidence to refute such slanders against the Lower Canada people as are now uttered in our legislature and echoed by some of the provincial presses. COLONIAL ADVOCATE, 8 December 1831.

THE CLERGY RESERVES

Up to Monday evening this really important measure has slept its way upon the order of the day of the orange-tory assembly—altho' rumour tells us that Lawyer Draper and others, who know as well as we do that no such bill ever will pass in this world, are about to angle for sectarian popularity, by ministering to the gullibility and avarice of the parsons, priests and preachers, and gravely proposing to divide the reserves and their proceeds among the Church of England and Scots Kirk Clergy, the Catholic Priests and Prelates, and the Ryersonian Methodist Preachers. Of course the crafty crew at 14 Downing Street would never consent to build up three sets of paid priesthoods, made independent of them by law, to wit the Kirk, which owns the jurisdiction of an assembly in Scotland, the Catholics, whose spiritual head is at Rome, and the Wesleyans, who bow the knee to a Conference sitting in Leeds, Sheffield or Manchester. An old man in his dotage, a girl in her teens, a profligate George Guelph, or Charles Stuart, or a lustful and beastly Henry 8th, these, or either of them may be in turn the "one shepherd", who, according to the creed repeated from Archdeacon Strachan's soft cushioned rostrum every Sunday, the faithful call *The Head* of the Holy Catholic Church—that church, with that head, would have the reserves if the Assembly willed it—but the others—Never!

But why divide the reserves in this way? There can only be *One True Faith*, there cannot be two, three, or four. Are we to pay the three protestant churches for teaching, as we ourself were taught in infancy, that the head of the Roman Catholic Church, in which the whole christian world worshipped for 1500 years, is the "beast, the man of sin, and *the scarlet whore*," mentioned in the Revelations? Are we to pay the Episcopalians, Methodists and Presbyterian Parsons for preaching and teaching, as they do in their pulpits, homilies, associations, confessions of faith, and Christian Guardians, that the God of Heaven bestowed these names upon the Bishops of Rome, and that the Roman religion is damnable in its doctrines and idolatrous in its worship? Upon the other hand, would it be right, that the King, Governor, two Houses of Parliament, Legislative Council, and House of Assembly should consent to pay out of the public lands the ministers and prelates of the Roman Catholic Church, the ancient religion of Christendom, for denouncing the Protestant churches as the propagators of a damnable heresy, those in their communion as unbelievers and heretics, and on the broad way to hell and eternal destruction?

Again—how vehemently does the Presbyterian system assail English prelacy—as the eldest daughter of the scarlet whore— popery in disguise—an anti-christian hierarchy!

Once more—Are the five and twenty denominations left out in this calculation—the Quakers, Mormons, Tunkards, Independents, Irvingites, Congregationalists, Baptists, Unitarians, Seceders, Menonists, Children of Peace, Christians, etc. to have no share?

Of all these there can only be one true faith. Are we then to pay alike for truth and error—for religion and idolatry—and thus prove King and Parliament of no moral principle at all?

Better would it be for the Assembly to follow in the wake of past parliaments, and give the reserves for the education of the people of the country. THE CONSTITUTION, 14 December 1836.

NEED FOR GOVERNMENT ACTION

What is the Legislature, and what are the different Religious denominations doing to promote Education among the people? Let no man trust in empty Despatches from the English Colonial Office. They are a pack of plausible lies. How can those who do their utmost to prevent the English people from being educated, in order that an Aristocracy may be necessary to control them, desire for us that moral, religious and educated population which would render the existence of an aristocracy in the Government unnecessary? One thing is certain—no free popular Government can exist unless the people are informed. An ignorant Republic would surely degenerate into a most corrupt and hateful Government. THE CONSTITUTION, 21 December 1836.

ON HIS OWN EDUCATION

I got an excellent education—several of my school-fellows are inhabitants of this city. Two of my uncles, with my mother's consent, articled me as a clerk to George Gray, the wealthiest as he was one of the oldest merchants of Dundee. I was at 15 admitted a member of the Commercial Reading-room. Before I arrived at that age I was an active member, and for some time Secretary, of a Scientific Society, of which the late Mr. Edward Lesslie was the Vice-President. We were members together for several years.

Although early instructed in the principles of religion and good morals, and kept constantly at school under excellent masters from the time I was five years old, I acknowledge that at seventeen I was reckless, wild, a confirmed gambler, and somewhat dissipated, (more so perhaps than I would like to own). But, even at that age, my thirst for useful knowledge was unquenchable. At twenty-one I paused, threw down cards and dice for ever, and became temperate.

       .   .   .

I have constantly identified myself with the common people of the country, have earnestly and anxiously sought to raise them higher and higher in the scale of intelligence, and will yet venture to believe with the Ayrshire Ploughman, that instead of encouraging Orange Lodges, Established Priesthoods, close Corporations, and delegated Tyrannies, mankind will become brotherly-minded. What else but this hope could have supported me through the struggles of the last fifteen years? THE CONSTITUTION, 8 February 1837.

Chapter Three

BOOKS AND NEWSPAPERS

EDITOR'S PREFACE *Soon after his arrival in Upper Canada, as his advertisements show, Mackenzie became active in the distribution of books, through store and library. And, as will be seen in this chapter, he never lost his faith in the educational power of the printed word. Easy access to books was to him a necessity.*

On 18 May 1824 he published at Queenston the first number of the Colonial Advocate, *and soon (2 September 1824) began advertising books for sale at the office of the paper. In December 1824 he moved the press to York.*

The early issues of the Colonial Advocate *appeared at irregular intervals, but within a few months weekly publication was established, and continued with two interruptions (16 June to 8 December 1825 and 8 June to 7 December 1826) until November 1834.*

The paper was usually of four pages (with occasional supplements), five columns wide, with type of varying sizes, sometimes, apparently, determined by the amount of material clamouring for publication. In the early years (1824-1826) a good deal of space was given to general information on such practical questions as agriculture, gardening, road and canal building, manufacturing. Later a great deal of space was found for news from Europe. During the agitation over the Reform Bill in England, the revolutionary struggles in France, and the war against Russia in Poland, long news reports were published as they arrived via London and Quebec or New York. Canadians were in this way kept in touch, not only with their homelands, but with public affairs generally.

British, American, and other Canadian journals were freely quoted, and sometimes these quotations take up the bulk of the paper. Advertisements usually filled as much as one and a half pages. "Fillers" often took the form of anecdotes, advice as to health, poems, and appeals from the editor for payments owed.

Mackenzie maintained very high standards of printing. There are few misprints, though much inconsistency in the use of capitals, punctuation, and paragraphing. His journeymen were skilled craftsmen, and in a letter to his deputy, Wixon, Mackenzie wrote from London (30 January 1833): "With some slight mistakes my letters and documents are correctly printed, and creditable to the compositors."

Some day a detailed study will have to be made of the advertisements in the Colonial Advocate. *A single issue (11 August 1831) is typical. On that day there were advertised for sale: a pleasure yacht, mills, houses, farms, a distillery and potashery; imported clothes, glass, hardware; patent medicines, farm implements, and groceries (in one instance "ashes will be taken in payment"). Advertised as manufactured in York are millstones, brass machinery parts, pot barley, and sleigh bells. A notice by Dr. John Rolph tells readers that he would like patients to "employ him by the year" and "before they are urged by existing sickness". A lawyer tells of his change of address; the Misses McCord announce their improved method of teaching young ladies; and J. L. Riddell gives notice of a course of lectures, three nights a week for "near five weeks", on Chemistry. There are three notices of lost and found cattle. The United Amicable Society of Bricklayers, Plasterers and Masons announce their monthly meeting for general business, including the relief of members "in case of sickness or accidents"; and the Journeymen Joiners and Carpenters announce a public meeting "for the support and regulation of trade". Several shipowners advertise their lines on Lake Ontario and across the Atlantic, the line of steamboats and stages to Prescott being appropriately owned by one Mr. Weller. For recreation there is the British Museum of York, with its stuffed animals, its stones and fossils, its Cosmorama and Phantasmagoria, and its Fancy Glass Blower, Mr. Smith. Opportunities for work included the building trades, turning and tool-making (axes and mill-wheels), blacksmithing, brewing and distilling, potash-making, and the handling of transport and retail trade on stages and ships and in shops and inns. The Canada Company, in spite of Mackenzie's often-expressed bitter hatred, advertises two-and-a-half million acres of land for sale. And what seems to have been a big-scale New York Lottery holds out prospects of valuable prizes for its "distant Patrons".*

The advertisement columns are spotted with cuts of suitable motifs: a house, a tree, a cow, a tailor, an auctioneer etc. Mackenzie had also a set of column-wide cuts which he used again and again at the head of articles: delicate little engravings of a farm-house fireside, children playing with hoops, men ploughing, fishing, and fence-building.

From January 1827 for one year, Mackenzie was "Printer to the Honourable the House of Assembly of Upper Canada". Both during this period and later, debates in the House of Assembly were reported in some detail. In *1830 and 1831 debates in the English House of Commons and in the Lower Canada Legislature on questions of Reform were also extensively reported. And, in preparation for his mission to England in 1832, he gave many columns to the Minutes of Town Meetings of the Inhabitants, texts of petitions, and the names of those signing them. Some issues of the paper were so filled with documentary material that there was little room for editorial comment.*

Up to the time of Mackenzie's departure for England in 1832, he had but little editorial help and it is safe to assume that all unsigned paragraphs are by him. During his absence the paper was edited by Randal Wixon, or Wixson (after the Rebellion sentenced to exile in Van Diemen's Land, but pardoned after thirteen months in captivity in Canada and England). Mackenzie wrote sixty or seventy long letters to Wixon and to John Mackintosh, chairman of the Committee of the Inhabitants of York, and many of these were published in the Colonial Advocate. *After his return, in August 1833, he wrote less, being occupied with his duties as Mayor of Toronto, but his hand is usually unmistakable.*

The Advocate *(the name had been changed in December 1833) came to an end on 4 November 1834.*

While he was in England he published his Sketches of Canada and the United States. *It is a compilation of articles and paragraphs from the* Colonial Advocate *and from his note books, put together in something of a hurry for the benefit of English readers. It is from his inclusion of passages which appeared in the paper over the signature of Peter Russell that we know that this was one of his pseudonyms (Sketches, p. 229).*

Early in 1835 Mackenzie sold his printing establishment to the owner of the Correspondent, *which took the name* Correspondent and Advocate. *Its editor was Rev. William John O'Grady. Mackenzie contributed articles and letters to this paper, until he resumed his role as editor again in July 1836, when he started a new paper,* The Constitution, *which he continued till the eve of the rebellion. This paper was closely filled with immediate Canadian concerns of both Provinces. There were no appeals to Governments, but many to the people. In July and August 1837 Thomas Paine's* Common Sense *was reprinted, almost in full. On 19 October 1836, Robert Emmet's last speech to his countrymen was published, and throughout these months ties were strengthened with Papineau and the* patriotes of

Lower Canada, and with the reformers and revolutionaries of England, Ireland, and France.

Books were scarce in Upper Canada in Mackenzie's time, but Robert Lamond's narrative of emigration from Scotland to Upper Canada in 1821 tells us that an appeal for Bibles and other books for emigrants appeared in the Glasgow Chronicle, *14 June 1820, and also that, though emigrants were told not to take furniture with them on board ship, they were allowed to take their private libraries of books.*

As might be expected, the editor of the Colonial Advocate *and* The Constitution *undertook as one of his responsibilities the task of filling the gap as best he could, by importing, publishing, and selling. Among the publications at his office were: treatises on Potash-making, Horticulture and Tobacco-growing in 1826, 1827, and 1828;* The Trial of William Penn *and* A Catechism of Education *in 1830;* St. Matthew's Gospel *in Chippeway and* The Mother's Primer *in 1831; the* New Testament *in 1837. (See the* Bibliography of Canadiana, *by F. M. Stanton and M. Tremaine, 1934, and the* Colonial Advocate, *22 September 1831.) Advertised as on sale at the office were sheet music for voice and solo instruments, the novels of Scott, Galt, Fenimore Cooper; the poems of Byron, Southey, Gray, Burns; works of history, law, science and theology. A few months before the Rebellion, Mackenzie was in New York buying thousands of books for his store, which in November 1837 contained 20,000 volumes (Lindsey, Life, 1862, vol. ii, p. 98). In the issues of 22 February and 19 April 1837 he printed passages from* Pickwick Papers, *which he must have read as the monthly parts arrived from London.*

Advertisements and news items in the Colonial Advocate *tell us something of the libraries of the time: the York General Library, opened on 3 May 1827; the Mechanics' Institute, December 1830. In the* Colonial Advocate, *7 April 1825, there is the announcement of the opening of a subscription library in the village of Cramabe, and on 7 December 1826, Mr. Joseph Elliot, from Ireland, announced a circulating library at Carradoc, London District, containing from two to three hundred volumes.*

The reading of newspapers and other journals was no small part of Mackenzie's daily work, and is reflected in the many articles reprinted or quoted in the Colonial Advocate *and* The Constitution. *In the 1834* New Almanack for the Canadian True Blues *there is a list of Canadian papers, classified according to politics, and in the news item on the reading rooms of Toronto there is a list of foreign Quarterlies which he regularly saw and read (*Constitution, *26 July 1837). Mackenzie was deeply concerned about the distribution of news-*

papers. His conviction that everyone had a right to a knowledge of world affairs made him very critical of Post-Office regulations, especially with regard to the postage of periodicals. His opinions on the inefficiency of the Post-Office date back to his earliest political activity. Agitation for reform had started in Upper Canada before his arrival, and an investigating Committee was appointed by the House of Assembly in 1821. In 1829 a second Select Committee was appointed, with Mackenzie as chairman. The Post-Office was controlled in London, and succeeding investigations exposed the fact that proceeds from the service went into the private pockets of officials or into the British Treasury. Thomas Stayner (Colonial Advocate, *29 August 1833*), *Deputy Post-Master at Quebec 1827-1836, was exposed as a profiteer. The whole question of Post-Office reform was taken up by Lord Glenelg, Lord Durham, and later by Lord Sydenham. (See* The Durham Report, *ed. 1902, p. 101;* Canada and its Provinces, *vol. iv, pp. 729-754.)*

PLANS FOR
THE "COLONIAL ADVOCATE"

In introducing to our readers our opinion of the main cause of whatever portion of wealth and prosperity we possess, "Agriculture", we have to state that, in the course of our Journal, we will devote a considerable space, from time to time, to this useful art. Practical utility is the object we will keep in view; and the notions of ingenious but speculative men, which may have a tendency to mislead, into rash projects, persons engaged or engaging in agricultural pursuits, will be carefully avoided. Nor will we introduce more of the theory than what may seem absolutely necessary to exhibit a view of those principles which long experience has dictated to men of sound judgment and correct observation.

It will be our study to render our details as concise as possible, in as far as may be found consistent with perspicuity.

We will carefully watch the progress of the art in other countries, and in particular will give a due attention to the improved modes of farming in the United States. From these Americans we have much to learn, ere we can rival them in the practice of Agriculture. But let us hope for the best; our senators may open their eyes; we may ere long behold Agricultural associations in Upper Canada; Agricultural improvements properly rewarded; Agricultural professorships, and a practical, yet scientific race of Farmers. We have a rich soil—a favourable climate—a population inured to labour, hardy and industrious; and even though we be, as Mr. Webster sneeringly terms us, the distant dependency of a distant monarchy, we may yet flourish, without hastily severing the ties which bind us to the land of intellectual grandeur—the country of our forefathers.

.   .   .

We intend, according as we have room, to copy into the "Advocate" articles on Roads and Bridges, Townships, Diseases, Scotch emigrants, Irish ditto, English ditto, American ditto, Sheep, Cattle, Agricultural Societies, Wheat, Barley, Oats, Corn, Buck Wheat, Potatoes, etc. We will likewise give some account of the following articles, and others, which may be termed properly articles of commerce: such as Flax, Hemp, Pot and Pearl Ashes, Bees' Wax, Honey, Lumber, Tobacco, Ginseng, etc. We have prepared for publication notices on Gypsum, Lime and manures, and we will occasionally touch upon the attendant science of horticulture.

.   .   .

To the subject of inland trade, rivers, lakes, canals, shipping, the circulating medium, bullion, banks and bank issues, we intend to draw the attention of our readers—we can only find room to state our intentions in this place.

We earnestly desire to see established, throughout Upper and Lower Canada, New Brunswick and Nova Scotia, efficient societies for the improvement of arts and Manufactures. We would like to see the manufacturer not quite four thousand miles from the farmer. We would like to see less apathy, not only in the government but in the governed, in regard to this important topic. Our foreign commerce, confined and shackled as it is, and as it has been, is entirely in the hands of the British capitalists; our lumber trade is merely encouraged to support British worn-out shipping. We are inundated—glutted with British manufactures. Luxury is encouraged and the simplicity of our manners lost, by the temptations of foreign gewgaws which we could as well, aye, much better, do without. Upper Canada at present is

> No land of Canaan, full of milk and honey,
> Nor (save in paper shekels) ready money.

And the whole together is a system revolting to the feelings of every independent thinking colonist. Our farmers are indebted to our country merchants, our country merchants are deeply bound down in the same manner, and by the same causes, to the Montreal wholesale dealers. Few of these Montreal commission merchants are men of capital; they are generally merely the factors or agents of British houses, and thus a chain of debt, dependence, and degradation is begun and kept up, the links of which are fast bound round the souls and bodies of our yeomanry; and that with few exceptions from the richest to the poorest, while the tether stake is fast in British factories. COLONIAL ADVOCATE, 18 May 1824.

PAPER MILL AT
WEST FLAMBORO'

The most important item of news in this journal today is Col. Crooks's advertisement, stating that he has determined to erect a paper mill, or rather to convert to that purpose a building already erected. COLONIAL ADVOCATE, 23 March 1826.

CANADIAN REVIEW
AND MAGAZINE

We are afraid that the time has not yet come, in which colonial periodicals strictly literary can command encouragement commensurate to the expense of their publication and to what is due to their compilers. The fourth number of the Canadian Review being for February of this year we have just looked into; it contains much useful and interesting matter—and if not in every respect the counterpart of those works of the same nature which have been warmed into existence, and idolized as it were into fame, by the people of England; yet is it a valuable trophy as proving the desire which the few literary men among us have to introduce into the colonies learned publications of native growth. We are well convinced that when our towns and villages are a little farther advanced, —when our Booksellers find it their interest to establish their shops in some two or three dozen of towns from Halifax to Sandwich, and when our academies have gained a name among the literati of the west; then—but not till then—will such a work as this prosper. Paper-mills, Typefounders, Printers, Bookbinders, and Booksellers should be encouraged by all classes.—Colonel Crooks's intended paper mill does himself as well as the legislature great honour—him for his enterprise, them for their liberality.—The Legislature of Nova Scotia lent their aid to a similar undertaking in that province some time since,—and it now succeeds so as abundantly to reward the proprietor. May it be so here. Every rag ought to be saved for the paper mill, and the good lady as she looks at her well filled basket, may say to herself "In saving these tattered and worn out garments, I am collecting the chief material for a Bible or a Testament, a Dictionary or a Geography. I am adding, in every rag, a new page to some useful work that may benefit my children or the sons and daughters of my country." Our limits do not allow us to enlarge on this interesting subject at present, but we may remark that it is indeed very surprising that such a work as the Canadian Review has only three subscribers in the capital of Upper Canada, namely the Lt. Governor, Doct. Strachan and the Atty. General. Its politics we put out of the question;—we do not like to see the writers in its columns quote letters to shew that the native Canadians have a "great want of knowledge and *capacity*." There is no use in their doing so;—had Mr. Sparhawk, Mr. Chisholm, and other juvenile politicians of the same school, not been over anxious to convince the world that the natives of Canada are a race of mortals vastly inferior to the English and Yankees who have condescended to dwell among them, the Union that was so much desired by the mercantile classes had long ere now been quietly and peaceably accomplished; and that too on fair and equitable principles. Now it is too late.—The newspaper friends of that measure acted as if they had been in reality its enemies—but found to their cost that the native Canadians would not suffer such contemptuous treatment with impunity.

It is not therefore on account of its local politics that we would recommend this publication to our townsmen,—but because it is the only colonial work that professes to analyze literature in general. For instance—The Geography and Geology of Lake Huron by John J. Bigsby M.D., F.L.S., M.G.S., a book printed in London in 1824! is reviewed in this number—and it is of the first importance that we should be made acquainted with every scientific work relating to Canada. Mr. Lymburner's speech, and several other articles, are not only worthy of perusal, but even deserving of a place among the choice books of such of our opulent men as are able to afford select libraries. The proprietor, whoever he is, sent us a copy of the second number in a compliment, the third we glanced into while crossing in the Queenston last fall to Niagara—and the fourth we have seen in the store of Messrs. Lesslie and Sons, the agents at this place. In the success of the Canadian Review we have no personal interest other than that which arises from a conviction that at this early day too little pains is bestowed by the country to reward literary talent. What would North America be at this day were it not for the moral influence exercised over her people by England?—What is America?—Read the annexed paragraph and it will help you to solve both questions.

"*Printing in Boston.*—In looking into Griscom's Tour in Europe a few evenings since, I met the following passage: 'It is supposed that the number of monthly publications which is sent off by the coaches and waggons, from Paternoster Row (London) and its neighbourhood, amount to fifty or sixty thousand.'

"This is indeed a large number, but having been at some pains to make inquiry, I find the monthly publications of Boston will compare, to great advantage, with what is here stated as to London. . . ." *Boston Palladium.*

Montreal ought to become at no late date the Boston of the colonies. We would like to see our colonial governors recommending legislative assistance to a type foundry to be located in that city. Education is and must of need be the basis of all free governments that look forward to permanence; not only a learning of the A.B.C., but also of every branch of science and art necessary to enable the children of Canada to cope with and equal the inhabitants of older settled climes in all that ennobles and distinguishes civilized society from savage rudeness, and mulish ignorance.

Britain was peopled from various lands but time has obliterated their distinctions.

"Love led the wild hordes in his flower-woven bands,
The tenderest, strongest of chains!
Love married our hearts, he united our hands,
One race we became."

So let it be with British America—let every national distinction cease from among us—let not the native Canadian look upon his Irish or Scottish neighbour as an intruder, nor the native of the British Isles taunt the other about stupidity and incapacity. Rather let them become as one race, and may the only strife among us be a praiseworthy emulation as to who shall attain the honour of conferring the greatest benefits on the country of our birth—or the land of our choice. COLONIAL ADVOCATE, 30 March 1826.

PRINTING, PUBLISHING, AND BOOK SELLING

A LETTER TO ENGLAND
BY PETER RUSSELL

Although the art of Printing has not received any very material improvements in North America, it has been the means of spreading knowledge widely over that vast continent. The unshackled institutions of the U. States, the freedom from censorship, licence, stamps, bondsmen, and those other incumbrances under which European Editors sometimes labour, has within the last thirty years multiplied the newspapers in America beyond all previous calculation.

Dr. Dwight informs us that the Boston Weekly Newsletter, now the Massachussetts Gazette, was the first newspaper published in the British Colonies. It was first issued in 1704. In 1765 there were 26 papers in North America.

The cities of New York and Philadelphia support between twenty and thirty daily prints, and so profitable has the proprietorship of some of them become, that it has been determined by the owners of several New York Journals, to send to England for Steam Engines such as are used to expedite work by the Times and other London prints. Daily papers are also published in Boston, Baltimore, etc., and there are perhaps 500 newspapers in the Union; which issue their numbers some twice a week, some thrice, but the greater part only once a week, and the sizes are, from the New York Albion, on a beautiful imperial sheet, and down to an Indiana or Missouri "Oracle" printed on a coarse piece of paper, something larger than common foolscap.

The utmost attention is paid by the National Congress to preserve entire the freedom of discussion, and in order that printers may be enabled to give the most authentic information to one another *throughout the Union*, they are allowed to exchange newspapers with each other *free of postage*. Sometimes the editors of daily papers exact a dollar or two of difference from a humble country printer in exchange, but they are in the main very liberal. The National Intelligencer stated some months ago that it exchanged with upwards of four hundred other papers, and the Postmaster-General of America would have extended this privilege to Canada editors last session had the hint been given him sooner.

In the British Colonies there is no fixed rule in respect to printers' exchanges,—but I believe that Mr. Sutherland expects all newspapers to be paid postage for by the printer who mails them, which is a great drawback upon the trade. In other respects the freedom of the press in British America, is as inviolate as in the Union.

The following specimens from that highly interesting newspaper the Colonial Advocate, are proof of the stability of the government, and of the extent to which freedom of remark may be carried by editors, unchecked in the Colonies. (The writer here does us the honour to quote No's 33, 39, 43, 44, and 27 of our series.)

Millions of newspapers are issued annually in Philadelphia, New York, &c. and if it could be ascertained how many are printed in the Union in a year, it would be a curious memorandum. Niles copies an item from the *Whig*, published in Richmond, Virginia, by which it appears that there were sent 150,624 newspapers from that one city, between the 1st January and 31st March last, through the post office, the weight of which the editor estimates at 27 tons. The same paper adds that 11,648 newspapers were, during the same time, received in exchange from other printers by the editors of papers in Richmond.

The price of a weekly journal, published on an imperial sheet, is, in most of the United States, so low as two dollars per annum; the subscriber paying half a dollar yearly extra for postage, *at the office where he receives the paper*, or (if demanded) a cent per number. A New-York daily paper costs $10 p. annum. Most of the daily papers in the large cities, select from their news columns, curtail their advertisements, and print a country paper, which they issue twice a week; all the additional trouble is the new arrangement of the matter already in type. The proprietors of the N.Y. Commercial Advertiser daily paper, print the Spectator for the country, at $5 a year, and circulate more copies in the Canadas than any other United States' journal, the Albion perhaps excepted; which latter is almost exclusively devoted to European news. The senior editor of the Spectator, Mr. Hall, was in this neighbourhood lately collecting; he is very obliging and polite to all Europeans who call at his office. I waited on him in New-York, and was presented with a file of the latest London daily journals to take to U.C. and my friend Mr. Taylor, then on his way to Glasgow, had given to him by Mr. H. a whole bundle of American papers to amuse himself with on his passage. The Albion seldom intermeddles with the local politics of the Union or of the Colonies, is moreover very loyal; and as it is decidedly the most elegant paper in America, both as to type, paper, (some would except the Montreal Herald, which is generally printed on very costly English paper) and arrangement of matter, so it is the most costly, being $6 a year though issued only on Saturdays. It admits of few advertisements, and therefore is, in my opinion, not a very profitable concern. The New-York American and Noah's Advocate, both for the country, are published twice a week, at four dollars a year, and are highly spoken of. The weekly papers, who charge $2, depend almost exclusively on advertising for support.

In British America there are upwards of thirty periodical publications, chiefly newspapers. Eight are supported in this Province; all weekly prints, on super-royal paper. The Colonial Advocate used to have the greatest circulation, (from 800 to 1150 copies) but at present it is asleep. [*There were no issues of the* Colonial Advocate *from 16 June to 8 December 1825.*] The Kingston Herald issues nearly 600 a week; its Editor, Mr. Thomson, is a native Canadian, a member of Assembly, and supports what are called popular measures, both in his paper and in the Assembly. The *Herald* is held in great estimation by all classes. The government press is in the hands of a Mr. Fothergill, a Yorkshire quaker, of a highly respectable family, and related to the late Mr. Birkbeck, of Illinois, Dr. Fothergill of London, and other eminent characters. Mr. F. is a member of the legislature, and on the popular side, so that our Lt. Governor has his own Gazette in the ranks of the opposition. In our Colonial prints, there is no want of *liberty*; of that be assured. The Old Quebec Gazette published twice a week, on a sheet and a half sheet, is owned by Mr. Neilson; it used to be the official paper, but opposed some of Lord Dalhousie's measures, and he, after giving the editor notice to change his tone, removed the Government patronage to the New Quebec Gazette, published by Dr. Fisher, by authority.

Mackenzie, in his Advocate, gives the following account of the ex-editor of the Albion.

"There is Dr. Fisher, (of New-York that was,) who with the help of an American press, and American printers, in an American city, on American paper, and with American types; all republican agents, animate and inanimate; with these did he set forth and extol, without ceasing, the ever memorable & never to be sufficiently praised blessings of the British constitution & government, not only as fully enjoyed by the freest and most favoured of King George's subjects, at home; but also, by us colonists, who, God knows, enjoy in reality a very minute portion of the former, but certainly are intimate enough with the effects of the latter, as administered in these dependencies, by earls, knights and others. Our brother editor, Carey, did not see far enough, when he termed the worthy doctor 'a crazy editor.' The doctor was all the while besieging Quebec, and where Montgomery fell and Montcalm gave up the ghost, did this editor, by a *ruse de guerre* fairly enter a conqueror."

.   .   .

In the old Gazette there are often very interesting and important original articles; as an opposition print it is ably conducted; the editor's father [*John Neilson*] is a member of the L.C. Parliament.

The Quebec Mercury, Montreal Herald, and Kingston Chronicle are of the unofficial journals, the most highly favoured by the Provincial Governments, the measures of which they support as well as they can. The Montreal Herald is extensively circulated in Lower Canada, it is issued thrice a week, in two half sheets and one whole one—price $5 including postage.

In many parts of the Canadas, and New Brunswick, the United States journals have an extensive circulation; the cause of which are their cheapness, and the early intelligence they convey. The lowest priced print in the Colonies is $3 per annum; but in general $4 or $5 is demanded. All the Upper Canada papers charge $4 if sent by post. It is somewhat curious, but true, that most printers here take all kinds of produce in payment; some of them take any thing, witness the editor of the Courier, Cortland, N.Y., who advertises that he will take rags and *old pot-metal*. I had like to have forgot the Nova Scotia journals. I see three of them regularly and am much pleased with the moderate and patriotic tone they assume. The Nova Scotian, conducted by a son of the celebrated agricultural writer Mr. Young, author of Agricola's letters, and the Acadian Recorder, by Mr. Holland, contain much valuable intelligence respecting the colonies in general. I have the pleasure of a perusal of the New Brunswick Courier printed at St Johns city, and esteem it.

If the British parliament would regulate our Post Office in the way the U.S. regulate theirs, it would be of great benefit to the Colonies. A general post office is merely a monopoly retained by the government for the public good, and ought to be conducted so as to be of the greatest benefit possible in its way. It is not so now; read the following extracts from a letter addressed by the editor of the Colonial Advocate to Capt. Mathews, a member of the U.C. parliament. (Quotations from the Advocate No. 26 are here made.) The truth is that there is no law for the regulation of newspapers *in the colonies,* and a law for this purpose is much wanted.

After writing Capt. Mathews, Mr. Mackenzie petitioned the House of Assembly anent the post office; the same was referred to a select committee who examined a number of persons and finally produced the following report, on which the house would have acted had it not been for the stormy discussion that soon after took place, (here Mr. Russell had inserted the report of the select Committee on Post Office abuses). I do not agree with these gentlemen in thinking the Colonial Legislature ought to have the Post Office in their own hands; it would be much better if the Ministry would send for the consolidate post office law of last session passed at Washington, and get a similar one for the colonies, through the British parliament, where all the colonies are concerned we must and ought to have laws from home.

To collect debts for newspapers in a country extending nearly 800 miles is often difficult, but I am fully persuaded that a manly, enlightened, and independent daily newspaper, published at Montreal, attached to the British constitution, a considerer of measures more than men, and not personal nor scurrilous in its remarks, would be a very profitable speculation to the proprietors, and an important acquisition to the colonies. No reflection is intended by this remark on the gentlemen who now conduct the colonial press.

The only legislative body in this world who *employ* and *pay* reporters to take down and print their debates is the House of Assembly in Upper Canada. Much juggling appears to have been the consequence of a competition between the printers for the office of printer and reporter; and I extract two very amusing and laconic papers from Mackenzie's Advocate, in illustration of the subject. He too was a competitor.

The late act passed in London allowing newspapers to pass between Britain and her colonies on payment of a small postage is a wise and salutary measure. It brings these distant parts of the British dominions nearer to one another; it enables the colonist to inform himself of what is doing at home, and affords the merchant, farmer, and politician, each a view of the Canadas, while sitting by their own fire-sides. This act is an honour to the member who introduced it, and to the ministry who supported it.—Would it not be judicious to allow newspapers to pass between editors in the colonies and their brethren in England free of all postage either way? —such a step as this would enable the British editor to judge more clearly of the wisdom of measures proposed at home affecting the colonies, and a poor colonial editor could at a less expense, add three or four additional British journals to his exchange list.

Pamphlets, and periodical publications other than newspapers, might also be authorized to be sent from one part of the colonies to another at fixed rates per sheet when the mails would admit of their passing. English periodicals might also be brought from Britain, and our reviews and magazines go thither regularly and without much expense.

This leads me to the subject of Reviews and Magazines. In a letter to my brother George, written from Ancaster in August last, there is an account of a society who are supplied with English periodicals, *via* New York, he will shew it you.

The Quarterly and Edinburgh Reviews were formerly re-printed in New York, but since Messrs. Kirke & Mercein's failure in 1820, they are re-printed by Wells & Silby of Boston, who send them by the U.S. mail, or a private conveyance, as per desire, to the subscribers in the Canadas and the rest of British America. I get my copy of Wells & Silby, and my bookseller is allowed 20 per cent off the retail price, which is $5 a year.

If the British Government would permit such works as these to come by the packet ships to the colonies, the British publisher would sell many copies here, & booksellers who advertise in sheets stitched to the Reviews, would obtain a greater circulation for their prospectus, which do not appear in the U.S. editions.

Blackwood's Edinburgh Magazine was reprinted by E. B. Clayton of N.Y. for several years, and as it abounds not only in resistless satire, but also in well written essays on important subjects, I felt sorry when they gave it up. A House in New York (Wilder & Campbell) fulfil orders for British editions of the most celebrated periodicals, and by this means I get an occasional peep at a stray number of a friend's copy of Christopher North.

The North American Review is in general conducted with much moderation, and the writers in its pages occasionally display a degree of talent highly creditable to their country. This work has a very limited circulation in the British Colonies.

In order that we might exhibit our judgment, and display our research in polite literature, we critics of the colonies, got up lately a colonial censor under the style and title of the "Canadian Review." It is or was edited by Mr. Chisholm, a Caledonian, printed at Montreal, and appears quarterly.

The three first numbers are undoubtedly a credit to the Province, to the authors, and, in respect of typographical execution, to Mr. Ferguson, the printer; but it is with regret I have to add that the merit of the work is much clouded by a disposition shown in some cases to decry and vilify personally those to whose politics it stands opposed.

A Magazine is also published in Montreal which takes its name from that city.

In Boston, New York and Philadelphia, there are edited and published several very useful literary journals; as also scientific, and religious Magazines, not a few. Nor is the Ohio country deficient in literary periodicals; knowledge travels westward among the "Backwoodsmen" with a rapidity unparalleled in former ages.

I had written this far when I received a number of the Nova Scotian, containing the heads of the American and Colonial Steam navigation act, and so firmly am I persuaded of the propriety of a more extensive, intimate and permanent system of correspondence being established between England and her North American colonies, that I hail this measure as one of those, which, under divine providence, are destined to unite these distant lands in a closer bond of Union. I would think it most advisable that the conveyance of magazines, pamphlets, reviews, and other literary and scientific periodicals were in the hands of government as a part of the post office system; but should administration think otherwise, a bill to incorporate a private company, with power to forward reviews, &c, even if it should cost £1000, would reward the proprietors. If it be objected that, by this means, the levelling abusive trash of political firebrands might come among us oftener and do more mischief, I would reply, that if all the republicanism of the United States has not yet extinguished our affection for the land of our sires, neither will the Dolbys, Hunts and Woolers, of England corrupt us; while on the other hand her divines, poets, philosophers, artists, and men of science, will be enabled to hold an early and useful communion with each other and with the British family even to the utmost bounds of her western dominions. I cannot for a moment doubt but that the Quarterly Review, Blackwood, and others of our essayists reprinted in the Union, have done there much good, as tending to remove from the minds of their orators, statesmen, and military men, the stupid but much cherished idea that they alone of all the nations of the earth enjoy true freedom.

Another proof of the rising importance of the western country was afforded me this evening, in the Black Rock Gazette of the 20th ult. It is there stated that fourteen years ago there was only one small newspaper published in the state of New-York west of Canandaigua, while now there are fourteen, chiefly of the imperial size, located west of that village; as also that in 1811 a house and half acre lot on the main street of Buffalo would sell for only $800 or thereabout, but that the same lots exclusive of the building, could not now be obtained for less than 6 or $7000; and further, that in the village of Rochester in the same state, which in 1813 consisted of only a mill and three or four houses and shantys, lots have been sold in some of the principal business streets this season at $100 a foot in front, extending only 70 or 80 feet deep!

The booksellers of New-York, Boston, and Philadelphia, print cheap editions of new English works of celebrity the moment they are received. Scott's new novel, "The Fortunes of Nigel", containing upwards of 500 pages 12mo. was put into the hands of workmen on Thursday morning, in New-York, and by eight o'clock on the morning of the Saturday following, printed, done up, and for sale in the different book-stores.

Of Byron's poetical works, the Waverley novels, Moore's Melodies, and other popular works, very cheap editions are to be had in the United States; for as the copy right of the authors does not cross the Atlantic, any one may reprint. Works so reprinted, as also the greater part of the old standard books, are sold to country book-sellers on a credit of six months, at a discount of from 33 to 40 per cent off the retail price. I have also had occasion to examine several booksellers' invoices where they bought for cash in New-York and Philadelphia; the charges were as follows: Tales of My Landlord, each series, $2, Waverley, Ivanhoe, Guy Mannering, The Entail, Reginald Dalton, Sir Andrew Wylie, 8s. Sterling, each novel in a 2 vol. edition; on all these 50 per cent was allowed off; so that the country bookseller only paid 4s. British for a very good edition of a novel which in London would have cost him upwards of a guinea. This discount of the one-half off, is regularly allowed where the invoice is paid down cash, by most of the wholesale houses.

In cases, however, where there is a copy right in the United States, the allowance of the trade is, as in England, at the option of the bookseller or author. The Americans carry on the book trade to a great extent. In many of their villages are to be found large and well filled book-stores; and I am informed that there are now two or three booksellers' shops located in boats travelling along the Grand Canal.

At Hartford, in Connecticut, there are a great many books printed for hawkers and pedlars, who travel about taking orders for works at double their value, and succeed in getting not a little cash for Yankee editions of Family Bibles, Histories of the United States, and other publications, not over accurate in the text, upon occasion.

Very few books of any sort are printed in the colonies. In all Upper Canada Mr. Peter M'Phail, of York, is the only professional bookbinder, and there is not one concern that depends solely on the sale of books, or of books and stationery, above Montreal. School books, bibles, and paper are to be found in most of the country stores; some of the shopkeepers keep on hand a supply of stationery and miscellaneous publications. Lesslie & Sons, formerly of Dundee, chiefly supply the parliament of Upper-Canada with stationery, which article formerly used to be ordered from London direct. For booksellers' shops you must go to Montreal, Quebec, Halifax, or St. Johns; even in these large towns the trade is not carried on but in retail; if your bookseller has not the work you want, he will get it for you bye and bye, from New-York, Boston, or England. I am not sure that an extensive bookseller would thrive in Montreal; but with a good capital to enable him to give credit to the country stores, he might succeed in diverting to that city a large portion of the brisk trade which now goes to the United States.

The demand for scientific works is not very extensive, but it nevertheless forms an important item in a bookseller's business here; what with priests, royal grammar and district schools, medical people, (and a college when we can get one,) hundreds of Greek, Latin, and Hebrew books are sold annually. The New-Englanders have attempted to reprint several of the classics, but their editions are not only *dearer* than those printed in Britain, but also less accurate, and the paper is less strong. The foundation of the Jewish city on Grand Island, above the Falls of Niagara, is now laid, so that I suppose we shall have Hebrew books bye and bye correctly printed by the children of Israel themselves.

Although the American Bible Society have been nearly ten years in operation, very few of their bibles are either sold or given away gratis, and as there are no bibles printed in the colonies, we have to depend on supplies from the British and United States societies, His Majesty's printers, and the U.S. booksellers. I saw Col. Wardlaw present a young boy at school, about a year ago, with one of the naval and military society's testaments. I have understood that the Colonel had a number at his disposal. $211 were remitted to the American Bible Society in New-York, in August last, by a society in the small village of Niagara, U.C. in payment of bibles.

I would expect many beneficial results from an act of the Imperial Parliament to protect, so as to render profitable to the inventors or proprietors, every new and useful improvement in the arts and sciences; and to invest in the authors or proprietors of new books, maps, engravings, &c. published in any one colony, a copyright, under proper restrictions, and for a limited period. A colonial act of this nature could be of small avail, as what had the right of a patent at Kingston or York, might be made freely by all in Quebec and Montreal. An act of the supreme government on the other hand, as it extends over and binds all the colonies, would secure to some future Cabotian the advantages which ought to accrue to genius and learning, when applied to useful purposes.

Notwithstanding the objections which I have seen urged by Longman & Co. as well as other eminent British publishers, to allowing "copies of works so secured to the British Universities," &c, I think it ought to be so ordered here also, in so far as sending a copy to at least one public library or seat of learning in each colony.

In the United States Congress two acts have passed, securing copy rights to the inventors; and the offices of the district clerks in each state are appointed as places of record or deposit of the works, engravings, charts, maps, designs or etchings, for which a temporary monopoly is desired. COLONIAL ADVOCATE, 6 April 1826.

THE LIFE OF A FARMER COMPARED WITH THAT OF A PRINTER

[*Thomas Smith was a young apprentice in the office of the* Colonial Advocate *who drowned himself in the York harbour, 23 April 1826. Mackenzie wrote a detailed and sympathetic account of the tragedy, and asked, "Who is there that can know, far less describe, the extent and measure of his grief?"*]

The death of Thomas Smith, with the circumstances that attended it, have in no small degree increased the dislike I have long entertained to the manner in which a country newspaper is and must be conducted in a small community. To publish a small political paper draws the attention of no one, and is time and labour uselessly bestowed.—To publish a large one, as I have done for some time, induces a great number of respectable persons to subscribe; and so far all is well. But the proprietor and editor is and must be a slave. He toils from day to day to get forward; he perceives that his ideal profits are accumulating; that the list of his debtors is *rapidly* augmenting; that his prospects are *slowly* brightening; but he still must remain *a slave*. What with writing for the paper, dunning careless subscribers in all directions, receiving and answering letters, reading foreign journals (as a task,) correcting the press, attending to the directions, or weekly addressing an immense number of papers to hundreds of post-offices, collecting ways and means for carrying on his business and maintaining those whose dependence is placed upon him, sitting up on one or two nights of the week to superintend his publication, giving an every day's constant attention on the spot, entering accounts and posting his books in a business carried on entirely by the ledger, and where very few indeed think of paying him in advance, continually displeasing some of those he wishes most to please, and pestered with their ungenerous and angry expostulations, independent only that he may be the more acutely made to feel his daily dependence on all classes. Such is his life for six days in the week *all the year round;* and how think you is the seventh disposed of? If I would speak for myself I might truly say, that I am often so wearied and fatigued with the toils of the working days as to be perfectly unable to enjoy the rest provided by a kind providence on the Christian Sabbath. That instead of being fit to attend church, read the scriptures, or in any way engage in the duties of divine appointment, I am glad to lay me down on my bed or on a sofa, as a temporary relief from the effects of incessant toil. All this is bad enough, but there is one circumstance connected with a country newspaper which is still worse; Namely, the slavish dependence of masters upon their journeymen. A large newspaper requires many hands; if one or two desert you, you are most awkwardly situated. Of journeymen printers there are, perhaps, more than in a great many other trades, of what may be fairly termed *tipplers*; men who will be sober one day, tippling the next, and useless for one or two days in the week, all the year round.

In Upper Canada there is no choice, except Hobson's, "this or none". A master printer is not like a carpenter or a shoemaker, who can at all times find abundance of working people in his calling. There are but few operatives; and consequently *you must* oftentimes introduce *among your apprentices* men who will make the printing house a scene of drunkenness and disorder; and, if you quarrel with them, your paper stops, and yourself must go off to the United States to hire at any price Yankee "helps" in their place, real water drinkers, but as stiff, as self-important, and as calmly insolent in their behaviour, as if they had, each in his own proper person, achieved their national independence, and brought about the peace of '83. These are facts in newspaper printing which I have long tried to disguise even from myself.

The farmer, on the other hand, depends directly on his maker; if he is a diligent man he may expect for the superfluous produce of his farm *the market price*, and his crops are ripened by the solar beam and refreshed by the dews of heaven, the grass springs up in due season to afford food for his cattle; he has continually before his eyes innumerable instances of the wisdom and goodness of his Creator. He trusts in no degree to the caprice of the multitude, and is perhaps the most independent among the lords of creation, as the country newspaper printer is the most abject slave, pursuing a phantom, sacrificing his best days to the pursuit of that *competence* which the contented mind can never want, and which the ambitious can never possess. I have not written for the multitude, nor desired to acquire riches as the chief good, nor will I ever do so. I have long admired the force of that passage in the works of an elegant writer which advises us whenever "the desire of wealth is taking hold of the heart" to "look round and see how it operates upon those whose industry or fortune has obtained it. When we find them *oppressed with their own abundance*, luxurious without pleasure, idle without ease, impatient and querulous in themselves, and despised or hated by the rest of mankind, we shall soon be convinced that, *if the real wants of our condition are satisfied, there remains little to be sought with solicitude, or desired with eagerness*". COLONIAL ADVOCATE, 27 April 1826.

THE LIBRARY OF PARLIAMENT

From a careful calculation, founded on an examination of the records of former Parliaments, we find that the Library has cost the country upwards of £3000, and perhaps we may have missed noticing some appropriations. It is now in a wretched state—the books are valuable, very valuable, but they are under no regulations whatever. A sum quite inadequate to the duties required is allowed the Clerk of the House of Assembly for attending to the books; better add that to his slender salary as clerk, and allow £6 a year to some respectable studious person *who has no other employment*, obliging him to attend constantly from eight in the morning till eight at night (meal times excepted) in the Library, day by day all the year round. And giving him rules for the regulation of his conduct regarding the books and regarding the Library.

The editor of this journal well remembers how greatly he has been indebted to the opportunities afforded him in his younger years of having access to an extensive and choice collection of books, and there is scarcely a member of Parliament but what must find the library of the house extremely useful in the course of the session for references. Besides this there is not in the colony another library to which they could have access, *half so valuable*. We hear of two libraries!—one for each house! Better, much better it were to extend the present one so as to include some of those late important works on various subjects which have appeared in England and America—together with the principal reviews, magazines, newspapers etc.

As there is no extensive library to which the youth of this colony can have access, we have the more need to have a good one to which our legislature may refer in their riper years.

We fervently pray that it may be enlarged and kept open at all seasons of the year not only to the members, *but also to those whom they may introduce to the librarian*. This is the practice of Lower Canada, and it is worthy of our imitation. For until our studious men can have access to proper books, we will never boast of profound scholars. Gibbon could not have written his "Decline and Fall of the Roman Empire", in Canada—no nor in any part of America. And why? Because he would not have been able to meet with the necessary authorities in any library; no, *nor in all* the libraries of this quarter of the world. And it must be obvious that the fewer the books are the evil becomes the greater. Were the editor of this paper a member of the provincial legislature he would require to consult authorities continually, so many are his imperfections; although there are few who have passed a greater portion of a short life in reading.

As the library is now managed, the books instead of being annually increased are scattered and lost, being taken away and no account kept of them. Look at the advertisement in the Upper Canada Gazette of stray books, and look at a similar notice in the Quebec paper. Our library lacks the most by ten times and all from improper management. We heard some of the members (Goths and Vandals) talk of *selling the books* the other day. God forbid! COLONIAL ADVOCATE, 11 January 1827.

YORK LIBRARY

A severe attack of our subtle and unyielding adversary the fever of the country prevented our having the honour of being present at the meeting for a public library on Monday last. We shall become a subscriber however, and shall look out twenty or thirty volumes as a present to the society if they institute a liberal and disinterested system. There are a number of gentlemen in town who could well afford to spare a few books towards the establishment of a public library, and we think it probable that they will do so. The Attorney General, as member for York, may be reasonably expected to use his influence on its behalf. Notices of meetings shall not be charged by us as advertisements. COLONIAL ADVOCATE, 3 May 1827.

YORK PAPER-MILL

About three miles out of town in the bottom of a deep ravine, watered by the river Don, and bounded also by beautiful and verdant flats, are situated the York paper-mill, distillery and grist-mill, owned by Messrs. Eastwood and Co.; also Mr. Shepard's axe-grinding machinery, and Messrs. Helliwell's large and extensive brewery. I went out to view these improvements a few days ago, and returned much gratified with witnessing the paper manufacture in active operation—as also the bold and pleasing scenery on the banks of the Don. The river might be made navigable with small expense up to the brewery, and if the surrounding lands were laid out in five acre lots all the way to town they would sell to great advantage.

There are two or three other paper-mills in the province. COLONIAL ADVOCATE, 9 August 1827; SKETCHES, p. 270.

THE LIBRARY OF CONGRESS, 1829

I was indebted to the general [*M'Comb, commander-in-chief*] also for an introduction to the library of Congress, and passed several hours very agreeably in examining the extent and condition of that invaluable appendage to a deliberative body. The library, as I have before stated, is placed in the Capitol—is exceedingly well arranged, each description of books being kept by themselves. There is but one library for both Houses. Occupied on the same deliberations, interested in the same cause, appointed by the same authority, a free, contented, prosperous and happy people, why should the senators require one apartment and the representatives another? It is enough that less enlightened and united bodies pursue that course.

The catalogues are upon a new, and I think, useful principle in large libraries, which not only facilitates your finding any author you want, but also other works treating upon similar subjects. I perceive they have got British copies of a great many Reports of Committees of the House of Commons; some of them well thumbed too. To a legislative body such as assembles at Washington, a choice collection of standard books is absolutely indispensable. There are a number of copies of several domestic works in the library, purchased to encourage the authors, and afterwards voted away from time to time, by joint resolutions of the two Houses assented to by the President, which serve in place of laws on such matters. SKETCHES, p. 39.

THE NEED FOR
READING-ROOMS

Albany Horticultural Society—We have read with lively pleasure an account of an anniversary meeting of the above named Society, which occupies upwards of two of the massy columns of the last received number of the N.Y. State paper, and is full of interest. But of what avail is it to mention such matters here? Instead of Mechanics' Institutes, Atheneums, Public Reading Rooms, Apprentices' Libraries, Agricultural and Horticultural Societies, Forums, Literary Clubs, and other Institutions of a similar nature, to delight, instruct and elevate the intellectual character of our artizans and farmers, or to employ the often ill-spent, because uselessly employed, evenings of our apprentices and other youths, we have a motley generation of upstart would-be gentlemen to set us the fashions—a race alike despised by and despising the great body of the Canadian people; rioting in luxuries this infant province can ill afford to spare them, and possessing as it were the soil and its serfs on a rack-rent lease, seemingly neither knowing nor caring who shall follow in their train after them.

These place-holding, place-hunting aristocrats, are headed by a batch of military heroes, who are, it appears, to have each his 1200, 800, or 600 acres of our best lands, while Sir John, the keystone of their arch, would fain persuade the Commons' House of Assembly to tax their constituents another million of dollars to pay the claimants for losses in the late British and American war; said claimants having been refused by Britain the proceeds of the above mentioned lands, part of which are, it appears, to be partitioned among men who never saw these provinces, and the rest having already been distributed among a host of political priests and partizans; one and all of whom would spurn the idea of entering a literary or scientific institution and there *herding* with Canadian plebeians, the mob, the canaille. Time may remedy these discrepancies, but we are somewhat impatient of its operations.

The writer of this article well remembers the many advantages he derived from the establishment of a literary and scientific institution in his native city, of which, at the early age of sixteen, he became a member. It was furnished with an extensive and well assorted library, a philosophical apparatus, and a museum richly endowed with minerals, shells, botanical productions, natural curiosities, &c. &c. Essays were delivered weekly by its members in rotation, and debates on scientific subjects ensued. Many a long winter's evening has the writer spent in the hall of this institution, endeavouring to acquire the elements of useful knowledge out of the abundant materials thus placed within his reach, while, had no such society existed, he might perhaps have been induced oftener to exchange his labours at the desk of his master's counting-room, for the deceitful gratification offered in the tavern or gambling house.

Imagine a society of 70 or 80 persons of all ages, from 15 to 75, of all ranks—from the mechanic's apprentice with his leathern apron, up to the city bailie or parish minister with his powdered toupee, met together on an entire equality, in a large hall full of books and papers, scientific apparatus, chemical tests, models of machinery, &c. &c., to give and to receive valuable information. Of the youths who then there congregated, some there are who sweetly sleep below the Spanish sod, others at this day rank high in the service of their country, and one among the number, an old and valued friend, to whom the writer paid a visit while on his return from Virginia, lately, has arrived at well merited distinction in the employment of the neighbouring republic. Much satisfaction will it give us to see (as we hope we shall) such institutions as we have alluded to, encouraged and promoted in the country of our adoption, more especially in this its rising capital. We hail the approaching period when our mechanics and their apprentices will meet with the sons of the true nobility of our land, to spend their winter evenings as we used to spend ours, in all the ardour of early enthusiasm, some seventeen or eighteen years ago. COLONIAL ADVOCATE, 1 October 1829.

THE EXAMPLE OF HOBBES

We do not copy so much into this newspaper from the Philadelphia National Gazette, as from some other periodicals, but we select from its columns and preserve in our scrap books, for after reference, until the numbers are often entirely riddled. We scarcely ever receive a Gazette but there is something in it well worth the remembering, and out of the ordinary line of news or newspaper quotations. In the number of the 20th November, we find another extract from Sir James Mackintosh's Dissertation on Modern Ethics, containing a notice of the celebrated philosopher, Thomas Hobbes of Malmesbury. The account given of Hobbes's success in the attainment of knowledge is very pleasing. He was nearly thirty years of age when he began to study the classics, yet he wrote well in Latin. It was after forty that he learnt the first rudiments of geometry. About his sixtieth year he began to publish those philosophical writings which contain his peculiar opinions; and at the age of eighty-seven he gave to the world metrical versions of the Odyssey and the Iliad!

There is scarcely any profession or employment on this continent but affords more or less time for the improvement of the mind; and the example of Hobbes, with many others, may be triumphantly offered as evidence of the duration to advanced life of the power to cultivate and improve the mental faculties. COLONIAL ADVOCATE, 9 December 1830.

THE AMERICAN LANCET

We have been favoured by the editors with a copy of the first and part of the second volume of the American Lancet, a journal devoted to the healing art, and conducted by "an association of physicians and surgeons" resident in the United States.

The Lancet is published in New York, twice a month, in sheets of 24 pages each, on fine paper, at $4 per annum, payable half yearly in advance. Extra sheets are occasionally presented to subscribers free of expense, and the postage is only one cent a number. Orders should be sent to Dr. John G. Vought, Agent, 294 Broadway, New York.

We will frankly confess, that so pressing are our various avocations, that we have not had leisure to read and form an opinion of the work, but we perceive that it contains a great variety of useful information, clothed in the language of the country, and among the names of the contributors we find Drs. Mitchell, MacNeven, Pascalis, Osborn, Reese, Mott, Akerly and Yates, all of New York. COLONIAL ADVOCATE, 9 December 1830.

"NO TIME TO READ THE PAPERS"

All men will find time for every thing that is really a gratification to them; and hence the complaint of "no time," it is in fact *no taste* for newspapers. Every man has time to read a weekly paper, during a rainy day, of a long evening, or sometimes when waiting for his meals; if he is not a slave, he certainly can find time to improve his mind.—His children, undoubtedly, have time enough to learn vice, and if he is not ambitious to raise them above the level of ignorance, they will certainly prove vicious. The most illustrious people will always find time to read, and it is the lazy and idle only who have no *time*. It is mysterious how many people employ their time, while not at their business, and especially some who do very little of any kind of business whatever. Such persons are a blank in creation, and society feels no loss when they drop away. POOR RICHARD, or THE YORKSHIRE ALMANAC, 1831, p. 15.

QUEBEC READING-ROOMS

In Quebec are two reading-rooms—one in the lower town, sustained by the merchants—the other, in the Bishop's Palace, connected with the library of the House of Assembly. I have often proposed to influential members of the present as well as the two last legislatures of Upper Canada, the establishment of a reading-room, and the annual augmentation of "the library," but always in vain. The representatives of our Upper Canada "superior intelligences," possess so much information already, that they appear to think an addition to the stock would occasion a superfluous waste of public money. Here the law-makers are more moderate. They live and learn. Instead of a few miserable odd volumes, the sweepings of some second-hand London book shop, and which form "the library of both Houses" of the legislature of the intellectual colony above M'Gee's Point, I find in Quebec an extensive and valuable collection of authors in the French and English languages, carefully arranged in boxes on shelves so that they may be expeditiously removed in case of fire. They are divided, in the catalogue of 1831, into seven classes, viz.—

1. Theology.
2. Government, &c.—Section i. Government, politics, and legislation. ii. Political economy, commerce and finance.
3. Jurisprudence.—Section i. Law of nature and nations, and treaties of peace. ii. Civil law. iii. Ecclesiastical and Canon law. iv. Constitutional and parliamentary laws of Great Britain and Ireland. v. Statute and common law of Great Britain and Ireland. vi. French law. vii. Colonial law.
4. Arts and Sciences.—Section i. Philosophy. ii. Physical and mathematical sciences and agriculture. iii. Mechanical arts, manufactures and trades. iv. Fine arts and art of war. v. Medicine, anatomy, chemistry, &c.
5. Belles Lettres.
6. Geography and Voyages.
7. Chronology and History.

.   .   .

Perhaps the day may yet arrive in which "the superior intelligences" who annually assemble at York will be content to take from the Lower Canadians the example of a well-endowed legislative library! To me it would be an inestimable treasure, a mine of the sort of riches I have ever coveted most. I never think of Philadelphia, without some friendly recollections of the Franklin library and its 25,000 volumes.

.   .   .

The Quebec Exchange and Exchange Reading-Rooms are chiefly upheld by the subscriptions of the mercantile part of the community, and the reading-room is abundantly supplied with newspapers from Europe, Lower Canada and the United States. Although the trade of the two provinces is extensive, only one Upper Canada paper, a journal of very limited circulation, is received. The second story contains the Quebec Library. In the room I found Almanacs of all sorts in abundance, also the Reviews, New Monthly Magazine, and Army and Navy Lists. The "Black Book, or Corruption Unmasked," with the supplementary volume, are placed in a very conspicuous situation, and the "Courant," "Vindicator" and "La Minerve" are subscribed for.

[*In the* Sketches *Mackenzie adds this footnote:*] The libraries of the Legislative Houses in Lower Canada are valuable literary treasures. The library of Congress contains 16,000 volumes; the library of Harvard University contains 35,000 volumes, and a considerable augmentation is expected from Europe; the library of the Boston Athenaeum numbers 25,000 volumes; the Quebec library in the lower town, and the public library at the Exchange, Montreal, are both of them valuable and extensive. But the library of the Legislature of Upper Canada has not had a volume added to it, except the journals, for nearly a dozen of years. It is indeed a miserable apology; not worth one-tenth of the private library which that ambitious priest who made a pilgrimage to London to accuse the people of Upper Canada and their clergy of ignorance and sedition has been enabled to purchase with the cash of the country.

In several sessions of the Provincial Legislature of Upper Canada, I made repeated efforts to improve and enlarge the library. The Legislative Council successfully opposed an attempt I made by a resolution which passed the Assembly, to order, out of the contingent fund, the "Edinburgh," "Quarterly," "Westminster," and "American Quarterly Reviews," and "Blackwood," the "New Monthly," and other leading periodicals of the day, for the use of members—they threw the motion under their table and refused to act upon it, and indeed manifested in all their proceedings the utmost unwillingness to put the country in possession of those British and Colonial publications for reference which the spirit of the age requires. COLONIAL ADVOCATE, 12 and 19 May 1831; SKETCHES, p. 183.

HAMILTON WEEKLY PAPERS

There are two weekly newspapers in the Gore District, both of them published at Hamilton. The name of the one is the Western Mercury, of the other the Free Press. The *Mercury* is the old Gore Balance under a new title, and is the organ of Messrs. Law and McNab the Wentworth attornies, and of a knot of petty magistrates, placemen, incorporated priests, and hungry office seekers, who would devour a province like a cloud of locusts if their power was at all equal to their inclinations. The *Mercury* is supported by the subscriptions of the executive faction who rule in York although opposed both to King and constitution; is upheld by the advertising of sheriffs, districts, governments, &c. and openly in the pay of those who have sought for thirty years to keep the people in ignorance, squander the fruits of their patient industry, depress the humbler classes under colour of law, and unite their efforts to crush every man whether judge or labourer, farmer or printer, who had dared to stand up for the British constitution and the good of the country. It is a part of the monopolizing system of the harpies who have long had the patronage of the colony in their hands, to establish slavish presses all over, and hire poor hungry sycophants who are only fit for dirty employments, as their "scullions." These mean fellows will bow and scrape, and fetch and carry, tell lies or babble nonsense, praise and flatter or abuse and scandalize, just as they are bid—nothing is too bad for them, so that they can get the means of existence. If you meet them in private they will acknowledge that they detest their trade, but like the finisher of the law can now get no other. Work they cannot, teach school they will not. Drudges, therefore, they must remain. A few of these soulless creatures, in the pay of those in authority, have been established with presses, out of the public funds. Some of their papers are dull lifeless things, as inanimate as torpid reptiles, and only awake to spue out venom before a general election. Others are conducted by more mercurial creatures, always ready for mischief. Such journals answer the very important purpose to a wicked faction of keeping independent papers in more limited circulation— but in the end they will assuredly bring about a spirit of enquiry fatal to their upholders. The Mercury will continue to slander the independent portion of the community, and cloak over the iniquity of the faction who squander six hundred thousand dollars yearly— it never will do the people's business and check and expose peculation and official knavery.

The *Free Press*, on the other hand, is evidently established on independent principles, by a young Englishman of good abilities, but who, so long as he pursues an honest manly course will have the sharers and dispensers of the good things in the Gore District for his inveterate enemies and merciless persecutors. We learnt seven or eight years ago what it was to contend with this mercenary class— and would advise the people of Halton and Wentworth, those who know and appreciate our principles and practice in the legislature and out of it, to give up the Mercury for the Free Press so long as the latter shall continue their advocate. We will even be a little more disinterested, and say to some of our supporters in the Gore District, "Rather than that a liberal journal should not be firmly upheld in Gore, if you cannot take both papers, drop the Colonial

Advocate and take the Free Press." The Town and County of York will keep up this journal if not a single number were sent beyond its confines. In making these remarks, we are actuated by a disinterested wish to benefit the country, without the least mixture of personal feeling, and we hope the advice here given will not be thrown away. One suggestion more and we have done—Let the intelligent and patriotic men of Halton and Wentworth, maintain the literary character of their beautiful district by frequent, able and spirited essays and communications addressed to its most independent press, and let the youthful editor be encouraged to stand to his colours, and rather to fall gloriously on the field of honour with the ensign wrapped round him than yield an inch by whatever weapons he may be assailed. COLONIAL ADVOCATE, 22 September 1831.

PAPER AND INK

DEAR SIR:—I have just received the Advocate of the 12th July. It has but one fault.—The paper is detestable. They would refuse it here to wrap up brown sugar with. It is a little fairer than the ink, and but very little. I am sorry to perceive that Messrs. Eastwood and Skinner would offer such miserable paper to any printing office. Surely the difference of profit to them can be no great object! The paper is actually coarser than one of the earliest numbers of the Observer, a work apparently coeval with the invention of printing and paper making.—The papyrus from the old mummy of Thebes in Egypt, 4000 years old, is *fair* when placed beside the improved productions of my friends of the Don Mills in America in the year of grace 1832, with all the aid they can invoke from Acid and Alkalies, Chloride of Lime and Oil of Vitriol!

Copy from the *True Sun* one or two extracts from Mr. O'Connell's address declining to leave Kerry for Limerick; also an extract from the Morning Chronicle about the three Scotch Whigs and the 42 Sycophants, or the virtues of reform. From the same paper give the scene of the royal marriage, and the expected arrangements concerning the East India Company's Charter.

Nothing can exceed the freedom of debate (within the rule of good manners) which is exercised in the House of Commons. Speaking of the East Indies the other evening, Sir Charles Forbes declared that wherever our government went in India we left the people poorer and poorer, sweeping as it were with the besom of destruction until we had left the native inhabitants a nation of beggars. I took down his words in the ante-room. [*From a letter to Randal Wixon, London, 21 August 1832.*] COLONIAL ADVOCATE, 11 October 1832.

TAXES ON KNOWLEDGE

The Relative Situations of the Periodical Press in England and America, briefly stated by an American Printer

TO THE EDITOR OF THE *True Sun* [*London, England*]:

SIR,—I was much pleased with a remark made by one of the candidates for the metropolitan districts the other day, who began his oration at the great meeting held in the London Tavern, for the purpose of ascertaining the public sentiment with regard to the expediency of discontinuing the house and window assessments, by assuring the electors, that, if elected, it was his desire to commence the good work of Reform and retrenchment by an immediate repeal of the taxes which impede the progress of knowledge.

Believing, as I do, that those taxes are by far the most dangerous to the interests of the humbler classes of society of any with which their productive industry is so heavily burthened, and that the very first act of the extended representation should be an Act to secure and extend the freedom of the Press, I purpose, with your permission, to place before the readers of the "True Sun" the particulars of a comparison I have instituted between the taxed Press of England, and the unstamped Press of the North American Union.

New York State, with a population under that of Scotland, maintains 263 Newspapers, of which 18 are printed daily,—one at Rochester, 500 miles from the ocean, four at Albany, and 13 in the city of New York. I do not remember having ever heard of a prosecution for libel being instituted by those in power against any Journalist of any party. "William's Register" estimates the whole number circulated in this State alone at 16,000,000 of sheets, or about 35,000 reams annually. The methodists publish an edition of a Newspaper, in which political news is blended with the advocacy of their peculiar doctrines, the subscription to which extends to 20,000 copies. If "William's Register" and a late tabular statement in the "Scotsman" are correct, New York State alone circulates as many as two-thirds of the whole number of sheets published annually in Britain. Scotland has but forty Newspapers, not one of which is published daily, while even the little town of Newark, in New Jersey, has its daily Press handsomely supported. Tax the Press in America, as it is taxed in England, and Newark would soon cease to have any Newspaper at all. Tax it as it is taxed in England, did I say? That would be impossible. All the fleets and armies of Great Britain were unable to collect twopence tax in the pound of tea from three millions of Americans threescore years ago; while it is evident that some two hundred and fifty excisemen are fully competent to enforce payment of a revenue an hundred fold heavier from three-and-twenty millions of Britons.

In the United States there are no excisemen to be found at the paper-mill, with their stamps and marks—there the manufacturer is placed under no restraint, nor subjected to a system of espionage, and heavy taxation laid in virtue of laws by far too intricate and complicated to be understood in a life time by many whose task it is to obey them; while in Britain there is an excise duty of three-pence per lb., varying from twenty to fifty per cent. on the original value, and falling, (as usual) with double weight upon such coarse editions as are only purchased by the poorer classes. In America the paper-maker imports rags, his raw material, duty free from all nations; in England he is taxed a crown per ton at the custom house. In the Union the bookseller may publish any work with or without the printer's name or his own—not so here. Beyond the Atlantic there is no duty on news-advertisements, no stamp on Newspapers, (there they kicked at it the moment a stamp was exhibited to them), no registration of proprietors at the stamp-office, no penalty against false affidavits, no necessity for resorting to fraud or collusion, evasion or trick—all is free as the air they breathe. The young American who was, perhaps, a journeyman or, it may be, an apprentice in a daily Newspaper-office in New York, Philadelphia, or Boston, yesterday, may, if he chuses, be the proprietor of a super-royal weekly Journal of respectable appearance tomorrow, in some thriving western village, which perhaps twelve months before formed a part of the silent primeval forest. Every possible facility is given to talent and industry. All the youth has to do is to employ his savings or his credit in the purchase of a press, and some £40 or £50 worth of type—new or at second-hand, as may best suit his finances, hire an upper floor, set agoing "The Tyrant's Foe, the People's Friend," issue "Number One", *and be steady*—he's comfortable for life. How different the printer's prospect here in England! A few individuals of wealth, credit, or enterprize, contrive to overstep the innumerable difficulties placed in their path—obtain the requisite capital—enter into security for good behaviour before they are accused—hire editors at large salaries—pay taxes, stamp duties, and penalties, and obtain a living—but thousands are kept back from the honourable and useful competition by laws enacted by an Aristocracy—ever cruel, jealous, and profligate, as a Government—for the protection of that supremacy their order had so long and so successfully usurped. Even in the Canadas, Nova Scotia, and New Brunswick, under British Colonial Government, there is to be found neither paper duty, advertisement tax, censorship, stamp, nor registration. The editor, who in general is also printer and proprietor, goes off to Albany, Boston, or New York, and selects his materials, then hires his journeymen and apprentices, opens his office often where never office was opened before, and suddenly comes forth in black upon white, Whig, Tory, Radical, or go-between, as taste, interest or inclination, may have prompted.

In the United States, Newspapers sent by mail, pay a halfpenny each sheet for postage, if sent to any place within the State in which they are printed, or if sent not more than a hundred miles into other States. When Newspapers are sent upwards of 100 miles in the mail, into other States, the postage is three farthings each number, and this charge is payable either by the printer or the subscriber at the printer's option. The utmost facility is given to the transmission of British Newspapers. I have sent many a number of the "True Sun" to the conductor of my Newspaper, in Upper Canada, at the expense of three farthings each for 3,000 miles sea, and 600 inland carriage. Sir Francis Freeling manages these matters differently.

Every Editor of a Newspaper in the United States is privileged by law to forward one copy of his Newspaper whether it be a weekly or a daily one, to every other Editor within the said States, who may choose to exchange Papers with him, and also to receive by mail the lucubrations of his brethren of the type, free of all postage charge. I can tell from many years experience that this is a most convenient arrangement. It certainly cannot be called un-English, for, although the advantage is not possessed by the printers of these kingdoms, it is the uniform custom in the colonies to exchange Newspapers postage free, and a good custom it is.

The price of a Weekly Newspaper in the United States and British Colonies varies between five and fifteen shillings a year. Daily Papers of the largest class are charged in New York forty-two shillings and sixpence per annum to subscribers, and in other large cities the price is thirty-four shillings, exclusive of 3d. a week paid by persons who live at a distance for postage. A single Daily Paper, much larger than the "Times", costs from twopence to twopence halfpenny—small country Papers vary from a penny to twopence.

In the circulation of the political periodicals, the London system of news agents is far preferable to the American custom of personal subscriptions, especially on the score of independence. In America, every Editor is unavoidably known to the whole city, village, or district in which he resides; in Britain the real conductors of the most influential Journals are known but to a few, comparatively speaking, either personally or by address. In London the editors and proprietors know little or nothing of their patrons; they sell their Papers at the counter to news-agents, and receive the cash in return; in New York there are annual subscriptions, expenses of collection, credit from six months to six years, bad debts, and sometimes total loss. Few printers in America have been in business for five or six years, without being able to exhibit thousands of advertising and newspaper debts in their ledgers, one or more years in arrear. Some of my news subscribers have not paid me any thing for these last seven years, but I know they can pay. This is the worst difficulty attending Newspaper printing in America, although it does not hinder many persons from acquiring great wealth. The sheet of paper costs us only a halfpenny at the paper-mill, and we neither need to give credit of stamps nor advertisement duty, so that bad news debts in America are quite a different thing from bad debts of the same description in England.

The "Times" of the 15th of June last has no doubt whatever but that the principal daily Journals, were they to study their own interests exclusively would gain by a removal of the stamp duty on Newspapers; but it expresses a doubt whether the public would gain much by the change. "If," say the editors, "Mr. Bulwer and some other Members clearly understood the question, they would see that the removal of the tax would at once create a virtual monopoly for all the present principal Newspaper proprietors; and who could conduct the business with such facility as those already armed with all the means of success?" The Journalist proceeds to deny that the present system confers any monopoly, and insists, that with the repeal, "We (the 'Times') should be quite certain that we and some of our morning and evening contemporaries, could immediately drive all the cheap rivals out of the market. Those who are so anxious for the repeal would, in fact, be the first to be ruined by it."

Those who are most anxious for the repeal of the taxes on knowledge are the great body of the people, and perhaps it would be difficult to convince the people that they would be ruined by receiving their Newspaper at threepence instead of sevenpence, whether they bought the "Times" or not. Venders of cheap publications would be free to exercise their callings without the interference of the informer or police; and Newspaper proprietors of talent and skill, with a small capital, would feel that they had had a new field opened to their exertions, a field now monopolized by the rich few, because of that wealth which would no longer avail them after the repeal—or, if it did avail them, would only do so by their affording the same information to the nation at the very lowest possible rate. Repeal all the taxes on knowledge, and the London public will have the daily Journals delivered, a copy at each man's door who may desire it, for £2 or £3 a year; their numbers and circulation will be greatly extended, their advertising custom increased, in many cases tenfold, and the profits on capital and talent employed will be found fair and reasonable.—The "Times" allows that the tax which prevents merchants and manufacturers from freely advertising their commodities, in a commercial community like England ought to be removed—but it would be willing to stop there—self-interest interferes. Sir Charles Wetherell said in the House of Commons, that to repeal the taxes on knowledge would be extremely ruinous to the large capitalists who now own the copyright of Newspapers.

The worst the change could do for them would be to enable them to continue their business with all the advantages of established character, withdrawing about two-thirds of their present investments, which might be placed in other profitable undertakings. The "New York Gazettes," that were established many years ago, still maintain the advantages they gained by their seniority, they do by far the most profitable business in the city, yet leave ample elbow-room for other and younger competitors; they need no such protecting monopoly as the "Times" seeks to uphold here. Advertisements are a mine of wealth to an old established Journal in America; their publication costs very little—no capital is expended in taxes to be balanced by bad debts—whatever is realized is clear gain.—The abolition of the stamp duty on Newspapers would injure the present daily Press more in its influence than its pecuniary character, for the competition of talent would be fourfold what it now is. Would not this increase of talent be a great public gain?

Speaking from the experience of America I would say, remove the taxes on knowledge, and you will speedily have one or more weekly or semi-weekly Journals, of more or less celebrity, in every little village or market town in the three kingdoms. Scotland will exhibit daily Newspapers in Glasgow, Edinburgh, Paisley, Dundee, and Aberdeen. England, in Liverpool, Bristol, Hull, Newcastle, Birmingham, Leeds, Manchester, Sheffield, Carlisle, Bath, &c. Ireland, in Cork, Limerick, Belfast, Londonderry, and other principal towns. The nation would soon have its thousand presses of every size and quality; many new openings to fame and fortune, honour, and celebrity would be instantly opened to men of talent and character,—perhaps it is not too much to affirm that 15,000 families, now idle, would find active employment in the trades of bookselling, book-binding, type-founding, paper-making, printing, and the arts attendant upon these trades. The best Emigration Committee England ever saw would be the one who would contrive to transport the greatest possible number of excisemen. COLONIAL ADVOCATE, 21 February 1833.

POST-OFFICE REFORM

I have long been of opinion that one way by which to unite two countries together, where the people or a majority of them speak one language, and carry on an extensive trade with each other, is by a safe, cheap, and expeditious post communication, and lines of post roads judiciously laid down.

This very obvious method of connecting the Canadas with England has hitherto been greatly neglected, or rather prohibited, for the restrictions have amounted to a virtual prohibition.

But the present is a good time to change these things for the better, and if we would even now take the hint from our republican descendants of the American Union, letters might soon be passing from the most distant parts of Ireland or Scotland to the western-most corner of Upper Canada for a postage of only a shilling or fifteen pence, and newspapers that have been stamped, duty free.

If it can be done, or if a better means of conveyance is not suggested, a line of packets should be made to run twice a-week between Halifax and Liverpool; the swiftest-sailing ships that can be built and the safest and most obliging captains. From Halifax the post-road should be improved, no matter at what expense, to Quebec, and settlements encouraged at every point where they can be begun with advantage. To improve such a road for such a purpose, the legislatures of the two Canadas would doubtless contribute most liberally and with great cheerfulness. Careful, experienced, trusty men should be chosen to oversee the road made. We would thus accomplish a speedy, safe, cheap, regular, and expeditious post communication with the whole of British America at all seasons of the year; and the Montreal or Quebec merchant, or the Upper or Lower Canada emigrant would receive his letters as soon and at a price as reasonable as if he had employed the New York packets and United States' mails. Pamphlets, magazines, reviews, and all other periodicals should also be allowed to pass by this conveyance between England and her colonies, and it should be an unalterable part of the post-office-law to allow no fees, perquisites or jobbing. At present the whole concern is a job from beginning to end.

Whenever you talk to the people at St. Martin's Le Grand [*G.P.O., London*] about reduced post-office rates, and a clear well-defined law, they tell you a long story about the magnitude of the national debt. What has that to do with the matter? Here we are [*in England*], a first-rate commercial nation, the first naval power in the world, justly desirous to keep up our influence beyond the Atlantic; yet with excellent means in our hands, arising out of the control of the post-office, we employ a code of laws which drives the whole of the colonial correspondence into the hands of the United States, to enrich their treasury, while the British monthly packets capsize once or twice a year, and charge such a price for the letters they carry, that it would seem as if their owners wished the Canadas beyond the Rocky Mountains. Why expend millions on wars, and canals, and defences, and be pennywise about the postage of letters, pamphlets, and newspapers? If the good folks of the colonies are wanted to be kept together, the more they know of England and English affairs, and the more England knows of them— the better for the connexion. The post-office is one of a very few monopolies that may be turned to great national advantage, if the rulers of the nation are not too busy to attend to such matters.
SKETCHES, p. 446; COLONIAL ADVOCATE, 29 August 1833.

POST-OFFICE REFORM

NEWSPAPER AND LETTER POSTAGES
REFORM IN THE POST-OFFICE DEPARTMENT
MR. STAYNER ORDERED HOME

One of the leading objects for which I was sent to England, was to endeavour to obtain an improvement in the management of the post-office department in the colonies, it having been for many years a matter of public complaint and legislative remonstrance.

Believing that it might become necessary to make application to the House of Commons on the subject, I requested of Mr. Hume that he would draw its attention to that part of one of the petitions from Upper Canada. He did so, and our memorial was ordered to be placed on the journals of the House. I afterwards laid before him such a statement of facts as induced him to move for those full and ample returns, respecting which addresses to His Majesty have since passed the House.

In several communications, personal and by letter, I continued to point out the defects of the post office system, but deferred more direct attempts at obtaining a change, until informed by the reply of Lord Aylmer to the House of Assembly of Lower Canada, that no answer had been received from England to the address of the House of the preceding session. Then on the 5th of March last, I addressed a note to Sir Francis Freeling, having previously obtained Mr. Viger's permission to make use of his name, requesting that an interview might be arranged to take place between him (Sir F.), Mr. Viger, and myself, with respect to the post communication, revenue, and management in the Canadas, and the complaints of the petitioners for a change for the better.

Sir Francis replied to my letter on the 9th of March, stating that the interview could take place, only through the permission of the Colonial Office.

On the 26th of March I enclosed Sir Francis's letter in another to Viscount Howick, and requested his lordship's permission that the interview might take place, Mr. Viger having previously approved of the request being made. . . .

On the 28th of the same month I addressed a letter to Viscount Howick on the state of the Post Office Department, and the complaints of the petitioners concerning its management; this was accompanied by a series of propositions for a general measure for its regulation. I took my letter to the Colonial office on the following day, having first added to it, for reference, the following documents, some of which I obtained from Mr. Viger:

1. Report of the Select Committee of the House of Assembly of Lower Canada, on the Post-Office, for 1831.

2. Ditto. do., September, 1832.

3. Ditto. do., House of Assembly of Upper Canada, 1825.

4. Ditto. do., do., 1829.

5. Ditto. do., do., 1831-2.

6. Copy of the discussion in Upper Canada legislature, session 1831-2, on the post office question.

7. Extracts from many newspapers in the Colonies exhibiting and complaining of the abuses of the Department.

8. Sir F. Freeling's letter to Mr. Armour of Montreal.

9. A letter from Mr. Sutherland, late deputy Postmaster-General, addressed to myself, concerning the defective state of his instructions from England.

10. Miscellaneous papers referred to in my letter to Viscount Howick.

I begged of Mr. Viger the favour of his opinion upon the various propositions contained in my statement, which had reference to the postage of letters, newspapers, magazines, and pamphlets, inland, to and from Europe, and to and from the United States; the responsibilities of the post office department; means of enforcing strict accountability; the appropriation of surplus revenue, if any, to grant new facilities in the conveyance of the mails; an improved and more frequent communication with England, and the means of bringing it about; franking powers; &c, &c. But that gentleman, after reading the papers, thought it best to defer any observations on their contents, because the House of Assembly, of which he is representative, had (in the annexed reports) expressed its sentiments in its then two preceding sessions, and had also at that time placed the subject under the consideration of a select committee which has since reported at great length. The request for a conference, was however, reiterated, and on the 2nd of April I ascertained that the whole matter had been left over for Mr. Stanley's decision, by the special direction of Viscount Goderich.

About this time I left London for Scotland, but took the precaution to write the Vice President of the Board of Trade from Manchester urging a speedy attention to the question of the Post Office, which I will do Mr. Stanley the justice to acknowledge that he did not for a moment neglect. On considering my statement, and still more especially the official colonial documents by which it was accompanied, His Majesty's Government decided, that previous to any conference taking place or the adoption of any new measures, Mr. Stayner the deputy postmaster-general should be requested to proceed to London to give the government the benefit of his experience. His Grace the Duke of Richmond accordingly requested Mr. Stayner to come to London, in which he arrived the day before I sailed for Quebec.

While with Mr. Stanley, at the Colonial Office, I placed in his hands copies of the address of the House of Assembly of Upper Canada of this year, and also the Lower Canada report and address of the 18th March last. He then told me that they expected Mr. Stayner daily, and was willing that the interview that had been requested as above should take place, and that additional suggestions might be made; but I found it impossible to attend to any engagements of that nature at so late a period, and besides, I had embodied my own views and wishes in the report of the 28th of March. What the improvements are that are likely to be made, and how far Mr. Stayner's journey and the remonstrances of the people may be of service to the country, a little time will probably show. That the department is not now on a footing suited to the wants of the provinces, all parties, *even Mr. Stayner himself*, will readily admit. Beyond the steps already mentioned, I could think of none, except that of directing public attention to the abuses that exist, through the pages of my book. [*Sketches of Canada and the United States.*] COLONIAL ADVOCATE, 29 August 1833.

CANADIAN EDITION OF THE SCRIPTURES

AN ADVERTISEMENT

W. L. Mackenzie has imported from New York a copy of the *Old and New Testaments* on stereotype metal plates, in beautiful order, warranted under the hand of the agents of the Protestant Episcopal Church in New York, to be perfectly correct and of the approved version in use in the Protestant churches, and as printed in Scotland and England under royal authority. This Bible consists of about 900 pages 12mo. (or small 8vo.) and will be found very suitable for schools or private families. The types are in excellent order, and will print off any number of copies, from one to one hundred thousand, either of the Bible and New Testament or of the New Testament by itself.

Mr. M. would agree with a binder or with any person having on hand a large quantity of paper of a suitable size, to print such a number of copies as might be agreed on, and he trusts that those associations and individuals who exert themselves in circulating bibles, will extend their patronage to the first edition, he believes, ever printed within Upper Canada. [*St. Matthew's Gospel was published in Chippeway at the* Colonial Advocate *office in* 1831; *the* New Testament *and* Apocrypha *was published by Mackenzie late in* 1837.] THE CONSTITUTION, 19 July 1836.

POLITICS OF SOME NEWSPAPERS

Novascotian, Quebec Gazette, Vindicator, Canadien, Minerve, Advocate, Reformer, Free Press, Recorder, Kingston Spectator, Grenville Gazette, Liberal, St. Francis Courier, Pictou Patriot, St. Catherines Argus, patriotic liberal journals.

Montreal Courant, Gazette, New Gazette and Herald, Quebec Mercury, York Courier and Patriot, Kingston Herald and Chronicle, Canadian Wesleyan, Antidote, Cobourg Star, Warder, Niagara Gleaner and Reporter, St. Thomas Journal, Canadian Emigrant, Cornwall Observer, and Gore Mercury, servile Tory papers.

Montreal Daily Advertiser, and York Correspondent, not decided yet. A NEW ALMANACK FOR THE CANADIAN TRUE BLUES, 1834, p. 10.

THE PARLIAMENTARY LIBRARY

Where are the thousand pounds worth of books for the purchase of which, for use and reference by the Legislature, there was a law passed last winter? No fear of J. B. Robinson, A. McLean, A. N. McNab and Sir F. Head being in a hurry to fulfil that enactment. Blind, dumb, and beetle deaf Assemblymen suit them best. THE CONSTITUTION, 26 July 1837.

NEWS AND READING-ROOMS

It is not perhaps generally known that there are two of these excellent Institutions open in the City, or they would be better supported than they are. At a very trifling expense, information from all parts of the world is within the reach of those entitled to admission, as well as the pleasure and amusement to be derived from reading the productions of many talented writers in every department of literature, which enrich and adorn the pages of the Periodicals of the day. On the tables of one are to be seen the London Constitutional, the Spectator, the Edinburgh Scotsman, and Dublin Register *liberal Newspaper*, also the London and Westminster, Edinburgh and Quarterly Reviews, the Metropolitan (edited by Capt. Marryatt) and Blackwood's Magazines, etc., etc. THE CONSTITUTION, 26 July 1837.

Chapter Four

THE SCENE ABROAD

EDITOR'S PREFACE 1. MACKENZIE'S TRAVELS ABROAD *By the time Mackenzie settled in York, Upper Canada, in December 1824, he had seen something of the world. From his home in Dundee he travelled, in 1818, to south-west England, and worked for a few months as clerk in the office of the Kennett and Avon Canal Company. In July of that year he was in Paris (Colonial Advocate, 18 April 1825), and between then and sailing for Canada in April 1820 he seems to have lived in London (Colonial Advocate, 5 January 1826). On his arrival in Canada, he worked first in the office of the Lachine Canal, then moved to Upper Canada. He joined partnership with John Lesslie, first in York, then in Dundas, selling books and drugs. In 1822 he moved to Queenston, where he opened a general store, became a school trustee with David Thorburn as colleague, and, in May 1824, started publication of the* Colonial Advocate. *It was to David Thorburn that he dedicated his* Catechism of Education *in 1830. In December 1824 he moved his press to York, which remained his home.*

From Dundas, Queenston, and York, his visits to the United States were frequent, and perhaps it was the easy travel to and fro between Queenston and New York State which quickened his political sense, and drew his attention to shortcomings in the government of Upper Canada. His objects in crossing the border were the purchase of type and paper, the study of institutions and systems of government, and the personal enjoyment of meeting interesting people, seeing the sights and talking with the inhabitants. His impressions, on the whole, seem to have confirmed both his Reform opinions and his loyalty to Britain. His general liking for the people must have encouraged Wixon, in Mackenzie's absence, to devote many small-type columns to the refutation of Mrs. Trollope's strictures in her book Domestic Manners of the Americans, *1822 (Colonial Advocate, May and June 1833).*

From June 1832 to June 1833 Mackenzie was in England, the bearer of the petition of the people of Upper Canada to the King and Parliament. It was a time of great poverty and of the terrible epidemic of cholera, and Mackenzie had no hesitation in advising any who could to emigrate (Colonial Advocate, *25 April 1833). A short visit to his native Dundee confirmed his conviction that Canada, with all its drawbacks, could offer hope to the wretched of Scotland, Ireland, and England.*

In London he enjoyed to the full every variety of sightseeing. He visited churches, museums, and galleries. He listened to debates in the House of Commons, and talked to members. But the greater part of his time was filled with trying to win the ear of the government on the grievances of the Upper Canadians, and with writing long letters home to York on his efforts.

During the four years after his return he does not refer often to visits to the United States, but we know that he was there in 1836, buying books for his store.

2. FOREIGN AFFAIRS   *There is little indication, in most of the accounts of Mackenzie available to students, of his broad interest in foreign affairs, nor of the pains he took to help his readers realize that their problems were not unique, but were shared in some form by the people of many countries. This interest is immediately apparent when the pages of the* Colonial Advocate *are turned over. News arriving by ship at Quebec or New York is obviously of very great importance to the editor. Upper Canada readers were able to get detailed accounts of what was actually happening, or rather what had happened five or six weeks earlier, in Paris or Warsaw, London or Dublin, Manchester or Dundee. From New York came news of slave risings in Jamaica and Virginia, accounts of the development of railways and manufactures, speeches of outgoing and incoming presidents.*

Because these news stories were usually printed without comment, the passages which follow give only a very incomplete indication of the scope of the paper. Mackenzie relied on the news itself having its impact on his readers, and, if he commented at all, often contented himself with a single sentence about "the heroic Poles" or "great news from France".

MODERN GREECE

It gives us great concern to observe the apathy manifested in these colonies towards the cause of the unfortunate Grecians. While England with her wonted liberality is raising money, arms and *men* to aid the Greeks—while even the most remote wildernesses of the United States are contributing their free gifts and donations towards

the attainment of Athenian freedom, and Lacedemonian liberty—
nay, while the New-York hatters are vending, and the people of that
good city wearing, *Hats, the profits of which has gone to Greece,* the
British North American colonies are looking on with the utmost
unconcern. . . .

When a boy at school, in our thirteenth year, we read Ray's
Dundee edition of Rollin's ancient history, and between that age and
sixteen, Pope's Homer, Barthelmy's Anacharsis, and Plutarch's
lives. From the many bright examples of patriotism, self-denial,
and heroic courage, which we found there recorded, we at that early
period learnt to revere the sacred name of freedom.

These volumes, combined with a knowledge of what our British
ancestors suffered from the bigotry and persecuting spirit of the
age in which they lived, implanted and nourished in our minds a
love of civil and religious liberty, and a correspondent hatred to all
tyranny and absolute power in church and state, (whether exercised
by one tyrant over a people, *or by many*) which principle we will
cherish to the latest moment of our existence; and as the cause of
Greece is that of suffering humanity we will exert our humble
powers to advocate that cause. COLONIAL ADVOCATE, 27 May 1824.

LAFAYETTE ON THE NIAGARA FRONTIER

The history of General Lafayette's visit to the United States in 1824
is before the public; but the enthusiasm with which that illustrious
friend of America and survivor of her Washington was received by
all classes must have been seen in order to be fully comprehended
by strangers. I was invited to come over to Lewiston by Colonel
King, Mr. Cook, and other gentlemen resident on the opposite
frontier, on the day in which the General was to make his entry
from the Falls into that town, and I gladly accepted the invitation.
The whole country, for many miles round, had assembled to welcome
the chivalrous hero who had left the voluptuous court of France,
and the wealth and titular splendour of his native land and ancient
lineage, to draw the sword of freedom on behalf of foreigners in a
foreign clime, struggling against the despotism exercised by those
of his own order, in the name of Englishmen, but without their
consent. In the hey-day of youth, in the glow of boyhood, at the
period of life when the sons of noble families are too often taken up

with frivolous and idle pleasures, did the good Lafayette devote his life, his fortune, and his utmost energies to rescue Englishmen and the descendants of Englishmen from that "gilded slavery", as Lord Chatham called it, with which a proud and selfish race then governing in England in the name of the nation, would have enchained the youthful Hercules of America. Lafayette gloried in the prospect before him, of extending happiness to the hut of the poorest settler; with him "virtue was its own reward;" he cheerfully entered a service where there was great danger to be encountered, no pay, considerable pecuniary loss, and a doubtful cause to be contended for.

But to return to the scene at Lewiston. The proudest of monarchs might have envied the homage that day paid to General Lafayette, by a people who felt themselves in the presence of one of their first, greatest, and most disinterested benefactors; it was indeed the homage of the heart. Half a century had elapsed since their aged visitor had combated in their defence, by the side of the fathers of their race; and I saw grey-headed men, surrounded by several generations of their offspring, shed tears of joy when the General reminded them of the deeds of other years, when the western world was struggling with the Butes, and Norths, and Burgoynes, and Sackvilles; the monopolists, directors, contractors, state priests, fools, and tyrants of a former age, for a name among the nations of the earth.

I was introduced by Colonel King; and as I had addressed a pamphlet to the General some months before he left France, he immediately recollected me, spoke with the utmost kindness, and earnestly urged me to prove myself the disinterested friend and advocate of liberty on the other (Canada) shores. He inquired as to the progress of liberal principles in the Canadas, and I assured him that the feeling of the people was strong and nearly universal in support of free institutions; and that whatever course the government might pursue, Canada would not be awed into slavery.

Although I consider this interview with the most persevering and consistent friend of freedom now alive, one of the most fortunate events of my life, it has since brought upon me many injurious imputations. A placeman in the provincial assembly quoted it as a proof that I was a rebel; and to this day the official presses in British America cast it in my teeth as a crime of no mean magnitude. Yet have the Lord Advocate of Scotland and other members of this government, as well as the presses which support them, given very strong proofs of the esteem and approbation with which they look upon Lafayette, "the hero of two revolutions" in France and one in America; and when at Paris, during the short peace of Amiens, the champion of the Whigs, Charles James Fox, visited him in terms of personal as well as political friendship. SKETCHES, p. 66.

FRIENDS OF FREEDOM IN NEW YORK

Under the head *United States* our readers will find recorded, from the New York *Truth Teller*, an interesting account of a public dinner given by the friends of *civil and religious liberty* on this side the Atlantic, on the last anniversary of *St. Patrick*. The proceedings of this assemblage of eminent men of "every country and every creed," are well worthy of an attentive perusal. The reflecting christian will here perceive that an all wise providence is bringing great *good out of evil* even in unhappy Ireland, and that one excellent effect of prelatic intolerance and tory rapacity exercised in and towards that much oppressed nation, is, that thereby the glowing embers of a pure and holy flame are fanned and made to burn yet brighter and brighter on *Freedom's* Altar in North America.

Loyal and staunch adherents, as ourselves and the far greater part of our readers are well known to be, in the cause of constitutional monarchy, due allowance must be nevertheless made for the republican prejudices of others in perusing the history of the St. Patrick's dinner. The Americans have national whims, but they are a grateful and kindly people; and truly they have a great deal to be thankful for. Speaking the English language, nursed and nurtured in English modes and customs, basing their political fabric on national intelligence and the inherent rights of the human race, and being guided by enlightened legislators and under the administration of equal laws; judged by judges of their choice, governed by rulers who study their will, taxed but by their own consent and their revenues frugally applied to the best of purposes, under their own direction; freed from the curse of an established priesthood, and absolved from the yoke of clerical patronage, our neighbours beyond the Niagara river only require the presence of a *Strachan*, a *Maitland*, a *Colborne* and a *Sherwood*, together with the other great and *exclusive* blessings we enjoy in Upper Canada, to become as wise, as happy, and as contented, as the dutiful and loyal subjects of March and Durham appear to be. It is alleged too that the republicans are troubled with frequent elections, while it would seem as if our paternal government were about to save us the necessity of any further legislative labour, by itself assuming and exercising without *control* all the powers of the constitution, with (as some think) a few extra powers to boot. No doubt this *restrictive system* will be productive of the best possible consequences, and probably the good natured democrats across the lines, struck by its beauty, and enamoured with its simplicity, may in the end adopt it also. COLONIAL ADVOCATE, 16 April 1829.

REVOLUTION IN FRANCE

"Another agony has begun. The streets of the French capital have again been deluged with blood. Charles X. has ceased to reign. The haughty Bourbons are again fugitives. La Fayette—almost *our own* La Fayette—is again at the head of the National Army. And France reposes once more in the arms of her legitimate sovereigns—*the People*." *N.Y. Paper.*

. . .

It appears that the people of Paris, were immediately seconded in their measures, in every section of France yet heard from. The moderation of the new Government is not less praiseworthy, than the glorious act by which they have preserved the liberty of the people.

The London papers state that the British Cabinet, on hearing of the measures resorted to by the people of France, immediately assured the French Government that they should in no way interfere in behalf of either party. COLONIAL ADVOCATE, 9 September 1830.

FRANCE AND FREEDOM

Altho' I dislike war and bloodshed, I must own that the late intelligence from Europe does not all displease me.—General LaFayette (like Samson with the Philistines of old) seems determined to make one other effort to crush the Hydra heads of arbitrary power in Europe before he dies; and the hearts and hands of his gallant countrymen are with him. Louis's ministry would rather wait patiently until the tyrant of the north had subdued the brave Poles, and Austria crushed in the dust the friends of freedom in the land of Cicero and Cincinnatus; they would then expect the aid of the allied despots to prevent the French from consummating their revolution and reuniting with Belgium; and would invite to their aid a prostituted priesthood, who like ours would, as heretofore, answer for spies and informers to the mock liberal government, and under the hypocritical mask of christian forbearance and pious submission, teach their flocks the exploded creeds by which European tyrants long have thriven. But it will not do. France is arming. Already she can count 500,000 well disciplined troops, ably officered, and united as one man in the cause of freedom. Italy is with her. The oppressed Poles look upon her as on the morning star of their coming day. The brave and generous Belgians are eager to fight their old oppressors under her banners. Ireland, whose ill-treated millions have for ages sighed in vain for civil and religious equality, will rejoice in every victory obtained by the genius of France; and Scotland my native land whose choicest patriots and truest friends were murdered and banished and fined and imprisoned and tortured by the tyrants and bloodhounds of 179-, in solemn mockery of the first principles of eternal justice, will offer up before the throne of the omnipotent, the daily prayers of her pious and long suffering children for success to "the cause of truth upon the earth." England, whose glorious and oft repeated efforts in favour of rational freedom, first illumined the benighted soil of France; England, the free spirit of whose institutions (tho' now perverted by the few) first taught America to rejoice in the enjoyment of self-government; England, once happy and prosperous, but now depressed by the efforts of a despicable aristocracy of wealth without merit, a faction hostile to every principle of virtue, justice and christianity; England too will be with France, and the Birmingham artist while he fashions the weapon of war with which the fortress of continental darkness is destined to be attacked, and, we would fain hope, for ever overthrown, will rejoice that he too had been made instrumental in bringing the glorious cause of human right to a happy consummation. Of the warm and generous feelings of the Canadians I surely need not speak; and the United States have testified their gladness at the progress already made in the good work of regeneration. It is honourable to our nation that we have now a ministry at the helm who sympathize with Frenchmen in this their day of renovation; and I trust that the machinations of the titled traducer of the gallant Moore, and the depraved and dissolute oligarchy by whom he is surrounded, will in vain seek their downfall. I have ever had the fullest confidence in the truly noble ministry now guiding the reins of state in Great Britain.

But who are they who will dare to oppose the progress of freedom in France? Who are they who would seek to crush her gallant sons while fighting on the plains of Europe the battles of the human race? —I can tell, for I have marked them well. They are they who seek to hold power solely for their own aggrandizement; that few who long have triumphed in the misery of, and trampled to the dust, the millions; that few who have in all ages striven to keep mankind ignorant, divided and debased.

Established priesthoods; titled misers and titled spendthrifts and debauchees; arbitrary monarchs, and the venal throng who bask in the guilty sunshine of their power; government brokers, bankers and state creditors; ambitious and unprincipled politicians; the proud, the haughty and the overbearing of all countries—these, with few exceptions, will make common cause against the people, and in secret conclave enter into an unholy alliance to perpetuate European bondage. Grave senators and princes, titled priests and hireling legislators, from Charles and his Cardinal in Holyrood, from Arthur Wellesley and his partizans at Strathfield, say down even as low as Father Strachan at York and his hopeful pupil John Robinson in the palace of *justice*, (with the very meanest of their tribe of provincial sycophants,) will view with horror and dismay the glorious attempts that are now making and about to be made in Europe to establish on a broad foundation the rights of man to equal laws; and all their emissaries will be at work under ground, in the dark and midnight hour sowing discord in the people's camp.

But I had forgotten to enumerate in the glorious host of Freedom's sons, the prostrate victims of a guilty a bankrupt unholy alliance. Will the camps of the confederate kings and emperors present the same unity of purpose as now directs the armies about to be arrayed under the soul inspiring banners of the genius of France? Will the degraded peasantry of Germany, Prussia and Russia, feel hearty in the cause of their haughty masters? We doubt it much. Has Poland cried aloud for freedom, only that the iron yoke might bind her gallant sons faster to the car of her despoilers? Is the remorseless lust of dominion by Russia destined only to be appeased by the life's blood of the unyielding and indignant Poles? Will it be said that the brave Kosciusko lived and died in vain, a banished hero? Forbid it Heaven! In the inspired language of one of freedom's bravest friends, I would say for Poland that its rising is not that of a people against their monarch "but of the oppressed against the oppressor, of the native against the stranger, of the betrayed against the betrayer, of the slave against the tyrant; of a nation, the victim of the basest treachery in the annals of mankind, against the traitor, the spoiler, the remorseless author of their suffering. Their cause is a triumph in itself; and may the great Being who 'hateth iniquity, and terribly judgeth the oppressor,' shield them in the day of struggle, and give a new hope to mankind by the new victory of their freedom!"

Let the readers of the Colonial Advocate keep a watchful eye upon the march of events in Europe; *the tide rises*. COLONIAL ADVOCATE, 28 April 1831.

REFORM REJECTED

We are anxious to ascertain the results of the rejection of reform, and most sincerely hope that that measure will yet be speedily effected without bloodshed. Corruption has assuredly taken deep root in England, and many powerful attempts have been vainly made to banish the very semblance of freedom from the soil, but they will not succeed. The Morning Chronicle of the 8th. October was in full mourning; the bells of the city of London were muffled, and tolled as if on the eve of some great national calamity; the shops all over London were closed and business abandoned.

. . .

That two hundred peers should attempt to stand in opposition to King, Government and People, and opposed to a hundred and fifty of their own order besides, even for one hour, and in a bad cause too, is indeed an exceedingly marvellous circumstance in British history! Surely corruption has indeed struck a deep root. COLONIAL ADVOCATE, 8 December 1831.

A LETTER FROM NEW YORK

310 GRENVILLE STREET
NEW YORK, APRIL 25, 1832

TO MR. WIXSON

DEAR SIR—We sail for London next Tuesday morning in the Packet Ship Ontario, Capt. Saber, expecting a voyage of about a month, as the winds are light at this season and often easterly. I have this day very good news for the friends of cheap popular free government in Upper Canada—there is little reason now to doubt the passage of the English Reform Bill, in an efficient and unmutilated state, thro' the House of Peers. I have my information, not alone from what you see in the public prints, but also by private letters from a person in high standing in England addressed to his friend here, on which I place much dependance. The Reform Bills for Ireland and Scotland will follow suit, and we shall see once free and happy England, again return to the old fashioned prudent and economical system of a former age, during the best days of her constitution. I perceive that imprisonment for debt, that cruel and barbarous law, is about to be abolished in Britain. The law commissioners have reported in favour of its abolition both on mesne process and executions; and parliament will pass an efficient statute which, without impairing public credit, will strip honest poverty of part of its terrors, and diminish 30 per cent the least desirable part of the business and gains of the lawyers. Doubtless this news will be gratifying to Messrs. Rolph and Bidwell who fruitlessly combined their useful talents in the legislature in opposition to Mr. J. B. Robinson and the colonial tories in endeavouring to take the poor debtor from the dungeon's cell and place him beside his weeping wife and helpless children.

I met in the streets of New York a procession entirely composed of coloured people, with drums, trumpets and a band of music;— there were hundreds of them—some bearing banners, others flags, and all decorated with badges, sashes, ribbons, etc. I felt pleased and gratified at their contented, joyous bearing, and hope that the day may soon come, in which the task-master shall no more dare to lift his whip to the unhappy African; and in which man shall cease to possess the power to buy, and sell, and torture his fellow-man. The philanthropic Clarkson's worthy name was inscribed on the insignia of one of the societies composing the procession. Were I a person of colour, and felt as I now feel, I would never rest nor cease my efforts until the last badge of degradation and inequality had been taken from the necks of my countrymen.

The quakers of England deserve to be honoured and admired for their anxious and unceasing efforts to remove the chain from the neck of the slave—I trust that Henry Brougham will never forget the pledge he gave to the free and truly English Electors of Yorkshire at the last general election. COLONIAL ADVOCATE, 10 May 1832; SKETCHES, p. 273.

O'CONNELL

I have heard Mr. O'Connell, the great Irish agitator and champion
of emancipation address a meeting of one of these [*Trades' Political*]
Unions, not less than eight hundred or one thousand members being
present. He has the most perfect self-command, and an inexhaust-
ible fund of genuine wit and broad humour; is one of those speakers
you can listen to for hours, and yet regret when you cease to hear
the sound of his voice. There is a quaintness in his manner of
expression which gives double effect to his jokes and witticisms.
Yet he can be lofty and majestic when he pleases; and I rejoiced
to perceive that his original and flowing eloquence, as he told in
strong and emphatic language of the wrongs of Ireland, drew from
an English audience the most enthusiastic sympathetic cheers. I
rarely ever witnessed a more successful speaker, in his popular
character of an agitator, than Mr. O'Connell. No wonder it is that
he roused Ireland to a sense of her wrongs. It is fortunate for
Ireland that the Duke of Wellington did not succeed in making the
catholic clergy pensioners to the state—and it is fortunate for the
three kingdoms that 68 of the Irish members, with Mr. O'Connell
in their front, were found among the original uncompromising friends
of reform when a majority of the Scotch and English opposed it.

In the House of Commons Mr. O'Connell divests himself of his
popular character, and as a legislator argues and reasons profoundly
and logically, and votes honestly. His eloquence in St. Stephen's
chapel at twelve o'clock at night is quite of a different kind from
his eloquence in Saville house at twelve o'clock noon. . . . I have
heard Mr. O'Connell blamed for using coarse metaphors or figures,
but it was by his enemies—no man could have been more circum-
spect in his choice of words than I found Mr. O'Connell on the
several occasions in which it was my good fortune to hear him
speak. The misconduct of the different Irish administrations has
added to his strength and power as a popular leader, and he *will*
succeed in his object of giving freedom and equality of rights to
his countrymen who almost idolize him, as well they may. I can
tell you that he is a firm friend to Upper Canada, as I shall have
reason to shew you by and bye.

.   .   .

Mr. O'Connell is a man of whom all Irishmen ought to be proud.
In their cause, in Ireland's cause, in the cause of civil and religious
freedom all over the globe, he is a powerful and consistent champion,

157

and likely to be a successful one. He has also manifested the warmest attachment to the Canadas; and the kind manner in which he spoke to me of our affairs, and the interest he manifested on our behalf, entitles him to my lasting gratitude. COLONIAL ADVOCATE, 16 August 1832; 13 September 1832; Lindsey's LIFE, 1862, vol. 1, p. 257.

LONDON STREET CRIERS

The cries of London are among its greatest curiosities, and are greatly increased in number since I was last here. Sometimes half a dozen of persons are found within a stone's throw of each other, males and females, tenor and treble and bass voices, each bawling at the top of his or her voice something to be sold. I would consider such proceedings a perfect nuisance, did I not remember that in this day of misery and poverty, and hunger and disease and crime, many are driven to this means of earning an honest livelihood, for their aged parents, for their fatherless or motherless babes, for a sick wife, or a husband in prison or in difficulty. One of the cries is by a boy who comes along the street every day, once or twice, with a fine large milch cow, and milking pail and measure, bawling in a peculiar dialect "Milk! Milk from the Ka-u." To prevent suspicion of adulteration the process of milking is [per]formed in the middle of the street, in view of the customer. An Irishwoman, neatly dressed, passes daily, calling out in a fine musical strain, "Buy my water cresses;" and an active little dame often crosses her path, crying "any brooms wanted today, ma'am," in a tone between laughing and weeping. She addresses no one in particular; knocks at no door, but passes quickly along under her burthen.

Salmon, cucumbers, baskets, shoes, cherries, gooseberries, strawberries, band-boxes, candlesticks, tongs, pokers, cheap-tracts, songs, sermons, flowers, pictures, and a hundred other sorts of ware are hawked about in this way—often much to my annoyance, although I feel that it would be cruel to stop the criers. COLONIAL ADVOCATE, 13 September 1832.

CHOLERA IN LONDON

The cholera morbus still rages here, and its victims are not few; dreadful, however, as are its ravages, I like it far better than I would have done civil war. The reform bills have averted the latter calamity, so that the hand of one brother is not lifted up against another, in deadly strife, nor likely soon to be; and as for the pestilence, the cholera, this new disorder so deadly in its nature, it is the hand of God, and in his own good time he will lift it off, when the purposes for which it has been sent are accomplished. The Cholera is a truly awful complaint; it is a perfect picture of hell. Dives is described in the new testament as having had full possession of his senses in the place of torment; and of being fully alive to his intense misery. In like manner, the sufferer under the pestilence, the cholera, retains the full and entire possession of his senses, while undergoing the most dreadful agonies which it is possible for the imagination to conceive.

I removed with my wife and servant from Westminster, near the public offices, in order to enjoy the benefit of a more healthy and elevated and agreeable part of the metropolis where no cases of cholera had been known. Yesterday the servant took ill, was in dreadful agony. We sent for a physician of eminence (Dr. Brydone) who at once saw that it was the blue cholera of India, and applied remedies under which the patient is getting better. Some say it is both contagious and epidemic, and that persons whose bodies are predisposed to disease will catch the infection—of which comparatively few recover. Be this as it may, I have no intention of again changing my lodgings. I am here on what I believe to be a good, honourable, and proper errand; and if it pleases the Creator to cut me or mine off, while in what we consider the way of duty, we can bear in mind that he is able to raise up other fit and proper persons to fulfil his wise purposes. Here then we are, *in the House with the Cholera*, and not dismayed.

.   .   .

I have most commonly attended the ministry of the celebrated Edward Irving; and although I do not like the interruption from persons speaking, as if inspired, in an unknown tongue, yet there is something so noble, so honest, so captivating about this eloquent divine that I always leave the church more firmly determined to go back next Sunday, and always do so. There is such a power and energy in his discourses, such a simplicity in his manner, such convincing proofs of great judgment and sincere good-will towards men in his language and actions that I cannot but feel the greatest regard for him as a minister.

He preaches 17 times a week, in doors and out, and his audiences frequently include the first families in the land.

He hesitates not to go where the cholera rages most; in the midst of infection, pain, poverty and misery, he may be seen administering the consolations of that holy religion, the power of which he feels, to the dying and the agonized, and strengthening the hopes of those whose hope in this world is gone, by an assurance of eternal happiness, life forevermore, in mansions of bliss beyond the grave. Mr. [*George*] Ryerson pursues the same course; heedless of risque, he spends most of his time in visiting and comforting those whom the pestilence has laid low. COLONIAL ADVOCATE, 13 September 1832.

COBBETT

I am not sure that I mentioned to you that I dined one Sunday last July with the celebrated Mr. Cobbett at his country seat, Kensington. I was glad to accept an invitation which enabled me to see a man who has filled a large space in the public annals of Britain for the last forty years, at home. Mr. Cobbett is the centre of a party, formidable in numbers and not deficient in talent. He is a keen and unsparing critic; reviewing and animadverting upon the plans of other men with great severity and unquestioned skill. He is likely to succeed in being returned for the two hundred thousand inhabitants of Manchester to the new parliament, which will give him great weight. *His plans* then will be exposed to the test of Legislative investigation, and we shall see how far he will be able to carry into practice his theory of an equitable adjustment of the national grievances, debts, bonds, and obligations.—Mr. Cobbett I consider a happy man. With the experience of three-score he possesses the vivacity of eighteen. He is pleased with himself, with his plans, and his prospects. Has a fine family, a comfortable fireside, and enjoys excellent health. He talks as much of trees, and flowers, and gardening and agriculture, as of matters of government—and has evidently made farming his study to a great extent. I should not be at all surprised if we find him not so great a democrat in the House of Commons as he is in the Weekly Register. Mr. Cobbett is tall and well made, ruddy complexion and good looking; his hair is as white as snow, and no sign of baldness. He is evidently a man of an ardent temperament, of strong and powerful passions—and I believe his object is to increase the comforts and lessen the misery of the great body of the people, but it is evident he is not very scrupulous as to the means of bringing about this great good. Mr. Noah of New

York, in his Advocate, and more recently in his Enquirer, and Mr.
Cobbett, of Bolt Court, in his Register, appear to me to have adopted
the maxim of "all's fair in politics"—they both put forth, in a
powerful strain of sarcasm or invective against political opponents,
statements not always so correct as they might be. Indeed Mr.
Cobbett has evidently acted towards both whigs and tories for many
years as though he considered them an organized band of public
plunderers, legalized by unjust statutes to oppress mankind, and of
whom nothing could be said that would be "too bad." Mr. Cobbett's
manner is kind and prepossessing, but I think he does not bear
contradiction so well as some men of less genius and power of mind.
COLONIAL ADVOCATE, 15 November 1832; Lindsey, vol. 1, p. 250.

PUBLIC AFFAIRS

19 WAKEFIELD STREET, BRUNSWICK SQUARE.
LONDON, SATURDAY, OCT, 20TH, 1832.

To MR. RANDAL WIXSON.

Dear Sir:—I wish you to publish from the *Morning Chronicle* of this
day, Cobbett's account of what he saw in Scotland—Western's
declaration of the views of government with regard to the Corn
Laws—and one or two extracts from Brougham's former speeches.
Also, take from the Chronicles of the 19th and 20th, a part of the
remarks about the Earl of Eldon and his intended victim, Thomas
Hardy, whose funeral was attended by 40,000 persons. The feeling
of pride and contempt towards common people shewn here by the
aristocracy is well delineated by the Editor. There is an article from
the Essex Independent in the number of today which would indicate
that the *Doctrinaires* of France and the Whigs of England are the
same species; give it a place in the Advocate; also another article
from the *True Sun* of the 8th instant, concerning Lord Brougham,
the leader of the Whigs. I remember that Mr. Henry Boulton, the
Attorney General, in reply to some remarks by myself or some one
else in the Assembly, stood up and prophecied that the Whigs when
in power would be Tories as far as they could, or words to that
effect. Mr. Boulton will peruse such proofs of his wisdom as I now
give, with pleasure. In the Chronicle of the 17th there is a good
article upon excessive taxation. The latter part of Colonel Stanhope's
Speech at the Tower Hamlets dinner is also very well worth perusal.
    It is as difficult for public writers to write for forty years upon

public men and public events and be consistent in all they say, as it is for a man to keep his temper and thoughts in one even unvarying tenure—of that Mr. Cobbett's sayings, which I sent you last packet are a proof. What I feel most is his remarks upon Muir the Scottish patriot. They were surely uncalled for from Mr. Cobbett. His reception in Edinburgh, however, is creditable to the metropolis of Scotland. The people, as is well said by the Editor of the Scotsman, regard him "as a man who has been a thorn in the side of corruption for a quarter of a century." Publish a part of the account given of him in the Scotsman.

I was not aware until lately that Quakers could sit in parliament, but it appears they can—and I beg the very particular attention of the Canadian public to the excellent speech of Mr. Pease the Quaker candidate for the County of Durham—*I am told he will be successful*. Read that speech ye Quakers of the County of York, those of you especially who have shewn no sympathy with your countrymen in their difficulties—contenting yourselves if your own personal interests flourished—beginning your charity at home and ending where ye began. Read and ponder well upon the manly good sense of one of your own sect, in the country of your ancestors. You have many amiable good qualities—I mean those household virtues which others sometimes lack—read the lecture of Quaker Pease, and resolve henceforth to add to your catalogue active benevolence as members of a respectable and respected political community. They who desire to share as much as they can of the benefits of a government, and to perform as few as possible of its more important duties, incur a debt to their fellow men. Quaker Pease seems to be well aware of this—like Penn of Pennsylvania, he is a rational, liberal man, of sound practical judgment, very benevolent—anxious, not that Quakers only should aid each other, but that such should henceforth be the rule of the whole human family. I speak to those Quakers only who have never attended an election, never signed a petition, never attended a public meeting—but lived that life which the petty tyrants of Canada wish every one to live, a life of selfish ease. They may say "we cannot sit in the Assembly." True, but you can vote. "We are enemies of war." Very well—come to the hustings and support that candidate whose private character you esteem, and who will pledge himself to be an enemy to war also. War is a rare game for governments—but the people are its dupes—they rejoice in victories that bring them no benefit, and toil and sweat for the honour of maintaining in affluence those who have deceived them and abused their confidence—this is a great evil.

Church and State here seem to be disposed to separate, and I am glad of it, for by all I can see and hear, the devil himself is not a worse enemy to true religion—the religion of the New Testament—than a richly beneficed clergyman or bishop. You will see by the True Sun of the 8th, that in Birmingham where half a century ago the enlightened Priestley was almost crucified for being a dissenter, the tables are turned upon his persecutors. Perhaps it will be so with us in Canada before long. The people knew when they elected *Shade* and *Chisholm* and *McMartin* and *Jarvis* and *Crooks* and *Burwell* and *Fraser* and *Ingersol* and *John Willson* and *Allan McNab* and *Hagerman* and *Boulton* and *Brown*, and their friends, that they were electing men who did not care a farthing for them and their rights—yet they elected them with their eyes open and better candidates before them for selection. I regret this—it has grieved me often, and even in this country I have had it cast in my teeth that it was of no use to reform the state of the representation for that the great counties did not in many places vote one whit more independent than the small places. But *I hope*—I hope when I see the change of feeling shewn in Grenville—I hope when I call to mind that the noble electors who have four times sent me into the legislature are the same persons who not long since sent such men as Colonel Thompson, Peter Robinson, Sir David William Smith, and Thomas Ridout. The progress of reason in politics is slow, but its triumphs are sure. York County will surely not again fall back into forgetfulness, profiting nothing by the experience of ages.

I have sent a copy of my report upon the War Losses to the Editor of the Hamilton Free Press, omitting some parts because of its great length; to that paper I would refer interested parties.

In the Morning Chronicle of October the 15th, you will find an article under the Editorial head upon the subject of Church Reform and the Abolition of Slavery—give it a place. Mr. Pelham is good authority as to the intentions of ministers. They deceived every body by the liberality of their parliamentary reform bill, and perhaps they may agreeably disappoint the enemies of free institutions on the subject of the church. All, all, however depends on the people—if they send good members to parliament and shew a firm determination to back their efforts, reform will be thorough. But if not, it will be as with us in Upper Canada—we sow the wind and reap the whirlwind.

I am told that the Duke of Wellington would certainly have taken office—dissolved the parliament and prevented all reform, but for two things, the organized combinations of the people, and the determination of the great monied reformers to draw every dollar of specie out of the bank of England and oblige it to pay in paper. It is understood that the Governor of the Bank waited upon His Grace, and told him that this would be one consequence of his return to power.

I can perceive from the tone of the Chronicle, that its intelligent and patriotic editor does not expect the ministers to do much for the northern colonies—he argues that they have the remedy of all their grievances in their own hands—and that if they are too slavish and pusillanimous to make use of it, they deserve the kicks that are so liberally dealt out to them from all quarters. I told a member of parliament the other day in conversation the history of the meeting at York on the 23rd of March last, and how the farmers acted— bearing with patience & resignation every species of contumely and insult. When I came to tell him how they were called "the Swine of Yonge Street", &c. &c. he interrupted me with—"can they stand all this with patience ?"—I said they wished to shew an example of order and obedience to the laws, *and hoped for relief from England.*— I was going to tell you his concluding remarks, but am afraid it would wound the feeling of many persons whom I highly respect, and therefore forbear. Speaking of ministers, Mr. Black remarks that sufficient allowance is not made for their difficulties, and that there prevails rather too great a disposition, in spite of their honesty of intention as proved by the reform bill, to lower them to the level of those who, if they had had their will, would have deluged the country with blood rather than have a reform.

I rather think there will be hot work in Holland. The Dutch have 150,000 well disciplined and well officered troops ready to resist France and England, and it is now generally understood that active operations will soon commence on the continent both by Land and by Sea.

It seems Ferdinand of Spain is not dead although his death was announced in the official journal of the French government.—Mr. Carey, when I announced Judge Boulton's death on a former occasion, said he supposed I had done so in order to have an opportunity of contradicting the report the week following. My notice in a former letter of Ferdinand subjects me to the same charge now.

By the way, the ejection of the Dutch from the Citadel of Antwerp has a good deal to do with a question on our side the Atlantic. Britain wishes the river Scheldt kept open, because she can by this means introduce her manufactures into Germany, &c. The Dutch say no—that as the Scheldt passes last through their territories they have a right to the sole navigation of it. This is the St. Lawrence navigation question over again, only that in this case Britain is retained as counsel on the opposite side, with a fleet and store of "leaden persuaders."

Publish Mr. O'Connell's third letter about the Wallstown murder, from the *True Sun* of the 16th of October. Give it a preference to other matter in the newspaper, for it is a remarkable document. Mr. O'Connell is taking the true way to free Ireland from her oppressors—he is representing crime in its *clear distinct* light—and the people are taking the hint—they are making the country too hot to hold the spies and pimps and informers and bloodsuckers, who would drench Ireland with the blood of the last Irishman rather than miss having the church revenues to support the young profligates of the English Aristocracy under the garb of holy men of God, ministers of the everlasting gospel, &c. There is too little principle in the governments of Europe—*the people have to do all.*

Ireland has been a colony for six centuries, and she is still used like a colony—Viceroys, Governors, Attornies General, Lords, Bishops, Turncoats, Vagabonds, Colonels, Generals, Strachans—all the scum and offscourings of these three kingdoms are sent to quarter at free cost upon her fertile soil. Wily priests are hired to set the people against each other—to say to the catholic farmer— "See how anxious these protestants are to destroy you!" And to the protestant tiller of the soil—"up and exterminate these blood thirsty papists!" Thus it is that the scene of Cain and Abel is daily renewed among the most noble free-hearted generous people in the world. There is an end to everything, however, and at length the Irish have resolved to kick in right earnest. Although their country is lashed alongside the most powerful nation of ancient or modern times, I learn, both from the conversation of private circles and the language of the press and the government, that Stanley considers himself defeated in Ireland, and I'm glad of it. Cowards and mean men are fit for slavery, God and nature intended them for nothing else, but that a whole hearted noble people like the Irish should truckle to foreign bondage forever was not to be looked for. Any people may enjoy freedom who will it, and are brave and united— it is the part of the hereditary bondsman to pray for the liberty to enjoy God's blessings from the favour of "his lordly fellow worm." Seldom did the children of Israel take the field in a good cause but they succeeded. When Switzerland determined to be independent she became free. When Holland felt degraded at being a miserable contemptible appurtenance to Spain, she successfully opposed the powerful monarchy by which she was environed. In like manner, Ireland has a mind to make the country too hot for the leeches who suck her blood, and she will wear 'em out in this way—*it is the only way*. It is understood in Ireland that before certain Lords would agree to the reform bill there was a sort of understanding that the revenues of the Irish Church should not be interfered with. Mr. Stanley got the management of affairs for the aristocracy of which he is one of the ablest and proudest members—and he is tired of his office. I try to believe that the present government are honest and that their pledges of economy have a meaning. Yet, with the misery that stares them in the face in this great city, how they could agree to give £4,000 a year pension for life to the Speaker, £100,000 a year for life to the Queen, the bitter foe of reform, in case she survived her husband, and a retiring allowance of twenty-two thousand two hundred and twenty-two dollars, to Lord Brougham, one of themselves, to be paid him for life, yearly, whenever he quits office out of the taxes, how they could agree to all this I do not understand. When I speak to liberal clever men of the extravagance of salaries with us, they are incredulous when I name a sum. Lord Goderich told me that he thought Governor Colborne's income very moderate indeed, and it is not far under 18,000 dollars a year. The dissenters, however, have more moderate notions. They have educated 800,000 children, yearly, and they are to vote next December, and have a voice in these things.

I perceive that the Canadian Methodists have passed resolutions, under which they intend to send an agent here next spring to endeavour to effect a negociation by which they may have their superintendent or chief bishop selected for them in England, by a body, highly respectable I admit, but every way unfit to make such a selection for a people of whose local situation, manners and habits they have a most imperfect knowledge. Could they not choose their Bishops in Canada themselves? Has the abuse, the foolish idle twaddle of the government hacks and their presses wrought this miracle, or am I in a dream? The more I see of the management of affairs on this side the Atlantic the less I incline to advocate European interference with our affairs. The government here minds me much of a certain Upper Canada storekeeper who would be every thing, would grasp at all trades, extend his business in all directions, monopolize every bargain of land or anything else. By an ambition to do too much he did a great deal to a disadvantage, & finally went to nothing. I shall not mention a name *for I dislike personality*, but it is just so here—the government want to legislate and govern the whole nation, that too for selfish party purposes, and they do two-thirds of their legislation and governing at midnight and to a disadvantage. However, if the Canadian Methodists must have a Bishop from England, let 'em. I shall only add that the folks here pay for their folly dear enough—they have imported pageants from a thousand a year up to a million! Perhaps these remarks will give offence. If so I shall regret it. I wish the Methodists well, for they have been faithful to the country—but I dislike this new move.

I have read the new American Tariff Law with great attention. It is a boon conferred upon Canada and a valuable one. It will give us tea at the cheapest rate; drugs, dyestuffs and a thousand other things from the best markets, duty free; it will do more, it will force a free trade to India for the colonies, which I doubt much whether our petitions would have done without it. The cheaper the farmer buys, the cheaper he can afford to sell with a good profit. I like this Tariff Law. It may be said that no conscientious man will buy American tea which is prohibited. *Did Canada consent to that prohibition?* Was our advice asked when the ports were opened to American provisions? Would it be just to let the American farmers compete with us in our own markets while we were enriching a monopoly by paying 80 cents for a lb. of the tea he can have at half a dollar?

The old parliament, as I learn, meets no more. It is prorogued to the 11th and will, it is understood, be dissolved on the 3rd of December, when the elections will immediately take place.

In the *True Sun* of October 15th, there is copied from the Times of this day week, the account of a dreadful slaughter of the Irish at Carrigeen by the military who were sent to post tythe arrear notices for the support of "our holy religion." I dare not trust my feelings in commenting on this transaction. Unhappy Ireland.! It is a frank and gallant nation and dearly is it purchasing with blood, innocent blood, that liberty which God hath granted to his creatures in his earth. Surely it is a truth that the people on this side the Atlantic have enough to do with their own affairs without attempting to regulate ours. If but the Canadians had my spirit, and abandoning all selfish and party interests would manfully and unitedly insist upon managing the whole of their domestic affairs under a free, cheap and economical government, it would be well for the country. We could then do England twice as much good as we do now, by purchasing her manufactures without putting her to the cost of governing us in every trifling petty matter.

I have marked one or two of the police cases, the heart-rending accounts of which fill the English and Irish papers. Society here is certainly composed of precisely the two classes mentioned by Mirabeau—those who have more appetite than dinners, and those who have more dinners than appetite. You cannot travel in any quarter of this splendid city without meeting squalid poverty, the aged and infirm or the young and helpless, exposed and miserable. The keepers of the workhouses are often the most cruel of jailors. Canadians, I beseech you forget your differences and disputes, and unite to avert such additions to the catalogue of human misery. Be assured that the splendid carriages of your Judges and Pensioners and Governors and Gentry will be followed by pauperism, poverty, vice and crime. It adds to the pleasures (mean and grovelling as they are) of such a man as Doctor Strachan, to have a hundred poor miserable wretches humbly attending at his gate or in his "soup kitchen" begging for a morsel. Their poverty forms *an agreeable* and striking contrast with the coach, the palace, the liveried footman, &c &c. But I fear much it will not gild the horrors of a death bed. History is a cheat and experience a deceiver if such men as Lord Eldon can sleep sweet, and feel, in the dark and gloomy evening of life no compunction for their crimes. Would that our legislators would remember their duties and responsibilities! I sat in the Assembly with Brant—he is no more; and with Jessup—his sun is set; and with Fothergill—already has the worm said "thou art my brother." And we that remain will not lay these things to heart. Never in life did I enjoy more robust health—yet, *I may be next.*

I read, from the Reformer, which I think I saw at Mr. Hume's or the new England Coffee House, the account of Priest Bethune and the projected union of the Orangemen and Ribbonmen against the Methodists. I read it with surprise. Is it not enough for these people to inflict John Brown and George Boulton on the legislature, but they must also propose to make Canada another Ireland! Most truly does O'Connell say, that the government and the soldiers care no more for Irish blood than the street waterer does for the water with which he lays the summer's dust. *Let it not be so in America.* Let us take away from all classes of men the power to amass unjust wealth with which to blind and delude the people.—I have heard astonishment expressed because the soldiers fired upon the people in Montreal and in Ireland—they were their fellow subjects—they were their fellow countrymen! I am not surprised at these things. The Scotch low country soldier, from Dundee, Glasgow, Edinburgh, &c. would in three cases out of four be willing to take the consequences of resistance in such a case, so would the well informed

Englishmen, in many cases. Not so the highlander. Obedience to his superior officer is his first law, and he would promptly *do his duty*, as he would consider it, by sending an unoffending population quick to eternity at the word of command. Such is the force of education. The French soldier, it appears, has *now* an opinion of his own. He is not a slave. Fortunate it was for the people of Paris that the troops had the feelings of men, and the manly intelligence of free citizens. They accomplished the revolution of July, 1830, which notwithstanding all I hear said against it, is doing much for France. The same name of *honour* that would lead the highland Scottish soldier to obey his officer in a doubtful case like that at Carrigeen would induce a lowlander to draw back—each would be brave in a righteous cause—the difference would lie in the notions of civil liberty, a term not very well understood in some parts of the world. We would fain hope for the dawning of a better day.

Mr. Ryerson, for months before I came to England and ever since, has devoted his whole time and attention to the assistance of the Rev. Edward Irving of whose congregation he is an active member. He passes the whole of his time in the exercises of religion, preaching to the poor, assisting those who stand in need of his aid, and teaching the doctrines of the church with which he is connected. I have already expressed my sentiments of Mr. Irving; he is, I think, an eminently good and gifted man. About 20 preachers connected with his church go and preach in the streets and lanes of the city, on Sundays and weekdays. In some places the police interrupt them and convey them to prison for preaching. The same police will allow vagabonds, disorderly women, criers of commodities for sale, to infest the streets on Sunday while those who would inspire the people with the principles of true religion they are directed to apprehend and incarcerate. This is the order of the Secretary of State for the Home Department. It is much easier for a church like that established here to flourish amidst crime and infidelity than when placed alongside truly pious and charitable christians. The chief superintendent is a namesake and perhaps relative of Gov. Colborne's new Sec'y.

A gentleman of high rank whose son was wild and intractable has disinherited that son because he changed his course, joined Mr. Irving's church and went to the streets and bye lanes to instruct others. This young man and another have been for weeks in jail here among criminals, in order to get them to promise not to preach the gospel in the streets, but they will not give that promise. Mr. Irving's congregation still retain the peculiarity of speaking in the spirit—some too, sing in the same way—it is the most beautiful music you ever heard. They think this right, and I do not know enough to say they are wrong.

Yours very faithfully,

W. L. MACKENZIE.

COLONIAL ADVOCATE, 20 December 1832.

DUNDEE AND ABERDEEN

There are too many people in this country—far too many—they are like the trees in a nursery which soon choke each other's growth unless transplanted and placed at due distances. If there is a farm to be let for 14 or 19 years, half a dozen of persons are ready to embark their capital on the improvement of the bare walls of the house and the acres that surround it, and to offer a rent which all experience tells them must be ruinous or at least unproductive to themselves. Is there a house to be built? Ten contractors are ready to underbid each other, and he who succeeds is generally in a worse state than his idle competitors. Is there any work to be done, in whatever branch of business or trade it may be, there are so many persons unemployed and ready to do it that they ruin each other, and become the slaves of a capitalist's interest, toiling without even the hope of better days either for themselves or their children. The farm servant works for a miserable pittance and fears to marry the woman of his choice, lest the blackest poverty should be their lot and the lot of their offspring. The weaver or other mechanic toils in hopeless poverty and neglect, and all the professions dependent on the working classes become equally precarious. Bankruptcy stares the most prudent in the face, and while a comparatively few riot in luxury the many are in despair. Poor laws appear to be the only remedy, and they are at best an inefficient one. The Scotch poor laws leave the poor to starve—the Irish have no poor laws. It is a melancholy fact, that in proportion as a nation becomes very rich and very full of people, with the wealth produced by its industry placed in the hands of a few, the very poor become more and more wretched: hospitality diminishes, the sight of the wretched becomes more hateful, and the habit of giving is less fixed. Such a state of things cannot exist in America for centuries to come, and to obviate its effects here, benevolence must be compulsory. Mr. Gourlay was no visionary when he spoke of the advantages of removing 200,000 a year annually from Britain to the Colonies; they would be unspeakably great. It is said that there are 800,000 paupers in Ireland, and I believe that there are not less than 200,000 in Scotland, the latter, very little better off than the former. Dr. McCulloch gives fearful testimony of the present condition of the poor of Scotland, and is borne out by the evidence of others. There is not a more cruel species of animals in existence than your very rich people. The Scotch and Irish absentee peers and landed gentlemen screw the last shilling out of their miserable tenantry, leaving the poor to die in ditches or starve by inches. People of Upper Canada beware how ye tamper with the privileges granted to you—"power is always stealing from the many to the few," and ye may bestow with your lands a curse on those who shall inherit them, because of your carelessness! —Abbé Raynal's advice contained in my Almanac for 1831 cannot be too often read and considered. It is of inestimable value.

I have probably talked too much politics in my letters, but it should be remembered by the reader that politics is the science which teaches the people of a country to care for each other. If a mischievous individual were to attempt to cut off his neighbour's hand, would that neighbour's other hand and feet do well quietly to permit the amputation of the limb if they could hinder it? All will say, No. This then is politics. That part of our duty which teaches us to study the welfare of our whole country, and not to rest satisfied altho' our own household is well off when our neighbours are in difficulty and danger. The honest politician is he who gives all he can of his time and means to promote the public good, whose charity begins at home *but does not end there*. The man who says he is no politician, is either ignorant of what he is saying, or a contemptible selfish creature, unworthy of the country or community of which he is a part.

The number of mills for spinning flax into yarn in Dundee is now very numerous. The smoke of their steam-engines darkens the face of the heavens, and many a poor and miserable boy and girl eke out a miserable existence by long and incessant toil in these ever to be detested establishments, the graves of morality, and the parents of vice, deformity, pauperism, and crime. Long may Canada be free of all such pests! Let our domestic manufactures be those which our children can easily carry on under the eyes and in the houses and homes of their fathers and mothers.

.   .   .

The Lords of Justiciary were holding the Circuit Court here when we arrived, and curiosity led me to the court house to see their proceedings. As I entered the lower hall, I found that the court was guarded by files of soldiers placed on each side of the lobby with drawn bayonets. On arriving at the Upper door by which the public are admitted I found it shut, and one of the town's officers, assisted by a soldier inside, kept guard. He refused to allow me to go in, and other persons were equally unsuccessful. Such of the audience as were in court were allowed to come out, but, although there was abundance of room, the people had to stand outside in the rain. There were very few constables. Their lordships rose at noon, and the soldiers attended them with military parade. I went back at 2. P.M. and got admission at the re-opening of the court. The body of the hall was filled with legal persons, witnesses, jurymen's seats, each seat supplied with papers, pens, ink, &c. the judicial bench, with the two judges fantastically arrayed in white silk robes with pink and scarlet knots, the invention of a darker age. The soldiers were there as before, but in fewer numbers. Few constables were present, and the appearance of the whole proceedings had a military air with them I did not like. What has a military band of music and soldiers with their guns, bayonets, swords, &c. to do with the administration of criminal justice in a free country? I never witnessed any such scenes in England, and hope I may not often meet with them in Canada. Soldiers are ostensibly kept up to protect us from foreign aggression, not to interfere with or serve as a police in the administration of the civil law.

On enquiry I find that the Provost and Magistrates of Aberdeen (a self elected junto) are sheriffs within the city and liberties, and very probably they have had something to do with the above red-coat parade. How deeply the ignorance and stupidity of mankind is to be deplored. The selfishness of our species ruins the best laid plans for their amelioration. In England, up to Edward Second's reign, Sheriffs, Coroners, and Justices of the Peace were, nearly all of them, elected by the free inhabitants of their respective districts. The reason why they have ceased to do so may be found by consulting Blackstone. By and bye it is possible that public opinion may be so far enlightened as to enable them to insist on resuming this great right. With us in Upper Canada public sentiment is in favour of the nomination of justices of the peace by the people, and if there were a little more of public spirit in some of the counties that boon would not be long withheld. But I greatly fear that when a new election takes place really disinterested farmers will hesitate to come forward as candidates, or if they do come forth, will scruple to take the pains necessary to secure their safe return. COLONIAL

ADVOCATE, 27 June 1833: from Letter 40 to Wixson. Quoted in part in Lindsey, vol. 1, pp. 284-6.

SLAVERY

The blessing of heaven can scarcely be expected on America while the disgraceful practice of enslaving the bodies and minds of the coloured population is allowed to exist. It must and will be abolished not by sending the slaves to Liberia, but by giving them equal rights with ourselves, and promoting the education of their offspring. THE CONSTITUTION, 8 November 1837.

Chapter Five

APPEALS TO THE PEOPLE

EDITOR'S PREFACE   *By "the People" Mackenzie usually meant "the freeholders". Sometimes he included the mechanics and apprentices living in the towns, but he was the spokesman for the farmers, and a member of the Upper Canada House of Assembly for the County, not the town, of York. He devoted much of his time and energy to learning, at first hand whenever possible, the circumstances, opinions, and grievances of the farmers, and giving expression to them in his journals.*

His Appeals to the People are paralleled in many cases by the Addresses to Government, which follow in Chapter VI. They reflect his relations with his constituents and with the settlers in other parts of Upper Canada. They often refer to elections, and the following dates may be useful for reference:

General Elections were held in July 1824, July 1828, October 1830, October 1834, and June 1836.

Mackenzie was a candidate in the last four; he was elected for York County in 1828, 1830, and 1834.

He was expelled from the House December 1831, January 1832, November 1833, and twice in December 1833. He was re-elected January and March 1832, November and December 1833, and in the General Election of 1834, and continued to sit in the Assembly until the dissolution of May 28, 1836.

In March 1834 he was elected Alderman of the newly incorporated City of Toronto, and in the same month was chosen Mayor by the new Board of Aldermen.

During the years covered in this book Governors-General, who also held office as Lieutenant-Governor of Lower Canada, were:

1820-1828	*Lord Dalhousie.*
1828-1831	*Sir James Kempt.*
1831-1835	*Lord Aylmer.*
1835-1838	*Earl of Gosford.*

Lieutenant-Governors of Upper Canada were:
1818-1828   Sir Peregrine Maitland.
1828-1836   Sir John Colborne.
1836-1838   Sir Francis Bond Head.
The institutions of Government were:
The Executive Council, appointed.
The Legislative Council, appointed.
The Legislative Assembly, elected.

ELECTION APPEALS

TO THE ELECTORS OF MEMBERS OF ASSEMBLY

On you alone, Farmers, does Canada rely. You are the sole depositories of civil and religious liberty. If you look to the provincial executives, they are foreigners, having an interest differing widely from yours, and are hardly able, even if we grant that they have the will, to reconcile jarring interests arising from a crooked colonial policy; but possessing patronage and power, having in their gifts, offices and emoluments, honours and dignities, lands and heritages; influence immense, if we consider the size of the country.

If we look at the Legislative Council, what do we find but a new edition of the Privy Council of England; a new but truly not an improved edition; something in fact as is the brown paper copies of Scott's Novels published by Mathew Carey of Philadelphia, to the splendid editions of the same works which issue from Constable's press. Have the members of our Legislative Councils ever been other than the most obsequious, cringing worshippers of power? Have the honourables and reverends and right reverends, ever attempted ought towards consolidating your liberties? Have they not, on the other hand, done all that in them lay to abridge, to curtail, aye, to crush them? . . .

Will the judges guard your rights? dare they do it? will they become the champions of your liberties? Remember Thorpe . . . .

There is an established church? There is so; but will its priests desert their churches and their revenues to suffer persecution for conscience sake, if need be, as many of your forefathers and their ministers did? Perhaps so; look to York; look elsewhere, and we can anticipate your reply.

We have still the bar to analyse. There indeed you have a few friends—we hope true ones. You have a Stuart, of Lower Canada; a Rolph; an O'Sullivan, and some more; and they may increase.

To yourselves, therefore, Farmers, in the hour of trial, must you look for aid. The eyes of the whole Colonies, and of America, are fixed on you. You are the only true nobility that this country can boast of. Through you only, by your Representatives, can the real state of things become known in the British senate. If ye choose the wisest, the honestest, the most esteemed of your body; men who have been long known as tried patriots, in whose souls the voice of freedom is not yet extinct; who hold no offices under, or receive any gifts from the Crown; and who, as fathers, as husbands, as members of society, are kind and brotherly minded; men of cultivated minds and discreet demeanour, *fearing God and hating covetousness.* If to such as these ye trust your liberties, there is yet hope for your country, that such representatives will assert your rights, recover your due influence, and be a means to consolidate your freedom. But if ye will, as heretofore, choose collectors and king's advocates, ambassadors, parasites and sycophants, to manage your affairs, you will dearly rue it; you and the generations that shall be hereafter. Look at Spain—Look at Greece—Look at Revolutionary France— Behold the sad effects of misgovernment, and beware! The errors were in the princes in the end, but sprang from an effeminacy in the people in the beginning. COLONIAL ADVOCATE, 18 May 1824.

TO THE ELECTORS OF UPPER CANADA

The important week which is to decide the character of our new house of assembly is at hand. . . .

The conduct of a majority of the members of the last parliament, of whom so much was expected, is known to you; the money they have squandered away mostly to useless purposes (little less than half a million of dollars) came out of your pockets; the state in which the province now languishes, and the apathy of those who are at the helm of affairs, you are well aware of. Up, then, and be doing. Stir yourselves, like men, and strike at the roots of corruption, in the persons of our late corrupt representatives. Send them to beg for the crumbs that fall from Sir Peregrine's table, but never again trust your religion, your liberties, your peace of mind, and indeed all you can or ought to love and admire, to worthless beings who have no claim to your favour unless it be on account of their having made a low bow, or given you a friendly shake of the hand previous to an election day. COLONIAL ADVOCATE, 8 July 1824.

TO THE ELECTORS OF THE COUNTY OF YORK

GENTLEMEN:—I have the honour to inform you that it is my intention to come forward as a candidate at the next Election of Members to serve for your County in the Provincial Parliament; and I most respectfully solicit your votes and support.

I have no end in view but the well being of the people at large—no ambition to serve, but that of contributing to the happiness and prosperity of our common country. The influence and authority with which you may invest me, shall always be directed, according to the best of my judgment, for the general good; and it will be my care to uphold your rights to the utmost of my power, with that firmness, moderation, and *perseverance*, which becomes the representative of a free people.

If honoured with your suffrages, it will be alike my duty and my pleasure to watch over the local interests of this great county—and to promote every public improvement and useful undertaking, which shall be found conducive to your prosperity and the general welfare.

I have ever been opposed to ecclesiastical domination; it is at enmity with the free spirit of christianity; and nations which have bowed to its yoke, are become the dark abodes of ignorance and superstition—oppression and misery.

That corrupt, powerful and long-endured influence which has hitherto interfered with your rights and liberties, can only be overthrown by your unanimity and zeal. An independent House of Assembly, to Upper Canada, would be inestimable.

I have been a careful observer of the conduct of the people's representatives in the colonial assemblies; I have seen men in whom was placed the utmost confidence, fall from their integrity and betray their sacred trust—men too, who had entered upon their legislative duties with the best intentions towards the people, and who evinced for a time a firm determination to support their rights. But there are others who continue to maintain and uphold the interests of their country, unshaken and undismayed; who consider it their highest honour to persevere in a faithful discharge of their public duties, and eagerly strive to deserve the good will, the affection, and the confidence of their fellow subjects.

Among this latter class I am desirous of being numbered; and, unless I shall be found deserting the cause of the people, I trust that the people will never desert me.

Accept my sincere thanks for the abundant proofs of kindness and confidence, and for the liberal assurances of support, with which you have honoured me, and, believe me,

Gentlemen, Your faithful humble servant,

W. L. MACKENZIE.

York, 17th December 1827.

BROADSIDE (Toronto Public Library); COLONIAL ADVOCATE, 3 January 1828; Lindsey, vol. 1, p. 143.

ELECTION PLATFORM

[Twenty-three Resolutions prepared by W. L. Mackenzie and submitted to a meeting in the Township of Markham to nominate candidates to represent York County, 26 January 1828.]

Mr. Mackenzie said that . . . he had prepared a series of resolutions, embracing his own opinions upon leading political topics, connected with the present state of the province, and of the district, which, with the permission of the chair, he would read to them: if the sentiments of the electors would be found to coincide with his own, he would come forward at the ensuing election as a candidate for their suffrages, but if not, he would immediately decline.

The first twenty-three resolutions were then read, one by one: as follows :—

1. Resolved, that a judicious exercise of the powers enjoyed by the freeholders of this province, freely to elect their representatives in parliament, is necessary to the unimpaired preservation of their rights and privileges as British subjects, and essentially promotes good government and the public welfare.

2. That it is exceedingly desirable to obtain an unreserved expression of public opinion upon the present situation of affairs in this province.

3. That for several years past, the income of real estate in this district, the profits of trade and industry, and the wages of labour therein, have diminished, and are still diminishing, and that no adequate encouragement is given to domestic manufactures.

4. That besides the ensuring to the subject the most perfect security of his person and property, the aiding and facilitating the diffusion of useful knowledge and the free exercise of industry and enterprise, are among the most efficient means of promoting the general prosperity and preventing its decline.

5. That the insufficient aid which has hitherto been afforded for promoting education has been partially and unequally bestowed, and that the large sums which have been appropriated by the present and by the last provincial parliament, out of the public revenue, or by resorting to expensive loans, the principal and interest of which must be liquidated by heavy taxes to be levied upon the people, for facilitating industry, and opening and improving internal communications, have produced no adequate advantages, nor been satisfactorily accounted for to the public.

6. That laying out many thousand pounds for making a ship navigation, chiefly for naval and military purposes, in one corner of the province, called the Welland Canal, while no effectual aid has been afforded to repair the roads and bridges of this district, and while the far more important navigation of the St. Lawrence remains unimproved, is contrary to sound policy and unjust towards this neglected part of the colony.

7. That under the present depressed circumstances of the province, when wheat, flour, ashes, and lumber, the staple articles of export, fetch a very low price, no taxes or new duties for the public use can, equitably, be imposed, and no dependence can be placed on any funds for aiding in the diffusion of education, and facilitating the exertions of individual industry and enterprize, other than such funds as may be derived from the existing public revenue of the province.

8. That, although the civil list of this colony has been hitherto paid by the British nation, a very large sum has been annually voted by the Assembly, and applied for several years, to the payment of the salaries, emoluments, and expenses, of the officers of the civil government, over and above ten thousand dollars per annum, placed at the disposal of the lieutenant governor, by the imprudent act of a former legislature.

9. That the said salaries, emoluments, and expenses, have been greatly increased for many years past, often without the concurrence of the legislature (such as in the cases of Judge Powell's pension of £1000, Mr. J. B. Robinson's expenses £500 sterling, etc.) and are in several instances paid to absentees and persons who have rendered no service therefor to this province—and in other instances, the said

salaries, emoluments, and expenses are excessive, compared with the services rendered, and with the incomes derived from real estate, and the usual recompense obtained by individuals of talent, character, and industry, equal to those of the persons who receive the said salaries and emoluments.

10. That besides the unnecessary and excessive salaries and expenses, FEES, increasing to a heavy and grievous amount, are paid by the subject to divers officers of Government, whereby individuals are burthened unnecessarily, the protection of the law and the benefit of government are lessened, and the resources of the country for its necessary wants diminished.

11. That a majority of persons, chiefly dependent for the support of themselves and their families on the salaries and emoluments of public offices held during pleasure, have been placed in the executive and legislative councils of this province, not a few of whom have a direct individual interest in maintaining and increasing the said excessive salaries, fees, emoluments, and expenses, and perpetuating other abuses profitable to persons in office.

12. That a majority in the said Legislative Council, chiefly consisting of executive councillors, judges, and other officers so holding during pleasure, have year after year rejected, refused, or neglected to proceed upon various necessary bills sent up by the representative assembly of this province, for the remedy of abuses grievous to the subject, for increasing the security of persons and property, and promoting the common welfare and prosperity; particularly:

A Bill to repeal the act under which Mr. Robert Gourlay was banished.

A Bill to repeal the permanent appropriation of £2,500 annually placed at the Lieutenant Governor's disposal.

A Bill to dispose of the clergy lands for the purpose of general education.

A Bill to declare emigrants who had complied with the various requisitions of the provincial statutes, or been born subjects of his majesty, and renewed their allegiance according to the provisions of the 30th. George IIIrd, lawful subjects of his majesty.

A Bill for facilitating the administration of justice, by improvements in the laws now in force regulating the formation of juries.

A Bill for allowing religious societies to hold land sufficient to build churches and meeting houses upon.

A Bill for the more equal distribution of the property of persons dying intestate, by abolishing the laws of primogeniture.

13. That the rejection, refusal, or neglect to proceed upon, these

and other necessary Bills sent up by the Assembly to the Legislative Council, by a majority of the said council, formed of Executive Councillors, Judges, and officers, holding their commissions during pleasure, must be held to be the act of the executive government of the province, and as such constitutes a public grievance, destructive of the ends of the constitution of government as by law established.

14. That this meeting, in common with their fellow subjects, regard as a fundamental and inalienable principle of the constitution, that the people should not be taxed without the consent of their representatives, and that to the legislature alone belong the controul and distribution of all monies levied on them, as also that the management of the post-office of this province ought not to be placed beyond the controul of parliament, and that the appropriation of its revenues from year to year unknown to the legislature amounts to direct taxation without representation.

15. That an established or state religion is not desired in this province.

16. That the clergy reserves ought to be sold, and the proceeds of the sales appropriated to the advancement of learning, and the improvement of the public highways.

17. That a university free from religious tests, and offering literary honours and distinctions alike to all classes of christians, is much wanted.

18. That it is the incontestible right of this colony to have, in like manner as many other British colonies have, a responsible agent of its choice, residing in England, who might at all times, watch over the preservation of its just rights and privileges, and the commercial and agricultural interests of its inhabitants; and that it is to the want of such an agent that must in part be attributed the unfaithful representation of the situation of this country, made in England on many occasions by persons interested, ignorant or prejudiced, and the impossibility which the mother country, in many cases, was under of knowing the desires and the true interests of the inhabitants of this province.

19. That the expenses of civil suits in courts of law in this province, both to plaintiff and defendant, are a grievous burthen, and in many cases equal to a denial of Justice—because verdicts are only to be had at an expense generally far exceeding the means of the parties.—Insomuch, that while in many other parts of this continent ordinary debts are collected by law with moderate costs, the legal charges here induce creditors oftentimes to lose the debt altogether, rather than, by prosecuting the debtor, to run the risk of selling his

cattle by sheriff's sale, while he and his family are thrown as miserable outcasts upon the world.

20. That the chief criminal judge of this province, holds, at the pleasure of the crown, the situation of speaker of the legislative, and chairman of the executive council; that the judges of the King's Bench depend entirely on the crown, and are perfectly independent of the people—receiving high salaries from England and looking thither for promotion and support.

21. That such judges are not constituted so as to afford a probability of their giving the most impartial and unbiassed opinion, in cases where the interests or power of the crown, or the interests of the local administration, or its officers and servants, are opposed to the rights and privileges of the people.

22. That the address of the House of Assembly to His Majesty, praying that the colonial judges might be rendered independent of the executive, and appointed during good behaviour, with power of impeachment by the assembly, and a fair trial, was dictated by a well founded conviction that the abuses which exist in our courts of justice would have been lessened by the alteration there requested.

23. That those members of assembly who voted their constituents aliens are not worthy of the support of this meeting at the ensuing election.

COLONIAL ADVOCATE, 31 January 1828.

ON SELECTING
REPRESENTATIVES

APPEAL TO THE PEOPLE OF UPPER CANADA

PEOPLE OF UPPER CANADA!

The day approaches on which you will again be called upon to choose your representatives; I therefore hasten thus to redeem an oft repeated pledge.

Farmers of Upper Canada! let the sentiment of continued devotion to the true principles of liberty—of sincere love towards the whole family of man—without distinction of caste, country or creed—forever animate your bosoms. Instruct your children in these principles in early youth, that the maintenance of social order may be to them a solemn duty even to their latest breath! Think of your fellow subjects beyond the Atlantic, with affectionate recollections of the land of your forefathers or nativity! Nourish no unkind or revengeful feelings against your brethren who compose the independent portion of the great English family on this continent, but may your earnest desire on their behalf, as of old, be "that peace and happiness, truth and justice, religion and piety, may be established among them to all generations." Cherish continually a sentiment of lively gratitude to the creator, preserver, and bountiful benefactor of the universe, for the multiplied blessings, the unnumbered comforts that surround you; and to that "righteousness which exalteth a nation," may you ever be enabled to lay claim.

Ye independent cultivators of the soil, watch unceasingly over the liberties of your infant country! A kind Providence hath cast your lot in a highly favoured land, where, blessed with luxuriant harvests and a healthful climate, you are enabled to look back without regret, upon the opulent nations of Europe, where the unbounded wealth of one class and the degrading poverty of another, afford melancholy proofs of the tyranny which prevails in their governments. Compare your situation with that of Russia, an empire embracing one half of the habitable globe, the population of which are slaves attached to the soil, and transferable to any purchaser; or with Germany, Italy, Portugal, and Spain, where human beings are born and die under the same degrading vassalage. Pass over into your parent state, into Great Britain, a nation in which the arts and sciences have been protected and encouraged, and where responsibility to public sentiment or constitutional rights, prevails in a greater degree than in some of the other European nations, and even there you will find the greater portion of the land divided into unwieldy entailed estates; and the people burthened with heavy rents, and taxes, and tithes; and the charges of increasing pauperism. You will perceive an inequality of the ranks of society, too great for the purposes of producing the greatest quantity of human nourishment, and the greatest sum of human happiness; in the poor laws you will recognize a cloak for oppression, an instrument for obtaining the greatest possible security for the rich with the least possible remuneration for the services of the poor. Despotism is at one end of the chain of society, and at the other slavery.

Traverse the wide world and what will you find?—In one place, a privation of liberty—in another, incapacity to make use of its possession—here, ignorance, vice, and political misrule—there, an immense number of your fellow men, forced from their peaceful homes and occupations "to fight battles in the issue of which they have no interest, to increase a domain in the possession of which they can have no share."—Contrast their situation with yours, and let the peaceful plains, the fertile valleys of Canada, your homes, the homes of your wives and children, be still more dear to you. Agriculture the most innocent, happy, and important of all human pursuits, is your chief employment—your farms are your own—you have obtained a competence, seek therewith to be content.

Mechanics of Upper Canada! beware of secret associations—they are unfit for a free country! Beware of the spirit of party, of sects, and of factions; they are ever injurious to true liberty by dividing the people against each other. Many there have been of the most distinguished among mankind, who having set out on life's journey as humble and obscure mechanics—by a careful cultivation of the powers of their minds; by employing their leisure moments in acquiring useful instruction—by cherishing in their breasts a sentiment of self respect—and by preserving their regular, industrious and frugal habits, have risen to honour and estate among their fellow men, and are held in estimation for their patriotism and probity, their benevolence and private worth. In every civilized country, ancient or modern, the mechanics have been found among the most steadfast friends of rational liberty, the most intelligent supporters of social order. At the hustings, in a few days, in the towns and counties of British America, they will doubtless prove to the world that they have not yet exchanged the symbol of their manly independence of character to put on the servile badge of sycophancy to arbitrary power.

"The rights of man, (observes Mr. Fox in his reply to Burke upon the Quebec bill) are, in fact, the basis and foundation of every rational constitution, and even of the British constitution itself, as our statute book proves; since, if I know anything of *the original compact between the people of England and its government*, as stated in that volume, it is *a recognition of the inherent rights of the people as men*, which no proscription can supersede, no accident remove or obliterate."

For the maintenance then, of these rights, people of Upper Canada, are you about to assemble in your several towns and counties; and I earnestly intreat you to manifest the high sense you entertain of the blessings of freedom by your general attendance at the polls, and by your anxious and careful selection of able and faithful representatives. Poor indeed in soul or in substance must that farmer or mechanic be, who, being in health, cannot in two or four years spare time for one day's journey to the hustings to express an opinion by his vote, concerning the persons chosen to watch over the public welfare. He should remember that an enlightened people are the only safe depository of the ultimate powers of society; that "The great object in the institutions of popular assemblies is, that the people may be fully and freely represented;" that the institutions of the mother country are every year becoming more popular; that improvements in the British system will be felt gradually in Canada; and that "in proportion as the structure of government gives influence to public opinion, it is essential that public opinion should be enlightened." Exert yourselves then at the approaching election, to find in your respective circles able and enlightened representatives—men of calm reflecting minds—devoid of little personal views—willing to support in the Legislature the measures you want to have supported. It is not a change in the form of Government which will remove any difficulties or grievances under which you labour; nor will railing at the United States perpetuate the dominion of your rulers. The grand panacea is self reformation.

. . .

In the last House, it was apparent that not a few of the members made their way into parliament, more to represent the losses sustained by certain individuals during the last war, and to endeavour to place a direct tax on every inhabitant of the colony to pay these losses, than for any other purpose whatever. Some of these warriors had heavy personal demands in this way and were by no means delicate in urging them, even at the risk of interrupting that tranquility and unity of purpose which ought to have distinguished the Assembly in the important struggle for good Government in which it was so meritoriously and anxiously engaged. In the next Legislature, some will doubtless seek seats to gratify certain private interests of their own, and others will be willing to come forward purely from a principle of love of country. If at all possible, send the latter. Set not your hearts upon returning any man who has not satisfied you that he can and will support your measures. I greatly lament the unfortunate custom which too much prevails in all representative bodies, of choosing men to represent the public interests, and advocate the most important rights, through the agency, not of personal knowledge of character, but of electioneering assiduity, without regard to qualification. Many lawyers can split a hair in argument, and make a bad cause appear to be a good one, they are able enough, eloquent enough, and could support your cause efficiently. But unless you are satisfied that they are with you in their hearts—that they will take up your cause, not as they would some chance client's, but with zeal, earnestness, and a settled conviction of its righteousness and importance, have nothing to do with them. If you find a lawyer who has tried to fill his neighbourhood with litigation—who is more famed for gaining causes than for scrupulous virtue in accepting their management, he is a "minister of municipal litigation, and the fomenter of village vexation"—avoid him.

The lawyer who has promoted and enlarged the quarrels of a county will not easily become the peacemaker of a province—or if he does, it will only be an assumption of that sham patriotism, which cloaks hypocrisy seeking for higher office. As it is far easier to do evil than good—to wound than to heal—to defile a vessel of pure water than to restore the liquid to its original purity; so also is it easier to mar the peace and prosperity of a province by means of able but unprincipled representatives, than to repair the injury.

But wherever a lawyer can be found among you, worthy of the high vocation whereto he has been called—learned, industrious, and faithful—less anxious for the fees of office than the peace of society—always willing to embark in the most perilous duties of his profession, the protection of property, personal rights, domestic peace and parental authority, entreat him to come forward as a candidate; elect him with acclamation; he will surely maintain your rights, and stand as a sentinel upon the watch tower of Freedom, to warn you of approaching danger. He will not be found sleeping upon his post. His education, his habits, his intimate acquaintance with the laws and constitutions of nations, will qualify him in a peculiar degree for fulfilling the duties of a representative of his country.

People of Upper Canada! you have hitherto set too little value upon the elective franchise. As individuals, in selecting an agent to transact your own private business, or to attend to your own immediate interests, you will overlook the claims of a personal friend, in order to obtain the services of a stranger, or one indifferent to you, who is more competent and can better serve you; yet in the important affairs of legislation you are too much inclined to be governed by personal predilection or mere incidental circumstances having no material relation to the merits of the case. It seems to me to be very discreditable to a county to send an ignorant, conceited, vain, foolish man, to parliament, and leave enlightened, prudent and capable men at home. Yet so it is, that ever since I have known Upper Canada, some men have been sent to the Assembly, who were so much captivated with a dinner, a smile, a gracious observation, or a nod from a colonial governor, that even their very boarding-house landladies could not help taking notice of the extraordinary effects the condescension had produced in moderating their zeal against misrule and the promoters of it.

Every county in the province has usually a certain quantity of minor business to be transacted—there are private and public bills which particularly affect it—and money to be divided on its roads and bridges—rights which it seeks to maintain and grievances which it desires to have redressed—petitions for various improvements in which it is interested—taxes to be laid on, of which it might be required, perhaps, to pay an unequal share—divisions and subdivisions demanded by surrounding districts in which it is concerned —privileges and immunities desired by certain of its citizens at the expense of others—and a hundred other incidentals too tedious to enumerate here. All this mass of business, it is probable, is either well or ill done according as its members are fit or unfit for their office. And a county either receives or loses some part of its proportion of legislative aid and patronage according as its representatives are more or less able, ingenious and industrious. All men are by no means, however, to be rejected in consequence of their want of splendid powers of speech or other shewy attainments. Many there are of little education, and ordinary acquirements, who yet possess a weight of character, acuteness of observation, industry, and perseverance, which will more than counterbalance the superior acquirements and more imposing appearance of those who would pass for men of wisdom and learning.

.   .   .

You have far less reason to complain of the defects of the established constitution than of the corruption, ignorance, carelessness and subservience of successive assemblies. Would *an honest parliament* have disturbed the peace of society and retarded the settlement of the province by passing the Alien Bill ? Would an honest parliament have passed the gagging bill, the spoon bill, the sedition bill, the permanent appropriation bill, the $12,000 mission bills, the York Bank monopolizing charter, the bill to allow judges appointed during the pleasure of the executive to regulate law fees ? Would an intelligent and patriotic legislature have involved the colony, situated as it now is, in a public debt of £120,000, and that too before it began to enquire into the appropriation of the money voted ? Would a firm and uncompromising band of patriotic legislators have stood passive for so long a period to the inroads of the protestant episcopal church upon the rights of the people—to the injury done by the crown and clergy reserves—and to the secret misapplications of the public revenue ? Would the representatives of a people jealous of its rights, have remained for years passive under the indelible stigma affixed by the high handed act of imprisoning a natural born British subject for eight months in a dungeon—refusing him the benefit of habeas corpus—and afterwards banishing him to the United States, without conviction of any crime whatever? Would they have tamely beheld the province deprived of a hundred thousand valuable European settlers since the late war, owing to the bad character and bad faith of the privy council, in disturbing the public peace, misgoverning the country, and raising the fees upon grants of land, from a trifle up to £30 sterling, suddenly, and in the teeth of publications by themselves all over the three kingdoms, inviting settlers to come and improve the Canadian forests, and to accept lands on liberal and fair principles!

These and many other results of legislative carelessness or subservience ought to awaken all your constitutional vigilance, and induce you to redouble your efforts for the general welfare. The last House was not all you could have wished—but it did some good. It protested against the Crown and Clergy Reserves—against the intolerant character of the provincial university—against the misapplication of the public revenue—against the extension of temporal power to the ministers and members of one particular protestant sect to the injury of others equally conscientious—against the late governor's conduct and character—against the insult offered you by the retention of evil counsellors around the present chief magistrate—and against the unlawful removal and degradation of Mr. Justice Willis, and the continuation of a judiciary system in which you had long ceased to have trust or confidence. Some of the towns and counties, it is true, sent representatives whose conduct was a source of much unhappiness to their fellow members—because their every effort was exerted to make the House a scene of strife and confusion, to degrade the character of the people, and render popular legislation a bye-word and a reproach.

To insure good government, with the aid of a faithful people, the following five things are essential:

1. The entire control of the whole provincial revenues are required to be vested in the legislature—the territorial and hereditary revenues excepted.

2. The independence of the judges; or their removal to take place, only upon a joint address of the two houses, and their appointment from among men who have not embarked in the political business of the province.

3. A reform in the Legislative Council, which is now an assembly chiefly composed of persons wholly or partly dependent upon the executive government for their support.

4. An administration or executive government responsible to the province for its conduct.

5. Equal rights to each religious denomination, and an exclusion of every sect from a participation in temporal power.

Were these fundamental principles of reformation once conceded to you, I think it probable that the assembly would have the means of effecting other improvements which you have desired, and securing to you good government and public prosperity. If Sir George Murray would see the "undivided attention of the executive government and legislature given to the advancements of the general interests of the province, in a spirit of cordial co-operation," and also "a cordial concurrence in all measures calculated to advance the common good, in whatever quarter such measures may happen to originate," let him set to work in earnest to remove the causes of discontent, especially those aforementioned.

It is best for the Assembly not to indulge at this time in too many new projects, lest the influence of public opinion be shaken, by having submitted to it too many matters upon which there may be a difference. And it is to be desired that the persons in power will not forever distinguish themselves by an indiscriminate zeal against reforms, but that they will endeavour to avert the tempests of revolution, by assenting to a gradual and prudent accommodation of your established institutions "to the varying opinions, manners, and circumstances of the age and country in which you live."

Without intending the least personal allusion to former legislative assemblies, or any of their members, I would intreat you to put your seal of disapprobation upon the intemperate and the debauched, if any such should presume to offer themselves to your notice. The litigious also, who are constantly to be found collecting their debts in the law courts, and those poor spirited men who are continually thirsting after office and its emoluments. Men whose conduct in their private dealings with their fellows, has been found to be regulated by covetous, unchristian, selfish principles, will be sure to make dishonest and unprincipled legislators—for, how can he who takes daily advantage of the necessities or follies of his brother, be a lover of mankind, benevolent, and kind? Mind not his boasted patriotism, nor his exclamations against existing abuses, for there is guile in his heart and deceit on his lips!

Beware of electioneering sycophants! for if they flatter you, they will assuredly flatter power after you elect them! Choose not your men, because they make a great profession of adherence to this religious denomination or to that—look rather to the effect which their profession has upon their conduct as members of society and heads of families. No person in embarrassed circumstances ought to be placed in the House of Assembly, unless he has given frequent and convincing proofs of his devotion to the public interests. Vain empty boasters, sometimes get inside the walls of the senate house, and prove by their inconsistent conduct, their senseless harangues, their unfitness for business, their being blown about by every wind of doctrine, that their constituents were unworthy or ignorant of their privileges as men and Britons. Empty vessels send forth the loudest sounds.

Lastly, avoid the placeman, the office-holder, the pensioner, and the acknowledged court favourite. The Assembly is intended as a check upon men in office—that because you cannot be all present in your proper persons to examine into and expose and check the corruption, partiality, peculation, misrule, or other offences of office-holders, where they exist, your representatives may do it for you. But if you send a Sheriff, a Judge, a Crown Officer, an Inspector of Licenses, a Clerk of the Peace, a Collector of Customs, or other person whose emoluments the very breath of the executive may annihilate, how can you expect that in one case in a hundred these functionaries will fearlessly check the abuses of which perhaps they individually reap the benefit; or mar those hopes of promotion in which they have put their trust? Yet, look not upon the candidates according to their personal appearance or riches. Wealth is no true criterion by which to estimate patriotism.

The very rich man is, perhaps, as improper a representative of a people situated as you are, as the very poor. The man to whom the prayer of Agur has been literally fulfilled will generally suit you best. I cannot for a moment believe that an Assembly of the best and most faithful farmers in the country would have been as easily assailed by the corruptions of a colonial administration, as were those who assented to some of the worst measures of this government.

"In truth," says Mr. Gourlay, speaking of legislative corruption in his Statistics, "with such tools (as the Assemblymen) the governors of Upper Canada have always been enabled to legislate at will; and the very thing which, theoretically, must have appeared a safe-guard to liberty, has tended to its extinction. No governor, left to himself, would have had the effrontery to act as some of the provincial governors have done; but, countenanced by the representatives of the people, the feeling of shame was taken away."

ON SELECTING REPRESENTATIVES

One of the greatest evils attending your system of elections, is the extent to which corruption can be carried, in the way of bribery, secret promises of reward to leading partizans, and after punishments to independent voters. This evil is so notorious that I need only allude to it. Another is the distance to which voters are obliged to travel to the poll in large counties, although it would be very easy for the executive, in the absence of a specific law, to accommodate the people by holding the poll, in a contest, three days in one section of the county and three in another. It would be easier for a returning officer, his clerk, and the candidates, to travel to Newmarket, than for five hundred voters north of the Oak Ridges to come to York, and the example holds good in other places. If the executive would take the hint, the indulgence would, I am sure, give many of you much satisfaction. COLONIAL ADVOCATE, 9 September 1830; Lindsey, vol. I, pp. 179, 181-3 (quoted in part).

PETITION THE KING

TO THE PEOPLE OF UPPER CANADA

People of Upper Canada! It would have given me unspeakable pleasure had I been enabled to congratulate you upon the progress of Education throughout the Province; the flourishing state of the public treasury; the disinterested zeal and unanimity with which your representatives at their latest session had successfully asserted your right to enjoy good government; and the firm basis upon which better measures on the part of the executive had at length placed the happiness and prosperity of our common country.

But although that satisfaction has, thus far, been denied to my most earnest wishes, I shall not relax my humble exertions to promote the welfare and advance the true interests of a gallant people, a people to whom I am under the greatest obligations, and from whose hands I have twice received the highest testimonials of their esteem and confidence.

When the order was issued for a general election last autumn I felt assured that the result of another appeal to the electors, even under the present defective state of the representation would be productive of the happiest consequences. The first session of the new parliament has passed over, and not one voice has been since raised throughout the province in its favour. It is indeed well known that its conduct as a whole has displeased and *disappointed* all parties, and that the language of complaint is heard both loud and deep throughout the colony. Of what then do you complain?

You complain that your interests, the great interests of the province, are sacrificed in order to promote the interests and augment the profit, pleasure and immediate advantage of a few. Your complaint is just—the prevalence of individual interests, over the general welfare is the fatal defect of this government.

.   .   .

It is true that the great body of the people cannot give their undivided attention to the acts of the government under which they live; but it is equally true that they may observe and remonstrate against those open those notorious abuses the existence of which is fatal to their prosperity and happiness. However perfect the constitution of any government may be, it will speedily resolve itself into an engine of tyranny and oppression unless there is intelligence, patriotism and manly virtue enough in the great body of the people to check the corruption engendered in man by the possession of power. Some of the South American states which obtained very liberal constitutions, went so far into anarchy and confusion, that the tenure of life and property became much more precarious than it had been under the old colonial yoke of benighted Spain. "The price of liberty is *everlasting* vigilance."

The next question I would propose for your consideration is— *What is to be done?*

My answer would be—*Petition the King*; approach the throne of your venerated monarch with dutiful loyal and affectionate addresses, from every town, township, village and hamlet in the colony; humbly yet firmly recapitulate your grievances, and patiently but perseveringly seek redress.

The present time is propitious to your wishes, the ministry have proved themselves honest able and determined men; they have deserved your esteem and confidence by the noble stand they have made, in power and out of power, for the rights and liberties of the empire. To petition the British House of Commons would imply a want of confidence in an administration whose every act deserves praise.

Petitions to the King as affording legal and constitutional means of expressing your opinion—the opinion of the people—on public affairs, and uniting you in the steady and undeviating pursuit of objects of common interest, praying for such remedies as are within the constitutional exercise of your monarch's prerogative, are the very best means of obtaining remedies for existing evils.

Never did a more favourable opportunity present itself for the province to express its sentiments. All men admire the amiable honest and patriotic character of William the Fourth. Your King, then, is with you; his ministers will cheerfully enquire into the sources of existing evils and strive to redress them, they too are with you. The eyes of the other colonies are upon you—Lower Canada will go hand in hand with you, and the Honourable Mr. Viger, her agent, will gladly unite his efforts with the exertions of the other friends of the colony, in your behalf. The present time is one of no peculiar degree of excitement. There are no foolish and wicked state libel prosecutions afloat, nor have reverses in the markets to which your staple produce is carried for sale embittered the minds of any among you.

This then is a time in which you should calmly yet actively contend for general principles; and if you decline doing so, it appears to me probable that your government will go on in its career of monopoly, mortgaging by accumulated provincial loans your persons, property and industry, impoverishing the agricultural and labouring classes, imposing upon them all the provincial burthens, and diverting capital from their support, until some violent result is produced by their rapacity and your indecision.

The only enemy you have to contend with is the faction in power here, and its fellow-workers the faction of disappointed state priests, pensioners, charlatans and tax consumers which now forms the opposition to the royal government in England. The executive government in this province, from its highest officer to its lowest and most ignoble minion, can ill conceal the hatred they bear to his Majesty's Ministers in England. The host of court locusts and servile parasites who swarm in this colony are in terror lest a moderate reform in England and *union of sentiment* among the colonists should be the means of putting a stop to their cruel rapacity.

This faction, though contemptible in numbers, are from necessity united in their efforts, and will stir up against you every private, personal, local and partial interest. They are accustomed to dictate and you blindly to obey. On this habit of blind obedience they depended in the last session of parliament and a majority of your representatives (so called) were generally the registrars of their mandates. It remains to be seen whether you, in your towns and townships, will manifest the same passiveness to oppression.

It is probable that out of a population of 230,000 souls a sufficient number may now be found in Upper Canada of independent and industrious inhabitants seeking nothing but equal justice for all, and the protection and benefit of good government, peace and public prosperity, to check the abuses of men in power, say at least *a majority* out of forty or fifty thousand qualified electors. They have the means of putting everything to rights under the present constitution; but *they must unite as one man, banishing all national, religious and local distinctions*, suppressing as much as possible all views of partial and personal interests, and insist upon their natural right to have a government as free as possible from sinister designs and distinctions acting solely for the peace and welfare of the country.

To pay off your debt and interest, to provide for the *real wants* of your government, and the necessary expenses of your country which cannot be provided for by the classes and individuals more immediately benefitted by the present system, you will have to insist—

1st. On having the control by your representatives, of all monies whatsoever coming into the hands of government, whether arising from Crown Lands, from Taxes or Duties.

2nd. On having the control over all local assessments, taxes or rates in your several localities, by the vote of the qualified electors at their town meetings.

3rd. You ought to insist on an equal representation of the qualified electors in the House of Assembly.

4th. You ought to vote for no man who will not pledge himself publickly to the Electors to support these principles by every constitutional means, as a member of the Assembly, in the event of his being elected: to allow of no preferences or exclusive privileges to any denomination; and to insist on a full control over all public money, to vote none of it but in consideration of a fair equivalent rendered to the Province.

5th. You ought to insist on a reduction of all law expenses, and the exaction of no fees the tariff of which is not established by an act of the provincial legislature.

6th. It appears by late authentic accounts that the Independence of the Judges is agreed to in England; but it is your bounden duty to insist on the establishment of a court for the trial of impeachments. Even if no better were obtained than the present Legislative Council composed as it now is, the terror of a public accusation by your representatives to be succeeded by a public trial for delinquency in his judicial station, would often deter a corrupt and partial judge from high-handed acts of oppression and cruelty in which he otherwise might be apt to indulge.

7th. You ought to insist on the regulation BY LAW of the land-granting system, and THE ABOLITION OF ALL RESERVES otherwise than for Education and Roads and Bridges.

If those among you who live by their honest industry will only set their minds on these things, and undeviatingly, quietly, and constitutionally insist upon them on all occasions, you will soon have all your reasonable desires fulfilled, and be indebted for your success to yourselves, the only power from which you can permanently obtain true freedom, and which alone can secure a just and good government, at least equal to any that falls to the lot of humanity.

In conclusion—permit me to congratulate you upon the quiet and undisturbed enjoyment of the unspeakable advantages attending a free and fearless periodical press. When this journal first saw the light many there were who doubted whether Upper Canada possessed public spirit and intelligence enough to appreciate the value of a free discussion of public affairs. The experiment has been made in its widest latitude and public opinion is triumphant.

W. L. MACKENZIE.

What is chiefly wanted to consolidate and preserve British institutions and British principles in all her North American Colonies is Education. All reforms in government must begin by enlightening the people themselves. Our church and state government is exerting its utmost force to keep them in darkness; its colleges, its prelates, its district schools, its boards of education, all, all have one distinct tangible object in view; the very same object for which in darker ages "seats of learning" were founded by priests and tyrants—namely, to impart to "the chosen few" a sufficient fund of knowledge by which they might afterwards be enabled to rule over their more ignorant brethren. Therefore, my friends, encourage Education in every township, and seek not to put off the teacher of skill, talent and moral character, with a miserable pittance, but reward him liberally. COLONIAL ADVOCATE, 2 June 1831.

WHEAT AND BACON

TO THE FARMERS OF YORK COUNTY

Farmers of York County, we have news for you.

LISTEN!

Last winter the Merchants and Millers, gave you high prices for your Wheat and Flour—they expected to have the same protection in duties against United States competition in June when making sales in Montreal as they had had by law in January when making purchases. Some of them borrowed at the bank to enable them the better to give you a high price—others employed their own ample means.

They will sustain heavy losses. And Why?

Not from the natural fall of the markets, but because a Law appears in last Thursday's Gazette of the following extraordinary character; a law too of which they had no warning, and which takes effect instantly—nay even before it was published:

This act authorizes the Americans to import into Upper and Lower Canada, *duty free*, for domestic use or export, American Flour, American Wheat, American Oats and Oatmeal, American Barley, also Indian Corn, and Cornmeal, American Live Stock, American Beef and Pork, American Hams and Bacon, American Lumber or Wood.

It also authorizes American Flour, Beef, Pork, Hams, Bacon, and Wood or Lumber, when imported into Upper or Lower Canada, to be from thence exported to the British West Indies, Bermuda, and the Bahama Islands, there to be received duty free.

But the new act does more than all this: it not only allows the Americans to harass, ruin and discourage our merchants and millers by bringing immense quantities of American produce into competition with the produce of Upper Canada in our own markets, while they refuse us leave to go to theirs, but also, according to the interpretation of the Custom House at Montreal, permits Americans to come here, erect flouring mills on the British side of the St. Lawrence, on the Welland Canal (made by our money for their use), or any where else in Canada, and there grind American flour, duty free, and then export it to England, our principal Market, *there to be received on equally favourable terms with the flour of this British Colony.*

The writer of this article addressed a letter to the Office of the Government on Saturday last, desiring a copy of the opinion of the crown officers in order that it might be ascertained whether they coincided in opinion with the Montreal Custom House. We regret that it has not been suitable for the authorities to enable us to give their interpretation publicity this week.

Some of the effects of the act may be:

1. To give increased value to property on the south shores of

Erie and Ontario, and to depress its value on this side. Millions of bushels will be raised in places in the west where never a bushel was raised before.

2. To drive speculators out of the purchasing market here, ruin or greatly discourage last year's buyers, and unless some favourable accident happen, bring the bushel of wheat to half a dollar. It is now dull at 3s. 9d.

3. Those who have purchased farms in the expectation of getting a dollar for their wheat will be deceived.

4. Flour which has generally kept about $1 to $1½ a barrel higher in the Montreal Market than in New York for years back, will fall like a shot. Even now instead of the common summer value of $7 or $8 it is dull at $5. The Americans can make the same use of the Lower Canada market with ourselves, and supply their ample domestic demand and foreign trade besides.

5. One of these days we will have American cargoes of Oats, Pork, Corn and Barley, free in the York market, to undersell our constituents of Markham, who pay a sterling shilling bounty to the East India Company on each pound of tea they drink, which the Americans do not.

6. These measures will help the Americans to pay their taxes easier than before, and oblige government to double ours, for Jonathan is cute and will look to his own interest.

7. The Yankees will take all the money out of the country—they will undersell us, and *for cash* only—and the money sent from England to purchase flour will get into their hands, to impoverish us as the reward of the loyalty of the last half century. Our revenue will be lessened.

And who is to blame for all this?

Solemnly and sincerely do we reply—THE GOVERNMENT OF THIS COLONY, and not that of England. Parliament after parliament and session after session have they cruelly and wantonly trampled under feet bills sent from the Assembly appointing commissioners to treat with the commissioners which L. Canada had appointed by law to treat and consider of duties, trade, and all matters of mutual importance. Yes, even, when last winter, Messrs. McLean, Berczy, and Gordon were named, they could not trust them. And when any of our Executive gentlemen went to London it was to get pensions, places, grants, and favours for themselves and their friends, and not to look to Upper Canada interests.

And what has Lower Canada, and the West Indies, and United States interests been about?

The United States had a polite, manly and accomplished commercial agent in their Minister, Mr. McLane of Delaware; the West Indians by their agents, of which each island has one, were indefatigable; Lower Canada will rather gain by the new law, for she is a trading colony; to us alone, to Upper Canada, the measure is as hideous as it has been sudden.

One Question more—What is the remedy both for the past and the future?

This we will consider of until the time of the township meetings —and we hope our readers will do so also. We mean to attend every meeting. COLONIAL ADVOCATE, 7 July 1831.

PUBLIC MEETINGS

TO THE PEOPLE OF YORK COUNTY

Mr. Mackenzie respectfully acquaints his constituents that he considers these public meetings highly expedient at the present time, and that it is his intention to meet the people at each of these places on the days above named, to consult with them for their interest upon subjects connected with the general welfare; to learn their opinions, desires and intentions respecting future road appropriations, the late British Act authorizing American produce to be brought free into Canada, the duty on salt, the condition of courts of law, the collecting and applying assessed taxes in the district, the expediency of further augmenting the provincial burthens by loans to the Welland Canal Company and for War Losses, and the best means of promoting education and obtaining the control of the whole revenue to the country, as well as of putting a stop to the sale of public lands in a secret manner and of obtaining the passage of laws for their future regulation.

Mr. Mackenzie is aware that the present is a busy season of the year; but it will certainly be to the full as inconvenient for him to leave home for nearly a month as for the farmers to ride each to a place of meeting in his own township and return the same afternoon; and Mr. M. considers the present time highly favourable for a general application to His Majesty's government for the practical recognition of those invaluable rights and privileges, for the advocacy of which on their behalf the freeholders of the Home District have repeatedly left their homes at most inconvenient seasons of the year to secure his return to the Provincial Legislature.

Lower Canada has gained much because her people and those they trusted have been united and consistent, and spirited in their exertions.—Lower Canada has this year sent the Hon. Mr. Viger to London as the agent of its Legislature, with petitions for the removal of the remaining obstructions to the public prosperity. Mr. Mackenzie had several interviews with Mr. Viger, at Quebec last spring, and has been authorized by that gentleman to state to the people of Upper Canada that he earnestly desires their happiness and would, if requested by them, use his utmost efforts while in London, to obtain a full recognition of the principles of the constitution of 1791.

The petition of many thousands of the people of this Province, to Great Britain, against the upholders of spiritual tyranny, has been placed in the hands of Mr. Hume, long the able and disinterested advocate of your rights, in the British Senate; and the advantage you are likely to derive from Mr. Ryerson's extensive local knowledge of the country, its wants and wishes, is evidently great.

If you can agree upon general principles to be maintained by the agents you may appoint in London, I am well satisfied that his Majesty's Government will exert its utmost powers to fulfil your just and reasonable requests; your king's noble efforts on behalf of your brethren in England, Ireland, and Scotland, are an earnest that you have in him a firm and powerful friend.

Your enemies continue to represent you to the British Government as perfectly indifferent to your own welfare, ignorant of your own best interests, and so phlegmatic as to be disposed to lose even now a third of your summer's labour to your active eagle-eyed neighbours beyond Lake Ontario, rather than take the trouble to walk or ride three or four miles to attend a town meeting called by most respectable inhabitants among you for your good. I trust the result on the present occasion will as much disappoint them as did your late elections. There are those in York who have boasted that executive dependants and base sycophants enough will be found in York to vote down any useful measure that may be proposed at the town meeting on Saturday next, and to frighten the farmers and mechanics from attending it. If there are, let them come forward in the face of the country and shew themselves, in order that the true character of York township may be made more fully known. The present proceedings are not done in a corner, nor in secret; and if Dr. Strachan and the executive council of Upper Canada can bring forward in any one township a majority of inhabitants who will say that they approve of his and their public conduct, they are hereby invited and challenged to do so now, or else admit to the whole world what we believe to be a solemn truth, namely, that public opinion is universally against them—because they have contemned and utterly disregarded its salutary admonitions.

There are those doubtless who fear the ignorance of the people of Upper Canada; I, on the other hand, stand more in dread of rulers like ours who are virtually independent of them. The people have an interest in good government, but the rulers have a gain by misrule. COLONIAL ADVOCATE, 14 July 1831.

AFTER HIS SECOND EXPULSION

TO THE ELECTORS OF THE COUNTY OF YORK

Gentlemen!—A vacancy having again occurred in the Representation for your County in the House of Assembly, I have the honour to inform you that I intend being a Candidate for your suffrages at the ensuing election, which is, I understand, to be held at the Red Lion Tavern on Yonge Street, on the 30th instant.

The House of Assembly have taken the trouble to express and record their opinion, that I am unfit and unworthy to hold a seat in this present Parliament; and if you have confidence in the judgment and conduct of a majority of the members, their sentiments thus gratuitously promulgated, will doubtless have due weight with you. The constitution, however, leaves the choice of a Representative to watch over your interests in the Legislature, in your own hands, and not to the discretion of a majority of the members for other sections of the Province.

A foolish and groundless report having been circulated, that the House had disqualified or attempted to disqualify your late Member from being again elected or taking his seat in case he should, as I trust he will, receive a majority of your suffrages, I beg leave to contradict it. Equally unfounded is the rumour that a candidate having a minority of your suffrages can be elected or sit in the Legislature.

Twice, in England, in the last century, was it attempted by the House of Commons to introduce the principle that persons chosen by the minority of the electors might sit and represent the interests of the majority, but the good sense of the nation speedily reversed the decision, and probably for ever.

AFTER HIS SECOND EXPULSION

It is expected that the present Session will terminate in a few days. I think it would be for the interests of the Province at large that the present members should never meet again in their corporate capacity, and trust that every constitutional means will be resorted to by the country in order to obtain another choice.

I remain, Gentlemen,

Your Faithful Humble Servant,

WILLIAM L. MACKENZIE

York, January 13, 1832.

COLONIAL ADVOCATE, 19 January 1832.

FOR A TOWN MEETING

AN APPEAL TO THE PEOPLE

It is with feelings of sorrow and regret I now address you; deeply deploring the unhappy course pursued by men high in authority in this country; their neglect of your humble petitions and remonstrances, their continued violation of your rights and privileges; and their unwillingness to identify themselves and their actions with your opinions, or to promote the objects of your dearest wishes.

Although, during the administration of Sir Peregrine Maitland, you had been subjected to much disquiet, and the country greatly disturbed and agitated by powerful and oft repeated attempts to interfere with your civil and religious privileges, you fondly hoped that his successor would have profited by the errors of the past, and listened to your humble but earnest prayers for the peaceable enjoyment of those inestimable advantages intended to be secured to you and your children after you under the constitution, solemnly guaranteed to you by the British Nation.

Your reasonable expectations have unfortunately not been fulfilled. His Excellency Sir John Colborne has listened to the advice and been guided by the counsels of the same men who led his predecessor from the onward path of political rectitude; your wishes have been slighted, and this fine country kept in a state of continual fever and irritation. Your best, your truest friends, whose services in the cause of rational duly restraind freeedom have been long and disinterestedly continued, in the face of the world; to whom you confide your dearest interests, and who are bound by every tie of honour, friendship and gratitude to promote your happiness; even

201

they are slandered, persecuted, insulted and degraded; their feelings wounded, and their usefulness impaired. Public opinion, clearly expressed, is set at defiance, and fundamental principles of the constitution openly violated.

The consequences of such a state of things all good men must lament; and I now call upon you to arise, bestir yourselves, and manifest to the world the high value you set upon the blessings attendant on a state of enlightened constitutional freedom. Your loyalty to your government, your ardent affection for your sovereign, your love of order and hatred of tyranny, have been too often and too well proved to admit of a doubt. But it is not for men who glory in the name of Britons to slumber at their posts when the fortress of the constitution is invaded, the freedom of the press endangered, and the rights of the electors of Upper Canada to a true and faithful representation in the councils of their country trampled on.

Up then and be doing! I hope all the independent inhabitants whom this Address may reach, young and old, whether they be landowners or not landowners, who feel themselves animated by the pure spirit of liberty, will assemble in this Town in front of the Court House on Thursday the Nineteenth instant, at noon, in order that due force may be given to public opinion, and measures devised, in concert with every other section of Upper Canada, for the maintenance and protection of your rights, and the speedy redress of your just complaints.

Remember that union, prudence and great forbearance are indispensable to your success. Your cause is good, your weapons therefore must be those of truth and conscious rectitude. Every act of the King's life is a fresh guarantee to you that his exalted justice will be extended the moment your complaints are known.

The high character of the present faithful and capable ministry; and the enlightened and honourable policy they pursue towards your brethren in Britain and in Lower Canada, are an earnest of what may be expected from their sense of your wrongs when your petitions and remonstrances reach England. In them be assured, you have prompt, energetic, efficient friends.

Let us then unite our efforts to defeat the sinister designs of those men who seem desirous to use their power, both here and in England to goad on this loyal nation to the very edge of the revolutionary precipice, if thereby they could a little longer contrive to retain a control over the people's dear won earnings. Let us be firm and patient, but persevering and determined. So shall the people of this lovely province be placed in the enviable condition of the most free and favoured spots of the vast dominions of the British Crown. CANADIANS! The objects for which this general meeting has been called, are threefold:

1. To address His Majesty and the Imperial Parliament on the present unhappy situation of public affairs.

2. To consider whether it would be expedient, under existing circumstances, to Address his Excellency the Lieutenant-Governor, requesting him to dissolve this parliament and call a new one.

3. To appoint delegates to carry authentic copies of the proceedings to the several districts, and invite the concurrence and active co-operation of the whole country therein.

The Special Committee will go more fully into details in their Address to you.

PEOPLE OF CANADA! Your cause is not the cause of one man or of one particular class of men, but of the whole country. The fate of the County of York to-day may be the fate of any other County tomorrow. An act of injustice to one man or body of men, is an act of injustice to the community of which he or they are members. Much excitement prevails in the country, and the minds of men are greatly disturbed and agitated. The provocations you receive from the high handed acts of men in the possession of delegated power are exceedingly irritating. But these provocations must be borne with patience, in order to avoid far greater evils. You have right on your side; you have faithful and trusty men at the helm of affairs in the parent state; you have a true hearted and paternal sovereign in William the Fourth, a king who anxiously desires to know and fulfil his people's wishes, and has deservedly obtained a high place in their affections; the excellent example, too, of Lower Canada, ought to stimulate us to new constitutional exertions. Never give up the ship! Victory awaits prudence and perseverance!

Courage then, noble Canadians! Pour forth your gallant and faithful population upon this capital on Thursday next; and heartily unite in seeking a constitutional remedy for your many wrongs. But see that ye subdue every passionate and angry feeling, forgetting personal injuries and burying all resentments and animosities against the men who have worked all this mischief. Pity their infatuation, but harm them not. Consider that man your enemy and the enemy of your free institutions who shall be guilty of the least act of violence himself, or found encouraging or abetting acts of violence in others. Let not even the appearance of intemperance be seen among you; it is a degrading and most unseemly vice.

The privilege you possess of meeting together in your primary assemblies to consult upon matters of national interest is itself a glorious badge of British Freedom. The right to embody your desires and opinions in petitions and remonstrances, can only be preserved by men who set a proper value upon it.

In conclusion: allow me to remind you that the eyes of the world are directed towards the Colonial possessions of Great Britain. The conduct and the actions of your haughty opponents are carefully watched and scrupulously weighed. Prove yourselves then worthy of your nation by a conduct void of offence towards God and towards man; and look steadily forward to a bright and glorious day of public and private felicity to your beloved country, as the reward of your manly virtue.

That Canada and England may long continue united in the bonds of kindness, mutual friendship and forbearance and good government; and that the crown he so worthily wears may flourish for many years on the head of our revered sovereign, will be the earnest prayer of every true friend of British Freedom, to the King of Kings.

Wm. L. MACKENZIE.

York, January 12, 1832.

COLONIAL ADVOCATE, 19 January 1832.

LEGAL WEAPONS

Let a requisition be signed by a number of reformers in whom the liberal party of the County of York have confidence, let it be printed and widely circulated, calling upon the inhabitants of the several towns in the county friendly to liberal principles, to meet in their several towns and choose three delegates in each town, to meet in county convention at the Old District Court House, York, on a certain day to be then stated, for the appointment of one or more delegates to represent the county in the Provincial Convention to be held at York on the — day of —, and for the nomination of fit persons to be supported by the people as members for the county at the next general election, as also for the transaction of such other business as they may deem expedient, such as petitioning, addressing their fellow-citizens, etc.

Let four or five leading reformers in each township cause notices to be stuck up and information given to the friends of popular rights to meet at a central place and time to be named to choose two, three, or more delegates to the county convention to be held at York, on the — day of —.

Through these proceedings, the sense of the reformers will be obtained, an extensive and useful correspondence established, public opinion concentrated, and idle and offensive persons prevented from intruding themselves and disturbing the meetings, as they would be apt to do if the scheme of political unions were fully persisted in.

The Reformers are to be known by their principles, which are, the control of the whole revenue to be in the people's representatives, the legislative council to be elective, the representation in the House of Assembly to be as equally proportioned to the population as possible; the executive government to incur a real responsibility— the law of primogeniture to be abolished—the principle of Mr. Perry's Jury Bill to be adopted—the Judiciary to be independent— the military to be in strict subordination to the civil authority— equal rights to the several members of community—every vestige of church and state union to be done away—the lands and all the revenues of the country to be under the control of the country— and education to be widely, carefully, and impartially diffused. To these I would add that we ought to choose our own governors, but I know that there are some reformers who have not made up their minds upon that question. I therefore advise that it be not pressed.

It must not discourage the Reformers of any township if they happen to find themselves in the minority as compared to the other inhabitants. Let them meet, few and small as they may be, and observe the above usages, the same as if they counted thousands. Time which does much is in their favour—they may be sure that Upper Canada will form no exception to the other parts of this continent, liberal principles must prevail—freedom is indigenous in our soil. A NEW ALMANACK, 1834, p. 19.

THE NEW CITY CHARTER

To the Citizens of Toronto.

My Friends:

I went willingly along with you in petitioning against the city charter in its present form, but as our memorials were disregarded and an act of incorporation passed into a law, I think our best course of proceeding would be to make united exertions from now until the close of the polls next week to place the civic government in the hands of a score of our most trustworthy reformers—sincere advocates of public improvement, yet disposed to be as careful of the public money as they would be of their own—friends also of justice mixed with mercy. The high church tories in Lower Canada cried lustily for city corporations to Montreal and Quebec, thinking they could bribe, treat, cajole or bamboozle the Canadians to throw away their votes, just as the Liverpool and other rotten borough freemen had often done for the like bait. But it would not do. The Citizens took the management of their affairs into their own hands, they were incorruptible; and as they began so have they continued. I need only advert to the late proceedings of the House of Assembly as an example to warn you to be careful to whom you commit the important trusts to be vested in those persons who shall be selected as your first magistrates, and as an inducement to you to afford the surest proofs of your fitness for free institutions by the choice of a discreet and prudent city council.

Some of the *worst* features of the incorporation act are, the unnatural union of extensive patronage with legislative, judicial, and executive powers in the same body of Individuals, without any adequate check to prevent the natural disposition of man to abuse power for his own advantage—the property qualification required from the elected—the power to raise five times the amount of the present taxes during the first year and also to borrow and spend perhaps foolishly within the same time, a sum equal to the whole probable revenue of the ensuing five years; such a course may end in bringing the town property to the hammer—the absence of that excellent friend to peace and order the Ballot Box—the giving one alderman two votes and the others only one—the withholding from the respectable citizens the power to choose their mayor—the changing a name for the city by which it had been known for thirty years, (altho' I do not dislike its new appellation,)—the absence of systematic checks to insure faithful returns at elections of aldermen, etc.; and the power given to arrest and summarily to inflict a disgraceful punishment on certain classes of alleged offenders without the shield of a jury. These defects, however, and many others, might be got over by the honest resolution and determination of the people themselves to choose careful moderate men to exercise power under the act. Bribery and corruption they should set their faces against; and the poor man should remember that if he votes carelessly or corruptly next Thursday, even those who profit by his imprudence will quote the return as a proof of the utter incapacity of the humbler classes to enjoy a share of the blessings of representative government.

This letter is written with a view to afford a more brief and popular explanation of the act than would be given by quoting a mere literal copy. I shall be amply rewarded for the trouble I have taken if I find that my suggestions have in some cases proved useful to those whose time is occupied in pursuits which leave less opportunity for study and reflection.

.   .   .

Hitherto the government of Upper Canada has legislated too much for its members, and too little for the people. It is chiefly upon the diffusion of sound political knowledge that the granting of political power is rendered safe. My object in writing this letter is to contribute all I can to the common stock of information upon the subject of the new incorporation. ADVOCATE, 20 March 1834.

GENERAL MEETING

TO THE MECHANICS AND LABOURERS
OF TORONTO

FELLOW CITIZENS!

Remember that when the tory members were passing the Incorporation Act for the disposal of your liberties and property, (in spite of your petitions,) they boasted and exulted that its very severe provisions would speedily crush what they called "the refractory disposition" of the "ruffian rabble" below their bar. They hated you for your free, manly independent spirit, for you were always on the side of justice, always for fair play. They looked on an "unwashed mechanic" as if he were a being of a different species, a degraded, inferior race or caste solely created for their menial service. I have carefully considered the incorporation bill, and am free to admit that its powers to fine, imprison, disgrace, injure and oppress the citizens, to assess and tax and involve them in difficulty and distress, would, if placed in the hands its makers intended, be a dreadful scourge to us "common people". But I bid you keep in memory that, if to the tail of a foolish and extravagant tory parliament, there were to be added a curse of tenfold magnitude in the shape of a wicked profligate vindictive tory corporation, *it would all be your doings.*

In you is the power over the fortunes of the city vested, and according as the majority of you shall now decide will be the character and bearing of our future rulers. The tories tell continually of your "ignorance, selfishness, habits of subjection and want of union"; they call you "rabble" and trust that you will act as if you were such. They may find out their mistake! The reformers of Upper Canada expect you to come forward like men and *like freemen*—they confide fully in your intelligence, judgment and integrity—and are convinced that you will not allow the powers of the city to fall into the hands of men who desire to convert it into a "Stanley coercion bill" on a small scale. I have been informed that the tories are greatly alarmed lest you get wakened up and become aware that your voices can turn the scale against them, and it is said that they have prevailed on Sir John to help them to steal a march upon you; and, instead of waiting for three months, to hurry on the city elections next Thursday week! Let them come on! I trust "the common people," whom they have insulted and benefited by, will be prepared for them. I will endeavour to give a plain account of the bill in Thursday's Advocate; and as it is the duty of every good citizen to contribute his share to the common fund of information I will afterwards print and distribute a thousand extras, through the five wards. Meantime I consider it of *very great importance* that the mechanics and labourers of the city and liberties should hold a general preliminary meeting to give the act a careful consideration, so that it may be made to work the best for the general advantage; and for this purpose I invite you to assemble, in as great numbers as possible, *at the Old King's Bench Court House* in St. David's Ward, on *Wednesday evening* the 19th inst., at half past six o'clock, when ward committees of vigilance can be formed, and ward meetings arranged and provided for.

There is an old anecdote about Doctor Johnson that he would not allow Scotland to derive any credit from Lord Mansfield, for he was educated in England. Much, said the doctor, may be made of a Scotsman if he be *caught* young. So it is with the incorporation bill. The tories deserve no credit for any thing good in it, for it was not intended, but I am well convinced that much may be made of it "if it be caught young". To the Chase then—Onward!

Yours Faithfully
W. L. MACKENZIE
Town Warden

19 Richmond St., March 18, 1834

ADVOCATE, 20 March 1834.

A LETTER

TO THE MEMBERS OF THE
CANADIAN ALLIANCE BRANCH SOCIETIES

I have been unable to reply to the numerous letters you have sent me during the winter, and the *Correspondent and Advocate* has been so full of parliamentary proceedings, that there was not room for many extracts from your Resolutions. These omissions will now be made up, and every effort used to extend the number and increase the usefulness of institutions which even now exercise no mean influence on public opinion. I will hereafter regularly correspond with all the branches, and concert measures with you for the diffusion of useful knowledge through the country.

I have received within the last fortnight letters from our agent in London, with a pamphlet containing the petition of the H. of Assembly of Lower Canada, and a full statement of all their complaints, which very much resemble ours. It has been widely circulated in London and must have produced an excellent effect. Lord Brougham presented their petition in the House of Peers.

I am this season at leisure to attend to political matters—unfettered by civic duties as a magistrate or by the neverending labours as a public journalist,—and I intend to exert myself in giving effect as far as possible to the intentions of the representatives of the people in the Assembly. To this end your Societies can contribute greatly, and the result must be the removal of that great political nuisance, the Legislative Council, as now constituted, and the substitution of a Chamber in its stead, by the freeholders, and controllable by public opinion.

I have accepted the office of a Director of the Welland Canal Company on the part of the Province, for the year ending in April next, as voted by the House of Assembly, in order that I may be enabled to inform myself fully of the true state of that work, its management, its importance to the colony, and the best means of rendering available the vast sums already expended on it, and for which the property of the Province is holden.

It is a cause of gratulation that the Province by its Representatives, has at length expressed in decided terms a correct opinion of Sir John Colborne. I have watched his conduct narrowly during the winter, without allowing myself to express an opinion, and I am more and more convinced that the same equivocal character he has hitherto sustained in his messages, and the same decidedly hostile feelings he has all along manifested in his actions towards constitutional liberty, will remain unchanged till the hour when the country will cease to pay him $24,000 of salary for neglecting its true interests, and to his polite and well bred Private Secretary other $3,216 in fees and so forth, for promulgating his decrees.

The conduct of Sir John Colborne and the legislative council in the matter of the county of Leeds; the open resistance made to the efforts of the House of Assembly for the protection of the freeholders in the exercise of their right of voting, I shall make the subject of another letter. In the mean time be it remembered that Sir John and the Legislative Council are essentially one and the same—his power over the places and emoluments of the members of the council—his influence as the confidential adviser of the colonial office—can do every thing with this creation of the minister for the colonies—and stoutly has the battle been fought against the yeomanry, and in favour of riot, bloodshed, Gowan, Jameson and Beverley.

I refer to a letter I have written this day to the electors of the 2nd Riding of York, and remain,

Yours faithfully
W. L. MACKENZIE,
Corresponding Secretary.

CORRESPONDENT AND ADVOCATE, 23 April 1835.

WINTER READING

TO THE FARMERS

This is the season of the year in which you have the most spare time to read; and as upwards of ten thousand books and pamphlets have been printed within the last six months at the public expense, by order of the House of Assembly, chiefly for your information in matters in which you have a deep interest, I would recommend that you procure as many copies of the publications as possible, to read and circulate them from family to family, so that you may the better understand how that share of your business is conducted which you delegate once in four years to be transacted by others.

There is first, the Statutes passed this year; this publication will show you what improvements in the laws and usages of the colony the legislative council, a body which answers very much the description given in history of "the thirty tyrants" of Athens, have permitted your representatives to make. Of these Statutes, about thirty copies have long since been delivered to each Member of the Assembly.

Secondly, there is the Report on Grievances, a book nearly as big as the bible, of which the House caused 2000 copies to be printed, and of these, thirty were sent months ago to each member for circulation among the people.

Thirdly, there is a pamphlet containing sundry bills passed by the House of Assembly, which your "thirty tyrants" tomahawked, such as the trial by jury bill, the intestate estate bill, the bills to protect the people of Leeds County from the violence of Ogle Gowan and Attorney General Jameson's mobs, and so forth; of this pamphlet 1000 or 2000 copies have just been printed and circulated among the members for your use. This book and pamphlet will tell you what the government is doing with your money; what bills your "thirty tyrants" have burnt or otherwise destroyed, which you wished to preserve and become laws, and will give you much useful information concerning the causes which operate in preventing that prosperity from reaching you which so industrious a people as you are, blessed with a fine and fertile soil, have merited.

A fourth pamphlet, 2000 copies, will inform you of the manner in which the "thirty tyrants" proceed in their systematic efforts to destroy good legislative measures; I may as well add in this place, that besides the salaries of its officers fixed by law, and the places and pensions and salaries and other things, your property, which its members unjustly enjoy, the legislative council demanded out of the public chest last winter, for silk curtains, velvet for their throne, tassels, hangings, Turkey carpeting, chairs of state, perfumery, gilding for a crown to their throne, presents to their servants, douceurs to some of themselves, and decorations for their chambers, a sum of money equal to about twelve thousand dollars, and got it too without a murmur or even an enquiry, three out of every four of your sapient representatives sanctioning the act of plunder, of robbery I might say, but I like to use mild expressions. Some think that your money voted to buy books to the parliamentary library has gone the same way; I have made a noise about it, but as Sir John Colborne usually covers the delinquents in such matters, I had to give up the chase until next month, when if the cup be not found in Benjamin's sack, it is probable it will be in "Beverley's."

A fifth book is a Report on Banks and Currency, signed Charles

Duncombe. I was on the Committee but dissented from the report. I voted for printing 2000 copies, however, because it conveys useful information. Every one of your members of Assembly had thirty copies of it for distribution among you long ago. Ask them for it. While speaking of Banks, I may mention to you that I am neither agent, partner nor director in any of them; that I owe them nothing but good-will, and have no great disposition to be deeper in their debt. I, however, would warmly recommend to all who may consider my opinion of any weight to encourage by all lawful means the Bank of the People in this city [*advertised in this issue as just opened*], of which Dr. Rolph is the President, Mr. Speaker Bidwell and Mr. Price the Law Counsel, and Mr. Lesslie the Cashier. If I had thousands to spare I would willingly deposit them with that institution or take stock; I like the principles on which it is founded, and above all, I admire the judicious selection of its directors and managers. By encouraging the circulation of its paper, by depositing monies in its vaults, by transacting business with it, and seeking its prosperity, the friends of cheap and good government will, in my opinion, be doing much to accelerate the triumph of that practical reform in Upper Canada. The notes also of the Bank of the People, an institution located at Montreal, deserve the utmost confidence—its proprietors are your friends.

A sixth book is called "the third Report of the Committee on Finance," and contains 128 octavo pages, with the celebrated resolution sent to London as the sentiments of the Assembly concerning the public moneys, the Canada Company, etc. It also contains a list of the commissioners who received £20,000 by the act of 1832, and £25,000 by the act of 1833, to lay out in improving the roads and bridges, many of whom appear to have drawn the money and forgotten to apply it to the public service, while others who expended a part have omitted to account for any of it. Two thousand of these books will give thirty to each member, and by perusing and circulating them you will make known who the defaulters are, and be enabled to spur up your representatives to the early appointment of such a searching committee on public monies as I tried to get established on the second day of last session, when I was supported by only one member. None to your profit was that vote as I shall prove to you when the proper season comes, which will be when we have borrowed and fooled away a few more hundreds of thousands. You throw away your money and your credit on that which brings nothing back—you are borrowing now in London to pay the interest there on the loans you had borrowed before—you entrust immense sums to knaves and sharpers, as I shall have occasion to prove when discussing the proceedings of certain incorporations in the course of a few days; and as sure as such a course of conduct would bring a family to poverty so sure will it bring a province to bankruptcy if not arrested by more prudent and judicious behaviour than either the legislative or executive authorities have as yet exhibited. Much of the evil can be readily traced to the operation of that moral pestilence, that worst of all official nuisances the legislative council as now constituted; and I rejoice that many of you who were long in the dark, now see this dangerous body as I have long seen it.

The Assembly's seventh publication I have just received; it is the new act relative to the appointment and duties of Township Officers. Like the others I have named it ought to be in the hands of the people, because they will be required to give effect to its precepts next townmeeting day; and the alterations from the former code of laws are many, important, and often very beneficial. It is also to be found in the Statutes of the last Session. One of its most valuable clauses was struck out by "the thirty tyrants," but they left much that was good untouched, and I do hope you will hasten to take advantage of their unusual neglect. On enquiry at the Clerk of Assembly's office, I learn that 15 copies have been sent to each Member by mail within a few days; and I hope before long to see every township in the colony choosing its Justices of the Peace, and selecting by the ballot vote its postmaster or postmasters.

I have just returned from a long journey in Lower Canada, and my time during the summer has been employed profitably in an investigation of the Welland Canal, in which £500,000 of your money is invested or at least, supposed to be.

Had I had leisure I would have visited many of you in your townships, according to my custom, especially the farmers of the Home District to whose manly independence, and firm and spirited proceedings I owe obligations not to be repaid. I do not forget my promise to the Riding I am more immediately connected with, but am as yet unable to make it good, by a tour thro' Toronto, Albion, Chinguacousy, etc.

We may look forward to the coming Session of the Legislature with hope and expectation. Every day last winter the House of Assembly became more and more unanimous in its efforts to obtain for the people their just weight in the scale of government. I trust those Members who were tried and found faithful have been made to feel that they acted for an intelligent and grateful constituency, and that they will return to this city, next month, animated with those ennobling feelings of patriotism which would serve to gladden the heart and better the condition of every good Canadian. There are yet many glorious days and years in store for Canada; let us seek for those things only which are just and true, and then may we expect that that great power whose attributes are "justice, goodness and truth," will be with and about us to counsel and direct our steps in the path of true happiness. CORRESPONDENT AND ADVOCATE, 3 December 1835.

RELIGIOUS FREEDOM

TO THE FIFTEEN HUNDRED PETITIONERS TO THE HOUSE OF ASSEMBLY OF THE DENOMINATION CALLED "CHRISTIANS"

FRIENDS AND NEIGHBOURS,

I duly received and faithfully attended to your Petitions for leave to your Preachers to solemnize matrimony among your people the same as other denominations; you and they acknowledging the Scriptures of the Old and New Testaments as the rule of your faith and practice. A Bill to grant all you wished for was brought into the Legislature, by a committee composed of Messrs. Gilchrist, Thorburn, Durand, Macintosh and myself, and passed and sent up to Sir Francis Head's dearly-beloved Legislative Council, who treated it with the utmost contempt, and threw it under their table.

Remember that this same Sir Francis Head; these same Legislative Councillors, and the Robinsons, Browns, Boultons, Macnabs, and others, the minority of the last parliament; and the Drapers, Ruttans, Jarvises, etc. who seek to get into the House to harass the majority in the next, are bolstering up the established Church of England—and that while your ministers and your religion are ridiculed, 57 rectories, 15 pensions, and a seventh of Upper Canada are being bestowed on the parasites of one sect to chain it to the wheels of the chariot of the State—remember too, that the Royal Instructions to Sir Francis enjoin tythes to be levied for that church, that a frail local bill is all that is betwixt you and the bayonet of the soldier at the back of the tythe-proctor, and that nothing but a reforming House of Assembly can save you from that curse of England and Ireland, which has caused so much bloodshed.

Up then and be doing—be the friends of those who are the friends of peace!—put down toryism by your votes at the hustings!—and by upholding reform and free institutions, contribute towards the great cause of civil and religious liberty, soon and signally to prosper in this our country.

I remain,
Your Faithful Servant,
W. L. MACKENZIE

CORRESPONDENT AND ADVOCATE, 15 June 1836.

LABOUR
THE TRUE SOURCE OF WEALTH

TO THE PEOPLE OF THE COUNTY OF YORK

MY FRIENDS!

Many a time have you told your fellow citizens in other parts of the province, by your selection of the humble individual who now addresses you, as your representative, and by your petitions to the King of Great Britain and his Parliament, and also to the Assembly here, that you were fearful that the paper dollar system would explode and injure thousands who placed their dependence on it. It is exploding, and the Colonial despotism will go with it. Had it not been for the paper money lords the people of the Canadas would at this day have been free and independent.

One of our most influential inhabitants called on me last Saturday and wished that I would state my opinion as to the best course to be pursued by the people in order to rescue the province from impending ruin. I instantly replied—"A Convention of the people of the two Provinces."

I was then required to reply to the following query, and to state the reasons on which my opinion was founded, through the press. I hasten to do so.

"Will the breaking of the Banks be an injury or a blessing to the country?"

Perhaps there is no one subject on which the people of America have laboured under a greater delusion than on that of Banks, Exchanges, and the instrument of Exchange, Bank Notes.

Labour is the true source of wealth.

The Farmer produces Wheat—the Miller converts it into Flour—the Labourer breaks Stones and Macadamizes Roads and these roads with the aid of Steamers and Boats convey the Flour to the place where the Foreigner will buy it at the highest price. The owner of the Flour receives his money, be it one thousand or ten thousand dollars—this is wealth; it was wealth before paper money was in existence—and I hope it will be so considered when a paper currency shall be no more.

To produce this wealth, the Farmer, the Miller, the Labourer, the Sailor, the Merchant, each contributes his share, by useful industry in an honest calling. The Weaver, too, and the Tailor, and the Shoemaker, and the Hatter, and the Smith, and the Waggon Maker, the Teamster, the Ship Carpenter, the Millwright, the Sawyer, the Mason, the House Carpenter, the Cooper, the School-master, and the Government lend their beneficial aid. The Farmer is up late and early, ploughing and sowing, and fulfilling the duties of a Husbandman—the Miller carefully prepares the grain for food—the Cooper curiously fashions and hoops the barrels which are to convey this food to the consumer—the labourer prepares the high-way for man's use, and toils with the Mason, the Smith and other craftsmen, powerfully assisting them by the strength of his arm and with the sweat of his brow—the Tailor, Hatter and Shoemaker clothe the body to preserve it from the inclemency of the weather or its too great heat, to keep the head from the cold of winter or the feverish excitement which might be produced by the heat of the summer's sun, and the feet comfortable under all the vicissitudes of the seasons—the steamer and schooner plough the sea or the lake to bear the food of man to the desired port—the merchant ships the produce, makes himself acquainted with the usages of other lands, their coins, their customs' duties, their most upright traders, ascertains who are the most trusty ship captains, what steamers or other vessels are the most sea-worthy, and the state of the markets—and the schoolmaster by his precept and example, and opening to the view of delighted and astonished youth the history of the past, endeavours to prepare them for enacting with honour, usefulness and integrity their respective parts in the work of this world, in which they are so soon to be called to take a share. Nor should I forget the Minister of Religion—he too is most useful, if he remind his fellow men at fit and convenient seasons, of the great and awful truth that they are but pilgrims and strangers here, seeking another and a better country, and looking forward to the enjoyment of happiness which this unstable world never can, never will afford.

In exhibiting the sources of wealth, I do not forget the important share of labour performed by woman. She is the nurse of infancy, a guardian in youth, a comforter in age and sickness. She prepares the food of man—she watches over his tender years—she preserves order and cleanliness through all her household—she smoothes down the asperities of life, and is the ornament alike of the palace and the cottage. . . .

I have now shewn the true source of a country's wealth—labour usefully and prudently applied—the result is national riches and individual prosperity. . . .

In what way are the services of a Bank, like the Bank of Upper Canada, the Kingston Bank, or any other institution issuing promises to pay gold and silver on demand in almost unlimited quantity, required to produce the wealth and prosperity I have shewn to be the result of labour and industry usefully applied?

In no way whatever. The country which charters such institutions, leaving their management to a few, privileging the managers for the partners to divide whatever share of their money or means they may choose to call profits, and to enforce payment of all debts due to them with usury, while they enable these partners to set all their joint creditors at defiance, which the members of private partnerships cannot do, the country which does this tempts the managers of these Banks to act partially, interestedly and dishonestly, and will sooner or later read its crime in its punishment.

.   .   .

Farmers of Upper Canada, depend on it you would be richer and happier, more wealthy and more contented and prosperous, were these vile Banking Associations swept from among you. They encourage and promote litigation, tax labour, cheat and defraud you out of the fruit of your industry, and are the infamous means of preventing your government from confining itself to its appropriate functions, the protection of life and property. In that way I have considered government (in the commencement of this letter) as useful, in compelling the obligation of civil contracts, preventing the strong from robbing the feeble, punishing the violent and lawless, enabling the industrious to labour in safety, and securing to him the fruit of his toil. . . .

The best course to pursue at this crisis would be to call *a Convention* of the people of Upper and Lower Canada, to devise means to rescue the country from its present distressed state. This course will very probably be taken when the true condition of England, after she has ascertained the late proceedings in the United States, shall have become known in America.

The mock parliaments of the colonial office do not represent the intelligence, wealth and population of Upper Canada. And if our assemblies were never so honest and capable, they are fettered. But a convention of the provinces, if properly attended, will be the salvation of our common country. Head and his folks have had trial enough now; their measures excite a mingled feeling of indignation, derision and contempt. Farmers and mechanics, you must look to yourselves—be honest and united and the day is won!

Your old and faithful servant

W. L. MACKENZIE

York Street, Toronto, May 22, 1837

THE CONSTITUTION, 24 May 1837.

SOCIETY IN
UNIVERSAL AGITATION

Canadians! It has been said that we are on the verge of a revolution. We are in the midst of one; a bloodless one, I hope, but a revolution to which all those which have been will be counted mere child's play. Calm as society may seem to a superficial spectator, I know that it is moved to its very foundations, and is in universal agitation. The question which is now debated, and to which entire humanity listens, is one which reaches infinitely further than the most celebrated of the questions heretofore debated. The question today is not between one reigning family and another, between one people and another, between one form of government and another, but a question between privilege and equal rights, between law sanctioned, law fenced in privilege, age consecrated privilege, and a hitherto unheard-of power, a new power just started from the darkness in which it has slumbered since creation day, *the Power of Honest Industry.* The strange name borne by this new-born power, may deceive some as to its strength and merits, but though they may deem it an infant, they may be assured they will find it a Herculean one. The contest is now between the privileged and the unprivileged, and a terrible one it is. The slave snaps his fetters, the peasant feels an unwonted strength nerve in his arm, the *people* rise in stern and awful majesty, and demand in strange tones their ever despised and hitherto denied rights. They rise and swear in a deep and startling oath that *Justice Shall Reign.* . . .

Not to this country and continent alone, nor chiefly, is this revolution confined. It reaches the old world. The millions down-

218

trodden for ages by kings, hierarchies, and nobilities, awake. Kings put their hands to their heads to feel if their crowns be there; hierarchies lash themselves and cry mightily unto Baal; nobilities tremble for their privileges; time-cemented and moss-covered state fabrics reel and totter; all who live on abuses seem to themselves to see the hand-writing on the walls of their palaces, and to feel *Every Thing Giving Way Beneath Them.*

Aye, and the puffed up, angry little creature, who sits perched upon a mahogany throne in a chamber up here in Toronto, playing the petty tyrant of an hour, might as well borrow Dame Partington's mop wherewith she sought to stay the ocean's swelling tide, as attempt to uphold the odious system of swindling, plunder, peculation and official robbery, whether by law or without it of which the many so deeply and bitterly complain. THE CONSTITUTION, 26 July 1837.

MEETINGS IN SUPPORT
OF PAPINEAU

Mr. Mackenzie presents his compliments to his brother Reformers in the several places for which Meetings of the people have been advertised in the *Correspondent and Advocate* and *Constitution* of last Wednesday, and expects to have the pleasure of being present at these meetings.

The following copy of the notices to which he refers ought to be widely circulated.

Public Meetings

The FREEMEN North of the Ridges, in YORK and SIMCOE, will hold Meetings on the following days, for the purpose of expressing their sympathy with Mr. Speaker Papineau and the brave and patriotic Inhabitants of Lower Canada, whose liberties are threatened with destruction by a profligate and treacherous whig ministry and a House of Commons who have repudiated those glorious principles which dictated the necessity of the late measure of British parliamentary reform.

It is then and there intended to choose Delegates to represent the interests and feelings of the people North of the Ridges in the Convention of the Canadas, soon to be held for the maintenance of

Justice and preservation of Constitutional Liberty;—to provide funds to defray their unavoidable expenses while in Convention— to enroll the names of all Reformers who desire to make common cause with the Friends of Freedom and Equal Rights throughout these colonies,—and to express that public opinion as to the measures of Sir Francis Head and his employers in the Colonial Office, which has not been, and dare not be expressed by the corrupt, bribed, purchased and pensioned bodies, most improperly denominated the provincial parliament.

[*Meetings called for Newmarket, Lloydtown, Albion, Caledon, Chinguacousy, Esquesing, Trafalgar, Churchville, Cooksville, East Toronto, Vaughan. Most of them attended by Mackenzie.*]

THE CONSTITUTION, 2 August 1837.

THE BANKS

TO THE LANDOWNERS OF THE COUNTY OF YORK

GENTLEMEN:

Last May I advised those among you who had the notes of the several Banks of this Province, or deposits of Gold and Silver in their vaults, to call and get specie, and take good care of it, as it would soon be a very scarce article—and I told you that the Banks neither would nor could continue to pay cash for their notes and other obligations, and that if you did not get the dollars the Montreal and New York Merchants would come and take them all away, and you would have to be content with worthless depreciated paper rags, the value of which no one would be certain of. Some took my advice—others abused me for giving it. If these latter have now on hand any notes of the Commercial Bank of the Midland District, they may consider them on a par with the vile Montreal trash with which Sir Francis Head's pet Bank, the Upper Canada, has flooded the colony, while the Baronet himself is mocking the sufferers by telling them that "the principle of monarchy is honour!" The Commercial, bankrupt before, has now parted with its last dollar, shut its door upon all its creditors, refused cash payments, and arrived at that meek and lowly condition in human affairs, in which to dishonour its drafts is no disgrace—for it has already paid out all it had to pay with. I think the Bank of Upper Canada must at no distant time follow suit, and how many more of them may qualify under the same act, is not yet absolutely known. There are many notes of the Agricultural Bank here in circulation payable in Montreal. I thought until lately that these were redeemed in that city in current money. Such, however, is not the case—they are only on a par with the uncurrent money afloat in Montreal, and paid in the notes of the Banks there, 100 dollars of whose paper is worth about 88 dollars in real money. The Farmers' Bank has begun to issue post notes, payable a year hence, without interest, and these, although really worth 6 per cent less than their nominal amount, pass readily in common transactions, the Bank itself also receiving them in payment of debts due at its counter.

The Banks here have a law in their favour, by which British silver sixpences, shillings and half-crowns will pass at a nominal value 11 to 14 per cent higher than their real worth as compared with any coin current by law in the United States. Even that ill-designed measure, which placed them on a par with the suspended New York Banks, cannot save them. They are unable even to pay in sixpences at 7½d. each!

In the late meetings, and in my newspaper, I told you that you had only begun to feel the hardness of the times—before the winter is over many of you will ascertain whether or not I am a true prophet. Those worthless characters who amidst the orgies of their lodge-rooms arranged plans by which they succeeded in disgracing some of your late public meetings, and the county itself, by conduct unbecoming a civilized country, and such as savages or even the brute creation would not have been guilty of, will probably find, that if they do not join with those who would oblige the government to act for the good of the governed, they will have to seek an asylum in our houses of industry or the land over the way from that "famine and pestilence" which follows Sir Francis, and of which they, the idlest and worst of our people, are not likely to miss their full share.

We will see whether 188 such outrageous, blood-thirsty characters as met at Churchville under the vile orange standard last August, will be as ready to turn out to bite their own noses off in August, 1838. Even fools learn sometimes in the school of experience.

Your faithful servant,

W. L. MACKENZIE

THE CONSTITUTION, 20 September 1837.

INDEPENDENCE

There have been Nineteen Strikes for Independence from European Tyranny, on the Continent of America. They were all successful! The Tories, therefore, by helping us will help themselves.

> The nations are fallen, and thou still art young,
> The sun is but rising when others have set;
> And tho' Slavery's cloud o'er thy morning hath hung,
> The full tide of Freedom shall beam round thee yet.

BRAVE CANADIANS! God has put into the bold and honest hearts of our brethren in Lower Canada to revolt—not against "lawful" but against "unlawful authority." The law says we shall not be taxed without our consent by the voices of the men of our choice, but a wicked and tyrannical government has trampled upon that law—robbed the exchequer—divided the plunder—and declared that, regardless of justice they will continue to roll their splendid carriages, and riot in their palaces, at our expense—that we are poor spiritless ignorant peasants, who were born to toil for our betters. But the peasants are beginning to open their eyes and to feel their strength —too long have they been hoodwinked by Baal's priests—by hired and tampered with preachers, wolves in sheep's clothing, who take the wages of sin, and do the work of iniquity, "each one looking to his gain in his quarter."

CANADIANS! Do you love freedom? I know you do. Do you hate oppression? Who dare deny it? Do you wish perpetual peace, and a government founded upon the eternal heaven-born principle of the Lord Jesus Christ—a government bound to enforce the law to do to each other as you would be done by? Then buckle on your armour, and put down the villains who oppress and enslave our country—put them down in the name of that God who goes forth with the armies of his people, and whose bible shows us that it is by the same human means whereby you put to death thieves and murderers, and imprison and banish wicked individuals, that you must put down, in the strength of the Almighty, those governments which, like these bad individuals, trample on the law, and destroy its usefulness. You give a bounty for wolves' scalps. Why? because wolves harass you. The bounty you must pay for freedom (blessed word) is to give the strength of your arms to put down tyranny at Toronto. One short hour will deliver our country from the oppressor; and freedom in religion, peace and tranquillity, equal laws and an improved country will be the prize. We contend, that in all laws made, or to be made, every person shall be bound alike—neither should any tenure, estate, charter, degree, birth or place, confer any exemption from the ordinary course of legal proceedings and responsibilities whereunto others are subjected.

CANADIANS! God has shown that he is with our brethren, for he has given them the encouragement of success. Captains, Colonels, Volunteers, Artillerymen, Privates, the base, the vile hirelings of our unlawful oppressors have already bit the dust in hundreds in Lower Canada; and although the Roman Catholic and Episcopal Bishops and Archdeacons, are bribed by large sums of money to instruct their flocks that they should be obedient to a government which defies the law, and is therefore unlawful, and ought to be put down, yet God has opened the eyes of the people to the wickedness of these reverend sinners, so that they hold them in derision, just as God's prophet Elijah did the priests of Baal of old and their sacrifices. Is there any one afraid to go to fight for freedom, let him remember, that

> God sees with equal eye, as Lord of all,
> A Hero perish, or a Sparrow fall.

That power that protected ourselves and our forefathers in the deserts of Canada—that preserved from the Cholera those whom He would—that brought us safely to this continent through the dangers of the Atlantic waves—aye, and who watched over us from infancy to manhood, will be in the midst of us in the day of our struggle for our liberties, and for Governors of our free choice, who would not dare to trample on the laws they had sworn to maintain. In the present struggle, we may be sure, that if we do not rise and put down Head and his lawless myrmidons, they will gather all the rogues and villains in the Country together—arm them—and then deliver our farms, our families, and our country to their brutality—to that it has come, we must put them down, or they will utterly destroy this country. If we move now, as one man, to crush the tyrant's power, to establish free institutions founded on God's law, we will prosper, for He who commands the winds and waves will be with us—but if we are cowardly and mean-spirited, a woeful and a dark day is surely before us.

CANADIANS! The struggle will be of short duration in Lower Canada, for the people are united as one man. Out of Montreal and Quebec, they are as 100 to 1—here we reformers are as 10 to 1—

223

and if we rise with one consent to overthrow despotism, we will make quick work of it.

Mark all those who join our enemies—act as spies for them—fight for them—or aid them—these men's properties shall pay the expense of the struggle—they are traitors to Canadian Freedom, and as such we will deal with them.

CANADIANS! It is the design of the Friends of Liberty to give several hundred acres to every Volunteer—to root up the unlawful Canada Company, and give *free deeds* to all settlers who live on their lands—to give free gifts of the Clergy Reserve lots, to good citizens who have settled on them—and the like to settlers on Church of England Glebe Lots, so that the yeomanry may feel independent, and be able to improve the country, instead of sending the fruit of their labour to foreign lands. The fifty-seven Rectories will be at once given to the people, and all public lands used for Education, Internal Improvements, and the public good. £100,000 drawn from us in payment of the salaries of bad men in office, will be reduced to one quarter, or much less, and the remainder will go to improve bad roads and to "make crooked paths straight;" law will be ten times more cheap and easy—the bickerings of priests will cease with the funds that keep them up—and men of wealth and property from other lands will soon raise our farms to four times their present value. We have given Head and his employers a trial of forty-five years—five years longer than the Israelites were detained in the wilderness. The promised land is now before us—up then and take it—but set not the torch to one house in Toronto, unless we are fired at from the houses, in which case self-preservation will teach us to put down those who would murder us when up in the defence of the laws. There are some rich men now, as there were in Christ's time, who would go with us in prosperity, but who will skulk in the rear, because of their large possessions—mark them! They are those who in after years will seek to corrupt our people, and change free institutions into an aristocracy of wealth, to grind the poor, and make laws to fetter their energies.

MARK MY WORDS, CANADIANS!

The struggle is begun—it might end in freedom—but timidity, cowardice, or tampering on our part will only delay its close. We cannot be reconciled to Britain—we have humbled ourselves to the Pharaoh of England, to the Ministers, and great people, and they will neither rule us justly nor let us go—we are determined never to rest until independence is ours—the prize is a splendid one. A country larger than France or England; natural resources equal to our most boundless wishes—a government of equal laws—religion pure and undefiled—perpetual peace—education to all—millions of acres of lands for revenue—freedom from British tribute—free trade with all the world—but stop—I never could enumerate all the blessings attendant on independence!

Up then, brave Canadians! Get ready your rifles, and make short work of it; a connection with England would involve us in all her wars, undertaken for her own advantage, never for ours; with governors from England, we will have bribery at elections, corruption, villainy and perpetual discord in every township, but Independence would give us the means of enjoying many blessings. Our enemies in Toronto are in terror and dismay—they know their wickedness and dread our vengeance. Fourteen armed men were sent out at the dead hour of night by the traitor Gurnett to drag to a felon's cell, the sons of our worthy and noble minded brother departed, Joseph Sheppard, on a simple and frivolous charge of trespass, brought by a tory fool; and though it ended in smoke, it showed too evidently Head's feelings. Is there to be an end of these things? Aye, and now's the day and the hour! Woe be to those who oppose us, for "In God is our trust." BROADSIDE distributed about November 27, 1837 (Toronto Public Library): Lindsey, vol. II, Appendix F.

Chapter Six

ADDRESSES TO GOVERNMENT

EDITOR'S PREFACE *On 5 December 1835, Lord Glenelg, Colonial Secretary, sent instructions to Sir Francis Bond Head, Lieutenant-Governor of Upper Canada, outlining the methods he should adopt in dealing with the* Seventh Report of the Select Committee of the House of Assembly on Grievances. *He made the observation that the greater part of the grievances were "now for the first time brought under His Majesty's notice" (W. P. M. Kennedy,* Constitutional Documents, *p. 412). Actually the* Seventh Report *(accessible in libraries, and therefore not given here) goes over the same ground covered in many previous petitions, addresses, and reports. A selection of these is given in this chapter. The repetitions may appear tedious, but a reading of them will throw light on the patience of the Reformers, and on Mackenzie's scrupulous respect for facts and opinions, and will help to place due emphasis on the steady movement for reform which preceded the Rebellion. It was this movement, extended over many years, and not only, perhaps not chiefly, the Rebellion itself, which led to the establishment of responsible government in Canada.*

It will be noticed that there is a high concentration of these addresses in the years 1831-3, the years when Mackenzie was preparing for, and carrying out, his mission to England. In London his hopes of obtaining redress were disappointed, and on his return he expressed his fear that reform could not come through petition. His next steps were continued appeals to the people, and the preparation of the Seventh Report, *which was presented in 1835.*

An important service rendered by the Colonial Advocate *was the publication of the text of Select Committee Reports, presented to the House of Assembly. Mackenzie was the initiator of various select committees, on many of which he sat, and of several of which he was chairman. The Reports of these committees were, with the exception of the* Seventh Report of the Committee on Grievances *(which was too*

long for the paper), published in full by Mackenzie, an indication of his
confidence in his readers' desire to inform themselves on the state of the
Province, and on the activity, or lack of activity, of their government.
The Reports themselves illustrate Mackenzie's thorough probing into
facts, figures, opinions, and actions. The Report on Roads and Bridges
(22 February 1831) is a good example of this.

Committees of which Mackenzie was chairman were: on the Post-
Office, 1829; on Privilege, 1829; on Prisons, 1830; on the Currency,
1830; on Roads and Bridges, 1831; on the Bank of Upper Canada,
1831; on the State of Representation, 1831; on Grievances, 1835.

The Seventh Report on Grievances *was published in book form*
along with the evidence, letters, and memoirs from Mackenzie to Lord
Goderich, titles of bills passed by the Assembly but rejected by the
Council or by the Crown, and other relevant documents.

ON THE EAST INDIA AND CHINA TRADE

The cause I am now to plead, is that in which much of the individual comfort and prosperity of more than a million of his
Majesty's dutiful and faithful subjects are involved; and if in me it
find a weak and powerless defender, I shall feel the greater sorrow,
because that, in my heart, I believe it just.

I mean first to direct your attention to the value of the trade of
those countries which are situated beyond the Cape of Good Hope
with these Colonies, and the loss which the latter sustain in consequence of the restrictions that exist by virtue of the present
system of British Colonial policy.

I shall next endeavour to prove the right which the colonies have,
in reason and justice, to the enjoyment of a *free* and *direct* trade with
countries beyond the Cape.

And lastly—I will attempt to point out the dangers, that, in all
human probability, will threaten the unity of the empire, if a refusal
of this right is persisted in, and palliatives only applied. FROM A
LETTER to George Canning. COLONIAL ADVOCATE, 27 May 1824.

⋅ ⋅ ⋅

Were I a native citizen of the Union, I would wish my country to
be the first in the world; as it is, I am equally consistent in desiring
to see the unity of the British empire maintained, and its vast power
and naval pre-eminence made as permanent as human foresight will

227

allow. Might it not be well to provide a check, a bridle, for these aspiring commonwealths? nature has furnished the means, (*and if the hearts of the people are with the government*) this means is British North America. If these colonies had advanced in an equal ratio with the Union, since the peace in 1783, we would have numbered three millions of souls, instead of one million. A union of *all* the colonies, with a government suitably poised and modelled, so as to have under its eye the resources of our whole territory, and having the means in its power to administer impartial justice in all its bounds, *to no one part at the expense of another*, would require few boons from Britain, and would advance her interests much more in a few years, than the bare right of possession of a barren uncultivated wilderness of lake and forest, with some three or four inhabitants to the square mile, can do [in] centuries. A colonial marine can only be created by a foreign trade, aided by free and beneficial institutions; these indeed would create it, as if by the wand of an enchanter. If that marine is not brought into being; if that trade, foreign and domestic, continues much longer shackled by *Supreme neglect*, and by seven inferior *Setts* of legislative bodies, reigning like so many petty kings during the Saxon heptarchy, England may yet have cause to rue the day, when she neglected to raise that only barrier, or counterpoise to republican power, which could in the end have best guarded and maintained her interests.

Were a war again to occur, were another Buonaparte to arise, on our frontier, the honour of Britain, would stand pledged to defend these colonies from foreign invasion and subjugation, and more blood and treasure would probably be spilt and squandered in the unholy contest, than all the advantages of the ministerial patronage of the colonies could repay for centuries. I dare not venture to anticipate the needless waste of human life, that might ensue. All these evils may however, be prevented by allowing us to be governed by institutions suitable to the genius of the people, and agreeable to their character and disposition.

Compare Upper Canada with the *western part* of New York state, both were peopled about the same time, namely, at the close of the revolution; the former is in no way inferior, indeed it possesses many important natural advantages over the latter, added to a more extended territory; yet the former counts its population under 200,000, while the latter contains over 600,000 souls; this single fact speaks volumes, and does more towards shewing that something is radically wrong in the management of affairs *somewhere*, than would the most laboured essay of the greatest statesman in Canada. . . .

The U.S. trade to countries beyond the Cape is very lucrative inasmuch as though they keep enough to answer the domestic consumption, they preserve their capital by selling to foreign countries the remainder, for very little less on the average, than they paid for the whole. If it be asked, how have these colonies deserved to be placed on an equal footing in this respect with the Union, I will answer the question with another, what have they done amiss, that they should be deprived of a free trade? They have kept good faith with Britain, and it will be for the interest of Britain to preserve good faith with them; I care not for British bounties, and bonuses, and largesses, give the colonies the controul of their own commerce, and then favours will not be wanted. The enterprise of the people of the U.S. would assuredly act as a stimulus to our Colonists if they were but placed on the same footing. FROM A LETTER to George Canning. COLONIAL ADVOCATE, 10 June 1824.

ON UNION WITH GREAT BRITAIN

That our country is suffering under the effects of great and unprecedented commercial depression your lordship well knows; that the supreme government desires the happiness and prosperity of these provinces is equally apparent. And if at a moment like this when the finances of England are straitened, she extends the hand of liberality and kindness to her colonies, strengthens their means of defence, and expends her treasure on canals to encourage their trade and agriculture; it is no less a duty than a pleasure to me to offer humbly and respectfully to the representative of my king an honest opinion as to the means whereby they may be for ever attached to our laws and government.

I have long been satisfied that if the North American colonies were rid of these inferior and subordinate legislatures, which are and must be for ever inefficient for the purposes for which they were intended; and allowed instead thereof a due weight in both branches of the British parliament, it would prove the foundation of their permanent and true happiness. FROM A LETTER to Lord Dalhousie. COLONIAL ADVOCATE, 26 April 1827.

FURTHER ON UNION

My Lord, I widely differ from those men who would separate England from her colonies—I am a constant and careful observer of the republican states—and I do think our great interest as a country would be found in a represented union with Britain, and a freedom from the endless squabbles, and idle contests which prevail in the democratic capital of federal America.

Your Lordship surely does not expect that Upper and Lower Canada, Nova Scotia and New Brunswick, will long remain satisfied as they are, and even if it were so—has Earl Dalhousie an enviable situation?—has Sir Peregrine Maitland a desirable government?—If civil commotion should agitate the neighbouring states are we safe and secure in our united strength and purpose of mind?—can we contemplate in calmness of soul the distant storm, with a certainty that we are safe from its widest devastations? Where is our refuge, where our strong tower?—Is it to be found in an armed soldiery? believe it not. In the fortresses of Canada? they may surrender.—But give the brave peasantry of these colonies their full weight in the national councils, let their voice be heard in the British senate, cease to trust in spies and informers, in foolish and feeble counsels and cis-atlantic hierarchies—*shew the people that vice and misrule in high places can be brought low by the impartial and outstretched arm of British justice, and Albion may rest secure in the possession of her faithful colonies for many generations.* FROM A LETTER to Lord Dalhousie. COLONIAL ADVOCATE, 11 October 1827.

ROADS AND BRIDGES

COUNTY OF YORK
Report on certain petitions concerning statute labour and Road Improvements in the Home District.
Select Committee:
MR. KETCHUM, MR. PERRY, MR. MACKENZIE (chairman).

Committee Room, Feb. 22, 1831

TO THE HONOURABLE THE HOUSE OF ASSEMBLY:
The Select Committee to whom was referred the petition of the Commissioners of the Kennedy Road, and certain other inhabitants

of Scarborough; the petition of John Bagwell, Esq. and certain other inhabitants of Toronto and the adjoining townships; the petition of James Boyes and 437 freeholders and other inhabitants of the County of York residing on or near Dundas Street; the petition of David Jardine and 347 other inhabitants of the townships of York, Etobicoke, Vaughan, Albion, Caledon, and the Gore of Toronto; the petition of Christopher Thomson and 39 other inhabitants of Scarborough; the petition of Stephen Pherrill and 35 other residents in the same township; the petition of a Committee of the Landholders of Scarborough, appointed at the last township meeting; the petition of John Judge, Wait Sweet, and 85 other freeholders and inhabitants of Toronto; the petition of John Lewis, Jacob Belfry, and 92 other inhabitants of York and Simcoe; the petition of Wm. Robertshaw, John Fletcher and 44 other inhabitants of the same counties; the petition of John Leflar and 116 other inhabitants of Chinguacousy; the Petition of Silas Fletcher and others of East Gwillimbury; the petition of George Barclay and others of Pickering, and the petition of Henry Crosby, S. Wismer, Calvin Cole, and 139 other inhabitants of Markham; have agreed to the following Report:

The freeholders of Markham, in their petition, state, in substance, that to change the statute labour laws so as to require a road tax instead of work, would be felt as a heavy burthen by a large majority of the people; that very many persons find it a hard matter to raise cash enough to pay the direct taxes already imposed by law; that to make ten years' improvements at once, by borrowing on the security of a cash tax would leave the poorer classes of persons assessed, without any opportunity for nine successive years, of paying their assessments in labour with the contractors; that in a country with a population thinly scattered over an extensive territory, it is expedient to allow each individual to work upon the roads he feels most interested in the improvement of; that the different persons through whose hands a cash tax would have to pass, would greatly lessen its amount: that to take from the freeholders the power they have so long enjoyed, of appointing their own overseers would be an encroachment upon their dearest rights as British subjects. That the settlers have a far greater interest in having good roads than any commissioner that could be appointed for hire, and that in all new settled townships the people have often to double or treble the amount of their statute labour, in order to render their roads passable through large tracts of unoccupied waste and reserved lands; that although it is and has been long and seriously felt as an evil of no small magnitude that the settlers have been thus obliged to spend their time in making roads through these wastes, and although it has been most earnestly desired by them that the rents and proceeds of the crown and clergy reserves might be applied to the improvement of the roads and schooling, the freeholders are not aware that anyone ever complained of statute labour or desired to commute it; that, had his Excellency's circular proposed to borrow money on the security of the sale of reserved public land, instead of imposing an additional burthen on the people, they have not the least doubt that a much larger sum might thus have been "raised for the immediate use of the province, and the statute labour" "left to keep the roads made by such monies in good repair, and the event would have been hailed with rapture by the whole population:" that in a new settlement it is difficult even for the settlers themselves to determine where a road can be made to the best advantage, and that to expend 10 years' statute labour now, would oblige the settlers to pay the tax to meet the loan and do statute labour besides. Your Committee concur in sentiment with the petitioners.

The petitioners in Markham consider it inexpedient to adopt the proposition of the government for changing the statute labour system into an assessment tax payable in money, and embody in their petitions the reasons why that change should not be made.

The petitioners in Toronto wish no alterations in the statute labour laws other than such changes as may be made from time to time at the town meetings; and pray that a tax in money may not be levied.

The petitions from beyond the Ridges express a strong degree of repugnance to the alterations proposed in the circular of the Government.

The petition of the Select Committee appointed by the Landholders of Scarborough to oppose the change proposed in the Road Laws, recites the following resolution as having been adopted in that township at its annual meeting: "Resolved, that [it] is the opinion of this meeting that in the present state of the province no plan can be adopted for the improvement of the highways, better calculated to attain the desired object, than the one now in use, of each inhabitant performing statute labour according to his rate upon the assessment roll."

The petition of the Freeholders and other inhabitants of the townships bordering on Dundas Street, sets forth, that it is expedient to improve that great thoroughfare by grants of public money, so as to render it "perfectly passable" at all times of the year, before legislative grants to any considerable amount are made to improve any roads parallel to, or side roads leading into the back country—that with a small sum granted for its improvement, the road between York and Dundas may be made a perfectly good road—that enterprising individuals have at great expense placed lines of stages on that road, which were for a long time attended with loss, and are only now becoming of any benefit to the owners—and that it is inexpedient to alter the route of the mails from Dundas Street to the Lake shore road.

All the other petitions referred to your committee are for Legislative grants of money to be made to improve the roads and bridges of the county of York generally, or for grants wherewith to begin or complete certain specific improvements in particular towns or places within the said county—and some of the petitioners express an opinion that the expenditure of the sums granted last year for roads had been obtained with very beneficial effects, and given much satisfaction to the country.

Two of the members of your Committee have during the last year examined the state of many of the bye roads through which the inhabitants of the back townships come to market with their produce, and find them in general in a wretched state. Were the revenue appropriated to pay the interest of a loan to Macadamize the great roads, and tolls afterwards established to keep them in repairs, it would enable the legislature to bestow a far greater sum, annually upon the bye roads, which would widen the circle in which produce is brought to this town, diminish the expense of carriage, induce new settlers to go back into the wilderness, enrich these settlers, stimulate the whole population to increased industry, and thus become a powerful means of adding to the wealth and prosperity of the country.

Your Committee are of opinion, that (however well meant) a more inexpedient mode of improving the roads than that suggested by the executive government could scarcely have been devised. It proposed to anticipate the next ten years' statute labour of the farmers of the colony by borrowing between two and three hundred thousand pounds upon the security of a tax to be substituted in place of road work, and that the sum to be thus borrowed, should be at once expended on the roads under the inspection of Commissioners to be named by Parliament. The Crown reserves, the Clergy reserves, the College lands and the Canada Company's conditional purchase, with the waste lands unsurveyed in the rear of certain Districts, comprise perhaps a fourth of the whole landed property in the colony. These lands pay no taxes, and produce little public benefit: yet by running the agriculturist in debt, as was proposed, they would have been at once raised in value 6d. to 5s. an acre, and the managers for the clergy, crown, college council, and Canada Company would not have been called upon to expend a farthing or sell a lot in aid of the undertaking. However unpopular tolls may be, they would be preferable to his Excellency's proposition, for they only who travelled would have to pay. Adam Smith's doctrine concerning roads and tolls appears rather more reasonable, as an abstract proposition. He argues that "the expense of maintaining good roads and communications, is no doubt beneficial to the whole society, and may, therefore, without any injustice, be defrayed by the general contribution of the whole society. This expense, however, is most immediately and directly beneficial to those who travel or carry goods from one place to another, and to those who consume such goods. The turnpike tolls in England, and the duties called peages in other countries lay it altogether upon those two different sets of people, and thereby discharge the general revenue of the state from a very considerable burden."

Several petitions numerously signed, were last year presented to the legislature, some in favour of, and others opposed to the establishment of toll gates on Yonge Street. The freeholders of Markham, in their petition before your Committee, represent that toll gates would be felt as a grievance of no small magnitude: for example, they suppose a man residing in Brock or Thorah or any of our new and distant settlements, sixty miles from York, should have one load of produce to carry to York in a year, and many of them will not have more, his county tax is 5s, his toll would be 1d. a mile going and the same returning, which is 10s; he performs the journey in four days at an expense for himself and his team of 5s. per day; his load is worth say £3, leaving him nett 17s. 6d. wherewith to furnish his family with a twelve months' necessary articles of merchandize, the like sum having been reserved for commuted statute labour and tolls while the man has also to work six or eight days in a year to keep his woody swampy roads in such a condition as will enable him to travel in his own neighbourhood.

In Lower Canada, the toll bar between Montreal and La Chine has enabled the trustees to keep that section of the travelled road to this Province in good repair. In winter the tolls are not collected. In England and Scotland tolls were established about 80 years ago, and were authorized by separate acts of parliament. "When a proposal is started for the establishment of a new toll in any County or Parish, a meeting of the proprietors of the lands thro' which the road is to run, and whom of course it is intended to benefit, is summoned: there the plans are laid before them, an estimate of the expense made, and it is then first discussed and put to vote whether the erection of the turnpike is advisable or not. After this is decided by the majority in the affirmative, Trustees, (each of whom must possess a certain annual income) are appointed to conduct a survey, to ascertain the best line, and make application to Parliament for a bill authorizing its establishment. The funds are contributed either by the landed proprietors themselves or by the Trustees borrowing money upon the security of the Toll." Such a system as this is inapplicable to a new country like Upper Canada, where the landowners are not sufficiently wealthy to pay the interest usually assessed in England upon the freeholders, when the tolls, as is frequently the case, will not suffice to keep the road in repair.

Perhaps the greatest thoroughfare, leading from York is Yonge Street. It might be worth while at some period not far distant, as an experiment, to allow a sum sufficient to Macadamize four miles of that road to be expended, and afterwards to place a toll bar with moderate rates of toll for two years within a mile of York, the tolls to be let by auction and the proceeds applied to keep the road in repair under the direction of the freeholders on or near that line of road. If found not advantageous, it might be done away at the expiration of the act.

The money value of wild land in the province is the price it will fetch when put up at public auction. The returns from the sheriffs of their late sales for arrears of taxes, shew sales of many thousands of acres in old settled townships, with a sure title, at from fourpence to a shilling per acre. Your committee would respectfully recommend, in order to raise the money value of lands, that the taxes on agriculture be kept as low as possible, and every possible inducement held out to settlers. Is it just, is it equitable to oblige a landed proprietor to pay yearly a fifteenth part of the actual monied value of wild lands he cannot dispose of, and afterwards expend this onerous tax, not to improve the remainder of his estate in the most judicious manner, but often foolishly by the justices, over whose proceedings no efficient check has been placed? If settlers from the United States were once more admitted to purchase and cultivate waste lands as formerly, or if good encouragement were held out by a well balanced government so as to induce emigrants from Europe to settle among us instead of going to the U. States, the amount of the absentee and other similar taxes would be less burthensome to the landowners than at present, for it is well known that the whole surplus population of the province is now altogether inadequate to settle more than a very small proportion of the millions of acres of uncultivated wastes in the province.

Your Committee would suggest that in apportioning the taxes upon land in this district, it is unreasonable that a 200 acre lot near York, worth from four to ten dollars per acre, should, if waste and uncultivated, be liable to no higher scale of taxation than a lot of the same size in the back townships which would not fetch £5 at a sheriff's sale. Such however is now the law, and the late sales have shewn its unfairness. It seems expedient that the whole of the wild land absentee assessment tax should be laid out in the township from which it was levied; by officers appointed by the resident freeholders at their annual town meetings. It seems expedient that a special provision should be made out of the district funds to pay three steady faithful labourers, one of them to be employed continually on Yonge Street, and the other two on Dundas Street, east and west, to fill up bad places, and otherwise keep in repair the worst sections of these roads.

Your Committee have heard complaints made in the Townships, that the Magistrates in their sessions, in some cases have caused pathmasters to direct the people to work on roads away from where they travel and have the greatest interest in making good, and that the consequence is that less than half the labour is done that would be performed under better arrangements. It is best to make in a township as many divisions as may be found useful, so as to correspond with the line of the principal roads, and choose a pathmaster to oversee each division, making the inhabitants do the statute labour in their several divisions. The passage of a law for the better regulation of the township meetings would be attended with much benefit in respect to this and other similar arrangements in the several towns in this district.

In case aid should be this season given to the roads in this district, your committee would recommend that the sums granted for township roads should be expended under authority of commissioners to be appointed by the freeholders at special township meetings to be held on a certain day to be named in the act to authorise the appropriation.

It appears to your Committee expedient, that authority should be given to the people of this district at their annual town meetings to assess themselves over and above their statute labour, any sum of money not exceeding in any one year on the whole £25 in any township containing less than 500 inhabitants, nor exceeding £40 in any township, to be expended in such road and bridge improvements as they may order or direct, by commissioners named at the meeting, where the assessment is voted. Each overseer of statute labour, ought to be furnished with an iron or steel shod scraper and plough, or one of them, where the work to be done requires these implements; to be paid for out of such an assessment as has been suggested.

In New Brunswick, Mr. Botsford, chairman of the board of supervisors of roads, proposes (in his report on roads, for 1828) that the covering of all bridges should consist of hewn timber or plank from four to six inches through—he recommends cedar where it can be had, and after it hackmattack or hemlock. He considers that it would be expedient to enact that no persons should drag timber or logs upon the principal roads in the spring and fall, unless when the ground is hard; and recommends a certain determined width (24 feet) to be adopted in making roads through the settled parts of the country, as also a certain width (18 feet) in roads through wilderness lands.—Your Committee have observed that no uniform system has been adopted by the commissioners under the act of last year, some having cut the roads very narrow, and others to a good width. Perhaps it would be expedient to make a rule.

The Road Acts, or a summary of their provisions, ought to be placed in the hands of every Overseer of Highways in pamphlet form, printed by contract, under authority of a statute. Your Committee have known many instances where overseers were at a loss how to proceed in the execution of their duties for want of such references.

In any act granting money for the roads of this District, provision ought to be made that the sum granted shall be expended as early in the season as possible, and that no turnpike be made after the middle of September. Some of the commissioners of roads delayed their operations last year to suit the convenience of individuals, so that on the post roads work was done at a season of the year so late as to render the highway almost impassable for carriages.

It should be an instruction to overseers of roads, not to cover wet and miry places with logs or poles placed crossways, but to lay them well with brush, and then cover the brush with a foot of earth about ten or twelve inches deep.

If Government will not give to the public use the reserved lands, as originally agreed upon, these wastes ought to be subject to absentee taxes like granted lands, and be liable to sale by the Sheriff if those who have the management of them and who receive the proceeds of their sales, do not pay out of these proceeds the taxes that may become due. Whoever holds a property in them, whether Clergy, College Council, Executive Council, or Crown Commissioner, ought to be bound to keep the roads passing through them in repair instead of leaving them so many wastes to burthen and injure the industrious and frugal settler.

On Dundas Street, not far beyond Cook's Tavern, there is a place called Barber's Hill where the unfounded opinion that a straight road is shortest, and that every deviation from the geodetic line passing through its extreme points is a loss, has induced the road makers to bring the road up and down a succession of steep slopes on the face of a high bank, instead of making one curve in the line and thereby preserving the top of the bank when once attained. In the present state of the settlement it will be a long time before this road can be made safe for wheel carriages by the annual statute labour; and it would perhaps be less expensive to level these slopes, than to purchase private property and change the course of the road. Accidents are continually happening at Barber's Hill, and mail passengers and other travellers in carriages are in constant danger of personal injury. If a sum of money could be obtained from the public treasury sufficient to improve this section of road, it would be well applied in removing the obstruction. Your Committee are of opinion that an inclination of 1 in 40, or $1\frac{1}{2}$ degrees, ought to be the greatest ever allowed on roads in this district made by legislative aid.

In Scotland and the North of England the roads have for the last half century been made of chip stone, that is, broken fragments of rocks. In the south eastern part of England, the whole soil is mixed with flint pebbles, and beds of gravel containing them in abundance are found near the surface. These when properly applied form the best and smoothest roads in the world. In Sweden, the roads are constructed like those of Scotland and are said to be superior to the roads of any other nation. Your Committee have seen large flat stones thrown upon and mixed up with the soil on Yonge Street and other roads in this district, a practice at variance with the true principles of road making, and the experience of other countries.— In the appendix to this report, marked A, your Committee have reported a synopsis of a few and simple principles of road making, in places where stone or gravel may be had. The common manner of road making here is to break up the foundation of the road to a great depth with a plough; and thus brought into the worst possible state for a foundation, the road is then made into a convex curve so flat in the middle that the water lodges, softens the road, renders it liable to form ruts, while it is so steep near the sides that a carriage approaching them is in danger of upsetting. Such a road, and more especially when large stones are put into it, and covered up with gravel, soon becomes worse than the natural soil for travel. If on Yonge Street longitudinal pieces of wood were laid to serve as tracks for the wheels, say pieces of wood 20 × 10, in the original form of the English railroad, and the space between Macadamized, there is reason to believe that produce could be transported at less than half its present price. At all events the experiment might be tried with one mile of road, and the results marked.

Roads are in most cases far beyond the reach of mere individual enterprize, and hence demand legislative aid.—They become permanent portions of national wealth, and add to the comfort and riches of this and future generations. They increase, when judiciously laid out, the value of the tracts of country through which they pass, and enable the owners of wild lands in the interior to bring them into market, although before unsaleable.

In the hope that legislative provision will be made for the improvement of the roads of this and the other districts, during the present session, your committee will defer entering into the particular merits of the several petitions for road money, until it shall have been ascertained what proportion of the public funds is to be expended in the county of York.

Your Committee recommend that Dundas Street East and West, and Yonge Street, the three principal roads communicating between the country and this capital should receive a liberal appropriation out of the Provincial Treasury during the present session, for their improvement.

FEBRUARY 28TH, 1831.

Your Committee have not expressed an opinion on all the petitions from the county of York praying for aid to the roads, because the consideration of these applications will come more immediately under the notice of the members for the Home District by the resolution of the House of Wednesday last.

Orders have been given by government that the survey prayed for by the freeholders of Pickering shall be made under the direction of the Surveyor General, and the Clerk of the Peace for the Home District has informed your committee that the Magistrates have consented to order the erection of the permanent boundaries and monuments desired by the Petitioners in East Gwillimbury.

W. L. MACKENZIE.
Chairman.

APPENDIX A

Mr. McAdam's Principles of Road Making

Synopsis of the few and simple principles on which good roads may be constructed, wherever gravel or stone are to be obtained.

1st. The stones should be broken until no separate piece weighs more than six ounces, and on the other hand all very small fragments, say beneath the size of a large pea, are to be rejected.

2ndly. The fragments are to be thrown on indiscriminately, until the proper shape be given to the road, and they attain the proper thickness; a depth of six inches is sufficient in any case.

3rdly. The best foundation is the natural surface of the ground, and a road is found to be the most lasting when the foundation is soft, as upon the natural sod of meadows. When the surface requires cutting it is to be dressed to a plane, and the whole shape of the road given with broken stone.

4thly. In remodelling an old road made of stone, the whole must be broken-up to the very foundation, and all the larger stones broken down to the prescribed size—no road is so likely to become bad as one made by laying large stones beneath, and covering them with smaller until the surface gradually becomes fine gravel. In this case the larger stones will infallibly work up to the surface and in our climate this process will be accelerated by the frost.

5thly. In relation to the shape or horizontal section of the road it should in no case be made a convex curve, but be always formed of plane surfaces, varied according to the nature of the ground—neither should the inclination of these surfaces ever be greater than is just sufficient to shed the water that falls upon them. In a road, the opposite sides of which are nearly upon the same level and the country open, the road is to be formed of two plane surfaces meeting at the middle of the road like the face of the roof of a house, a ditch is to be cut in the natural soil on each side, and the earth carefully thrown from the road. In a hollow way, the two surfaces should incline to the centre of the road, and a single ditch be cut in the middle. On sloping ground the road should be formed of a single plane surface inclined towards the higher ground, between which and the hill a ditch is to be made—the water is then to be carried off by culverts made from place to place beneath the road.

Such are the few and simple principles adopted by McAdam from the experience of many years on the best roads in England. In that country there were many in which the same excellent material was disadvantageously applied, but the whole has now been reduced to a common system.

If roads so formed are considered the best in such a moist climate as that of Great Britain, it is not an unreasonable inference that a similar formation of road in Upper Canada, the climate of which is comparatively dry, would answer every purpose. The experiment is worth the trial; and if it is made, it should be understood that Mr. McAdam's rules will be strictly followed. "Every road," he observes, "is to be made of broken stone, without mixture of earth, clay, chalk, or any other matter that will imbibe water, or be affected by frost; nothing is to be laid on the clean stone under the idea of binding." COLONIAL ADVOCATE, 10 March 1831.

ADDRESS TO HIS MAJESTY

At a general town meeting of the people of the Town and Township of York, convened by Mr. Joshua Van Allen, Town Clerk, upon the request of one hundred and eight respectable inhabitants, and held in the public Market Square of the said Town, on Saturday the sixteenth day of July, 1831, at eleven in the forenoon, after due notice had been given in the public prints and by handbills, the Town Clerk presided, and James Doyle, Esquire, acted as Secretary.

Mr. Mackenzie read, and submitted to the meeting for its adoption the draft of a petition and address to the King. . . . It was unanimously resolved to adopt the said address.

TO THE KING'S MOST EXCELLENT MAJESTY

We deem it a duty we owe to Your Majesty, to our families and to our fellow subjects, to lay a brief statement of our complaints at the foot of Your Majesty's throne, and earnestly to request that Your Majesty, in Council, would cause a strict enquiry to be made without delay into the administration of the government of this province; so that, forming an integral portion of the British empire, we may at length fully share in its equal and exalted justice.

When, in 1792, Lieutenant Governor Simcoe, the representative of your illustrious father King George the Third, called together the first parliament of this colony, he gave to the legislature in the name of his royal master the most ample assurances that it had been summoned together under the provisions of an act of the parliament of Great Britain which had established the British constitution and all the forms which secure and maintain it, in this distant country.

But we would humbly yet earnestly represent to Your Majesty, that the *Constitution* thus settled, and our just title to the rights and benefits of which is recognized, "and guaranteed to us by the supreme authority of a powerful and generous nation, under the auspices of its most illustrious citizens," has been acknowledged in theory, but, in a great degree denied in practice; for there is not now, neither has there ever been in this province, any real constitutional check upon the natural disposition of men in the possession of power, to promote their own partial views and interests at the expense of the interests of the great body of the people.

The infancy of the country, the poverty of the first settlers, the command over the waste lands, and the civil and military expenditures derived from England, left all the power in the hands of the executive government, and rendered the constitutional check derived from the power of electing a branch of the legislature altogether nugatory, or perhaps *rather mischievous than otherwise*, it serving as a cloak to legislative acts for promoting, in many if not in most cases, individual and partial interests at the sacrifice of the public good, and that too with an apparent sanction from the people through their representatives.

The undue advantages thus possessed by persons in authority, open a door to the practice of bribery and corruption in every department of the state; encourage in the people a servile spirit of dependance on persons in office, quite unlike the leading characteristics of British Freedom; and have left our representatives not even the nominal control over a revenue, complicated and very unsatisfactory accounts of the receipts and expenditure of some part of which are partially submitted to their inspection and published as a mere matter of form. Large sums of money annually raised for local purposes by the imposition of taxes and assessments on houses, lands and other property, and by the sale of uncultivated lands already granted, and on which these assessments had not been paid, are expended by the district magistracy, consisting of persons appointed by the colonial government during its pleasure; and in this, as in nearly all other cases of taxation and revenue, we are deprived of the privilege of disposing of our property as we think fit.

We most humbly suggest to Your Majesty, that the adoption of the following propositions as the rule of law in Upper Canada, is essentially necessary to its freedom and happiness as an integral portion of the empire; and we earnestly beseech Your Majesty to direct Your Ministers to give the measures we have suggested their hearty and efficient support:

1. That the qualified electors of the colony may be fairly and equally represented in the House of Assembly.

2. That the people may by their representatives have the control of all monies whatsoever coming into the hands of the government, whether arising from taxes, duties or crown lands.

3. That the land granting department (concerning the operations of which very little is known to the province), and the sale and disposal of all lands and other public property, be regulated for the future only by law.

4. That the Crown and Clergy Reserves, and all reservations of land, otherwise than for the purposes of education and roads, be abolished.

5. That the control over all statute labour, and over all other local assessments, taxes, rates, and imposts, raised or levied in the towns, townships, counties and districts of this province, be placed in the qualified electors at their town meetings; or in commissioners duly authorized by the said electors, when for county and district purposes.

6. That the undue preferences and exclusive privileges and immunities allowed and extended by the colonial government to certain religious sects or denominations, be abolished.

7. That a less expensive and more prompt and efficient system be established for the free and equal administration of justice; that matters of small amount and difficulty may be disposed of with as much regard to the legal rights of the parties as matters of greater amount and difficulty, but at a less expense; and that no fees be exacted, the tariff of which is not established by an act of the provincial legislature.

8. That the right of impeachment and the mode of trial be fully and effectually recognized and established.

9. That none of Your Majesty's Judges, nor clergymen of any denomination, be enabled to hold seats either in the executive or legislative councils, or in any way to interfere and concern themselves in the executive or legislative business of the province.

10. That the real estate of persons dying intestate may not descend to the eldest son, to the exclusion of his brethren, but be equally divided among the children, male and female.

11. That administering to your faithful Colonial people that justice which Your Majesty has dispensed to our fellow subjects in Great Britain, Your Majesty will cause the same constitutional principle which has called your present Ministers to office to be fully recognized and uniformly acted upon in Upper Canada; so that we may see those only who possess the confidence of the people composing the executive council of Your Majesty's representative.

We humbly pray Your Majesty to disallow, annul and make void a bill passed in the last session of the parliament of this province, entitled "an act to repeal an act passed in the fifth session of the sixth parliament of this Province, entitled 'an act for granting to His Majesty a sum of money towards defraying the expenses of the civil administration of the government of this province,' and for granting to His Majesty a certain sum of money to be applied towards the payment of the expenses of the administration of Justice and the support of the civil government of this province;" as also another bill passed in the said last session entitled "an act for investing in Trustees the Market Square in the Town of York, for the benefit of the inhabitants of the said Town."

We would also humbly intreat Your Majesty's protection against the passage of laws in the United Kingdom Parliament, (where we have no agent legally elected by us of our free choice, to act and advise us for our interest,) effecting sudden changes in our commercial relations with Great Britain and with foreign countries; changes by which the capitals of our merchants and manufacturers are in danger of being sacrificed, and our trade, commerce and agriculture discouraged; and most especially against the passing by that Parliament of any act interfering or assuming to interfere with our internal affairs, over which they have constitutionally no legislative power whatsoever.

We are desirous that the East India Company may not obtain the renewal of their charter in such form as would secure to them a further monopoly of the tea trade of this country.

Deign, Most Gracious Sovereign, favourably to listen to our supplications for a practical recognition of the principles and usages of the established constitution, and to adopt such measures for the future equitable government of this province, as may be within the limits of Your Royal Prerogative, and best calculated to maintain the unity of the empire, promote the happiness of your subjects, and establish on a sure foundation all public and private felicity:—so that, obtaining a full acknowledgement of our constitutional rights, we and our posterity, feeling deeply that we shall be indebted for the same to the noble efforts of our beloved monarch, shall ever hold dear and sacred the name and memory of Your Most Excellent Majesty. COLONIAL ADVOCATE, 21 July 1831.

TO LORD GODERICH

OFFICE OF THE GENERAL COMMITTEE
YORK, SEPTEMBER 16, 1831.

MY LORD:

I herewith enclose copies of the proceedings of [public meetings] held in Esquesing, Halton County; Hamilton, Wentworth County; Dundas, Beverly, Dumfries (Galt), Waterloo, Guelph, Flamboro' East, Nelson, Trafalgar, Halton County; together with duplicates of original certificates, signed by the Chairman and Secretary of each of these meetings.

Copies of the above documents have been this day delivered to the address of His Excellency the Lieutenant-Governor of this Colony, at the office of the Government here.

I also enclose the note sent by Mr. McMahon, Secretary to His Excellency, acknowledging the receipt of accounts of the proceedings of other townships in this colony, and one of the advertisements from the Gore District newspapers.

A few printed copies of brief extracts from the petitions to His Majesty and the provincial legislature, shewing the objects prayed for, are enclosed for more easy reference.

I have the honour to be, My Lord, Your Lordship's Most
  Obedient Humble Servant,
    W. L. MACKENZIE, Convenor, York Genl. Com.
(Approved in Committee—Present: Messrs. MORRISON, CAWTHRA, KETCHUM, TIMS, MILNE, SHEPARD, AND MACKENZIE.)
    COLONIAL ADVOCATE, 8 March 1832.

TO LORD BROUGHAM

YORK. UPPER CANADA.
DECEMBER 19. 1831.

MY LORD:

I have the honour to address these few lines to Your Lordship at the request of Mr. Stephen Washington, formerly one of "the Grey

Coats of Westmorland," but now a farmer and landowner in the township of Scarboro' in this province.

Mr. Washington desires me to state, that he voted for your Lordship, and against the Lowther family, at each of your (three) contested elections in Westmorland; that he preserves carefully your Lordship's medal of July 4, 1818: and that he rejoices that your Lordship is now placed in a station wherein you can greatly promote the happiness and prosperity of your fellow men.

Mr. Washington has a favour to ask of Your Lordship—not for himself individually, for he has a fine farm, a fine family, and is blessed with health and strength to labour, and with several grown up sons to aid him in the toils of the field. He supported your Lordship upon public grounds, firmly believing that the welfare of the country was your grand aim—and he remembers that on one of your three election contests you told the electors from the hustings that wherever any of the grey coats of Westmorland might be, *in any country or in any clime*, you would, if in your power, be their friend.

He thinks that many of the troubles which afflicted England are fast coming upon Upper Canada—and that it is the duty of those whom oppression has driven from thence, to take every lawful means to prevent that accumulation of wealth, power and influence here, in the hands of a few selfish individuals, irresponsible to public opinion, which has caused so much evil by being permitted at home.

He, therefore, humbly requests your Lordship to present the enclosed petition from the people of Scarboro' to the King, and to support its prayer, so that, instead of having the enemies of the present British Cabinet in authority here, a governor and executive council may be given to Upper Canada who will possess some sympathy with the people they govern, and aid them in their efforts to obtain good laws, and perpetuate free institutions.

Many similar petitions, from other places in Upper Canada, have been forwarded to Joseph Hume, Esq. and the Hon'ble Dennis B. Viger, to be presented to His Most Excellent Majesty; and the undersigned joins Mr. Washington in expressing a hope that they have not been sent in vain. I have the honour to be,

My Lord,
Your Lordship's
Most obedient, humble servant,
WM. L. MACKENZIE.
Convenor, York General Committee,
on State of Upper Canada.
COLONIAL ADVOCATE, 8 March 1832.

ON THE REMOVAL
OF SIR JOHN COLBORNE

19 Wakefield St., Brunswick Sq.
3rd Aug. 1832

When such men as Colonel Talbot begin to call meetings and endeavour to give a bias to public opinion, it may be inferred that they have strong fears that the public opinion is not with them. On the 39th page of this memoir I have placed an extract from the London Sun journal edited by Mr. Talbot one of the magistrates of that District. Surely such language as he reports Colonel Talbot to have uttered on the occasion of the public meeting he called last April was not well calculated to tranquillize the excited feelings of the settlers and avert that rebellion which he (Mr. Talbot) states he had stood in fear of. Sir John Colborne's abuse of the dissenters is echoed by his friend Colonel Talbot, who insults them as cold water societies of rebels, seditious trickery quakers, etc. Rest assured my Lord, that such expressions, proceeding from men subsisting upon the industry of the inhabitants (Col. T. has a pension of £400), will not soon be forgotten by the yeomanry. Such triumphs over public opinion and the laws of society will be very short lived. Is it by dividing the present inhabitants, the one against the other, that British authority is to become formidable in North America? Is it by rude language to the Methodist, who is, in general, studiously excluded from every office of honour and emolument, or to the Quaker, who is deemed unworthy even of a seat in the legislature of his country *because he is a Quaker*, that that harmony is to be produced, that bond of union created which will make the millions of the money of England, which have been expended in fortifying Canada, available to perpetuate the integrity of this great empire? LETTER to Lord Goderich. MS. in Canadian Archives: R.G.5, A.1, vol. 113. (Paragraph in Official Correspondence omitted from published edition of the Seventh Report.)

ON REPRESENTATION

TO LORD GODERICH,

On the State of the Representation of the People of
Upper Canada in the Legislature of That Province

My Lord:

Having been informed by Viscount Howick that Your Lordship

is convinced that all classes of the Inhabitants of Upper Canada are fairly represented in the House of Assembly, and having obtained Your Lordship's permission to state in writing the facts and circumstances a knowledge of which has led me to a different conclusion, I hasten to submit to your favourable consideration the following memoir:

The British Statute authorizing the establishment of a popular form of Government in Upper Canada was passed upwards of 40 years ago, when the Inhabitants were few in numbers, poor, and far removed from each other—consisting perhaps of two thousand families scattered over many hundred miles of a frontier yet in a state of wilderness. At this time the civil and military expenses of the colony were defrayed by England, the waste lands were in the gift of the Government, and in the King's Viceroys or Lieutenants were perhaps necessarily united extensive civil and military powers. The country thus situated and the means of internal communications throughout the province being very imperfect, a Commons House of Assembly could effect very little either to check extravagance, or reward merit, although it might, and as the statute book shews, did serve as a cloak to various legislative acts for promoting individual interests at the public expense with an apparent sanction from the colonists through their Representatives. The results of this state of things, being continued with no great variation to the present time, are correctly set forth in the extracts from the petition and address of the Inhabitants of York, dated the 16th day of July, 1831—which form No. 1 of the appendix to this memoir.

By reference to the several Editions of the Provincial Statutes from 1792 down to 1827, the period at which the resources of the colony were held to be sufficient to meet the whole expenses of the Civil Government, it will be seen that they abound with acts giving permanent powers to Governors, Judges, Sheriffs and Justices, and many other functionaries to levy from the Inhabitants in various ways, and under many pretexts large sums of money with no other accountability than the Lords of the Treasury at 3,500 miles distance or the collectors to themselves or to each other. It will scarcely be doubted but that a few individuals dividing among themselves the almost unlimited powers of Government in a new country would oftentimes abuse the trust committed to them and cause dissatisfaction to prevail among the settlers. In course of time as the province increased in wealth and numbers the existence of this spirit of discontent was more clearly shown, and is said to have induced the neighbouring republic to attempt the invasion of the Territories of

ON REPRESENTATION

Great Britain during the late war, in the course of which the Canadians gave ample demonstrations of their sincere and unalterable attachment to the British nation. Soon after the Peace, however, the existence of the discontents, which had been forgotten during the years 1813 and 1814, was seen at popular assemblages, and in the Legislature, and proclaimed aloud through the medium of the press. Moderate but liberal men upheld the doctrine that it was essential to the welfare of the Colony under the form of its Government that the Assembly, "should be placed under the influence of the great body of the respectable and intelligent people of the country," and not guided and controuled by a few individuals in possession of the government and its offices whose conduct appeared to warrant the assumption that it was their purpose to extinguish every vestige of independence in the Representative Branch, deny the blessings of constitutional liberty to the Settlers, and govern by the mandates of arbitrary power, a faithful people who had twice received the thanks of the English nation for their bravery in war and their attachment to the Crown; and who—from the concessions made to the revolted Colonies—were driven from their homes, their fortunes and their country, but promised as their reward, "the free and full enjoyment of the British Constitution."

The only effectual check to misrule in the Colony would be a House of Assembly freely and fairly returned by the qualified electors, nine-tenths of whom are landowners holding their estates in freehold and residing on their own property. (What better constituency could any government wish?) The voice of complaint from a House which would speak the sense and truly represent the feelings of the country, might reach England, might be listened to and might bring about a reform of those abuses by which persons in authority profit—this was speedily perceived by the Government and its Officers, and by their partizans, they therefore turned their attention to the various means whereby they might be enabled to command majorities in the Assembly on every important question, and besides the exercise of the usual influence of a Colonial Government they had recourse from time to time to various expedients to effect their objects some of which I will now state.

I

Up to 1820 the Representation consisted altogether of County Members elected by the owners of the soil, a class which may be safely trusted with the elective franchise in an agricultural com-

249

munity as having the deepest, the most permanent interest in the well being of Society.

But in that year the Government had influence sufficient to obtain the passage of a law bringing into existence a Borough interest in enacting that every village holding the Quarter Sessions of any District, (of which there are twelve, including Prince Edward,) should be represented in the Assembly by one member as soon as it contained 1000 souls; the same law laid the foundation for the present inequality in the County representation, for it authorized Counties formed, or to be formed and organized at a future period to send a Member each when the population had reached a thousand, and two Members each so soon as they numbered four thousand, but beyond that it made no provision, except that the County of Lincoln should continue to send four Members. (*See revised Statutes, pages 258 and 259.*)

This act also provided that whenever an university should be organized it was to be empowered to send one Member. The views and intentions of the local authorities, and of the species of University representation they would have sent from King's College, may be readily inferred from the charter of that Institution and Dr. Strachan's celebrated letter to Mr. Horton the present Governor of Ceylon, against both of which documents the country very unanimously entered its protest. The University, had it gone into operation as projected, would have become a nomination Borough under the especial patronage of Church and State.

The effect of the new clause for regulating the number of County Members has been the enabling counties where there are comparatively few voters, and towns where there are few inhabitants to outnumber the delegation for the large, populous and wealthy Counties, and consequently to increase executive influence.

The judges of the King's Bench interpreted the law for the payment of wages to members of the Assembly to include county members only, and every effort of successive Houses to ensure a certain degree of pecuniary independence to the new village representation has been rendered ineffectual by the Legislative Council. There are now four Boroughs, and there will soon be a dozen of them in operation, with perhaps not more than 1000 or 1200 voters in the whole twelve, including the district officers and many others whose daily bread depends on the breath of the Executive Government or its political partizans.

No. 2 of the appendix refers to a public letter addressed to Your Lordship by Mr. Attorney General Stuart of Lower Canada in which he appears to me to consider corruption of the representation of a borough in that colony, as a matter of course in Colonial Government.

The Appendix No. 3 goes to show the anxiety of the Government in favour of a village representation, and to make manifest its extreme unfairness towards the Colonists.

2

An attempt was made by the officers of Government who had seats in the Assembly to deprive the landowners of the legal power of addressing themselves to pay their members wages—this was in 1821. (See Assembly's Journal, Page 10.) The present Solicitor General introduced the measure, the present Chief Justice, the Collector of the Customs for Port Talbot, the Collector of Excise for York, and the Clerk of the Peace for Stormont supported it but it failed although the Lawyers were five to one in its favour.

3

In the same year another effort was made to injure the constitution of 1791, by means of a parliamentary adjudication in favour of allowing all persons to vote at elections who were or might become possessed of tickets from the Government containing a sort of agreement that the ticket holder was entitled to settle upon a certain lot, half lot, or quarter lot of waste land, and that if he made certain improvements and paid certain monies to government he would receive a deed from the Crown in fee simple. The agreement specified a year, 18 months or 2 years for the period after which the non-performance of his part by the settler would annul the contract. Had this scheme succeeded the franchise would have been extended to a class expressly excluded by the constitution, the most embarrassed and dependant of the population whose chief dependence for their lands was upon the forbearance of the local authorities. These would have out-numbered the real freeholders in many counties and could have been increased upon an emergency to any extent as long as Government had lands to sell or barter, by the distribution of these tickets of occupation to persons who had not the most distant idea of becoming settlers. The temper of the Assembly was tried on this question by setting up the brother of the present Attorney General as a candidate for the County of Durham. His opponent had the most freehold votes and was returned—the question was contested, the (present) Chief Justice argued that these location tickets holders were real freeholders, so said the Crown Land Commissioner, so said the

Solicitor General, so said Judge Jones. But the House resisted and declared the practice illegal. (See Assembly's Journal, page 93.)

Although their scheme thus fell to the ground at that time, the present Chief Justice (the Attorney General) did not lose sight of the principle it involved: accordingly we find him, in 1827, reporting to the Assembly in favour of giving the same class of persons authority to vote at elections (page 96 of Assembly's Journals 1826-7) they being resident in the District of Bathurst. There are indeed few, very few instances where the rights and liberties of the people are concerned in which those men who are now in the highest judicial and executive offices of Upper Canada have not leaned to, or advocated the undue increase of the power and influence of the rulers. There is fortunately no part of the complaints made by the people with reference to the representation which the local legislature will not be able perfectly to provide a remedy for whenever the measure to be proposed shall have received the sanction of the government here, with the exception of the emancipation of the Society of Friends and of Tunkers, Moravian brethren, Menonists, and all that extensive and highly respectable class of landowners who have conscientious scruples against taking an oath. They are excluded by the Constitutional Act from seats in the Assembly, and altho' an enactment in their favour was brought into the Assembly upon petition, it was found that no power short of the Imperial Parliament could afford relief. "It is obvious that no people can be satisfied with a Government from the constituent parts of which they are excluded."

4

At the Lower Canada elections the freeholders can elect any candidate in whom they have confidence—there is no property qualification for the elected—yet it is very seldom they select any other than the owner of the soil. Not so in Upper Canada. The officers of Justice found it expedient to narrow the power of the electors in making a choice both in towns and counties to that order of freeholders who are possessed of an unencumbered estate in land and tenements assessed to £80 or upwards. This law supplied them with the means of harassing Mr. Randal, one of the members for Lincoln, with a trial for alleged perjury in 1823.—They failed—& at the next general election the freeholders of the District marked the sense they had of the conduct of the Government by electing Mr. R. with the greatest number of suffrages ever given to a representative in the Province. By means of this law the local government diminished the number of persons capable of being elected, except in so far as a choice might serve the purposes of the executive. The possession of millions of acres of public land under no public controul gave them the means of bestowing lands to qualify a favourite whenever it might be considered expedient.

5

Another successful effort of the local authorities to diminish the numbers of persons capable of electing and of being elected, was the Upper Canada political non-intercourse act, as it had been called, (see revised Statutes, pages 340, 341, 342,) a regulation which has exposed the country and its government to much ridicule in the United States, and which I consider a tacit acknowledgement of the dread in which the executive holds the political institutions of the independent part of the great English family in America.

It has been enacted that any native-born subject of His Majesty, who, either on account of business, pleasure, health or for any other causes, has been a *bona fide* resident in any country out of the King's Dominions, shall, altho' qualified by property, talent, and the approbation of his fellow-citizens, and altho' he had at no time become, or intimated the least desire to become a subject of the state in which he had so resided, be incapable of sitting in the House of Assembly until after he has been actually resident for seven full years in the Province (and no other part of his Majesty's Dominions); at the expiration of which probationary state there is a restoration of his civil rights. All native-born or naturalized British subjects are by the same statute deprived of the right of voting at elections, either as freeholders or householders for seven years after they shall at any time have resided in the United States or other foreign country. Thus it is that British Capitalists, Merchants, Farmers, Mechanics, and Artizans who make a trial of the United States and afterwards on personal absentation choose to become permanent settlers under the Government of England in Canada and carry thither their industry and their means are treated at the very outset of their journey. Driven from the polls as aliens and intruders, and if perchance the freeholders of any county should elect one of them the elected shall incur a fine of £200, and a daily penalty of £40 for every day he offers himself to the legislature as a representative.—An Englishman who would be eligible in any county in the three Kingdoms to be elected to the Imperial Parliament, or in Lower Canada to the House of Assembly, may meet fine or imprisonment if he offers to come forward as a candidate in a Colony to which this nation guaranteed the full enjoyment of the British Constitution *about forty years ago!*

6

The Government commenced prosecutions against the Press and its Conductors for promulgating political opinions which they did not like; thus did they at an early day. In 1817-18 they succeeded in destroying a press which had opposed their system and had incarcerated the Printer and Publisher in a damp unwholesome cell for an example to others who might incline in like cases to offend.

7

They brought two or more actions against a well known native of Scotland for the expression or publication of offensive political opinions upon the state of the Province, failed in each case to persuade the Jury that he had broken the law, but at length succeeded in effecting his banishment as *an alien*, after having sent him for a long time to jail for refusing to go away. Many persons whose bravery in defending the Province during the war of 1813-14 had been acknowledged by grants of lands, had a mark of disapprobation set upon their heads and their grants taken away because they entered into this Exile's views on questions of civil right, others were struck off the roll of the Commission of the Peace, and in some cases individuals holding Commissions in the Militia were disgraced. Thus an attempt to express the opinion of the landowners by a convention was quashed and put down.

8

So very general was the discontent felt throughout Upper Canada with the measures of the administration so far back as fourteen years ago that the government held it indispensable to the public safety (or rather as I would consider their act, indispensable for the preservation of abuses in the administration) on the 27th of Nov. 1818, to pass a law prohibiting public meetings of the people in their several Townships and Counties, or of any part of them, for the purpose of petitioning the King and Parliament for redress of alleged grievances. This statute prohibited all political conventions and made it highly criminal in the landowners and other inhabitants of the Colony, His Majesty's subjects, to appoint, attend or assemble together any public meetings, "under pretence of deliberating upon matters of public concern or of preparing or presenting petitions, complaints, remonstrances and declarations and other addresses to the King, or to both or to either Houses of Parliament for alteration of matters established by law, or redress of alleged grievances in Church and State," because, as it was alleged in the act, such meetings of the people might "be made use of by factious and seditious persons to the violation of the public peace, and manifest encouragement of riot, tumult, and disorder." (See the old revised Statute, Edition 1819, page 42 &c.)

Upon what principle of honour and justice towards Upper Canada any Ministry in this country could have approved and sanctioned this extraordinary statute, I know not. In the space of two years or thereabouts "the Gagging Bill", as it is called in the province, was repealed, but not until the local executive had made far more permanent, and, I think, *prudent* provisions for the suppression of the opinion of the resident landowners concerning the measures of the government. COLONIAL ADVOCATE, 10 January 1833.

ON UNHEEDED PETITIONS

TO THE HOUSE OF COMMONS

The Humble Petition of William L. Mackenzie, Printer; Member Representing the County of York, in the Legislative Assembly of Upper Canada; (and deputed to this Country as the Agent for the Petitioners to the King and Parliament, praying for a Redress of Grievances) sheweth,

Addresses to His Majesty from Upper Canada.

That between the months of June 1831 and April 1832, the people of Upper Canada, having full confidence in the gracious disposition of His Majesty early to hearken to the just complaints of his subjects throughout his widely extended dominions, met together in their respective towns and counties for the purpose of petitioning His Majesty on the State of the Province, and of laying their grievances at the foot of the Throne.

At upwards of a hundred general meetings of the Landowners and other Inhabitants of the districts, counties, towns and townships into which Upper Canada is divided, Memorials to His Majesty were adopted, and subscribed by between twenty and thirty thousand persons, a considerable majority, as there is reason to believe, of the whole male adult population. And it was a request of the Memorialists, unanimously made at all their Meetings, that your Petitioner should proceed to England in charge of their Memorials, and endeavour to obtain a favourable answer.

Petition to the House of Commons, 1832.

That your petitioner was the Bearer of a Memorial to your Honourable House, agreed upon last year, and subscribed by 10,000 of the Landowners and other Inhabitants of Upper Canada, praying that an Enquiry might be instituted into the State of the Colony and relief extended—said Memorial was presented by one of the representatives for Middlesex a short time before the close of the last Session, but the investigation prayed for was not gone into.

Applications at the Colonial Office.

That your Petitioner was introduced to the Secretary of State for the Colonies on the occasion of presenting the Addresses from Upper Canada, last July, and has had the honour to obtain several audiences of His Lordship, and been permitted to address many communications on the State of the Province to the Colonial Office; but has not been able to perceive during a stay of nearly nine months in England, that the Memorialists, of whom your Petitioner is one, are likely to be benefitted, or existing abuses lessened, by any efficient measure of reform proceeding from the Colonial Office. He fears that he has been unable to convince the Secretary of State that there are any grievances worthy the attention of the Government.

Petition to the House of Commons, 1831.

That your Petitioner is a Member of the Central Committee of Friends of Civil and Religious Liberty, who forwarded the Memorial of ten thousand of the Freeholders of Upper Canada to one of the Representatives for Middlesex for presentation in your Honourable House, in 1831. The Petition was ordered to be printed, but there has been no enquiry. The Memorialists have requested your Petitioner to endeavour to obtain the attention of Parliament to the prayer of their Memorial.

Petition of 1828.

That your Petitioner was a Member of the Provincial Committee who forwarded to one of the present Representatives for Middlesex for presentation in your Honourable House in 1828, the Memorial of eight thousand of the Inhabitants of Upper Canada, stating their grievances; and that he has been required to act as their Agent.

Petition of 1829.

That about five thousand Inhabitants of the County of York, of whom your Petitioner was one, transmitted Petitions for redress of grievances for presentation in the House of Lords and Commons in 1829, but because of some informality in the wording the Legislature would not receive or listen to them.

Recommendations of the Canada Committee neglected.

That the recommendations made by the Select Committee of your Honourable House, to whom was referred, in 1828, the consideration of the state of the Civil Government of the Canadas, have not been complied with as far as Upper Canada is concerned. On the contrary, the abuses then complained of have greatly increased, and are increasing, with perfect impunity to the wrong doers. The attention of the Province is anxiously turned towards the deliberations of Parliament, in the confident expectation that your Honourable House will at length favourably listen to our humble prayers, cause enquiry to be made, and grant relief.

Persecution for Opinion.

An opinion is very generally entertained in Upper Canada—and, as your Petitioner believes, with good reason—that wherever the Government or its officers have an opportunity to injure in their business or prospects in life those persons whose names are attached to petitions calling the attention of His Majesty or your Honourable House to the misconduct which prevails in the Colonial administration, or who take a prominent part with the complainants, they seldom fail to use it. It is well known that for years together the right of the people to meet together and petition for redress of grievances was suspended, at the request of Sir P. Maitland, (now governing Nova Scotia and residing in England;) it was made a criminal act for any number of the Landowners to assemble together to petition the King, within the limits of Upper Canada; and the royal grants of public lands to Canadians, bestowed as the reward of their bravery in defence of the Province in time of war, were rescinded by General Maitland because they ventured to meet and petition Parliament for a redress of grievances, in time of peace!

Difficulty of Petitioning.

Petitioning England, and sending Agents, to London from year to year, is attended with much difficulty, trouble, and expense to a people 4000 miles distant from the supreme authority—and it is a duty at all times unpleasant to have to complain of the conduct of others. Although, however, the act of petitioning is unpleasant, the right is nevertheless dear to British subjects; and I humbly request

I

permission to recapitulate some of the grievances felt by the Inhabitants of Upper Canada which have been embodied in their Memorials to the King and Parliament, and to the Lieutenant Governor and Provincial Legislature. Having been honoured with the confidence of the Landowners, in whom is the right of suffrage, so far as to be five times successively chosen to serve as a Member of the Legislative Assembly for the most populous Shire in the Canadas, that in which is the Seat of the Government of the Upper Province—having been unanimously elected last November while absent in this country endeavouring to obtain the attention of the Colonial Department to the Petitions of the Freeholders, I may reasonably be supposed to speak their sentiments.

[*A restatement of the grievances enumerated in the previous Petitions to the King and House of Commons follows.*]

British Colonial Expenditure.

The Annual Expenditure occasioned to England by the present mode of Government in the North American Colonies has been estimated at about three million sterling, inclusive of the tax occasioned by the discriminating duties on timber—this is in time of peace. Even if no return were made to the colonists in merchandise, the whole exports of British America to all the rest of the world would scarcely amount to this sum—and as for the territorial revenue accruing to Britain it is not worth naming.

The Petitions of the people of Lower Canada to their Government, and of the House of Assembly of that Province to the King and Parliament, show that most of the evils of which we complain they also are afflicted with; and that they seek the same simple remedy—the power of "self-government." The other North American Provinces doubtless feel in a greater or lesser degree the pressure of a Colonial system unsuitable to the liberality of the age in which we live.

The Colonies contrasted with the United States.

The majority of the North American Colonists are neither of British birth nor descent—nor are they members of the established Churches of England or of Scotland. British America furnishes no suitable materials for splendid costly Governments—its inhabitants evidently have no wish for them. The people of Upper Canada are in view of the United States, in daily intercourse with its citizens; they are the same race of men, speaking one language; they see the people on their adjoining frontier thriving and contented under domestic Governments instituted for the common benefit and protection; and they are persuaded that it is the wish of the British nation that they should have no just cause to envy the condition of their neighbours. In Ohio, New York, and Vermont, the military, (of whom there are very few) are seen in strict subordination to the civil power—the laws are known to be a faithful expression of the public will—the penal code is humane and merciful—the judiciary are independent, and the people satisfied with the administration of justice—taxes are raised, and public expenditures appropriated only according to law—the public functionaries require neither extravagant incomes nor burthensome pensions to induce them to fulfil their several duties—population, wealth well distributed, and the value of real estate rapidly increase—to all the citizens are ensured the blessings of education—and, without establishing any one sect over the others, a suitable maintenance is obtained for the ministers of religion from the voluntary contributions of their several congregations.

*The best if not the only means of promoting the
prosperity of Upper Canada.*

Your Petitioner humbly submits, that unless the people of Upper Canada shall be entrusted with an influence in the management of their own affairs something like which prevails in the adjoining country, and the burthen of any disadvantageous comparison which they may draw, thereby thrown upon themselves, the difficulties which now surround the Colonial government will speedily be multiplied. Under a frugal Administration the value of landed estate in Upper Canada would be greatly increased, and the settlement of the country much facilitated by a numerous and intelligent class of capitalists, who will neither entrust their property nor take up their abode in a land in which the Settler is continually liable to be involved in the troubles attending a struggle for the possession of a government able and willing to protect persons and property and secure to the community the blessings of civil and religious freedom.

Prayer of this Petition.

In laying their complaints, year after year, before your Honourable House, the people of Upper Canada have constantly appealed to facts, and earnestly requested that an early investigation might take place, always reposing, as in duty bound, the fullest confidence in the wisdom and magnanimity of Parliament. And your Petitioner, for the several reasons hereinbefore set forth, humbly prays your Honourable House to cause an enquiry to be instituted into the condition of the Province, so that justice may be done, and relief extended to its much injured inhabitants.

Your Petitioner will ever pray.

W. L. MACKENZIE.

2 Poland St. Feb 21, 1833.

COLONIAL ADVOCATE, 25 April 1833.

Chapter Seven

CURRENT COMMENT 1824-1829

INTRODUCING
THE "COLONIAL ADVOCATE"

We will never flatter power, nor become the assassins of private character. Like Farmer Giles, we are perfectly exempt from all unfriendly personal feelings; and if we speak of men, it will solely be in reference to their public acts. Of these we propose to speak according to our own unbiassed opinion of their deservings. We are far from saying, or even thinking, that the nobleman now at the head of the Colonial Government in North America, is other than an able and a prudent ruler. It is the system we condemn, and few numbers shall go forth until we make ourselves distinctly understood on this head. Lord Dalhousie we believe to be a humane, well designing and amiable aristocrat. We respect him for his moderation and good temper as much as we do any other British peer. But it is a system of cross purposes that the colonies are governed by.

.   .   .

The proposed Union Bill, heretofore agitated in the House of Commons in England, pleased nobody. It was withdrawn; and it is possible the next may be founded on more just principles of colonial policy.

What is it, other than the system so stedfastly pursued by the British Government in Lower Canada, that has caused all the debate and disunion which has existed in its legislature, from the first session to the last, and which is transmitted to those that shall follow? Well might the noble Lord say, in his speech at closing the session, that "*these disputes have caused incalculable mischief to the Province.*" We do not agree with his lordship in his argument, though we can give our hearty assent to the conclusion he has drawn. But, wait a little, and we will, to use a homely phrase, put the saddle on the right horse.

We conceive ourselves as independent as editors well can be. We are not in want, neither are we rich. We have never been disloyal subjects nor radical reformers. . . . But we have made our election: it is to have only one patron, and that patron is the People:—the people of the British Colonies. . . .

Sincerely attached to freedom, we yet think it not incompatible with a limited monarchy. We would never wish to see British America an appendage of the American Presidency; yet would we wish to see British America thrive and prosper full as well as does that Presidency. We trust to see this accomplished, if Britain does not fall into the error of considering her colonists as much her slaves as Virginia does her Negroes.

We dislike much to hear Mr. Daniel Webster, of Massachusetts, gibe us as "the distant dependency of a distant monarchy," etc. etc., and hope the time will come when Canada will be pointed out as a model for other countries—not pointed at with scorn, as the King's printer has it.

We like American liberty well, but greatly prefer British liberty. British subjects, born in Britain, we have sworn allegiance to a constitutional monarchy, and we will die before we will violate that oath.

It has often occurred to us to enquire, while we perused the works of a political writer, or national historian, what religion did he profess? of what church was he a member? In some instances we could divine this ourselves from the bias he gave to his writings. But we have read authors, Protestants, aye, and Catholics too, who did in no instance suffer their religious creed to interfere with their political writings, and we are ambitious of being found amongst the latter class. It may not be amiss for us here to state, that we are Calvinists, and profess to believe the Westminster confession of faith as now adopted by the church in the northern part of our native island of Great Britain.

Having stated this much, it is fit we should declare our opinion on two subjects, which have caused some contention in the British Provinces, namely, the Clergy Reserves, and an Established Church.

.   .   .

In no part of the constitution of the Canadas, is the wisdom of the British legislature more apparent, than in its setting apart a portion of this country, while it yet remained a wilderness, for the support of religion. We believe that the late lord Melville, (then Mr. Dundas) was the first adviser of this measure. . . .

There is no doubt in our minds but that the English parliament, when it set apart these reserves for the use of a protestant clergy, intended exclusively to establish the English church, and to endow it with the lands so reserved; unless among the Catholics who, excepting the King's supremacy, reserved in the Quebec act, were left in the enjoyment of their rights, and had their title to tithes, from their parishioners, fully acknowledged by law.

Without going into an argument whether such was really the intent of that clause in our constitution, it is well known that those in authority here have so interpreted it; and it is moreover evident from the act itself that the clauses respecting religion are left open like every other part of the bill, for alteration and improvement by our legislatures, subject of course, to the control of the British Parliament. . . .

But when we reflect that our population is not like that of Scotland, a body of people nearly unanimous regarding the fundamental points of christianity, and undivided in their manners and customs; when we consider that (we except the Catholics in the lower province) the Canadas are peopled by emigrants from many countries, and that they have been accustomed to enjoy many different religious opinions and forms of worship, or have perhaps left their respective countries that they might be enabled here peaceably to worship their maker according to their consciences; when we thus reflect we are compelled to acknowledge that the imperial parliament did not consult the best interests of the people nor of Britain, when it endowed the professors of one faith, with the rents and emoluments of the lands belonging to the ministers of religion, thereby establishing in the nineteenth century, a militant dominant church.

. . .

We are clearly of opinion that Catholic and Protestant, Episcopalian and Presbyterian, Methodist and Baptist, Quaker and Tunker, deserve to share alike in the income produced by these lands; and we trust we shall yet see a law enacted by which the ministers of every body of professing christians, being British subjects, shall receive equal benefits from these clergy reserves; for we conceive it would remove a grievance which, if suffered to remain, may be a means of much evil—and indeed may be the cause of greater injury to British interests here than we choose to anticipate. COLONIAL ADVOCATE, No. 1, 18 May 1824.

LOYALTY

It is a very great mistake to imagine that the farmers and country people in Upper Canada lack general knowledge. They are a thinking people, and I verily believe that not in an equal number of the people of any English county is there more general information diffused than in the Province of Upper Canada, the population of which, is brought together from the four corners of the earth. What then can we expect, if this people are scoffed and mocked at by the satellites of government? I fear not to reply to the question—but it needs no answer.

The difference between passive obedience and non-resistance, to a tyrannical government, as compared with free discussion of the public measures of a represented and responsible one, is known by our meanest peasants. . . .

Loyalty is an odd sort of a word, and really admits of many definitions, there is for instance a sort which consists in keep[ing] up a connection with the party that have places to give away.

There is another species, disinterested in its nature, and which consists more in acts than in professions. It is likely from what I have heard that Mr. Robinson's father practised this sort of loyalty, and I wish I could say as much of the son. My ancestors too stuck fast to the *legitimate* race of kings, and though professing a different religion, joined Charles Stewart, whom (*barring his faith*) almost all Scotland considered as its rightful sovereign. Colin Mackenzie, my paternal grandsire, was a farmer under the Earl of Airly in Glenshee, in the highlands of Perthshire; he at the command of his chieftain willingly joined the Stewart Standard, in the famous 1745 as a volunteer; my mother's father, also named Colin Mackenzie, and from the same Glen, had the honour to bear a commission from the Prince and served as an officer in the highland army; both my ancestors fought for the royal descendant of their native kings; and after the fatal battle of Culloden, my grandfather accompanied his unfortunate prince to the low countries, and was abroad with him on the continent, following his adverse fortunes for years; he returned at length; married, in his native glen, my grandmother, Elizabeth Spalding, a daughter of Mr. Spalding, of Ashintully castle, and my aged mother was the youngest but two of ten children the fruit of that marriage. The marriage of my parents was not productive of lasting happiness, my father, Daniel Mackenzie, returned to Scotland from Carlisle, where he had been to learn the craft of Rob Roy's cousin, deacon Jarvie of the saltmarket Glasgow, or in other words, the weaving business, took sickness, became blind, and in the second year of his marriage with my mother died, being in his twenty-eighth or twenty-ninth year.

I was only three weeks old at his death, my mother took upon herself those vows which our church prescribes as needful at baptism, and was left to struggle with misfortune, a poor widow, in want and in distress. It is among the earliest of my recollections, that I lay in bed one morning during the grievous famine in Britain, in 1800-1, while my poor mother took from our large kist (which is an article of furniture of a sort only to be found among the Scotch and Irish) the handsome plaid of the tartan of our clan, which in early life her own hands had spun, and went and sold it for a trifle, to obtain for us a little coarse barley meal whereof to make our scanty breakfast; and of another time during the same famine, that she left me at home crying for want and hunger and for (I think) 8s. sold a handsome and hitherto carefully preserved priest-grey coat of my father's to get us a little food. How the mechanics and labourers contrived to exist during these times, is what I cannot tell, my recollections of this period are faint and indistinct. Well may I love the poor, greatly may I esteem the humble, and the lowly, for Poverty and Adversity were my nurses, and in youth were want and misery my familiar friends; even now it yields a sweet satisfaction to my soul, that I can claim kindred with the obscure cottar, and the humble labourer, of my native ever honoured, ever loved Scotland.

> Long may thy hardy sons of rustic toil,
> Be blest with health, and peace, and sweet content!

My mother feared God, and he did not forget nor forsake her: never in my early years can I recollect that divine worship was neglected in our little family, when health permitted; never did she in family prayer, forget to implore that He, who doeth all things well, would establish in righteousness, the throne of our monarch, setting wise and able counsellors around it. A few of my relations were well to do, but many of them were poor farmers and mechanics, (it is true my mother could claim kindred with some of the first families in Scotland; but who that is great and wealthy, can sit down to count kindred with the poor?) yet amongst these poor husbandmen, as well as among their ministers, was religion and loyalty held in as due regard, as it had been by their ancestors in the olden time. Was it from the precept, was it from the example of such a mother, and such relations, that I was to imbibe that disloyalty, democracy, falsehood and deception, with which my writings are by the government editor charged ? Surely not.

If I had followed the example shewn me by my surviving parent, I had done well; but as I grew up I became careless, and neglected public and private devotion. Plainly can I trace from this period the commencement of these errors of the head, and of the heart, which have since embittered my cup, and strewed my path with thorns, where at my age I might naturally have expected to pluck roses.

Earnestly did my mother desire me to honour my heavenly king, to remember my creator in the days of my youth, and I at this distant day have much greater cause to regret the little attention I then paid to her well meant admonitions in that respect, than to take blame to myself for either thinking or speaking disrespectfully of our anointed sovereign. COLONIAL ADVOCATE, 10 June 1824.

THE LATE LORD BYRON

Lord Byron had succeeded in stirring up among the people in that part of Greece in which he resided an almost inconceivable enthusiasm. His exertions were incessant in their cause and the gratitude of the people was proportioned to them. [*Lord Byron died on April* 19, 1824.] COLONIAL ADVOCATE, 8 July 1824.

EMIGRATION FROM THE UNITED STATES

We would recommend to the attentive consideration of all classes of our readers, the essay in another part of this paper, on the present system pursued by government, of virtually prohibiting emigration from the United States. Excepting the York junto, all classes of people would be benefitted by a change of measures in this respect, which would give new life to our agriculture, our manufactures, and our commerce, by attracting to the Colonies persons of skill, capital, and scientific information, of industrious habits, and of useful and productive callings. COLONIAL ADVOCATE, 19 August 1824.

A STAR-CHAMBER CREW

Were I at this moment immured in a dungeon, and denied the privileges of the lowest hind that breathes the vital air, and crawls along, I would not exchange places with our high-born ruler, surrounded by such men as he now delights to honour; no! I would spurn—I would loathe the very idea of such a prostration. I am the son of an humble, obscure mechanic, bred in the lap of poverty; but not to inherit the noble blood which flows in his veins—not to possess the ancestral grandeur that surrounds his name—not to wear the star that adorns his breast, nor the honourable orders that mark his valour—no! not for worlds, would I exchange situations with him, surrounded by men whose whole career is like "vanity tossed to and fro of them that seek death."

Representatives of Canada! Your constituents await your meeting in Assembly; they expect much at your hands; O! disappoint them not. I will tell of your labours in their service—I will, through the medium of a free and unshackled press, make known the sentiments of your loyal, honest, and independent breasts; and though there is one who is called of your number whose presence among you I shall deeply deplore, yet ye are many, and his machinations shall surely go for nought. I will sit in the gallery of your house; and, whether as your Reporter, or not as your Reporter, record and promulgate the language of truth, as it is elicited by your body in argument and debate, until the most distant boundary of our land shall echo back the tidings. I will not desert my post—never! never! COLONIAL ADVOCATE, 28 October 1824; Lindsey, vol. I, p. 62.

A DEFENCE OF
THE "ADVOCATE"

To CHARLES JONES ESQ.—BROCKVILLE
SIR,

I thank you for the plain manner in which you have pointed out, what appear to you as the greatest defects in the publication I conduct. It accords so well with my own views of propriety to speak what I think, that I derive pleasure from seeing others do so likewise. You seem to think that I have formed an erroneous opinion of the Attorney General—and that acting on, and being influenced by that opinion, I do him injustice as a public character.—There is only one remark needed from one in support of this opinion so freely given. The Attorney General went to England as the accredited agent of this Province, and he recommended, nay I am informed he himself drew out a clause in the Union Bill, making £500 in property a necessary qualification in a member of Assembly. For this one action of his, even if I refrain from uniting with it his advice to the English government (see his published correspondence) to do away in part the dependance of the executive on the Colonial Houses of Assembly in money matters, he deserves to be pointed out as a dangerous person in that house where the interests of the people are required to be guarded with peculiar and unceasing care against the encroachments of rulers and crown officers, of which he is one.

The parliaments of England have enacted many wise laws to prevent placemen acquiring an undue ascendancy in the Commons house—and when a crown officer tells his constituents—I will do as I have done before—such conduct as Mr. Robinson has seen fit to adopt, being the standard of excellence so referred to—if these constituents forget their duty to their country or are ignorant thereof and elect that officer to the legislature—it is the bounden duty of an independent editor not to overlook the past, thus made voluntarily the ensample and pattern of the future. Such has been my view of the matter, and acting thereon, I have let my knowledge of Mr. Robinson's humanity and forbearance as a crown officer when going the circuit—his proverbial probity as a lawyer, his high and unblemished character as a private gentleman lie in the shade—and have by argument, advice and satire, each in their turn endeavoured to remind my readers of Mr. Robinson when brought to the test—not only in the last parliament—but in England as its (the house's) organ. If Mr. Robinson's political creed is sincere—so much the worse for the country if they again trust him to another English mission. Possibly in that case a house of assembly had better be entirely dispensed with. You argue, if I aright understand you, that I do no honour to the judgment and penetration of the members of Assembly by supposing him capable of swaying their judgments, to the loss of their constituents. If you mean the last house I really cannot bestow great praise upon them collectively. Able and honest and independent members there certainly were in that house—but what could they achieve when overpowered by the majorities amongst which I so often counted *J. B. R.* and that Hagerman whose assurance the public prints tell me you, once at least, checked in warm but most appropriate language, language, Mr. Jones, that endeared your name to many in Canada—language that made not a few of those high spirits whose approbation is worth thousands of grovelling selfish souls, rejoice in your re-election to parliament. When you and six others on that great question "A free trade to India" were guided in your votes and speeches by sound constitutional principles, what am I to think of the majority who offered as an alternative to purchase thro' the U.S.—truly I am almost tempted to borrow your phrase "dolts indeed." If I were to ask you what roads were planned and executed by the money voted by the last legislature, if I were to enquire what they did with a million of the public money, (less or more) that in four years passed thro' their hands I think you would almost agree with me that there was little to praise, much to censure. Now having seen the gentleman whose name you think I have made an improper use of—the foremost of forty to spend uselessly as I think the public funds—having seen that a majority always enabled him to carry money bills with small enquiry I think that I stand justified in saying that this crown officer is out of his place when in parliament. Your ideas and mine may be different on the scope and meaning of the word personalities. If I meddle with none of Mr. Robinson's private affairs—if I do not disturb the sanctuary of his private friendships, his likings and dislikings, then I conceive I do him no injustice.—Mr. Robinson as Attorney Genl. *cum* M.P. is fair game. Or if he is not you will need to shew me my error, in the £500 qualification—that is with me the first test of his principles—especially as he offered it to those who were unaware of the vast disparity between the value of property in Britain and in America.—This letter is written in a hurry—and that hurry I cannot get the better of. The Advocate has still a great and unexampled circulation, but I am poorly paid, the agents in most places having little interest in the prompt payments of the accounts, and being often engaged in their own affairs to a degree sufficient to preclude much regard to mine, this joined to the evils of an ill-regulated post-office, renders my situation in a pecuniary point of view very irksome. *I am not able to pay the necessary number of hands to get the paper out regularly.* I often write half the paper, with several dozen letters, read 100 newspapers etc. etc., write 900 directions on papers to the respective addresses of the subscribers and paste and tie up 100 different mails to 100 offices and agents *in one week.* If to this be added correcting the press which I always have to do—mak'g out and dunning accounts of those due me, you may suppose that I repose not on a bed of roses. You have not, I hope, in reading thus far got tired—I have done all this for a long time, and I will do it for a still longer period if I can afford it—but never, never, shall I in public or in private approve a law for interest or private advantage, conduct which I think not right. I have in the Advocate recommended religion, I have never I think admitted the usual immoral trash which fills newspapers, to pollute its columns. It (the Advocate) is not to my mind—I would rather leave petty local politics to go into the field of general and constitutional information at any time—but I am not an independent editor—in every point of the word—if I were—I would give you an Advocate every week regularly, and as my time, now taken up providing for the passing day, would be more my own, I could the better be enabled to polish those periods which you, and not you alone but many others think a bar to the utility of the work as a colonial publication. In conclusion I beg you will not be offended at my freedom. I believe you wish me success in my undertaking—or you would not have taken the pains you have done in writing me—for this kindness again be pleased to accept my thanks—and believe me

Sir,

Your obliged and very humble servant

WM. L. MACKENZIE

York, U.C.
December 1st. 1824.

CANADIAN ARCHIVES: MG 24. E 1.2 (copy).

MARMORA IRON WORKS

There was no one clause in the bill of last session, for regulating our intercourse with the United States, and which has been reserved for his Majesty's approbation, that displeased me so much, as that for allowing pig-iron to be imported from that country duty free. I do not know what member it was, that introduced it into the Attorney General's resolutions, but if passed into a law (which I am inclined to think it will not be) it would be likely to discourage European capitalists from vesting their funds in Canadian manufactures in future. The Marmora iron works were established in the township of that name in 1820 (the operations commenced in May that year) and they now consist of two blast furnaces and a forge of four fires. Bar iron of all descriptions is made, as also potash kettles of a very fine texture, and all sorts of castings; these works have furnished government with about 300 tons of pig-iron in part of a contract of 750 tons. The price of pig-iron is £15 a ton, while in the United States it can be had for £8.15.0. Some years ago the price of pig-iron in New York State was as high as it now is at Marmora, but the Americans encouraged their own manufacture and a reduction of price is the consequence. It would surely be the worst of all policy for us to crush an establishment like this, by putting foreigners on the same footing as the native manufacturer. COLONIAL ADVOCATE, 7 April 1825 (Appendix).

ON THE WAR OF 1812

I went on board the great ship St. Lawrence [*Sir James Yeo's Flag-ship, 1812-1815*], and although none of your warlike sort of people except in a quiet way and upon paper, I do hope that if she is ever again put in commission, she will give these noisy brethren of ours on the other side the lake such a broadside as they may remember; so that at the peace which will be thereafter, I may hear less of their glorious and uninterrupted line of victories by sea and land—General Hull's campaign to the contrary notwithstanding. COLONIAL ADVOCATE, 7 April 1825 (Appendix); Lindsey, vol. I, p. 68.

RESTATEMENT OF POLICY

As to my sentiments in politics in general, they are on record in my past numbers: I think the British empire the greatest and the wisest that ever has been; but am of opinion that we colonists *do not enjoy* our just privileges as members of that empire—I think that taxation and representation ought to go hand in hand; that the best and safest substitute for *nobility here* is a general education, widely diffused; that, as the colonies *cannot* be represented in England, they ought to be allowed more freedom from oppressive and arbitrary enactments; that there is no danger either to the interests of religion, or to civil rights, likely to arise from our putting down that black and dark shadow to a free country, a political church establishment; that all religious denominations ought to be, for every political purpose, in the eye of the law *equal*; that the colonies ought to be united for general purposes, and have a Legislature which could pass laws binding on the whole in certain cases, such as the Post-Office, internal communications, patent rights, bounties, draw-backs, wild lands, copy-rights, etc.; that after a seven years' residence in this province, Americans are naturalized if they comply with the formalities of the provincial statute—that a free and cheap exchange of newspapers between editors in this country and Great Britain would have done more for the colonies than most people are aware of; that it was unwise to prevent this by half measures; that the contest between the court party in this colony and the representatives of the people is, on the one hand, a struggle for political power, and on the other for political existence—might against right. If I am told that Britain pays *this* expense and *that* expense for us, I reply that England actually impoverishes this country, by *preventing* our establishing home manufactures, and by large and improvident grants to persons who never saw the colony, or saw it only as Judges or Generals, for a few years or months, and who scrape and scratch all they can out of those poor wretches who are so unfortunate as to purchase on credit, at a high price, from their agents; it is inconceivable the sums that leave the colony in this way. To crown all, the wastes of the colony are to be sold to a monopolizing set of English speculators who like as the East India Company do now, will no doubt hereafter make the most they can of us, and be a second edition of the Holland Land Company, who *have conferred such vast and precious benefits on a portion of the people of a neighbouring state, by removing the root of evil* in *some places effectually out of the country almost as fast as it* grew. COLONIAL ADVOCATE, 8 December 1825.

TRUE PATRIOTISM

Ortus a quercu, non a salice, exclaimed our trusty aide de camp, Peter Russell; "I am a bough from an oak, not from a willow." I'll try your mettle, Messrs. Sinecure, Pension, Place and Post,—come forth with your aiders and abettors, and I will shew what a true Patriot is. A Patriot is none of your raving, railing, ranting, enquiring, accusing radicals—nor is he one of your idle, stall-fed, greasy, good for nothing sinecurists or pluralists,—he is in deed and in truth a friend to his country. He studies the laws and institutions of his nation, that he may improve others, endeavours rather to cultivate the acquaintance of, and shew a correct example to the better informed classes; he associates only with those whose private conduct is in unison with their public professions. Is not a mob hunter, nor a lecturer of the multitude; desires rather the secret approbation of the enlightened few than the ephemeral popularity of the many.—If he is a member of Parliament he looks carefully into the merits of the question and votes consistently with his conscience, whether with or against the ministry. He is neither a place hunter, nor a sinecure hunter. He promises his constituents very little, but tries to perform a great deal. Finally he is among the last of men who would countenance political *"gamblers and blacklegs"*; but a wise, manly and vigilant administration is his delight.—Is there one among your ranks who answers to this description, let him come forward? He alone can save you from confusion and defeat. COLONIAL ADVOCATE, 4 May 1826; Lindsey, vol. I, p. 76.

THE TYPE RIOTS

LETTER TO MATTHEW CROOKS, MERCHANT, ANCASTER

QUEENSTON, JUNE 26, 1826

I have your letter of the 9th, and return you my sincere thanks for your kind services as my agent during the reign of the Advocate and until twenty-four hours after its annihilation. Your conduct when compared with that of my pretended friend Gurnett raises you in my estimation and does you honour.—*Secrete amicos admone, lauda palam;* says Publius Syrus. But it was not enough for him to omit the praise—no—the adjutant could do no less than appear in that virtuous paper he so greatly despised, (or said he did), for the purpose of giving the editor of the Advocate a kick, the moment he thought he perceived him tottering! Very different was Mr. Cameron's demeanour—he too disliked the late papers—but contented himself with stating in a friendly letter his complete disapprobation. Mr. Cameron felt it due to himself to make no *public exhibition* on the occasion—And as for the other, I trust he will be well rewarded from the proper quarter for his officiousness—I have been reading human character for not a few years but must own that I was far from appreciating duly the disposition of your friend Mr. Gurnett. As to Riley and the rest I do not think them worth even a private notice. They are a common coin sure enough.

As to what you say about low and contemptible servility etc. etc.,

etc., the uselessness of the Advocate, and where *you compare me to a dog*, I suppose you mean well, when I take these expressions in view and compare them with your former letters, and general friendly conduct towards me. I do not see the late numbers of the Col. Adv. in the same light as you do—for I consider them among the most useful and instructive I ever published—but it is possible I may be wrong and you right.

On reading your letter of the 9th June I think it proper to state to you, that you have my full permission to publish it in the Observer if you think fit so to do.

I do not remember that up to the day on which the Advocate was destroyed I lost one single subscriber in the Niagara district, and in the main the number of subscribers were on the increase throughout the colony.

The outrage on my property on the 8th. inst. was committed by persons with whom I had no quarrel, and is unequalled in atrocity in the annals of printing, yet I very much doubt whether it will call forth the *printed* indignation of an Ancaster [*gap in MS of one word*] Tanner, Taylor, and Yankee Beer seller—That's the wrong side of the question.

As to my misfortunes of which you speak, I do not see that I am now more unfortunate than I have been for these few years past. I have been engaged in a cause ever likely to decrease my means and add to my embarrassments—I was the ass in the fable who performed his duty while he bore in silence all the kicks and cuffs offered him, but the moment he began to resent and kick again his master sold him to a tanner for the price of his skin.

I think you had better enclose all my papers and send them to me by a safe private hand to the care of David Thorburn Esquire Post office Queenston, I shall not want agents in future.

You have at different times mentioned your intention of paying me the small balance now in your hands, but it has hitherto escaped perhaps your recollection. To be candid with you I am really very much distressed for want of money, and if you could enclose such sum as may be in your possession *by return of mail* addressed to me, "care of David Thorburn Esquire Queenston" I would esteem it the top stone of the many favours already done me.

Your friend Judge Boulton's trial got a place at last when the paper was in a train for admitting that species of news. I believe your manuscript was faithfully followed.

I am not [*gap of one or two words*] aware that I have not deserved good at the [*gap of one word*] hands of the people of Upper Canada—

I am sure if I have been (as you tell me) an unprofitable servant, I [have] employed myself (with my eyes open) on an unprofitable service.

I remain
Your sincere well wisher and obliged and obedient servant
W. L. MACKENZIE

P.S. I have no fears for the future, none.—I will surely get justice of the government people for destroying my property, and if so, I will be able to pay all I owe and begin the world anew with a cargo of experience for my stock in trade. I am glad it is only with my journal you find fault, for as it is dead and drowned and ended you will of course scold W.L.M. no more. LINDSEY PAPERS.

JOURNALS OF THE HOUSE OF ASSEMBLY

MOST IMPORTANT PUBLICATION

The publisher of the journals of assembly, having determined to print an *extra number* of copies, in addition to the 200 required for the use of the legislature, *will receive orders* from those who may be desirous of possessing themselves of the *most authentic* and *valuable record* of the proceedings of their representatives in the last memorable session of this parliament, that ever can be offered to the public.

As this *great national work* could not be printed at so *very moderate* a price as it is here offered at to subscribers, under any other circumstances than in connexion with the very limited official edition, the publisher trusts that a deep and lively interest will be felt in *promoting* and *encouraging the subscription* for extra copies, as an excellent means of rendering more perfect our constitution, by causing the great body of the people more seriously to consider *upon proper premises*, the conduct and character of those to whom their *temporal* and *eternal* welfare is in no small degree entrusted: namely their representatives in parliament.

The work now offered to the public, although it shews the political feelings of all parties in their resolves, motions and votes, has *no bias* or party feeling to either side, but faithfully records with official exactness, all that was done or proposed to be done during the session.

To the intelligent yeomanry of the colony, enough has been

already said in regard to the merits of a work of such manifest importance as the journals of parliament. To them is entrusted the power of negativing burthensome taxations and impositions, and wisely directing the provincial revenues, by sending as their representatives men of principle and information—and in the journals they will learn to whom they can entrust their lives, liberties and estates, and also who those are that have proved themselves by their votes not trustworthy.

When a farmer wants to know how his representative behaved last session, he should not trust to newspaper report, *but to the journals.* There he will find out whether he was absent or present on important occasions; whether he slipt below the bar at voting time, or remained above it—whether he gave a vote such as the farmer himself would have given, whether he voted straight or crooked, whether he did his duty or omitted it—all is minutely recorded in that book of books—*the journals.*

The journals are the unerring touchstone of truth, for while the news give some sketches of what parliamentmen said, the journals tell you every thing every man of them did from the morning on which the garrison guns announced the lieutenant governor's arrival to open the session, and until the evening when the same noisy instruments gave notice at the highest pitch of their warlike throats, that that excellent personage had taken his departure from the tenantless hospital after adding to our statute book, and bidding the Lawmakers an annual farewell.

The past session has been pregnant with *important events,* and the journals shew these in their course:—such as the votes, motions, resolves and divisions on the naturalization bills *or Alien question,*—on *the Welland Canal* affairs,—the *St. Lawrence* navigation (proposed and defeated) improvements,—the *Rideau Canal,* a stupendous undertaking of 133 miles,—the *war losses* on the frontier,—the *Clergy Reserves,*—the far-famed *Abolition* bill *of imprisonment for debt,*—the Burlington Bay Canal,—*roads and bridges,* the proceedings, reports, resolutions etc. upon them, and how petitions for aid were treated,—the *cost* of a session *of parliament,*—provincial revenue affairs,—resolves and motions on *colonial trade,* and many other interesting subjects,—the votes for and against certain measures,—the *changes of opinion* among members,—messages from the king to the lieutenant governor and parliament, and from the lieutenant governor to the assembly;—addresses to the lieutenant governor and the British government, with replies from Downing-street, and the government house,—proceedings with refractory or *obstinate printers,*—questions of order and disorder,—resolves on *civil rights,*—district court proceedings,—*School houses,*—*improvement* of the *highways* (attorney general's plans for)—Hail Columbia, —Yankee Doodle,—coinage,—debtors' *jail limits,*—*trial by jury* (regulations for),—intestate estates,—whipping and the pillory,— *register offices,*—*police of towns,*—lateral cut to Niagara,—Kettle Creek and its harbour,—*guardians* to minors,—Major Randal's petition,—*dower* to wives,—physicians and surgeons,—leave of absence,—the *Kingston pretended bank,*—Hamilton court house,— *Libel,*—Marriage bill,—Mill-dam bill,—Patent rights—Prince Edward County division,—Methodists, Presbyterians, Baptists, etc., their right to hold lands (resolves on),—Replevin laws of England,— Newcastle district waters,—*Sedition laws,*—borough-members and their wages,—the Canada Company,—the York bank,—contraband trade,—*returns of population,*—Lincoln county division,—the library, —public stages,—tavern debts,—Valentine Gill and his map,— Matthew Leech,—ale houses,—Ensign Roach,—the new port of entry,—*assessments,*—confiscated estates,—the post office bill,—the new fees to magistrates,—members' postages,—*insolvent debtors' relief,*—on real estate,—new member from the Bathurst district,— *county courts,*—and on five hundred other topics of more or less general interest.

Every member's vote on every one of those questions which were put to the vote is to be found in the journals, and a farmer on getting through with a copy of the journals, and a copy of the statutes of the province for this year, would really sit down full of amazement, not at seeing so little done in the way of legislation, but at seeing so much perfected and how much more is under way.

From the journals the father of a family might teach his children, and himself learn the acts, customs and usages of a free people as shewn in the exercise of their constitutional civil rights.—He who is in possession of the journals has got a political treasure, a key to the conduct and character of every man in parliament, and will be at no loss how to bestow his vote next general election;—and as that *great event* may in case of the demise of his majesty, be more near at hand than is generally supposed, by reason of the king's feeble state of health, such a work is the more essential,—for a *third session* is generally the touchstone whereby an M.P. is *best tried.*

[*Throughout 1827 the* Colonial Advocate *title line described William Lyon Mackenzie as Printer to the Honourable the House of Assembly of Upper Canada.*] COLONIAL ADVOCATE, 1 March 1827.

THE DECLARATION
OF INDEPENDENCE

It is rather remarkable that the idea we expressed in our last letter to Lord Dalhousie, of a reunion between Great Britain and her former colonies, should have been spoken of by our friend Mr. Gourlay as a probable and desirable event in his letter to the editor of the Morning Chronicle, *almost of even date with ours* to the governor-in-chief. Mr. Gourlay expresses himself as follows:—

"I do wish that reconciliation could be brought about between Britain and her progeny—I do wish for re-union with all who speak the English language—even re-union with the States of America; and am assured that these could be brought about by wise colonial policy. Readers may be startled with such an idea but it is not one of a moment, or of hasty growth."

Our sentiments respecting the course now adopted by the general government and combined sovereignties of republican North America, have already been briefly explained—and a perusal of the *ostensible* causes which induced the British Colonists of 1776 to separate from their mother country, as set forth in their declaration of independence, may be the means of preventing or lessening some of those abuses to which colonial governments are yet liable. We have therefore printed entire that ancient historical document, *in another part of this day's Advocate,* (being the only instance in which it has appeared in a colonial journal, within our remembrance) and would respectfully request of those friends of the monarchy now in authority, information—how many of the wrongs complained of in 1776 are yet in these remaining provinces unredressed?

Since our last week's paper we have copied from New York and other papers the arrival in the United States, of about 1700 passengers from Britain, Ireland and these colonies, to which may be added perhaps as many more, by land, and to ports from which we have no regular accounts.—Three thousand a week is a powerful immigration.—Let colonial manufactures be encouraged, and the tide will turn northward. COLONIAL ADVOCATE, 19 July 1827.

ROBERT EMMET

Every one must recollect the tragical story of young Emmet, the Irish patriot; it was too touching to be soon forgotten. During the troubles in Ireland, he was tried, condemned, and executed, on a charge of treason. His fate made a deep impression on public sympathy.—He was so young, so intelligent, so generous, so brave, so every thing that we are apt to like in a young man. His conduct, under the trial too, was so lofty and intrepid. The noble indignation with which he repelled the charge of treason against his country; the eloquent vindication of his name; and his pathetic appeal to posterity in the hopeless hour of condemnation. All these entered deeply into every generous bosom, and even his opponents lamented the stern policy that dictated his execution. COLONIAL ADVOCATE, 10 January 1828.

GOOD NEWS

CIVIL GOVERNMENT OF THE CANADAS

[*The occasion was the publication in England of a Report of the Committee of the House of Commons to inquire into the State of the Civil Government of Canada (see Doughty and Story, Documents 1819-1828, p. 466). The Report (reprinted by Mackenzie in the same issue) recommended many of the reforms repeatedly demanded by Upper Canadians, such as placing the public revenue under public control, reforming the constitution of the legislative council, affirming the right of the government to extend the use of clergy reserve funds beyond the Church of England, changing the charter of King's College so as to remove religious tests for professors.*]

We congratulate every sincere friend to Great Britain, on the prudent, just, and conciliating report which has emanated from the select committee of the House of Commons appointed to inquire into the state of the Canadas. The enemies of our country may raise the old war cry of "sedition", "disaffection" as much as they please; hereafter it will go for nought. If such measures as are here recommended be carried into effect they will afford the best bulwark against invasion or aggression, namely, the affections of an intelligent, free, happy, and therefore loyal population. There may be some measures recommended in the expediency of which we cannot fully concur, but we are so well satisfied with the general tenor of the report, and with the patriotic and honourable conduct of the imperial parliament towards this country as therein made manifest, that we shall not qualify our humble yet sincere tribute of approbation, by pointing out a single fault. The report is, in truth, an extraordinary document, and if followed up may save millions upon millions in lives and treasure to Old England. The time fast approaches when ample justice will be done, by all parties, to the patriotism and sincere attachment displayed by the independent part of the public press in the Canadas towards Great Britain and British institutions. The agents from Upper and Lower Canada have deserved well of their country. COLONIAL ADVOCATE, 25 September 1828.

LETTERS TO JOHN NEILSON

Nov. 27, 1828

DEAR SIR

It was expected here, previous to your arrival from England, in Montreal, that you would have visited Upper Canada on your way home—this expectation, I believe, arose out of some conversation you had had with Mr. George Ryerson, agent for the Dissenters, before he left London. And so well pleased were the people here with your exertions on behalf of the colonists, that it was intended to have given you a public dinner in honour of the cause you had so ably and indefatigably espoused. You did not come, however, nor have I learnt that you, or Mr. Cuvillier, or Mr. Viger (if he be returned) have written to or corresponded with any of the members of Assembly who form the opposition to Doctor Strachan's system of government.

During the last two years I have written either thrice or four times to Mr. Samuel Neilson, but only once received any reply; I have, therefore, presumed that he has no time to answer requests out of the line of his profession, and tho' not personally acquainted with you, more than with Mr. Neilson, Junior, have, this time, addressed you—and that, because your active assistance given to the cause of the Lower Canadians induces me to think that you will also be willing to give us of Upper Canada such information as you can furnish for our guidance and good understanding with the sister province.

It has been expressed to me within a very short period by Mr. Rolph, Mr. Randal, Mr. Bidwell, Doctor Baldwin, Mr. Cawthra, Mr. Ketchum, and several other members of our provincial legislature, that to cultivate a good understanding with the Independent

Members of your parliament, would be very advisable, and might be conducive to the mutual interests and advantage of both colonies. Such also is my own opinion. If, therefore, we could receive authentic copies of such of the proceedings of your legislature, as might concern the interests of both provinces, or as might be to us a precept and example by which to profit—and also occasional individual suggestions, upon important questions, it would be well and desirable. Letters and packets addressed to assemblymen during the session are all paid for by the province—printed papers come free when there is room in the mails—and at other periods than the sitting of parliament, no one of us would think of the expense of conveyance of any papers that might be sent us for general information. Should you, therefore, write, to myself, or any of the other members whose fixed residence is at York; or should Mr. Cuvillier write—we will at all times be happy to hear from you, and to join with you in any measure that may be for the common good.

Would not one agent, if a Canadian, or one long resident in Canada, serve in London, for both provinces?—I consider the residence of an active agent at the British seat of Government as indispensible to Colonial interests, and wait with no little anxiety for your proceedings below on that question.

Elected to parliament, in the teeth of all the weight power and influence of government, and that too for the most populous and wealthy shire in the Colony, and the immediate seat of the local administration, I afford to you a convincing proof in my own person how unpopular the measures of the late lieut-governor and his advisers must have been. In the Advocate of this day you will see Sir John Colborne's replies to two addresses, from which, and private information, I judge he is to pursue popular and friendly measures—and some of us think it would be well for the legislature at its meeting to assert *that principle* so long in use in Britain, which, though it does not dictate to the sovereign (or his representative here) the ministry he must choose, yet informs him that a change of confidential advisers is thought needful, and that such change, as will induce parliament to repose with confidence in the integrity of the successors. It is in contemplation to assert this principle *here*— and we wait with anxiety for your example in L.C. I could wish to possess your sentiments on the subject, in a letter, not private nor for printed publication, but such as I might shew to the other members at my discretion. Nothing is more certain than that the best regulations, by Parliament, may be and are set at nought by vicious executive councils. With Doctor Strachan and his scholars in the management of our revenues, no good could be expected from any parliament that could be assembled.—Only to think of the Welland Canal, what a humbug of a direction they have had all along. Ignorance, folly and cupidity, united with avarice, and the canal as it stands is their monument. I wish Lower Canada would make some enquiry into the affairs of this waste—their £25,000 is sunk in it and they will probably look to it. The Deep Cut is tumbling in, *avalanche* after *avalanche* ($20,000 to $30,000 damage)—and the whole when looked into, will, or else I greatly deceive myself—prove to be a disgraceful job to some folks. Of the Report of your British-Canadian Com., with the evidence, (See *Advocate* of this day, etc.) no one official copy has as yet reached us here—perhaps you could procure us one from Lower Canada. I have seen extracts of part of the evidence in the papers of that province. Sir John Colborne keeps up a correspondence with Sir James Kempt. I hope they two will decide upon pursuing measures calcula[ted t]o allay the late and present discontents. One thing is certain, [the] people of late receive less abuse from official and demi-official news-venders in both colonies than formerly came to their share, and perhaps the Halifax Free Press is correct in anticipating that Sir James Kempt will not tolerate the old calumnies to be longer propagated. The Advocate newspaper has a circulation evidently superior to any other journal in the colony, but I would at once resign it if I could find some person capable of conducting it on liberal principles and in such a way as would continue to it that influence which independent public prints ought to possess on the public mind. This is my day of publication, and I have taken an hour to myself to write this hasty scrawl, before the post departs at eleven, for Quebec. That hour is at hand, and does not allow me to read what I have written, far less to get my letter written in a fair hand. Your goodness will excuse these defects, however, in an Upper Canada Printer—and—

Believe me—I remain
With much respect
Your obedient and humble servant
W. L. MACKENZIE

P.S. A member of Assembly *privately* suggested to me that Mr. Stanley, late under-secretary, might be with advantage appointed provincial agent. It is possible you may know him? I doubt the propriety of such an appointment.

2nd P.S. The member referred to in this day's paper, from whom I had information yesterday, that the damage already done at the

Welland exceeds $20,000 or $30,000, and that it is only a sample of what is to follow, was W. Woodruff, Esq. St. David's.—What must the engineer have been and what the director, who allowed Yankee speculating contractors—(or perhaps shared their gains)—thus to impose on Britain and the Colonies!!! I speak on the information I have. LINDSEY PAPERS; Doughty and Story, DOCUMENTS 1818-1828, p. 464.

YORK, Jan. 19, 1829

There must be a responsibility in the Government; by the constitution, *somewhere*—and the more I read the more I think that I have mistaken hitherto the persons in whom that responsibility rests in these colonies. It is, perhaps, after all in the Governors alone (in a few cases excepted). The Governors are their own premiers, they sign all treasury warrants, they can (remove or) suspend any other officer or judge at their pleasure. If the representatives of the people complain of an officer or other public servant, it is the governors alone who can remedy the abuse, and if they decline to do so the Houses of Assembly may refuse to entrust the public monies to their disposal, and in the end, on their complaining to the British Government, the governor so acting must go home and answer the charges made against him by the assemblies: for I perceive by your proceedings that the British Government will not hereafter sanction the taking of monies from the provincial treasury without a parliamentary vote.

Your Speaker, Mr. Papineau, in one of his speeches compares the executive council to the British Privy Council—Is he not somewhat correct? Is not the power of *hearing* their advice and taking his own still left with the Governor? May he not *severally* suspend them also, if he thinks them deserving of suspension, and appeal to England?

I of all things wish to perceive where the responsibility does rest, and if you will do me the favour to refer me to any authority for my better guidance, or write a letter that I may shew to other members I will feel obliged.

I brought forward a measure the other day for enquiring into the way in which Peter Robinson manages his crown land system—I think it a great grievance that all the waste lands of the crown should be in the hands of one man, at his absolute disposal, without the interference of the colonial Assemblies.

I think your finance resolutions will in due time, all (one about tithes excepted) pass our House, verbatim. I could have wished that such printed papers (parliamentary documents) as you order to the press for the information of your house should have been sent me—

They might have afforded much information, and I would cheerfully have paid for the trouble and expense.—None of the British Journals of Commons or Lords are to be found in our Library, and not one American book.

I have been carefully enquiring into the management of the P.O. department, and have caused the substance of the Postmasters of this town's examination to be forwarded to Mr. Stayner by this day's mail. Your Mr. Cuvillier told me, in Montreal, years ago, that the British Government were fully authorising to have a mail for their own convenience, but that we also had constitutional power to establish a provincial post-office if the King's Post did not suit us. Otherwise it would be a tax without our consent. Do you think that a provincial establishment would be advisable? I doubt it, under present circumstances.

This Welland Canal is a shameful job—we shall endeavour fully to enquire into it. I see you give committees power to send for "records"; we do not generally in U.C. draw out motions for committees in that way. I wish I knew more of the powers of the House.

23 MARCH 1829

I am sorry the Commissioners Bill is lost, because it renders yours which passed useless—a dead letter.

The bill went to the Upper House with the names of Mr. Speaker Bidwell, Mr. John Rolph and Mr. Thomson of Kingston in it—all old members and of the independent side, and, strange to tell! the Peers, who a few days before had agreed to appoint the commissioners in the act (see joint resolutions), changed their mind, and instead of striking out any of the above names and putting another, or others in their place or places, they struck out the clause of appointment altogether, and put in a new one leaving the choice òf commissioners to Sir John Colborne. The act, by the way, gave them authority for three years. These amendments came down on the last day, and were read once and then the bill was dead. Our road bill too, an excellent and valuable measure granting $54,000 to repair roads and bridges was lost up stairs—and in fact they passed no bill of any consequence to the great body of the people.

．　　　　．　　　　．

You say in your letter, you have laboured hard and made little headway—and well may we say so also; for myself as one I can truly say that I have come from the House night after night, at 8 or 10 or 12 P.M. after a twelve hours attendance, so tired and worn out that when I went to bed I could not sleep for perfect fatigue. I am a *little diminutive creature,* and I really could not have conceived it possible that I could have undergone the fatigue I have endured during the last ten weeks. I had to write all the original matter necessary for my newspaper, reports of proceedings etc,—I keep no clerk, consequently had to keep my books etc., and as we publish from 30 to 35 quires of news every week I get involved thereby and with other business, and when the Lt. Gov. got through with his closing speech I felt like a bird escaped from a cage.

In the House my principal object has been enquiry, and the result of that enquiry is, and I speak my mind candidly, that the present system is too corrupt to last long, its rottenness will in the end cause it to fall to pieces. Justice is difficult to come at—our local magistrates are often a nuisance in their neighbourhood,—our revenues are wasted on worthless parasites—our roads and bridges are the worst in the world and use may not improve them—our public works, when we plan any, cost five times what they ought—a particular clergy are encouraged and pampered as spies on their less assuming neighbours, education languishes—the costs of law courts, from the least to the highest, are enormous to a proverb—even our very monopolies are (the Canada Company for instance) made a means of adding strength to what is called the court party, instead of adding to our means for public improvements—the people have no check upon the public expenditures—no remedy for abuses, but to bear them—England, as you say, means us well—but she is not at our door—and justice even in England is a costly commodity. I am, from habit and education, very aristocratic in my notions; but observation and reflection has of late years greatly lessened my veneration for the heroes and heroines of ancient date and the pomp and shew of feudal grandeur. Our House of Lords here is the most wearisome piece of lumber ever invented to clog the wheels of a youthful state. Our peerage are literally a nuisance—if they were elected in some way or other there would be some check upon them of public opinion—but as it is, they appear to me to be deficient even in common sense. Here, as you may suppose, the great mass of the people are displeased, nor do I believe that Sir John Colborne will mend matters—very likely he is a good soldier—I do not doubt his fighting powers—but otherwise I do not see he is good for much. Our House of Assembly has not been required to grant any supplies this year, His Excellency having supplied himself, as you will perceive by his speech.

As I have this year a very good foreman in my office, I can be spared, and mean to devote a few weeks to a short tour thro' your province and the neighbouring States, to observe what may be worth remembering. If I come to Quebec, where I have not been for six years, I will take the liberty of waiting upon you.

Your agents bill has been lost in your Legislative Council. Be it so. Nothing can be more essential to England than an accurate knowledge of the wishes of the colonists—that knowledge would be well obtained by the accredited agents of the colonists—yet so it is they cannot be appointed in such a manner as to represent the people. Here we made no attempt at appointing an agent—it would have been *a waste of time*. LINDSEY PAPERS.

A CORRUPT ADMINISTRATION

WHEN BAD MEN CONSPIRE GOOD MEN MUST UNITE

It is very evident that the British Government, either from ignorance or design, treat the people here as *something below* the rank of freemen; and the person almost officially announced as having been chosen Chief Justice, only a few days ago, compared our popular elections to the Saturnalia of the Romans, where the slave and bondsman could with impunity insult the sovereigns of the world.

One and twenty years have elapsed since Mr. Justice Thorpe was driven from our shores in disgrace, to seek in England that redress for his own and his country's wrongs, which he sought in vain. His unfortunate wife and family, supported for a time by the charity of a few individuals, at last followed her husband. The people soon forgot that a judge had been among them whose noble mind and manly Irish feelings unfitted him to be an instrument of oppression. Judge Thorpe and his wrongs were speedily consigned to oblivion; no succeeding Canadian *Saturnalia* produced in parliament even a compliment to his memory. The few rioted in luxury. The many remained wrapt up in inglorious forgetfulness. Cases of individual and general wrong continued to accumulate. War ensued, and the Canadians fought; not for their liberties, for they *in reality* had none to fight for; they warred for the continuance of a system which had built up an established priesthood in the midst of them, rendered the popular voice of none effect, crushed education, impeded public improvement and formed a bar to population. They took arms to protect the judiciary, and their blood was spilt to defend what a

Chatham, a Fox or an Erskine would have denominated "a gilded despotism."

Peace followed and Robert Gourlay came amongst us. Like a Thorpe and a Willis, he had every thing to gain by uniting with the faction in power, every thing to fear if he opposed its combined strength. He did oppose it. But the people early forgot their benefactor, for such he surely was; and their worthless representatives humbled themselves in the dust, and prayed for executive vengeance to fall upon his devoted head; he was persecuted, tried again and again, sent to a dungeon, and finally banished like a felon, to the United States, denied the privilege of trial by jury, and convicted by means of old Powell of the heinous crime of being a Briton and refusing to leave a British colony. This was another political sacrifice, yet in Mr. Gourlay's extreme distress the people forgot him, and when he fell a victim they bowed the head and left him to his fate. Full of truly generous and disinterested affection towards them, however, he went to London, and in 3 octavo volumes, gave to the British public a faithful and eloquent record of their wrongs. Deaf to his advice, and scorning all counsel, the government and its agents have continued to treat the Canadians "as an ignorant multitude"—"a province of slaves."

Since then the executive has greatly narrowed the exercise of the people's imaginary rights. They are now taxed without their consent and the taxes appropriated without their approbation; their judges are appointed, pensioned and dismissed, and new appointments made at variance with their wishes. Their executive officers are constituted legislative counsellors for life, and the nominal servants of the public have thus become its real masters. Attempts at pointing out or remedying flagrant abuses or manifest oppression and misconduct in persons clothed with power, or their connexions, is usually productive of ruinous consequences to the party aggrieved, and justice *such as it is* has become so costly as to be far beyond the reach of the humble farmer. The people at last have cried out—their complaints went to *the foot of the throne*—they complained of misrule, of injustice, of tyranny, of oppression; and the persons complained of were justified and promoted, lauded, encouraged and rewarded.

Such is colonial usage in America.

Judge Willis came among us a stranger, highly recommended, sworn to administer justice, bound to resist oppression. He did act justly, he did resist oppression. He had an opinion, and as a conscientious man he stated his determination to do no violation to his oath. In eight short months he was disgraced, dismissed, traduced and vilified by persons in authority—he sought justice for us and for himself from the King of Great Britain; he laid his case before the persons who are there placed by the boroughmongers in authority over the people. Disgrace and dismissal are his recompense, accompanied probably with a pecuniary loss of thousands of pounds; and the man who was most violent and most personal in his opposition to his mild and noble conduct, even John Beverley Robinson is about to be appointed Chief Justice of Upper Canada!

Had Mr. Justice Willis chimed in with the despicable faction who rule the country, honours and riches, the wealth wrung out of the colony would have been his;—but he had a noble soul, a generous, a feeling heart; he was an Englishman of the right class and could sympathize with those who had suffered wrong—and therefore it is that he is ruined. Perhaps some ancient family connexion, some noble relative among the sinecurists and placemen who suck England's best blood, may, through court favour or bedchamber influence, procure him a Presidency among the Hindoos or Bramins, or a Judgeship (like Mr. Thorpe) in the murderous climate of Sierra Leone. If such should not be the case, Mr. Brougham in his famous speech upon English law and English injustice has given us to understand that subserviency to the powers that be is his only refuge.

.   .   .

In the debate on Canada, in this day's paper, the ministry seem to know only two things about this country, viz.—how many regiments are required to keep it in their possession, and how much cash it will take to maintain these regiments. Are they ignorant of our numerous petitions and of those of the sister Province? Not they indeed. But they are deaf to our entreaties, and count as their best friends those men whom the country *if it durst* would spue out of its mouth as the very scum and offscourings of mankind. And is not Sir John Colborne a prime actor in this political drama! Be assured, gentle reader, that Murray will neither order an appointment to be made, nor a measure of consequence to be taken in the colony without having first received the advice of his friend Colborne. To borrow a figure from arithmetic, we may say—As was Maitland to Bathurst so is Colborne to Murray. The faction have first to shew the present tenant of Elmsley House that they are the most pliable tools he can find in the province, and then the road to preferment and to the ruin of the patriotic Willis is an easy beaten path.

The people of Upper Canada are well aware that they now enjoy neither British liberty nor indeed any other species of liberty whatsoever; but that they are the very Gibeonites of modern times, the hewers of wood and the drawers of water to a worthless crew whom they could extinguish by the very breath of their nostrils. They look to their representatives, but it is of no use—their representatives can only echo their sentiments—if they go farther their labours will not be acceptable.—Let the farmers therefore look to it—if they form in every township or neighbourhood corresponding and constitutional associations—if they put on the attitude of freemen, their remonstrances will be heeded, but if not, some twenty years hence their children may be found in Bondage, bitterly lamenting the sacrifice of another Willis, or the immolation of another Thorpe.

That every means in the power of General Colborne, at the head of an administration of his own choice, surrounded by Strachan, Robinson, Boulton, Hagerman, Macaulay, Sherwood, Powell, Markland and their sort as his divan, will be made use of to induce the next session of parliament to consent to severe and arbitrary militia and other laws, new and oppressive taxes, and such other strong measures as the present system requires, we can very readily believe; of the success of his endeavours we are somewhat less certain. *On the conduct of the people themselves, however, will in a great measure depend that of a majority of their representatives.*

That the country is in a dangerous and unsettled state none will deny; that we are in the hands of a merciful creator all will be ready to acknowledge. Let us then remind the ministers of everlasting truth, the unbought and unpensioned among the clergy of Canada of whatsoever sect or denomination, that it is their especial duty, in the present alarming crisis, in their churches and in their chapels, to join with their congregations in humble and fervent prayers to the ruler of the universe; to implore His especial protection to this our infant country, so that we may enjoy the inestimable blessings of civil and religious liberty under a well balanced constitution, and transmit it unimpaired as a legacy to our children; and that the workers of mischief amongst us may be confounded and put to shame. COLONIAL ADVOCATE, 7 May 1829.

FOR UNION OF THE PROVINCES

To JOHN NEILSON   YORK, DEC. 7, 1829.
SIR

The last letter I wrote you was, I think, during the last session of our provincial legislature, one evening when I was tired and heavy after leaving the House. I have not heard from you since, and I presume my letter was not upon matters of any importance. I now again would feel a pleasure in hearing from you upon a subject designed by yourself, but baulked by our legislative council last winter, I mean the profit from a meeting of committees from the two provinces to consult upon matters of mutual importance to the two Canadas. Experience has told me not to trust in the passage of a bill in our legislative council next session, but the more I consider the thing the better I like it, and the more satisfied am I that it would be productive of good effects. Mr. Rolph called upon me last Saturday night, on his return from Kingston, where he had been on a visit to the Speaker of our H. of Assembly, and he thinks that the only way to bring about an interview of the sort, would be for your house of assembly to nominate and appoint a committee of its members to meet a committee of our house half way betwixt Quebec and York,* immediately upon the opening of your session, which is just two weeks later than ours. If you will write that you like the measure, a resolution will pass our house, I believe, by a vast majority, the moment we meet, and also a resolve appropriating a sufficient sum from the contingent fund to pay the expenses of the committee. Mr. Rolph informs me that it would not be parliamentary to name the committee in session and then defer the meeting till after our adjournment, and I think that it would be, moreover, very injudicious to do so.

I write at this early day, in order that I may have your opinion, if you will do me that favour, before our house meets. Your experience will perhaps suggest difficulties to which we have not adverted, and your advice may enable us to overcome them, if such exist.

I may also call your attention to the contents of my newspaper (the Advocate) of Thursday next. It will contain the continuation of Judge Willis's correspondence with the Colonial Minister, down to the 22nd. Sept. last, and I am sure you will read it with interest. (The letters are authentic, in Mr. Willis's handwriting.)

I feel anxious for the meeting of the committees to which I have alluded above, because it would lead to a knowledge and communication of the actual wishes and objects of the leading men in both provinces, and enable them to act together for the public good. It might also be the forerunner of a general convention of delegates, from all the colonies, authorized and recommended to meet for the common welfare, a measure I have long and anxiously desired to

* If you like the proposal, name the place of meeting, and the time, in your answer, perhaps the sooner the better.

see carried into effect. In the Quebec Gazette, conducted by your
son, I think I have seen a remark hazarded, that these colonies must
either be dependent on Great Britain or become an integral part of
the American Republic;—I must confess that I have allowed myself
to dream that a connection could be formed by which we might
greatly benefit the country of our forefathers, keep on friendly terms
with the Republic to the south of us, and yet be in a great measure
independent of foreign influence. You have great hope in the
British ministry, so say your letters which I have again read. Now
Sir, I have not that hope. And, I speak it with great deference to
your superior knowledge of mankind, and more particularly of the
British Court, as well as of the [*illegible words*], that on these colonies
themselves, and on the prudence and sagacity of their public men
will in a great measure depend almost every measure of reform in
the abuses of the present system. Although I praise the Americans
in my newspaper, I do not wish us to become more nearly connected
with them to the disadvantage of our British connection, but I am
desirous to see us more our own masters in regard to our local
concerns, and think that while the local legislatures are continued
in each province, a federal system might be now set on foot between
the colonies by which their connection with England might be at
once rendered more secure, permanent, and beneficial to both
countries while their slavish dependence on her ministers would be
done away. The currency, the post-office, the bankrupt laws, the
poor laws, the naturalization laws, post-roads, and many other things
now unattended to or ill-done, would be perhaps properly placed, I
think, in the hands of a federative union. Now we are found dis-
jointed, disquieted, dependencies, liable to become the prey of
revolution, and oppressed by a government which ought to protect
us. Our judges, the expounders of our laws, are exposed to beggary
and ruin if they but dare to act up to the obligations of their oaths,
our laws are anything that the minions of power choose to make
them; a system of espionage prevails, and we have but a nominal
command of the funds raised for our good provinces. Our Assemblies
meet but to quarrel and wrangle, and to demonstrate to the people
their utter inefficiency for the purposes for which they were created.
Yet were we boldly and unitedly to determine to continue *the friends
and the helpers* of the British *people*; to raise our voices against misrule from one end of Cabotia to the other, in a proper legal manner,
we *would* be heard. United to the States, the vast revenue raised at
our seaports would go to swell the funds of congress; their southern
and northern generals would be ours; their slave questions and

immense territory might not add to our happiness; they are not, like Great Britain, our natural customers, nor would we be theirs. Greatly therefore, although I admire them as a people, and *I do admire their course as a nation, and glory in their success,* as affording a proof of the practical utility of *the representative system of government,* yet do I believe that these colonies might be fully as happy separated from them; but if better measures are not taken, and a more statesmanlike policy pursued by us (by the colonists), disunion among ourselves will end only in making us conquered states, sneered at though received into the Union. I have travelled through the States a great deal during the past summer, and am convinced that Great Britain undervalues their strength, and afraid that when too late she will find out by dear bought experience *their unity of purpose.*

I remain

very respectfully

your obedient humble servant

Wm. L. MACKENZIE

LINDSEY PAPERS.

Chapter Eight

CURRENT COMMENT 1830-1833

LETTERS TO JOHN NEILSON

YORK, FEB. 8, 1830

The resources of this colony yet within hands of the executive are vast and valuable but very ill managed—the means in our hands (in the hands of the House) are literally nothing—We want to aid the roads and canals, but have nothing to do it with, and are £100,000 in debt already. Our expenditure to public officers is enormous, but we cannot control it in any way, for whatever we refuse out of one fund the government pays out of another. The very nature of the system prevents the passage of laws which under a more responsible government would be eminently useful.

Your letter to me recommends moderation and unanimity, and Sir we have need of it. We are a different sort of people here to what the Canadians are—Essentially different in many things. . . .

We have nominated Mr. Dunn of the Council, and our Speaker and Mr. Rolph of this House to the Committee to meet your Committee—the two latter are our best men and I hope they will do some good for the country.

YORK, FEB. 18, 1830

The Legislative Council will do nothing we want. The Commissioners Bill to treat with L.C. they have refused to accede to, and say they will accede to no bill of the kind which does not give the executive the sole appointment of the Commissioners.

The Road Bill, so much desired, and indeed all our bills and winter's labour they have thrown under the table, with a few trifling exceptions.

The only thing they appear willing to get in debt for is the

Welland Canal—and that, as you will perceive, not because it will increase the comforts of the people, or add to their income.

There is a full and particular account of many of the parliamentary events of the bygone week in my paper of this morning—to which I refer you. . . . They vote us no supplies—administer justice or injustice as best suits the expediency of the moment—and indeed I may truly say that here legislation is a farce and who are these councillors?—Why, men who under a free government would not weigh a feather in the scale of public opinion.

If our House breaks up on 2nd. March, I think I shall come down and see your legislative system at Quebec.

YORK, APRIL 25, 1830

I now take the liberty to request of you a copy, if you have one to spare, of the rules, regulations, constitution, and system of management of the Quebec Agricultural Society, of which I perceive you are the president. We are about to organize an association of the same sort here, and the only information we have, as far as I can see, is the newspaper accounts of other and similar institutions—which accounts are less full than could be wished for. A printed copy, if the regulations have been printed, could be sent up by the mail free of cost—and it is possible that the secretary could put us western folks into a way of communication with places from whence you of Lower Canada get plans and models of new-fashioned agricultural implements—choice seeds, etc.

I am somewhat surprized that you do not pay a visit to this province in the summer time—travelling is cheap and speedy in most places—and you would be surprized and pleased at the improvements of late years. This is truly a fine country.

In the beginning of the last session I took your statutes of last year and copied out the act appointing commissioners to consult with commissioners from this province, *leaving the necessary blanks.* Doctor Baldwin had drawn another bill, but I prevailed on him to substitute *a copy of yours,* in order that the precedent of its passage might, as being *in print,* operate the more against the Legislative Council if they refused it. The bill passed the Assembly—one Legislative Councillor and two assemblymen were appointed, and the council threw the bill under the table, assigning as their reason that the mode of appointment was contrary to usage of parliament.

This refusal on their part to co-operate with the assembly for the improvement of the province, may become a cause of complaints hereafter—and indeed we had many other reasons for finding fault with the system pursued here. But the latter part of the session was unfavourable for a cool and dispassionate discussion of such topics. A number of the members were persons who had suffered severely by the late war, or else had taken the securities of those who had suffered by it in payment of debts or demands, and they made so much outcry about their losses that it all but drowned their patriotism—and effected a temporary schism in the otherwise unbroken ranks of opposition—Besides, we thought it best, upon the whole, to let the British Ministry alone for one season to see what all their fine promises would amount to. There will be nothing lost thereby, for the people of the colony are well determined to stand up for their rights, and will have them too—I have as good means of ascertaining public opinion as most people in the colony, and it flows in a sound and healthy channel. What the English government will do I know not—but it is abundantly manifest that the persons who eat of the public loaf here, begin to see the necessity of studying to obtain a larger share of public good will than heretofore they had deemed necessary in their several stations. Much of our revenues, however, and means, continue to be uselessly wasted, and a great part of our time in our legislative sessions is employed in going again over ground that is tiresome for its sameness year after year.—I wrote Mr. Hume thrice during the last session, and Mr. Peel once—both gentlemen had acknowledged my former letters—I advised them to modify the system—and the latter would do so—but the former dare not—at least I think so from what I read.

I perceive that shiploads of industrious and active mechanics are arriving with their families from Scotland—and truly I am right glad of their immigration.—North America will hold them all, and the curse of poverty, oppressive taxation, and corn bills they will feel no more. I have found much reason to rejoice and be glad of the day when I left my native town for this country, now ten years back—and when I read of the hunger and hardships which an industrious and hard-working race of people are enduring at the hands of that landed gentry and borough-mongers of Scotland, I regret that the means of emigration, both from highlands and lowlands are not more easy and extensive—many are too poor to come here.

.   .   .

The situation of Europe is very critical—we have London dates to the end of March and Liverpool to the 1st. of April, incl.—the French are truly a spirited brave and manly nation—whether in

France or in Canada—I hope they will be able on both continents to obtain a government in which political power and responsibility will be united—and in which the happiness of the people will cease to depend on the personal character of the ruler for the time being. LINDSEY PAPERS.

TAXATION IN ENGLAND

Every thing that has an existence on the face of the earth, or under the earth, or in the firmament of heaven, is heavily taxed; and these enormous taxes are laid on and expended by a body called the House of Commons, the majority of the members of which are neither directly nor indirectly the representatives of the people, but are the nominees of lords, bishops, and wealthy gentlemen. So that if the representatives of every great county, city, and populous borough in England, Ireland, and Wales were to vote for a reduction of standing armies, tithes, and taxes, and for retrenchment and economy, the rotten borough and Scots close county members could and would outvote them and uphold corruption.

Yorkshiremen in Upper Canada, think on these things!

"Laws grind the poor, when rich men make the laws."

POOR RICHARD, 1831, p. 12.

TAXES AND REVENUES

We went into a full explanation on this head last year. The taxes being chiefly indirect, are far greater in amount than people in general are aware of. The Post Office is a tax of several thousand pounds yearly; the East India Company's monopoly is a tax of several thousands of pounds paid to that Company; the employment at high salaries of persons having no intention to remain long among us is a grievous tax; there are also assessed taxes about $50,000 yearly paid to district treasurers, and expended by the justices; and duties or taxes on still and tavern and shop licenses, and on imported goods of nearly every sort—half a dollar on every barrel of salt, to pay the war losses; so much of a tax on imported spirituous liquors, wines, sugar, coffee, molasses, iron, iron ware, horses, crockery ware, glass and glassware, tobacco, snuff, castings, soap, drugs, oils, paints, cloths and all sorts of dry goods, books, paper, etc., etc.; also a tax on dogs in towns; a tax on wild lands; a tax in shape of high official fees for what could be done far cheaper; the pedlar's tax; the tax on auctioneers; tax on physicians, and surgeons' licenses; police town tax; assessed taxes on dwelling-houses, shops, stores, saw-mills, grist-mills, oxen, cows, storehouses, horses, pleasure carriages, etc.; tax on marrying by license; tax on Quakers, Menonists and Tunkards.

These, with militia fines, excessive costs in civil suits, Fines, Forfeitures and Ferries generally, crown reserves, clergy reserves, absentee proprietors, and the legislative council as now constituted, amount to a good round sum yearly.

Then from the revenues of the colony are paid, pensions enormous, high salaries to official functionaries of various kinds, salaries to the church of England clergy, besides one-seventh of the lands; salaries to the bishop and clergy of the church of Rome, salaries to the church of Scotland ministers, and all these chiefly without the interference or control of the people or their representatives, who are very seldom informed how much revenue has been collected, or to what purpose one half of it has been applied.

In addition to the taxes above mentioned, our consumption of an immense quantity of English manufactures, is an indirect tax of great value paid to the British government, while the carrying trade being in the hands of English merchants, enriches the nation. Canada Wheat and Flour are allowed to be imported into Great Britain at a lower rate of duty than from other countries, to enable the Canadians to pay for the British goods sent hither. POOR RICHARD, 1831, p. 10.

RIGHTS

DEMANDED BY THE CANADIANS, BUT ACTUALLY WITHHELD BY THE GOVERNMENT

1. The entire control of the whole provincial revenue to be vested in the representatives of the people in parliament.

2. The Independence of the Judges of the land—their removal to take place only upon a joint address of the senate and assembly— their appointment to be from among men not intimately connected with the political business of the province.

3. An independent Legislative Council or Senate, instead of the assemblage of priests, placemen and pensioners, now employed as lawgivers.

4. An administration or Executive Government responsible to the province for its actions.

5. Equal rights to every religious denomination, and the exclusion of the priesthood from a participation in temporal power.

6. The right of voting by ballot, and in places convenient to the people, instead of obliging them to vote at distant places, often inconvenient and expensive to attend at.

7. The power of amending the constitution and laws, so that the representatives of less than one-third of the people, would not (as at present is the case) be enabled to pass laws binding (in every instance) the other two-thirds, even when against their will, as expressed by their members.

8. The right to exclude from seats in the House of Assembly, official persons depending on the executive for their daily bread, and liable to be removed from office at pleasure.

Were the above fundamental rights recognized, there can be no doubt but that a prudent appropriation of the revenue to objects of public improvement would follow:—also, laws authorizing the property of persons dying without wills to be divided among their children; establishing local banks under judicious regulations; diminishing the cost and trouble of obtaining justice, in civil and criminal suits; simplifying the law of libel, and jury trial system; diminishing or doing away heavy fees of office; placing the control of education in the hands of persons elected by the people; establishing a marriage law equal to all denominations of christians; and an administration which, as it would have to depend on the people, would necessarily strive to obtain their esteem, by turning its back upon official slanderers, rewarding honesty, merit and ability, punishing the guilty and protecting the innocent, promoting piety and virtue by precept and example, and doing away the heart burnings that exist among the people, who see clearly, that as things are now ordered, the only road to promotion is that of servility and meanness, and that before a man can be esteemed worthy of promotion by the rulers of the people, he must become deservedly unpopular among his neighbours—then, but not till then, is he a dutiful and loyal subject, of the genuine stamp—*a brother* of the few who assume power without right—yea, a brother, worthy of all acceptation! POOR RICHARD, 1831, p. 9.

NEW YEAR'S EDITORIAL

On this new year, the 11th of the series, the 11th colonial parliament is about to assemble in order to unite their deliberations for the public welfare. We will therefore briefly advert to a few of the leading topics which may be likely to engage their attention.

Education, with a view to an amendment of the existing system.

The Administration of Justice, its cost and character.

The Revenue and resources of the Colony.

The public expenditure.

Commerce.

The practical responsibility of public functionaries.

The present state of the Legislative Council.

The existence and assumed powers of a dominant church.

The quantity, use, and future appropriation of public lands, denominated crown reserves, clergy reserves, etc.

The law of arrest in civil cases.

The law of primogeniture.

The law of marriage.

The post-office department.

The militia system.

The extension of the system of Bank accommodations to other sections of the province.

The state of the current coins, and the banking system generally.

The improvement of the Statute Labour Laws.

The improvement of public roads, and opening canals.

An enquiry into the best mode of obtaining a proportional control over the revenue raised at Quebec, and over the present provincial seaport.

The system of voting by ballot for members of Assembly, and in the township meetings.

And the very unequal and incomplete state of the representation of the people in the House of Assembly, together with the means whereby public officers of the government seek to obtain seats in it.

The appointing power, as exercised with regard to Magistrates and other officers.

The appointment of a provincial agent.

To interrupt useful business, and do away whatever degree of harmony might be supposed to exist among the discordant materials of which we believe the present House of Assembly to be composed, we fear that the war losses, new pensions to idle persons, Strobridge's claim, Horne's claim, Smith's claim, and fifty others of the same nature, contested elections, personal pique, and official folly, will be brought upon the carpet. The province will, in such case, look on with displeasure, and sensible men will regret the continuation of a system of political misrule and parliamentary extravagance, and with confidence will predict its certain downfall.

The Welland Canal is now navigable, and its benefits to the colony may be safely tested without another grant of public money. Yet it is likely that Government will be in favour of a further appropriation of £25,000 to that work, in order to accommodate American produce and enable the farmer of Ohio to compete more successfully with the agriculturist on the north shores of Lake Ontario.

Our own opinion is that the improvement of the roads, and the opening of the St. Lawrence to ship navigation, are the two *leading objects* of a public nature which ought to occupy the attention of the ensuing session. For these purposes we would cheerfully consent yet further to pledge the provincial revenue and resources, because they are of public and acknowledged general utility. The only difficulty, next to obtaining funds at a low rate of interest, is in laying down and executing judicious plans for the expenditure of whatever appropriations might be made. The consent and active co-operation of Lower Canada in a ship Canal can hardly be called an uncertain contingency, and the uniting of the great lakes with the Atlantic by a canal to be navigated by square-rigged vessels is so truly noble and useful a measure, that to defer it much longer would, in a manner, be to retard the prosperity of the world. COLONIAL ADVOCATE, 6 January 1831.

SPEECH ON REFORM

MR. SPEAKER:

For now nearly half a century have the people of England been endeavouring to reform their political institutions, so that "the British constitution" the theory of which has been so much lauded may be brought into practice, and the House of Commons be in reality, what it has so long been in name, a full, free and fair representation of the people of the three kingdoms. An administration composed of men of talent and character, men in whom the country has the utmost confidence, is now at the helm of affairs; and perhaps ere now that great question which powerful majorities triumphantly negatived from year to year, that measure for the accomplishment of which the people have long and anxiously looked, and hitherto looked in vain, may have been conceded, and a reform in the representative system become the order of the day. To obtain this golden prize; to effect this great and lasting good to society without the aid of revolution, and in order to neutralize the revolutionary principle which has gone abroad among the people, the ministry of the present day, and many of their supporters in the legislature, have laboured hard and struggled long with arbitrary power and the corruption inherent to office held without real responsibility. Nor have they struggled in vain. Education has increased both the moral and physical resources of the great body of the people, and made them more and more fit to resist oppression—the old system being in reality unchecked has become more and more intolerable—the example of regenerated France has done wonders, and England at length has determined to be free.

Will we, Mr. Speaker, remain inactive while so glorious an example is set before us in Europe? I trust not. We too have need of enquiry into the corruptions of the Legislature, and let us begin with ourselves, seeing this House professes to emanate immediately from the people. Shut up a captive in the dungeons of the adjoining Bastille, and he will soon be found exclaiming in the bitterness of his heart, "How lovely is freedom! How invaluable is liberty!" Let us then prize that liberty and those rights which are the especial inheritance of freemen; ever bearing in remembrance that an elective government bottomed on corruption is the worst possible species of tyranny.

When it pleased England, forty years ago, to confer on Upper Canada a form of government in which the people had a voice, the inhabitants were thinly scattered over a frontier many hundred miles in extent; the constitution was determined on without their knowledge; adopted without once asking their consent; and put in operation by the proclamation of the general commanding on this station. There was no enquiry made of the people as to their approval or disapproval of the charter; if one person declined to go to the polls, his neighbour's vote went so much the farther in electing a representative. Even then, in those days of primitive simplicity, it was declared by Governor Simcoe, who himself had aided in passing the constitutional act, that England had in that act given to this her infant colony a constitution which was a transcript, an epitome of that of Great Britain.

Was all this a dream, or was it a reality? Is this Assembly, in which we now sit, half as pure and unexceptionable in its composition, even, as that unreformed House of Commons of England, the corruptions of which in buying and selling seats were, as Sir Francis Burdett stated in his place in Parliament, as notorious as the sun at noonday?

One of the first acts of the Canadian Parliament was to adopt the Laws of England as they then stood for a rule of decision here. By these laws no person concerned in the collection of the excise and customs revenue can sit in Parliament, yet here I have a collector of customs at my elbow; and another of the same class of officers is contesting the election of a pensioner of the crown during pleasance, although the rule of decision in England adopted by us, and acted up to so far as it suits a judiciary also removable from office at the pleasure of the executive, expressly declares that neither of these classes of persons shall ever sit or vote in the people's House. No postmaster in England dare so much as come near an election to give his vote, under a penalty of £100, far less can he sit in Parliament. Here, on the contrary, we have half a dozen postmasters who have left their bureaus to the care of deputy postmasters of their own appointment in order to legislate for the country in defiance of these very laws which it was the earliest care of the Province to adopt.

.   .   .

Another defect in the composition of this House is the inequality of the representation as compared to the population. I could name fifteen members in this House who have not altogether so many constituents as the honourable member for Lanark, my honourable colleague, and myself. I could show that twenty-six of the members of this House, being a majority of the whole, are returned by a population consisting of less than one third of the inhabitants of the province, while the other two-thirds are only permitted to send twenty-four members, or less than half the representation. Is it fair towards the freeholders that Hastings, Dundas, Haldimand, Niagara and Brockville should send hither *seven* members, *each having one vote*, while York County, with more than double the population of *all these places taken together*, sends only two members, each having but one vote? While the gentlemen from Lincoln have come into parliament with the direct suffrages of 700, 800, 900 and upwards, the representation from Haldimand obtained each 20, 30 or 40 votes.

Perhaps, in all, one person in every fifteen of the population gave a vote at the last general election; and if property alone were the basis of representation, the inequality of the present system would be still more apparent. Let us suppose the case of a town meeting where one candidate for office would receive 100 votes and another 50; would it be considered fair to elect the latter and exclude the former? Surely not! Yet such is our practice in effect. A bill of importance is laid on the table of this House; fifteen members vote for it, and twenty-four against it; it is thrown out, and the sense of the country is supposed to be declared upon the principle it involved. Yet such may be but seldom the case. The bank, for instance, has a charter affording very little security to the bill holders, as I shewed on a former occasion, yet when I made an attempt to enquire into its management the other day, believing that an institution which has three quarters of a million of its notes afloat among the country people, ought to be looked after, the proposition was negatived, 15 to 24. On examination, I found that the 24 who were for hushing up enquiry represented a smaller number of the Canadian people than the 15 who voted in its favour.

Such are the fruits of an unequal and unfair state of the representation; and the longer it is permitted the worse it will grow.

In his late speech to parliament the King uses the following expressions: "I place without reserve at your disposal my interest in the hereditary Revenues, and in those funds which may be derived from any Droits of the Crown or Admiralty, from the India Duties, or from any Casual Revenues, either in my foreign possessions or in the United Kingdom." In explaining this passage, Mr. Hume informed the House of Commons that the whole of the revenues, at home and abroad, thus placed at the disposal of parliament, had produced only £24,000 in the preceding year; and even of that sum part had been given to support the colonial priesthood or hierarchy as he called it.

What does the hereditary, territorial and casual revenue mean, Mr. Speaker, in this colony? It means a secret job, Sir; of the ramifications of which I believe neither the home government nor colonists themselves are rightly informed. It means fines levied on the people, lands made valuable by their persevering industry, public ferries rented at certain rates, fees on certain instruments signed and sealed on behalf of the country by the executive, town and country lots reserved for public uses; and, in fact, generally speaking, every species of public revenue, positively denied by our public functionaries to be under the nominal control of this house. Ought this powerful means of corruption to be vested in the hands of an irresponsible government, a government that supplies the public servants at its pleasure out of the taxes and asks this house not one farthing?

The honourable and learned member for Wentworth, some days since, declared the schedule of township grants on our journals, altogether useless. I think it a very useful public document. I perceive by its disclosures, that members of present and past parliaments have had grants made them of 500, 700, 900, 1000, to 2000 acres and upwards for no good reason therein stated that I can perceive, except the payment by them of a few shillings of fees. Is it consistent with the preservation of the people, that an irresponsible government like ours should continue to enjoy the power of thus rewarding its adherents with the public property, without any legislative interference with such a corrupting system? Surely not. Is it right that many thousand pounds a year should be at the absolute disposal, either of the executive council here, who know what they are about, or of the administration in England for the time being, who are without personal knowledge or the advice and consent of the country to direct them, in the disposition of the people's money? And this money, too, secretly disposed of, and all information concerning its expenditure refused to our repeated requests!

Sir, this is not the only country in which a suspicion on the part of the people has existed, that revenue usurped from the control of the country has been used for purposes which would ill bear the light. In France, last June, the people became suspicious; made enquiry; and the report of the chamber of deputies abundantly proves that their suspicions were well founded.

.   .   .

Such were the proceedings of the infatuated ministers of the Bourbons—they are now in a dungeon—or have perhaps been tried for their lives, and punished for their daring attempt to prostrate the liberties of the people of France. What must have been their agonized feelings, when, in October last, Polignac and his guilty colleagues saw their prison surrounded with an infuriated populace, with torches in their ranks, and demanding loudly the heads of their victims. Yet three short months before, these men were "governing France amidst all the enjoyments of luxury and power", unapprehensive of the coming change. Louis XVIII and Charles X profited nothing by adversity. While these infatuated monarchs were hiring their myrmidons to bribe the public functionaries and pointing their cannon at the breasts of the people in the streets of Paris, they were base enough to refuse a recompense to a friend who had suffered by his generosity to them in the day of their adversity.

Surely the recollection of these events ought to induce this House to order a rigid enquiry into the state of the representation. The power of the executive of this colony to qualify whomsoever they please for a seat in this House, by a present of 400 acres of land free of fees, is dangerous to liberty and ought not to exist. The unlimited power of the imperfect representation I have described, to involve the people in debt and pledge their farms for purposes not assented to by themselves, is also inconsistent with the enjoyment of free institutions.

To the power of lawyers, by the present grievous system of law fees and legal proceedings, and of merchants who have many farmers on their books, to influence the electors, I need only allude in general terms; the ballot box is perhaps the only remedy for this evil.

Merchants of a certain class, be it remembered, will be enabled by an official bank to give long and extensive credits, while others of a different class will be excluded from bank support, though equally responsible.

Why is our system so fruitful of controverted elections? We have three here to one that takes place in Lower Canada—we have ten to one in the State of New York. Who ever heard of a contested election lasting three or four weeks, to the interruption of all business, except in this Legislature? Nowhere in America at least. But thus we go on. Well might Mr. Canning exclaim, that the colonies of no nation on the globe were worse governed than those of England.

Many independent men, in whom the country has the utmost confidence, have retired from this House, from a belief that their opposition to the worst possible measures could and would be of no avail. Others have declined to come forward at elections, being deterred by perceiving that every application to the government for redress of our grievances had been in vain; that we had met year after year to wrangle and quarrel and vote no supplies and do no good; that all the good bills the most popular house of assembly could pass would be laid under the table elsewhere and come to nothing. There is Mr. John Rolph for instance—all sides of the House will admit that he would be an ornament to any legislative body—born in England; educated at Cambridge; a British Barrister of the highest character; he laboured for the good of the government of this colony unremittingly for six years, in this House. He absolutely refused to be a candidate for the chair you now fill, although his success would have been certain; he brought in and obtained the passage of an address to His Majesty recommending the reinstatement of Judge Willis and the appointment of Judges from England; his whole conduct proved that he had at heart the good of the country of his adoption. But we find him replaced in this House by [*space of one line in the* Colonial Advocate]. Why is this? Three deputations came to him from Middlesex; the leading men of Lincoln anxiously desired permission to put him in nomination for that great county; the Wentworth farmers again and again urged him to come forward; and who is there that will allege that his chance of election in Halton was not greater than that of an Honourable Member now absent? Why then did he not come forward? Doubtless, Mr. Speaker, because he must have felt that in such a system as prevails here, and with such a ministry as existed at home a few months ago, he could be of little service to his king and country. I have no doubt whatever but that these were his motives for declining a seat in this House.

It is believed by many that opposition to bad measures in this house, will be in vain, unless our constitution can be finally brought to recognize a solemn expression of the will of the people; until we can see this House in the possession of a degree of power sufficient for the business of effectually checking bad government; until this House shall possess an identity of interest with the community, its representation being equal; and until placemen and pensioners be excluded.

Under existing circumstances it may be admitted that an irresponsible government will just go as far in injuring the people in their persons, property and labour, as the spirit of the people to resist them would allow them to consider safe.

If in the course of my remarks I have said aught that was unpleasant to the feelings of any honourable member, I hope that he will consider that the question before us involves the great interests of the country and requires strong language. Individually, I meant offence to none. The private and personal character of all the public servants of Government to whom I have alluded is highly respectable; and doubtless in their several stations, they perform the duties of office by deputy, to the best of their skill and ability.—What I object to is, that they are here; and that their being here is a violation of the letter and spirit of our laws and constitution.

Will then the House this day order a full and free enquiry to be made? Or is this inequality of representation, this undue influence of the Executive Government, and all these departures from the spirit of the constitution, to be passed over as matters of no moment to the public welfare?

SPEECH ON REFORM

I now move that it be resolved *"That a select committee be appointed to enquire into the state of the Representation of the People, in this House; with power to send for persons and papers and records, and leave to report by bill, address or otherwise."* (Yeas: 28; Nays: 11.) [*This speech was made on 22 January 1831.*] COLONIAL ADVOCATE, 3 February 1831.

PULPIT v. PLAYHOUSE

There has been for some years a hot warfare in Birmingham, Sheffield, and some other great towns, between the pulpit and the playhouse. The question ought to be stated fairly. The Methodists wish to make all people serious—that is, they wish to kill them here to save them hereafter. The players give long life here, whatever may happen hereafter. But then a man may have every joy too, above. It is difficult to laugh when one is hungry, or when a dun is at the door. If a man give too much to the purchase of mirth, he may have seriousness forced on him whether he will or not.

But at all events, the man who wishes to have a long lease of his life, should shun all serious long-visaged people, as so many assassins. All brimstone merchants should be considered as more dangerous than mad dogs. COLONIAL ADVOCATE, 7 April 1831.

LETTERS TO JOHN NEILSON

YORK, FEB. 17, 1831

Our House is to be prorogued on the 9th March, and I intend to come down to Quebec immediately on the prorogation. I wish to see and hear your members in Assembly—I wish to have some conversation with them—and if it be possible I wish to go to England immediately afterwards. Our religious petition of 10 or 12,000 is now ready to be sent off, and an agent (Mr. George Ryerson) is to be sent off with it immediately. . . .

The events in Europe are of great moment, and must and will have an effect here.

P.S. In the Advocate of this day and last Thursday, you will find as full an account of the parliamentary proceedings here, as my time permits me to give. The people of Upper Canada are very independent and manly in their principles, and there is a great deal of information spread among them in one way or other, but the scheme of the government is such that it is next to impossible for us to get a truly independent house, and if we have one the Legislative Council are a barrier to all improvement, the opinions of which or their supposed opinions materially influence all their legislation.

YORK, FEB. 23, 1831

The Welland Canal Co's £50,000 or £200,000 question will, I think, result in giving them nothing this year—or only a trifle. They do not deserve to have all the credit of the colony lavished on them in preference to the far more useful improvement of the St. Lawrence, which would extend the commerce of your cities and benefit this Upper country, by enabling us to send flour and all produce cheaper down and to get goods cheaper up. . . .

If I can get away from home I will immediately come down to Quebec and see your legislative proceedings. I very much wish to see your legislature in session. We of the minority here are doing great good to our cause, and the ministerialists by their incapacity and the course they take are becoming more and more odious all over the province.

P.S. Our Lt.-Governor, with great professions of moderation, does all that in his power lies to neutralize the popular interest, and render the representative branch a mere name.

YORK, MARCH 7, 1831

There is much irritation prevalent among the people at the proceedings of this House but the system is so corrupt, that with a bad governor, £50,000 of revenue out of our control, bank loans, wild lands, all public places held at pleasure, rotten boroughs, a church establishment, pensions, enormous law fees, clergy reserves, crown reserves, the Canada Company, and so many other sources of patronage and indirect bribery, besides the rottenness of the legislative council, I do not at this moment see our remedy. The people would petition, but what does it avail? Yet the more I see into the system the more I dislike it, and feel disposed to do all I can (and that is but little) to bring about a better state of things. You go gradually but on a sure foundation to work in reforming abuses, and you have patriotic Assemblies. What our Assembly is let this winter's voting shew. I have written this in great haste, for I am much fatigued.

CORNWALL, APRIL 2nd, 1831

I very much desired to have seen the legislature of Lower Canada in session, but it was not possible. I left home last Thursday week at 1 a.m. and this is all the length I have been able to get, although a willing traveller. I never saw the roads in such a condition. No stages pass from this to Kingston—it is impracticable. The depth of the mud is really extraordinary, and bridges and pieces of the road have been carried away altogether. I left my baggage in Kingston, borrowed Mr. Bidwell's saddle bags and took horse. It took me a whole day to ride from Ganonoque to Prescott, altho' only 46 miles. On the evening of Thursday last, I set off at eight at night from Prescott in order to reach the outgoing mail from here, but could not, for there was no stage. The roads at the province line were impassable even for horses—eight miles of the journey has to be performed by the courier on foot thro' a morass with the mails on his shoulder!—I took only 12½ hours in the night to ride the fifty miles; but the roads were awful and the night very stormy. On arriving at this place I found by [*word illegible*] Gazette that the prorogation of the Legislature was about to take place, and that you had appointed Mr. Viger in the very way I once suggested to our Assembly to appoint an agent, but which was privately discussed and rejected as being *unconstitutional*. If we of Upper Canada can by petitions and addresses—public meetings and remonstrances— usefully second the views of your assembly *we will do it generally cheerfully and speedily*. The people here are not the careless ignorant race you would imagine from the present state of the representation. But they cease to have any expectations of good laws from an assembly and council constituted as ours is, and such men as Mr. Rolph though repeatedly urged decline taking a part in such a farce or burlesque on legislation as is commonly exhibited at York.

GOODENOUGH'S HOTEL, MONTREAL
APRIL 9TH, 1831

I have seen Mr. Papineau, with whose frank affable and candid manners I am much satisfied.

If you have had time to peruse the pamphlets I sent you with a letter from Cornwall on the Coteau du Lac on my way down, you will see that the state of our representation is such that little or no hopes can be safely entertained of hereafter ascertaining public opinion through the medium of the House of Assembly. Of this Mr. Papineau seems fully aware, and has said that should it be the wish of the people of Upper Canada to petition the King and parliament by towns and counties, he believes Mr. Viger would cheerfully consent (at their request) to act with Mr. Ryerson as their agent in London for explaining their complaints, which are far more general and grievous than they can be with you, who have a more equal system of representation, the virtual control of the revenue, and no wholesale introduction of English Stat. Law to be interpreted by a dependent and ambitious bench. I wish much to see Mr. Viger before he sails for England and for that purpose shall come down by the first steamboat for Quebec. I wish also to see you, in order that I may have the benefit of your experience of the state of England as to the extent to which it would be prudent to go in petitioning ministers. Legislation and interference with our constitution by England you deprecate, in the speeches attributed to you in parliament. What then is to be done, if, (and I think you say so) it is inexpedient now to allow the people to remodel their constitutions ? —The older I get the more clearly do I perceive that the constitutions of these colonial regions were made by the few governing to be administered for their own benefit; and what I am at a loss [in] is as to the means whereby they can be so altered as to preserve our connexion and friendship with the land of our forefathers and of our birth and yet give to men of talent, enterprise and genuine patriotism that fair field which is now engrossed by ambition and sycophancy.

I think the new Ministry honest and candid, and admire their wisdom in sending £400,000 of the old civil list estimates into the channel of the annual votes instead of voting it permanently. It will enable them to reduce the pensions of useless and idle persons after they shall have achieved reform, without alarming the peerage at once in such a degree as to endanger more and more their own stability and the improvement in the representation which I think they contemplate.

One thing is certain. If *the present Governor*, Legislative Council and House of Assembly of Upper Canada shall be allowed again to meet without an exertion of the people for an alteration of the system, the bank monopoly will be extended and doubled in the hands of the court politicians—the pay of the members of Assembly abolished, and more evil done in regard to the liberty of the press and of the people than future years will be able to undo.

You will then have your own almost prostrate political factions, *who are already in close alliance with the ruling party with us*, uniting in everything that could or might prove injurious to your country and to the freedom of Upper Canada. Such at least appear to me to be the too probable results. LINDSEY PAPERS.

MAY 31, 1831

We intend getting up township meetings and addressing the King from every township. In a sort of annual address to the people of the Colony I have (in the *Advocate* of tomorrow) endeavoured to prepare the public minds for such a proceeding. I have incorporated into this Document many of your opinions, as I believe them to be important truths—I therefore shine in borrowed feathers—but it is of no consequence so as the truth is elicited. CANADIAN ARCHIVES: NEILSON PAPERS, vol. 7, p. 228.

JUNE 25, 1831

When our public meetings here go into operation I am anxious to combine with them organized societies for the promotion of education and also the diffusion of political information. CANADIAN ARCHIVES: NEILSON PAPERS, vol. 7, p. 248.

THE BANK GENTRY

There can be no doubt but that the government officers, in their anxious chase after money, wealth, power, will strain every nerve to get a bill passed during the present session to allow them to circulate exclusively another million of their paper dollars at the expense of the country, and it may be to its lasting injury, but assuredly for their own individual advantage. Even now, by keeping up a monopoly of the rate of interest on government loans, and on loans to districts, they gain nearly £5,000 a year out of the very poverty of the people. They can curtail their discounts, or increase them at their pleasure; they can raise the price of property or lower it at will, by increasing, or withdrawing from circulation, their paper money. They cannot, say some, influence the vote of members of the assembly—but they can ruin them and break their bank credit if they do not vote to suit the interests of those who control the money loans. They cannot vote at elections, but they can punish mercantile people if their votes and exertions are not directed in favour of candidates who would sell the rights of the people for a mess of pottage. "We know very well how notes are black-balled in the Bank of Upper Canada." said Mr. Solicitor General Hagerman in the Assembly, last winter. "Two black-balls will cause a most respectable merchant's paper to be refused."—"You could not select in Kingston (retorted Mr. Attorney General,) a board of directors equally fit with those of York to direct the concerns of a bank." The Attorney General is Bank Solicitor; and Mr. Hagerman, looking down upon him with a smile of pity mixed with a shade of compassion, declared his conviction that there were in Kingston, men infinitely more fit than he (the Attorney-General) to direct a bank. COLONIAL ADVOCATE, 17 November 1831.

THE ELECTION RIOTS, 21 MAY 1832

I am sorry that you have been entirely silent as a public writer with regard to the military outrage committed at Montreal. Not that I blame the soldiers, (they were mere instruments in the hands of a higher power,) but because the example is a dangerous one. The Magistrates of Montreal are of the class opposed to the people of the country, and have few feelings or interests in common with those among whom they live. It is evident there was no need for troops; no disturbance which the civil power could not have quelled; and it is injurious to the government the reflection that the only use to be found for British soldiers in America is to spill the blood of the citizens of Montreal, while exercising their elective franchise. (*From a letter to Randal Wixson.*) COLONIAL ADVOCATE, 11 October 1832. [*See also* Colonial Advocate 31 *May* 1832, 11 *October* 1832, 20 *March* 1834; Constitution, 14 *December* 1836; Durham Report, 1902 *edition, p.* 90.]

LETTER TO RANDAL WIXSON

19 WAKEFIELD STREET, BRUNSWICK SQUARE,
THURSDAY, NOV 6, 1832

DEAR SIR:—The last knell of the last borough monger parliament of England has been rung—the dissolution of Monday is the beginning of a new era in the annals of the British Empire—the commencement of the representative system of government—still imperfect it is true, but incomparably more likely to be productive of good to the people than the tyranny of the cruel, jealous, vindictive oligarchy, from the mandates of which it is about to deliver them. Scotland will send up economical reformers, almost to a man—O'Connell and the radicals are sure of carrying the day in Ireland with a high hand—and as for England, I wish you could but see the enthusiasm that prevails. Even Sirs John Hobhouse and Francis Burdett have had reason to doubt of their own election because they refuse to give pledges for the future. I was a witness not long since to a curious scene in the crown and anchor tavern in the Strand, in the great room of which the members for Westminster were hissed and hooted far worse than Mr. Washburn was at the meeting of the 19th of January last and the York county hustings a few weeks after. Not one syllable they uttered was listened to. The people of England will send pledged, tried, firm men—men who will do their work well, and to the satisfaction of the country—they will send these men because they themselves have been impoverished and distressed—taxed and tithed and robbed and plundered—but, so long as only the poorer classes suffered, the middle classes gave themselves no concern—and were just as willing to put down radicalism by the application of another 10,000 redcoats to the army list from time to time as was the rankest tory bishop that ever sat in the House of Lords. The English rotten boroughs, however, being now disfranchised, and the great cities and towns very fully represented you may depend upon seeing great changes the moment parliament meets. Either the ministry will conform itself to an enlightened and united public sentiment or it will dissolve in thin air. I regret, that reform was not carried sooner— had it been so it would have shewn the middle classes in a less selfish mercenary point of view.

I have some curiosity about the result of the elections for Oxford and Haldimand—Haldimand shewed rottenness at the beginning, and Oxford exhibited an utter indifference to the public welfare at the last election which gave me much pain. In place of candidates who, as members, had borne with insults of the grossest kind from the satellites of government, in order that they might honestly and faithfully fulfil their promises to their constituents, by their conduct in the former house, they elected two men who had—the one in the legislature and the other out of it—done all they could to make the farmers aliens, and not only them but their brethren in other parts of the colony. Will these Oxonians shew a sense of contrition for this? Or will they not rather follow suit for this parliament at least? I have more hopes of them than of Haldimand. I hope a free press will do something in Upper Canada—I trust it will instil a sense of duty and obligation into those large constituencies of farmers whose cruel and ungenerous behaviour at the last general election has inflicted so many evils upon their country.

A writer in the Nova Scotian whose remarks are copied into the Cobourg Reformer of last summer ascribes to European *emigration* the rottenness of the Upper Canada Legislature. He is mistaken. It was not emigrants who returned a *Shade* for the 18,000 people of Halton—nor who sent Wm. Crooks instead of Jacob Upper for the

20,000 people of Lincoln. It was not *emigration* that put James Crooks in the place of Hopkins—Werden in the shoes of Peterson—Burwell and Mount in the room and stead of Rolph and Mathews—and that gave a Jarvis for a Baldwin. I confess I regretted as much to see the lukewarmness of some men who had sat in the former parliament, as I did the carelessness and folly of the people. The former found the path of duty strewed with anything but garlands—they found that no progress was to be made, no war losses to be carried, and they staid at home and gave up the ship. They would have made bad missionaries to the heathen for they cared only for little toil and great success—who indeed cares for ignorance and folly? They waited till the people should be wise, enlightened and ready to do all for themselves; instead of manfully filling the breach they allowed the enemy to scale the walls and take the citadel without firing a single shot. I complained to the government here of the inequality of the representation—but it was a melancholy truth I did not like to dwell upon *that the large constituencies had in many places shewn as much rottenness and corruption as the small.* The fault lay in the people and in some in whom they trusted—both got "weary of well-doing," and hence we have jealousies and divisions, a tory government and a tory assembly, at a time when Upper and Lower Canada might have otherwise advantageously united their efforts for the general welfare.

I confess I was astonished at reading this forenoon in the North and South American Coffee House that Mr. James Rogers Armstrong had joined with the president of the bank and the tory crown officers to pass resolutions likely to involve the two provinces in a quarrel, for the ridiculous and scarcely plausible purpose of annexing 60,000 French Canadians with the Island of Montreal, and a vast mass of property now happily free from primogeniture laws and costly English usages, to Upper Canada!

The local government has doubtless a hand in this disgraceful job—if Sir John Colborne did not countenance the crown officers they durst not thrust themselves forward for the accomplishment of such an object. They say they have not revenue enough. I wish they had a great deal less. The revenue annually squandered in Upper Canada is one of the greatest evils the people have to contend with—it furnishes the means of bribery and corruption to a degree that, joined with the apathy and carelessness of the farmers in many counties, has made the country very unhappy. More revenue! Look at the permanent salary bill!—the bank bill!—the refusal to pass my resolutions for enforcing economy in the legislative council!—the

enormous contingencies of the assembly!—the pensions!—the sinecures!—A province which has not the courage and manhood to send
representatives, even from such counties as Glengarry, Stormont,
Oxford, Middlesex, Kent, Essex, Halton, Durham, Simcoe, &c., as
would make even a shew of retrenchment and economy!—A province which passes resolutions from year to year, for a third of an
age, about the government expending the revenue without its consent, and the moment it has a shilling at its disposal gives that
shilling away at once and for ever by an everlasting grant! For such
a province as this to desire to dismember Lower Canada, the people
of which have acted a noble and highly honourable part, in public
matters struggling as one man against oligarchial aggression, and
that too, successfully, would be, I must say it, for I never did flatter
the colony, mean and selfish in the extreme. If it is not the sense
of the country that such men as Messrs. Boulton and Hagerman
speak (and I think it is not,) let the people shew it immediately by
their petitions sent per mail to a reformed parliament in hundreds—
they will be heard, fairly heard, of that I have now no doubt. I fear
much, notwithstanding all the manifestations I have seen to the
contrary, that the mass of the population do not possess sufficient
enterprise to act together, nor enough of intelligence and patriotism
to appreciate the difference between a government for all—equal
rights—the abolition of monopolies in the law, in the church, in the
bank, in the legislative council, in offices and in honours, and such
a government as they now live under.

In saying this I do not speak to their particular disparagement—
these three kingdoms, with 23 millions of inhabitants, are to this day
in a similar situation. The agricultural classes *here*, always the best
and most upright, are always the most careless of their rights and
privileges—if they had had enough to eat and drink they would
never have become reformers, but would have been ready, like Mr.
Burwell's electors, to pitch upon the *blackest* sheep in the whole
flock as a substitute for the bonniest Teviotdale.—At length, however, from servile instruments of the enslavers of their country they
have become, through misery and poverty, incendiaries in many
places, and in most situations radical reformers.

If I could think, even for a moment, that the yeomanry of Upper
Canada, would require to drink from the same bitter cup of adversity
which Ireland has quaffed to the very dregs, before they would
unite for their common advantage, and the general happiness, I
would not continue to toil and labour as I have done for these last
9 years, often with many great personal privations contending—but

I trust they will not require to be stimulated with so unpalatable a beverage, and would fain hope that by their unanimous and spirited petitions to the Commons of England they will speedily wipe off the blot which the past conduct of a majority of their present representatives has attached to their history, and prove themselves as worthy of free institutions as their fellow subjects, faithful and gallant and generous inhabitants of Lower Canada, who, with less of the advantages of education than their brethren in the Upper Province, had after 40 years legislation under the same imperfect constitution, proved themselves—I dare not deny it—by far the most disinterested and worthy of the freest institutions, and the best form of government, which has yet blessed mankind in any country or age of the world. While Upper Canada submitted with scarce a murmer except from the county of York, to the unspeakable degradation of having Judge Willis dragged off the bench by Strachan and Robinson for having defended those inestimable rights the people had not the sense to value nor the courage to maintain, and to this day consents to pay and pension and pamper that unfortunate judge's traducers, Lower Canada has driven Mr. Stuart from his £5000 a year into exile, followed him here by her agents *properly upheld*, and cashiered him for ever, at the very moment when he hoped as the reward of his base treachery to step, like Mr. Robinson, into the seat of the Chief Justice.

In mentioning these things I do not wish to wound the feelings of the many thousand noble and worthy men and women who like me call Upper Canada their home, but rather to arouse that fine and free spirit of emulation which, passing by selfish, worldly, and grovelling objects, would lift the lovely country where my most active years have been passed, the land of my adoption, the birthplace of my children, to a more respectable rank on the American continent and in the estimation of sensible and reflecting men here, than can possibly that wretched policy we have so long too tamely and meanly submitted to.

. . .

The writer in the *Nova Scotian* laments the want of able and temperate political leaders in Upper Canada, and regrets that there is no Papineau in the Senate. He is misinformed. In point of intelligence, spirit, and good temper, few men are equal to Mr. Bidwell. Never has there been a Speaker in the Chair of the Assembly who was fit to tie the latchet of his shoe, in that situation. Even Mr. Papineau's commanding influence was not acquired in a session—he has been the Speaker during 8 parliaments, if not 9. Mr. Bidwell has unquestionably the first place as a public man in the estimation of the reflecting part of the community of any individual in Upper Canada, and he will keep it, for he deserves it; but even when in the chair he could not do all he wished; nor will he be able to accomplish all the good he desires to do when again, as I hope and trust he will be, elevated in the next house to the highest place in the gift of the people of the province, as the reward of his first rate talents devoted faithfully and perseveringly to the public service, in the worst of times.

Of Mr. Rolph, it may be said that in coming forward in the House of Assembly on the popular side he made a much greater sacrifice of personal interest than Mr. Bidwell or any other member who has sat in that House since I first knew the colony. It is probable that he met with a very ungrateful return from the landowners for his six years disinterested exertions within doors and without, but for all that I have never ceased deeply to lament the misfortune the country suffered by his withdrawing from his most useful and appropriate sphere of a representative of the people. He well knows that he never would or could have been unsuccessful at the hustings, and although to be returned with Mahlon Burwell and to have sat in one house with Allan McNab would have been humiliating to a highminded man, yet would it have enabled the colony to steer clear of some of the worst difficulties with which, since 1830, it has had to contend. Such feelings as may be supposed to have actuated Mr. Rolph in 1830, probably induced Sir F. Burdett the other day to write to the electors of Westminster that he would rather be turned out with Sir J. Hobhouse than returned with Col. Evans.

On reading over what I have written, I can readily perceive that my language is not likely to make me a greater favourite with the good people of Upper Canada. I do not see, however, that my remarks can be softened down; and as I am one of that class of old and trusty servants who expect scarce any other reward than the privilege of saying what they please to their employers, I will conclude my epistle admonitory by assuring them that the more kicks and cuffs a man submits to with patience the more kicks and cuffs are sure to fall to his share; and that it is pretty much the same with a kingdom or province, witness Ireland, Upper Canada, and the Cape of Good Hope.

I am, Mr. Editor,
Yours truly,
W. L. MACKENZIE.
COLONIAL ADVOCATE, 21 February 1833.

INTERVIEW WITH
LORD GODERICH

To MR. JOHN MACINTOSH

CHAIRMAN OF THE COMMITTEE OF THE INHABITANTS, &C, &C.

The first subject on which I spoke to him was the War Losses, in relation to which I had sent in the memorial of which a copy of the most essential parts had been sent to an Upper Canada Journal for publication. His Lordship said he had read the memorial, but he thought the scheme I proposed impracticable—difficult to carry into execution—and interfering with the present plan of land sales. I proceeded further in explanation, answered the objections he offered —reminded His Lordship of the manner in which these debts were contracted, of the troublesome results of the everlasting agitation of the war loss question upon the legislation of the province, and of the promises of His Majesty's Government. He had had an idea that the losses were entirely occasioned by the enemy, and at first doubted my assertion, that a large share of the losses was occasioned in one way or other by the acts of the King's troops, or by the non-payment of property forcibly taken from the owners for their use. I assured him it was so, and offered instantly to prove it, by a reference to the documents I had appended to my memorial. He then said that the matter had only been a short time under his consideration—that is, from the date of the Niagara petition of last March—but I reminded him that the present Chief Justice had originated an address from both Houses of the Legislature so far back as 1829, in which it was asserted that the Province was unable to pay the debt, and that upon that nothing had been done.

As I proceeded, he told me he better understood the bearings and effects of my proposition for payment than at first, and that it would have a careful consideration. I reminded him that the legislature was then in session; that while I was here with the petitions of a large body of the people praying for a dissolution of the legislature, and writing home accounts of the interviews I had had with His Lordship, the first answer I received was a casual notice *via* Canada that the Provincial Parliament had been called at an earlier period than it ever had before; and that if any steps were to be taken on the War Loss question, on which the Assembly of the colony would be required to act, no great delay could take place without frustrating the intentions of the government, as the session would probably be a short one. His Lordship observed, that with regard to the publication in newspapers of what passed at such interviews, if it were done he would have to say nothing in respect to any matter brought under his notice.

I said that copies of my letters to Canada stating what passed at the two first audiences had been appended to my request for the present interview. That I had asked for it with the view of ascertaining as far as I possibly could His Lordship's intentions towards those of whose petitions I had been the bearer, in order that I might state the same distinctly by letter to Canada. That I felt highly honoured by the permission His Lordship had given me to state the complaints of the people in a quarter where they could best be relieved, but that I owed it to His Lordship to state that as soon as I had seen the notice for the calling of the Legislature on the 31st of October, I had advised the people of the colony to lose no time in receiving and forwarding petitions expressing their wants to the House of Commons of the reformed parliament. That Mr. Hume, and other influential members, were ready and prepared to have brought the question of enquiry into the state of the province at great length before the house, when His Lordship induced them to stay all proceedings by promising an immediate investigation, the result of which, on one important point, was the re-assembling of the Provincial Legislature at a most unusual period, the refusing any information to me whatsoever, and *in so far* the expression of the approbation of His Majesty's Government of the high-handed acts of the local executive and crown officers in my expulsion and re-expulsion, and the consequent disfranchisement of a large body of freeholders, because I happened to be the proprietor of a newspaper which had expressed the political opinions held by my constituents.

His Lordship did not deny that the refusal to order a new election under the circumstances implied all I had alleged—he passed over that point without remark—but said that my statements (those statements I have sent to Canada within the last 6 weeks) were too high coloured, and embraced many points which could not be considered at once. I cannot repeat the exact words His Lordship used, but I state the substance. I owned that my memorials did embrace many points, but reminded His Lordship how long most of these matters had been before him, and how well he was aware of the state of things in Upper Canada, so far back as the period when he offered to present and spoke upon the petition of the county of York, in the House of Peers, five years ago, which petition that House had refused to receive because of some technical informality of which people in America could not have been aware.

I also adverted to the many addresses, petitions, and memorials, which had been sent to England since that period and lain utterly neglected by the government, while every opportunity had been given to an irresponsible local executive to trample upon the people's rights and strengthen itself by increasing their divisions at their own cost or with the money of England paid to priests who could not otherwise obtain a living; I told him that it was a legislative council, a political machine the parts of which, as it appeared to me, were entirely under the control of His Lordship's department, that prevented the war loss bill of last session from passing into a law, and that for this government to hold out a promise to pay one half the war losses, if Upper Canada would pay the other, while some twenty persons under their control prevented Upper Canada from moving a step one way or the other, was a very great grievance. I added, that for year after year, the Assembly had passed bills altering the law of primogeniture, the law of libel, the criminal law in an essential particular, and amending the jury and town officer laws—that His Lordship had, on a former occasion, admitted that he was bound to believe that the assembly as constituted expressed the will of the colonists—that he had the evidence of their journals and proceedings, annually copied by the order of his department for its use and reference, (and to which he had refused me access,) as a proof of this public will—yet, that although instructions from England, in accordance with the desires of the colonists, as he himself understood them, and as the assembly had expressed them, would, as in the case of the Alien Bill, have accomplished their wishes, these instructions had been constantly withheld, and a few placemen enabled to defeat the wishes of the country by being constituted into a co-ordinate legislative body.

I said further, that I could have no wish whatever to see His Lordship again unless some new matter arose, or unless I should be requested to wait upon him, for that to be writing to Canada about interviews which ended in nothing fed expectations which had never been realized and prevented the people from making those united personal exertions by petition to the House of Commons which I trust a reformed parliament would not only listen to but also render unnecessary for the future. That I was a very humble individual and could only advise, but that I had advised the colonists to unite in petitioning the new house for liberty to manage their affairs for their own advantage and freedom from established priesthoods and other monopolies, and that I had done so after consulting with some of the most influential members of the House of Commons who had engaged to bring forward and support their reasonable requests, so that full investigation might take place. His Lordship observed, that he trusted that the House would hear both sides.

(I could have replied, that I regretted there should be two sides in such a case, but of course I forbore, for nothing could exceed the kindness and mildness of manner displayed by the minister. I really believe him to be naturally a kind, liberal, and benevolent man.) He added, that he should at all times be willing to see me on the subject of the colony, when his other avocations permitted—that it was his wish to give those who had complaints to make from Canada full opportunity to state the grievances, which *any part of the colonists* considered themselves to labour under. I said I did not doubt it. That Mr. Ryerson and others had been delighted with the easy access they had had to His Lordship's ear, on behalf of the petitioners for religious freedom—but that unfortunately *nothing was ever done that the petitioners desired.*

I also adverted to the case of the Hastings petition, as a specimen of the trouble and cost there was in getting a memorial into the hands of the government, and to the case of Neil McKinnon. On the latter affair I dwelt at considerable length, in the hope that I would be able to obtain a reconsideration of His Lordship's decision, *but I failed.* I stated that it was publicly reported, in 1825, that those British subjects who had the means of conveying themselves and families to Upper Canada, would each receive a free grant out of the many millions of acres of waste and desolate wilderness with which that country abounds; that Neil McKinnon, who was the father of a family of six children, resolved to leave his native land, with his wife and infants, for the wilds of America, and to expend all his means in conveying his family thither; but that he first obtained the royal promise, thro' His Lordship's predecessor, in writing, that he should have a free grant from the Colonial Government under the usual engagement for the performance of settlement duties. There was no word of a £30 payment under the name of a fee. Mr. McKinnon and family bade farewell to their native shore, and went straight to York *via* Quebec. Arrived on the wharf—their limited funds almost exhausted—without friends—scarce able to articulate a word of English—these poor people presented at the Government Office Lord Bathurst's letter, their supposed passport to good fortune, and received an answer which they understood to be a refusal —and I dare say it was so, for there was then no check upon the idle and careless in the government offices—and the forms to be gone through were so tedious and vexatious (besides the payments,) that those who had the means usually employed a practised agent to perform them.

I referred His Lordship to the petition of Neil McKinnon to Sir J. Colborne, in which he states that receiving neither advice nor assistance from government he was unable to remain idle in York with a large family; he therefore went upon a reserve in Markham where he remains to this day. I put the case to His Lordship, whether it was probable that this man, would have gone and paid a yearly rent for a reserve if he could have had crown land of his own free to cultivate, which was then vacant near the capital. I said it was extremely hard that this man should be induced to embark his small fortune in such an adventure and be kept six years cultivating lands for the church of England, of which he was not a member, with the royal promise unfulfilled in his pocket. His Lordship interrupted me by the remark that it would not do to depart from the new regulations. I said that McKinnon was no party to these regulations, they could not have a retrospective effect upon his claim, which he prosecuted again with my assistance as soon as he heard of my success with Sir George Murray for Neil Morrison; that Lord Bathurst's letter fixed no time of emigration; that the land was as desolate as when first promised, at the time when McKinnon exchanged the prospect of poverty in Scotland for clerical servitude in Canada.

I adverted also to Dr. Strachan's book—the sudden change of the tariff from that therein exhibited, and the cruel and disheartening character of such changes to poor settlers, and urged the propriety of placing the public lands under the control of a reformed colonial legislature, as they produced no money to England now. I said there were many such cases as McKinnon's; mentioned the £30,000 granted the year McKinnon emigrated, for the purpose of carrying out settlers from Ireland to be placed and supported upon free grants; and expressed an opinion that while this was done parliament never could have intended that a Scotsman who went out at his own expense should be turned off as a tenant to the church clergy. His Lordship betrayed some impatience while I was speaking of the petition of McKinnon and the land granting system. He would do nothing for him—he would not interfere.

I took this occasion to say that it did seem as if the government wished to discourage the settlers from petitioning either the King or parliament by the representatives of their choice, and I instanced

His Lordship's answers to the handful of abusive partizans who had insulted the country, under the name of "catholic inhabitants," and "protestant inhabitants" of the town of York. The addresses emanating from these old tories were received by the minister of a whig government as bright testimonies of loyalty and attachment, and as such acknowledged in the most marked manner, [while] the [f]rank and manly statements [of] a majority of the whole adult population were scarce deemed worthy of a note, barely stating through the under secretary that some fifty or sixty of them had been received. I told His Lordship, that I did not care about such distinctions on my own account, but that the people of Upper Canada were a more pitiful race than I took them for if they did not feel and show too that they felt such treatment. I added, that the people were from several countries, but that it did not appear to me that it would long be in the power of any government or administration to divide them so as to continue the present degrading and slavish system, and that government would have to enquire and put a stop to difficulties their neglect had caused, perhaps when it would be too late. I made some further remarks respecting the continuance of tory governors to mar and embarrass reform and real reformers, but my memoranda does not enable me distinctly to state their purport.

We next spoke of trade, and here His Lordship appeared less to differ from me in opinion. He said that in regard to the heavy duties on the trade of the Canadas, inclusive of the tea taxes, he would communicate with the Board of Trade, and admitted that the present high and discouraging monopolies ought to be removed. The China trade in tea would be revised with the other regulations affecting the East India Company, and the interests of the colonists would not be forgotten. I mentioned, that unless the Canadians were forced into the arms of the United States, it was the interest of no party to have a closer union with them, for that instead of free trade we should then have the high tariff of congress, by which the farmers of the colonists, who have no manufactures to protect or which are protected, would be obliged, like the South Carolina folks, to pay a tax to the manufacturing states upon all their purchases, instead of obtaining goods duty free at Quebec. That the natural channel of our trade was England. Free trade, in the true sense of the word, if accompanied with a freedom from military government, would, I said, be the best guarantee for the friendship of Canada, the legislative councils of which, I plainly told his lordship, would not (and ought not to) stand a week longer than they had the protection of the bayonet of the soldier paid from Europe. I daresay that many interested persons will be angry with me for remarking, that the Canadas suffered far more from other monopolies than they benefitted by the timber trade, and that in so far as it forced the English people to buy bad timber from a distance which they could get better and nearer hand, I wished it swept off with the rest.

I concluded my remarks by calling it to His Lordship's attention that England pays annually upwards of two millions sterling more than she receives, to keep up the bad government of the colonies under which so much dissatisfaction prevails, and that that important fact could not possibly escape the notice of a reformed parliament. On leaving His Lordship, he again assured me that I should be admitted to an audience at all times when it was suitable for him to give attention to the matters brought before him; that the written statements I might forward would be attended to, and that it was his earnest desire to promote the happiness of Upper Canada, accounts of the prosperity and rapid improvement of which he was receiving from time to time. I said I would send to those who had sent me a statement of what I had said and done, and that after I had learnt the early proceedings of the local legislature, I would most probably avail myself of His Lordship's kind permission, for which, under the circumstances, I expressed myself grateful.

I have received the Guardian of the 31st October and the Advocate of the 11th and 18th of that month, and have read the New York Journals of the 8th November, Boston of the 10th, and Quebec of the 3rd, but nothing later of Upper Canada affairs. Had I been a recognized and accredited agent from the House of Assembly, the government, or a select body of any kind, I could not with propriety have stated the above facts for publication, exactly in the way I may now do—but, as the Quebec Mercury justly remarks, I stand on quite a different footing from Mr. Viger, and those who sent me have a right to be acquainted with my public proceedings in their name, on their behalf, and at their cost, the same as if they themselves were present here and acting. As my interviews at the colonial office were entirely on the account of the people they ought to know what is to be expected, and although I have nothing very flattering to tell, yet a plain brief statement of facts may be useful.

In respect to public men acting in a public capacity on this great theatre of action, I would say to the committee that little of their real sentiments can be generally known, so much are they obligated to put on an artificial political exterior suitable to the parties they are influenced by—I say this particularly of the whig ministry, in whom I confess I have but little confidence as a body, although it is probable that the premier and some others of them are really friendly to substantial reform and cheap and honest government. Their proceedings will be guided by the new elections. If a majority of true reformers shall be returned, the ministers will, I daresay, come forward at the opening of the house next February with a large and comprehensive practical reform; if otherwise, corrupt influences will not be wanting to keep things as they are. Mr. Stanley is spoken of as being about to be called to the House of Peers and placed at the head of the Colonial Department. How this is I know not. Much will depend on the ensuing elections, which will be over in a few days. I have no doubt but that they will be terminated to your entire satisfaction.

I perceive that a great ado is made in York about attaching Montreal and 60,000 people who speak French to Upper Canada, in order that we may have more revenue!!! I am as willing as any one that we should have more revenue, whenever the great counties who send Chisholms and Crookes, and Mounts and Burwells, and Morrises, McNabs, Willsons and McLeans, Frasers and McMartins, to vote EVERLASTING salary bills shall have shewn themselves a little more worthy, and a little more able to appreciate the uses of revenue. These men would never have voted as they did had they not felt confident that their constituents were either too ignorant to understand their conduct, or too careless and indifferent to the public good to cashier them for it. The men who were elected after voting their constituents foreigners and aliens could entertain no very elevated opinion of the principles and dignity of their constituents. These are my frank and candid opinions, stated without fear or favour; I did my best to procure a new choice for the country, but not without considerable apprehension that, even if successful, the rotten timber and sapwood of the next House would outweigh the solid and the wholesome. As it is, the old members have had another trial, and I confess I cannot greatly blame Viscount Goderich for giving it to them. He has yielded much to the united voice of the people of Lower Canada—has changed their governors, restored their magistrates and militia officers, assented to their acts for parliamentary reform, and the improvement of the jury laws, allowed them to assume the entire control of the revenue, delivered to their control the Jesuits' Estates, turned Attorney General Stuart adrift at their impeachment, and hesitated to create a new Canada Land Monopoly to which they were opposed. *I have good reason to believe* that the new crotchet about dismembering their country is utterly unknown at Downing Street except through the newspapers. It will assist us in bringing on enquiry and do no good to its originators or promoters.

I am Sir,
> Your most obedient
> Humble servant,
> WM. L. MACKENZIE.

COLONIAL ADVOCATE, 14 February 1833.

INTERVIEW WITH MR. STANLEY

On returning to London, early last May, I sought an interview with Mr. Stanley previous to my return, on the questions of the Post-Office, the Bank Acts, the Executive and Legislative Councils, the Reserves, &c. . . .

The first thing I spoke to him about was the Post Office department; the inconvenience and comparative inutility of the British packet system to Halifax; the superiority of steam-ships or packets like the Americans', with a suitable internal communication with the Canadas, or failing the establishment of these, a contract with the United States weekly packets between Liverpool and New York and the abolition of the Halifax monthly mail altogether; the secrecy of the department in its management of the revenue and other proceedings, contracts, &c; the perquisites of the persons conducting it; the absence of all domestic control on a domestic branch of taxation; the newspaper and letter postages, their extravagance; the surplus revenue; the insufficient post accommodations as compared with the United States; &c. I handed him a letter from Mr. Hume respecting the delay of the post office returns ordered by the House of Commons on the month of August preceding, which he promised to enquire into, and did so. I stated my conviction of the competence of Mr. Stayner to act as an efficient head of his department, praised his diligence, but censured him severely for the shuffling manner in which he had acted in order to conceal the amount of an income to which he knew himself not entitled. I do not remember that Mr. Stanley dissented from any opinion I presumed to offer, except where, after adverting to the expense of the postages of the addresses from Port Hope and Hastings, I suggested that it might be expedient to allow members of Parliament to receive addresses and petitions from bodies of the people of Upper Canada, relative to matters wherein they may feel aggrieved. I remarked at same time, that parliament legislated in matters of colonial commerce, and that it was not unreasonable to ask, on behalf of those affected by their legislation and unrepresented, that their letters and representations might be free. Mr. S. did not seem to like the proposition.

I next proceeded to speak of the Executive and Legislative Councils, and the tenure under which the public functionaries hold office, referring at same time to the changes which it was understood Lord Goderich had effected. I urged, that persons in authority should always be such as possessed the confidence of the country; and asked of what advantage a change of Ministry or of governors had been to us, when all persons in office in our colony remained the same, whether with or against our will? Adverting to his own, Mr. Macaulay's and Lord Althorp's opinions on this subject, as shewn in the Mirror of Parliament, I submitted the difficulty the province would have to contend for any length of time against the corrupt influence of those persons composing the executive government, when it was seen that they could retain their official influence notwithstanding any changes of the ministry or of government. I quoted to him the false and deceitful returns of the income of colonial officers which I had been enabled to peruse through the kindness of his predecessor, and he took notes of what I stated. I then asked him, what dependence the colonists could possibly have upon an honest and faithful return of the receipts and expenditure of a revenue in the hands of men who had not hesitated to deceive His Majesty's Government, and into whose alleged mal-practices the people of the colony had no possible means of enquiring? He made many observations, but I cannot say that they amounted to an admission that he was favourable to a change of the system.

When I came to speak of the Legislative Council, the materials of which, and its impudent address to the Lieutenant Governor, censuring Lord Goderich's despatch, I did not fail to expose, Mr. Stanley produced a written list of the members not holding any office, among whom he named Mr. Burnham and Mr. Macdonell. I informed him that Mr. Macdonell was a pensioner, and the excise officer of the county I lived in, and that Mr. Burnham was an emigrant from the U. States who had the merit of having voted thousands of his countrymen and constituents aliens, for which they had left him out of the Legislative Assembly; he had then been placed in the Council, and held the office of Treasurer of the District of Newcastle. Some names in his list I said I had never heard of, and others were half-pay officers, liable to be removed out of the country, like Captain Mathews, on a brief warning. A majority of the persons who form a branch of the legislature, actually attending in session as a Council, were, I affirmed, interested in the maintenance of the abuses of which the people complained, and dependent on a part of the local executive.

Perceiving, that he expressed no opinion favourable to an elective council, and being aware that despatches favourable to some change in the councils, had been sent out, I reminded him of his often repeated sentiments, as well as those of Viscount Goderich, Mr. Fox, Lord Howick, Mr. Labouchere, Sir J. Mackintosh, and Mr. Ellice; and added, with great plainness of language, that if I had not formed a false estimate of the sense and intelligence of the people of Upper Canada, they would not long endure a system which was considered an insult to the age and continent in which they lived; and that if obstacles to reform were made by the new Whig Government the population would perhaps proceed summarily to remove all difficulties in the way of their attainment of the enjoyment of a pure representative government in which their wishes and wants would be attended to in a different manner from what they were at present.

I added that the fact of my coming to and remaining so long in England seeking the redress of real and substantial grievances on the part of the colonists, was itself a substantial proof of my anxiety for a continuance of a friendly connexion between Great Britain and Canada, and that enough of knowledge was now diffused in the colonies to ensure for those who desired the changes prayed for by the petitioners, a substantial and efficient support.

I mentioned the boundary question, the currency, the St. Lawrence navigation, patents, emigration, a bankrupt system, defences, public lands, the Rideau Canal, inland trade between the colonies, the colonial post office, &c., and said I did not see how these important matters could be regulated to the general satisfaction unless there were a colonial conference assembled, composed of persons possessed of the confidence of each colony and possessing the general and local information necessary to enable them to express an enlightened opinion, and guard the important interests now neglected, or only kept up as means of increasing improper influence; and I reminded him that the colonists were at once the proprietors and the cultivators of the soil; that there were not many mobs as in Europe, nor a body of slaves like the cultivators in the West Indies, but men who would see and follow the true interests of their country, and who ought to be freely permitted to do so.

He assented to my remarks concerning the character of the

yeomanry, and I passed on to speak of the revenue not under the control of the legislature, namely the sums necessary to pay the interest of the provincial and district debts, the proceeds of the timber duties, seizures, forfeitures, fines, ferries, Canada Company's Payments, Clergy and Public Lands Rents and Sales, Crown Fees, Fees and Incomes to public officers made permanent, the assessed and Wild Land taxes, the post office revenue and the college funds, Rideau Canal receipts, timber sales, & naval and clerical & military expenditure derived from England. I admitted that the control of a revenue comparatively so large, and under no efficient public responsibility, might give and doubtless had long given an undue influence to the persons who monopolized the powers of government, but endeavoured to shew that continued mismanagement would add to the existing discontents, and serve more and more to estrange the colonists from the mother country. I said I was convinced they would not submit to it; and that they would deserve to be slaves if they would so submit to it. I placed in his hands a copy of Bishop McDonell's letter to Mr. O'Grady, shewing the sort of influence attempted to be exerted through the payments made to colonial priests, and quoted Dr. Doyle's testimony in the House of peers on the same subject.

I admitted *that it was obvious* that with such means as they had the executive might corrupt and lead at their pleasure a majority of a colonial assembly, and thereby convert, as they often had done, colonial legislation and enquiry into a solemn farce, but added that the result would be political unions, volunteer associations, conventions, and perhaps the annihilation of the colonial system, by the entire loss of public confidence in British Justice. Of the attempts that had been made to organize, as in England, in military fashion, bodies of catholic, presbyterian, episcopalian, methodist and other priests, depending on the executive and its officers for the whole or the greater part of their livelihood, and ready to excite discord and mischief in the country, I said that in common with my constituents I had a great abhorrence of all such means of supporting a government, and that if the whig administration were to continue to sanction such undue preferences and expenditures of public money upon the priests of the minority of the colonists, contrary to the wish of the petitioners with whose memorials I had been entrusted, the result would be intestine divisions and perhaps bloodshed, as in Ireland, but that British influence in America would gain nothing in the end, by such means of upholding a selection of contradictory creeds.

Mr. Stanley informed me that with regard to the matters that had been brought before the government full enquiry would be made and means taken to satisfy the reasonable desires of the country—that as soon as Mr. Stayner arrived the post office question would be taken up—that the returns ordered by the House of Commons would be produced—that the abolition of the tea monopoly was then before parliament which would dispose of it—that the fullest information the House of Assembly could desire would be laid before it as to the revenue and expenditure—and that His Majesty had disallowed the acts of the provincial legislature relating to the York and Kingston Banks. I enquired whether the people would at length be permitted to amend their choice of representatives, and made reference to what I understood to be the real state of the case, but on that subject he would give me no information whatever. Before I left the Colonial Office he requested me to send him a statement in writing concerning the revenue and the erroneous returns made from Canada, and on some other questions in his notes, and I drew it up and sent it.

His manner towards me was exceedingly kind and friendly; I had been led to believe that he would be hasty, and impatient of my observations. Nothing could be more remote from the fact, for, although an Irish Archbishop was kept in the next room for the last half hour waiting for an interview, and my audience had been a very long one, Mr. Stanley asked me when I took leave of him whether there was no other matter of which I wished to speak to him. COLONIAL ADVOCATE, 5 September 1833.

Chapter Nine

CURRENT COMMENT 1834-1837

DIVISIONS IN LOWER CANADA

LETTER TO JOHN NEILSON

YORK, FEB 7, 1834

DEAR SIR

I am grieved for the divisions[1] that appear to have sprung up in the midst of the worthy and good men of Lower Canada who by their united exertions within the last few years, have effected so much good for this as well as your own colony. Doubtless these divisions are deeply injurious to the good cause of reform, and the knowledge that you are opposing Mr. Papineau and the Canadian party will continue, as of late, to be productive of the greatest injury to them in the minds of the English Ministers, and prevent their obtaining many concessions they would otherwise (I think) have readily obtained. I have since my return been, (at this distance) an anxious reader of the Quebec Gazette, and am grieved to see Mr.

[1][The division between Papineau and Neilson came to a head in 1834 on the question of the character of responsible government. Papineau had been moving in the direction of independent responsible government in all branches, legislative and executive. Neilson, while for a long time able to work with Papineau on specific grievances, became more and more committed to advocating reforms within the existing framework of the constitution. In the campaign of 1834 the Ninety-two Grievances drawn up by Papineau's party were the main issue. Neilson disagreed sharply with most of the statements and continued to campaign for a more moderate approach and for compromises with the British government. Papineau's party won a sweeping victory in the election. Mackenzie's comment three years later on Neilson's defeat was: "Mr. Papineau and the Canadians did no more than their duty when they dismissed him (the senior Mr. Neilson) from the legislature." *The Constitution*, 4 January 1837.]

Papineau reduced to the necessity of complaining of the hostility of an ancient and faithful and powerful ally of the people's best interests. I would distrust my own judgment, but Mr. Bidwell and those other gentlemen for whom I have long felt esteem, deeply sympathize with Mr. Papineau and those who act with him under the difficult circumstances in which they are placed. They seem to be honest and faithful in a good cause, and whether they are or are not successful the sympathy of many will continue to attend them.

You are made (in the papers) to say that you have not yet despaired of seeing the British Constitution in practical operation in *the Colony* of Lower Canada. How can that be?

Can you regulate your foreign commerce? Can you establish the laws of entail, primogeniture and half-blood?—the poor laws?—the Church of England?—the bankrupt laws?—the hereditary peerage?—tithes etc.? Can you obtain the control over the troops, so that at a month's notice you could disband them? I could name a hundred old and fundamental features in the system of alterations and changes known by some as the English Constitution which you would never think of ingrafting upon the Canadian mode of government, but we, your anxious onlookers here, are at a loss what you mean by proposing to give us the British Constitution. Mr. Macaulay defined it to be a series of reforms in the Government. Yet you appear to oppose reform. Even now, this session, your Legislative Council have rejected useful and salutary laws, and done little that is good, yet you seem to think the Canadians erring for trying to get rid of them, and *I know* that your opposition has great weight at home and is doing them great injury and *influencing those who influence* the ministers against them. I did not suppose that an elective council would be granted at once to their wishes, at a time when the British Peerage are alarmed for things established, but I did suppose that the demand would be less ungracefully refused, and that other reforms would be conceded, and more care taken in selecting future councillors—and my firm impression is that your opposition in the House and the course taken by the Gazette out of it is doing not only the Canadians below, but also us here great mischief. While united under "Neilson and Papineau", the Canadian body were to the enemies of good government here a terror. Divided as you now are, the spirit of the people may be broken down for years, and the most unfavourable influences exerted on our ensuing elections, next summer. I deeply lament this, and the more so that Mr. Stanley's despatches were announced in the Quebec Gazette in a tone of triumph, and the paragraph read in our House of Assembly as a proof of the bad feeling that exists between those to whom the country looks up for advice and good counsel.

At an inclement season of the year, I travelled 500 miles to get your advice, you received me kindly, and your opinion proved good and sound; our Upper Canada affairs have often been with you a subject of remark, and your spirit has been that of kindness and friendship. I am grateful. I presume not to oppose my judgment to yours, but I could no longer refrain from telling you in this private letter, that those who call themselves reformers here grieve at the opposition and censure given to Mr. Papineau and the worthy and good men who appear to seek free institutions for their country. If I know my own heart and mind I feel a sincere and abiding friendship for the land of my birth, but I have never yet seen any paper either in print or in MS attempting to prove that we in these colonies, *as colonies,* could possibly obtain the practical operation of what is called the British Constitution. I have read the article in the Quebec Gazette dated the 2nd. Nov. last, on legislative councils, and I feel that we must either be colonies of England or submit to the pleasure of Congress, but it does not thence follow that the shameful abuses in these colonies are to continue and that those who try to abate them are to be censured for so doing. In seeking a convention, the House of Assembly only sought a remedy for the positive evil of a legislative council which does much mischief and is composed chiefly of bad material, and in their tactic to the Supply Bill they exercised their best judgment in endeavouring to stop pluralities and sinecures, yet for so doing they are censured by Mr. Stanley and the censure echoed in the Quebec Gazette! These things amaze me.

I have hastily penned these few lines, and hope you wont be angry with me. I not only mean well, but I try to act from the best information I can obtain, and as I have often had to repent a premature judgment given on political matters and the actions of men, I merely send this letter as my present impressions on a matter in which I take a lively interest. LINDSEY PAPERS.

EXPULSIONS WHOLESALE!

In compliance with the wishes of many of my friends who had blamed me for not making an effort to obtain a seat in the House, and in obedience to the request of the freeholders of York and

Toronto at their late meetings, I resolved to avail myself of the legal opinion of the Attorney General and Sir John Colborne's arrangements in pursuance thereof, and accordingly waited last Saturday on Mr. Beikie, Clerk of the Executive Council, for the purpose of taking the oath as a member, when that gentleman informed me, that he had neither received the commission mentioned in Colonel Rowan's letter nor any letter intimating that it had issued. I immediately called at the Government Office and mentioned what Mr. Beikie had said. The same evening I received the following note:
(COPY,)

GOVERNMENT HOUSE, 8TH FEB. 1834

SIR,—Mr. W. L. Mackenzie having intimated his intention to take his seat in the House of Assembly on Monday next, I am directed by the Lieutenant Governor to request, that you will immediately transmit to Mr. Beikie, the Commission which His Excellency signed on the 18th of December last, appointing Commissioners to administer the oath of allegiance to members of the Assembly.

I have, &c
WM. ROWAN

S. P. JARVIS, ESQ.

GOVERNMENT HOUSE, 8TH FEB. 1834

Sir,—I am directed to forward to you the accompanying copy of a letter which has been addressed to Mr. S. P. Jarvis, Deputy Secretary and Registrar.

I am, &c.
WM. ROWAN

W. L. MACKENZIE, ESQ.

On Monday at ten I again waited on Mr. Beikie at the Council Office, and he shewed me the commission which had just been sent him by Mr. Jarvis, with an explanatory letter. He then offered to administer the oath, by virtue of an old commission authorizing him to administer it to emigrants, but acknowledged that he was afraid of getting into difficulty if he did so under the new commission. On this I had to go back to the government house and state the facts in writing for the information of the executive government. The Attorney General was speedily sent for, and the Governor and, I think, all the members of his council met and considered the matter in the Council Chamber. Mr. Beikie came into his room and again offered to administer the oath required by the 29th clause of the 31st Geo. 3rd, but when I asked him, under which commission? he would not say. I had previously shewn him my indenture and quoted the Attorney General's opinion, and he went back once more to the council. On his return, Mr. Jarvis the clerk in chancery came in, and he asked him if I had been duly elected. Mr. J. said I had. Mr. Beikie then told me that he would administer the oath to me as a member of the Legislature, in virtue of the Lt. Governor's authority to him to do so, dated the 18th of December last, and he did so and granted a certificate of the transaction duly attested, which I also signed and carried with me to the House of Assembly. It was now three o'clock, and I immediately walked into the Assembly's Chamber and took my seat, the House being then in Committee on the St. Lawrence question, Mr. Donald Macdonald in the Chair. Mr. McNab the Sergeant at Arms followed me shortly after and said that I was a stranger and must retire. I insisted that I was a member legally elected, duly sworn, and charged with no offence or irregularity which could disqualify me from sitting and voting, and shewed him the attested copy of the oath, bidding him interfere at his peril. He said he must use force and he did so in as gentle a manner as was consistent with the act. Although his proceedings were illegal, his whole conduct in carrying them into effect was marked by a discretion wisely adopted in the excited state of the minds of the dense audience by whom he was surrounded. I almost immediately returned to the seat I had occupied, and while on my way was seized hold of by Colonel Frazer, Collector of Customs at Brockville, and obliged to change my route. Before I had got well seated, one of the members, I think Mr. Boulton, moved that the Speaker take the Chair. He did so, and I addressed him stating the insult I had received while in the performance of my duty as a member. To this he made no reply, but said that the Sergeant at Arms must know his duty. He then left the Chair; the committee resumed, and I was a second time forced from my seat by violent means. After a little reflection I decided to resume my seat; was a third time forced from it by the Sergeant at Arms; and when the Speaker had returned I was placed at the Bar, charged by the Sergeant at Arms with refusing to leave the House.

Mr. McNab rose and declared his intention to vote for committing me to the common jail; that I had called the House a trained band of robbers in my newspaper; and that my object by this insult was to be sent to jail; he added that those who were there assembled under my banners were a band of ruffians who came there to intimidate the House.

Mr. SAMSON proposed to send me to jail, but was for allowing me a hearing first.

Mr. MERRITT rose in much anger, and said "Drown his voice. He ought to be put out of the House and two men stationed continually at the door to keep him out."

Mr. SHADE was of the same mind.

Mr. McNAB said we shall hear nothing he has to say; he cannot change our purpose.

Mr. PERRY moved a resolution in favour of my taking my seat, which was lost, 15 to 21, Mr. Archibald McDonald voting against it because "I had been legally expelled." In another speech he said he viewed my expulsion as unconstitutional. I wish he would explain.

My opinion of Sir John Colborne's general conduct is unaltered, but I must do him the justice to say that I think he was from the first in earnest to have me sworn in, and that the delays which took place were not attributable to the government office. He was bound to take the Attorney General's opinion on the point of law, and if his instructions were to be guided by his legal adviser in such cases he deserves neither censure nor praise for the performance of an ordinary act of duty. During Monday's debate, however, Mr. *McNab* said that the Lieutenant Governor had interfered very improperly, and in a manner no way creditable to himself and he might yet find that, like the Vicar of Bray, by taking both sides of the question he may fall through between. Mr. *Bidwell*, in one of the most eloquent addresses he ever delivered, spoke of His Excellency's conduct on that occasion as worthy of high respect. Mr. *Merritt* would remove the seat of government to a place where the mob could not intimidate the House as they do in York. Mr. *Morris* made a very bitter and unkind speech. I am credibly informed that when he was last at the hustings, he told the electors of Perth "that I was a revolutionary scoundrel who, if elected, ought to be expelled the House, and that he would use his utmost efforts to effect my expulsion." Mr. *Samson* said that my charges against the conduct of the House "were drawn out in the closet with all the coolness of deliberate malice." He, however, would vote against his own motion for giving me a hearing before punishment. Mr. *William Robinson* declared he would be for punishing and sending me to jail, and not allowing me to say one word in defence of my outrageous proceedings. (Hisses in the Gallery.) He added, that I would not have come to that House if I had not had His Excellency's sanction in my pocket. His Excellency's conduct was very unjustifiable. Indeed he (Mr. Robinson) could hardly think it possible that His Excellency should have thought of taking such a step without consulting with the Speaker of that House. And now that he is told that we (the House) do not recognize that right of the executive he trusted he would not persevere. Mr. *Samson* inveighed against Sir John Colborne with great vehemence. "I do say," quoth Mr. Samson, "that His Excellency had no right whatever to have interfered. I do say that he acted a most improper part; and I do not know but that this House ought to take it up. The proceeding on the part of His Excellency was a most unwarrantable one, as he knew perfectly well that Mr. Mackenzie had been expelled by us, to appoint a third commissioner to administer the oath to him." (It is indeed curious to see a chief magistrate censured by his bosom friends for doing only one lawful act in strict accordance with his instructions. They seem fearful that he inclines to run with the hare and hold with the hounds.) Mr. *McNab*, in the course of the debate, had to apologize for calling the people below the bar a band of ruffians, and I think it was the especial duty of Mr. Ketchum and Sheriff Jarvis to have required that explanation of him. The former however never once opened his lips, and the latter had too much fellow feeling with the member for Wentworth to complain. Messrs. Morris and McNab said a great deal about my having called the members a trained band of robbers, through the newspaper, but I never used any such expression, nor any thing like it. In the House no one expression of mine on any occasion was ever made the subject of parliamentary censure. Out of the House I have a right to speak of things as they are, subject to the verdict of a jury if I abuse that right.

Mr. *Perry* spoke nobly, and moved a resolution to dissolve the House, a step Sir John was bound in honour to have taken long ago. It was lost. Mr. *Bidwell* called for the rescinding of the entries on the journals of my last expulsion. That also was lost. Mr. *Berczy* prefaced a motion with some very spiteful and personal reflections. He was for admonishing me and not allowing any defence or explanation on my part. This carried. I protested against the usage my constituents had met with, and against the violent proceedings of the House, and then Mr. McLean from the chair tried to justify them and convince me that I was wrong. Thus the matter ended for the night, the debate having lasted full seven hours.

It is probable that the provoking language of some of the members would have ended in a disturbance had I not warned the people through the press, personally at many of their dwelling houses, and in the House before I took my seat, to preserve perfect silence whatever the members said or did. They were very orderly, and it is creditable to them that they were so. If public opinion will not avenge our cause violence and tumult will not help us. What I have seen at Brockville convinces me that to encourage violence would be to raise up among us an untameable power well calculated perhaps to gratify a momentary feeling unworthy of our better natures, but destructive of social order, personal security and comfort, domestic happiness and the rights of property.

In conclusion, I beg to say that I never once received the least advice or counsel to take my seat, either directly or indirectly from any member of the Assembly, but acted as I did because I believed it to be my duty. I greatly desire personal liberty, but the fear of a prison, or of poverty, or of danger to life or limb, will not, I trust, make a coward of me, in a good cause.

ADVOCATE, 13 February 1834.

YORK INCORPORATION BILL

We think it extremely unlikely that His Excellency will make his government still more unpopular with the people of this town and county, by assenting to the incorporation bill in its present shape, and forcing upon 9,000 people in Canada a close rotten borough government of the most odious character, in the very teeth of their public meetings and petitions and committees praying to the contrary. We are actuated by no party feeling or personal consideration in giving our feeble opposition to the present measure. We oppose it because on a careful consideration of its bearings we are convinced that it will be injurious to the peace and prosperity of our fellow townsmen; and it surely is not at a time when Borough Reform has become one of the main supports of His Majesty's Government in England that the King's representative here will hasten to wound the feelings of the people still further by allowing such a measure as this to come into operation. At the large and highly respectable meeting of our fellow townsmen held yesterday in the Court House we were politely allowed to state at length and in detail our views of the probable working of the bill, and after the meeting had listened to Dr. Baldwin and Mr. Ridout in its favour, and to several influential speakers against it, it was voted with acclamation that a select committee of the towns-people should wait on His Excellency with a petition that he would withhold the royal assent from it. The meeting was unanimous in its opposition, with the exception of Dr. Baldwin and one other, whose hands were held up in its favour. Should it pass into a law, the people will get up petitions against it to the House of Commons, and when its provisions are laid before a select committee of parliament, its odious character, and the sentiments of that government who could force such a bill upon the people will be fully made manifest. The petition to the Lieutenant Governor omits the most serious objections to the bill, but not choosing to offer an amendment at this stage of the proceedings the writer of this article signed it, reserving the right at the fitting time to propose a memorial elsewhere which should contain his reasons why this local change ought not to be sustained in opposition to the wishes of the parties more particularly interested. ADVOCATE, 6 March 1834.

CITY ELECTIONS

The first annual election of magistrates to serve for this city took place last Thursday, when two Aldermen and two Councilmen were returned in each of the five wards. A majority of the persons elected are of decidedly liberal principles, not at all disposed to use the great powers entrusted to them for any other purpose than that of promoting the true interests of every class of citizens. For a victory so important in its consequences Toronto is indebted (under providence) to the patriotism, union, and intelligence of its inhabitants. The citizens did their duty nobly, and will receive the reward of their fidelity.

We have given below the names of some of the public officers who took part in the contest, to shew the interest they felt in the result.

The greatest order and decorum prevailed throughout the city during and after the election, and among the friends of peace and quietness none were more conspicuous than our fellow citizens natives of Ireland, both catholic and protestant. ADVOCATE, 3 April 1834.

"BANEFUL DOMINATION"

[*The letter referred to, written on 29 March 1834, was published in the* Advocate *on 22 May 1834. It contained the phrase: the "crisis which is fast approaching in the affairs of Canada, and which will terminate in independence and freedom from the baneful domination of the mother country, and the tyrannical conduct of a small and despicable faction in the colony." See* Lindsey, *vol. 1, p. 300.*]

I have been so constantly employed of late in attending to the duties imposed on me by my fellow citizens, that I had not so much leisure as formerly either to read or reply to newspaper paragraphs. I find, however, that the British Whig, the Hamilton Free Press, the Courier, Guardian, Patriot, Western Mercury, and the Quebec Gazette and Mercury are displeased with the contents of a letter addressed to me by Mr. Hume, and dated at London the 29th of March last. I beg to state that my reason for giving publicity to that letter was a belief that it would be attended with the most beneficial results. I am satisfied of the truth of the statements made by Mr. Hume and heartily accord with the sentiments and opinions he expresses concerning the present condition and future prospects of the Canadas.

Mr. Ryerson smarts under the lash—it has been fitly applied. His three laboured columns in the Guardian, and his attempts at freeing himself from the charge of base ingratitude towards a generous benefactor sink him lower and lower in my estimation. I know him now. He can deceive no more. If he had (as he says) told me of his dislike to Mr. Hume while he was entreating his aid in London, or even after his return, I should not have publickly and privately urged his re-election last fall to the editorial chair of the conference he has so much dishonoured. I was led to believe the conference this year would be held at Toronto, and in that case intended to make a personal application to be heard against Mr. Ryerson's proceedings. I find, however, that Kingston is their place of meeting, and will delay further comments on his and their proceedings until their course can be ascertained.

As to Mr. Hume's reference to the example of America in 1776, it does indeed furnish an excellent and salutary lesson to the statesman—and with regard to his prediction that freedom from life legislators, military domination, land jobbing, established priesthoods and irresponsible government must be the result of the continued misconduct of the authorities here and their abettors in the Colonial Office, I do sincerely believe it is the truth. I am sure I have been acting the part of a sincere friend of the empire to which I belong while seeking the independence of Canada from the baneful domination of the Colonial Office. If revolution, violent revolution is to be avoided—if an honourable and beneficial connexion with Great Britain is to be maintained, it must be in the way proposed by Mr. Hume, namely, by conciliating the people and allowing the colonists the management of their internal concerns. Those who hold a different language are manifestly working to drive Canada into the arms of the United States.

June 9th.

W. L. MACKENZIE

ADVOCATE, 12 June 1834.

LETTER TO A. N. BUELL

[*This letter is written on the back of a heavy-paper leaflet, announcing the formation of the Canadian Alliance Society. See* Lindsey, *vol. i, p. 319.*]

TORONTO, DEC. 15, 1834

DEAR SIR

Unless we get societies up having one common object to be pursued by the same means depend on it this parliament of ours in U.C. will disappoint our hopes—but if we enlist the people in the cause we are safe.

Reformers here can find no better mode of combining the strength of the liberals than by the mode herein proposed—I trust it will meet your approbation.

It needs no public meeting to commence—only the signatures of a few reformers who think alike—if you have energy your numbers and influence will soon increase—we are nearly 400 strong in this city alone.

There is no other test required than an approbation of the views of the society—and as to privacy, it may be distinguished from secret meetings by the mark that women *may* be present, and that no member is enjoined to secrecy, nor obliged to continue longer than he thinks fit.

I regret the loss of the Recorder—If you publish these proceedings send me the No. If I were able I would be a subscriber, but I am not yet on the road to wealth.

Urge the people, through the press, to interest themselves in the election of Mr. Bidwell as Speaker. An effort is required to secure his election and the hint should be given to the people to spur on their members.

Yours faithfully

W. L. MACKENZIE

LINDSEY PAPERS.

LETTER TO SAMUEL NEILSON

MONTREAL, NOV. 18, 1835

SIR

I think your satire and ridicule of my late visit to your city was ill timed—I wished much to have called on you, but was impressed with the idea that one who could write so bitterly of those who had never injured him would not hesitate to offer an affront to them on a visit. And yet, why should I have thought so? From you and from your father I at one time experienced great kindness, and felt and remembered it. When I returned to Quebec from England some said you had changed your principles and turned. I combatted the sentiment, and it was not until I had the proof in your Journal that I conceded. Your talent and experience, however, might be better employed than in exhibiting me in an incorrect point of view—I have not deserved such usage, and I complain of it.

If there is, *and I begin to imagine that you have some shadow of cause for saying so* (for the Canadians have been very ill used and feel it), a French-Canadian party who would wish to obtain the ascendancy in Canada, for the purpose of visiting on the heads of the population of your origin and mine the sins of the old tyrannical governments of unreformed England, believe me, for I say it most sincerely, I am the last Scotsman in Upper Canada who would be their tool or their slave—but in as far as it is sought by the House of Assembly of Lower Canada to educate all and give all equal rights, why should there be two opinions? Why should a man so enlightened and experienced as you are, the son of an individual distinguished above many for his intrepid defence of popular rights, sacrifice to party, and personal feelings, the noble opportunity of healing divisions and uniting all who honestly seek the welfare of their fellow men. Life is so chequered that those in your situation, on whom wealth and happiness has been bestowed, as an inheritance, should try to sweeten the cup of bitterness called "local politics", leaving less gifted men like me to shew the littleness of our minds by a wordy warfare useless alike to the readers and the authors.

What reason had I in London or Quebec to believe you would take the course you have done, two years ago? What reason had I for supposing that when I wrote you my sentiments in a private letter you would treat the humble writer and his arguments with derision and contempt? You did wrong in these things—and I hope

342

you will yet think so. What ill have the U.C. reformers ever done you?

After you had ridiculed and derided the reformers of U.C. with whom you once acted until I could no longer condone it, I formally gave up your paper—but wishing to see whether you had good reasons for ascribing a feeling to Mr. Papineau akin to hatred of your country people and mine I moved formally for the Quebec Gazette and Morning Courier to be taken by the Parliament of U.C. I have since read very carefully all you have said and noted down and compared your reasonings with the results of my own observation. I am not sure that there is not more in what your father wrote me than I could have imagined; ill usage has, I fear, originated some feelings which never ought to have existed, but that cause has not perhaps produced all the bad effects you state, therefore permit me to beg of you to try to moderate parties rather than irritate, and exhibit the noble qualities of your nature rather than the unamiable ones which I would get rid of if I could, *but cannot.* . . .

For the course taken by your press there may be reasons I ought not to seek to learn, and which time will best unfold; but why are you so very bitter? Such bitterness were in character with me—a sort of misanthrope—but with you I hope it will be like the winter apple, ungrateful to the taste until the latter time, and then the most sweet and mellow when most to be desired.

Perhaps these few private lines will be excused. I seldom will intrude on you—but I do sincerely and unfeignedly wish the happiness of your father's roof-tree and all under it. LINDSEY PAPERS.

LETTERS TO JOHN NEILSON

On board the steamer Canada
between Quebec and Montreal,
18th Nov. 1835

HONOURED SIR

If any one had told me three years ago that I would have remained nearly three weeks in Quebec without seeking the honour of an interview with you I should have deemed it an impossibility. Yet so it is, I am on my return from that city without having sought or obtained that honour. So much for politics.

Your own remarks, in a letter of Feb. 1834, and other circumstances have induced me in my recent visit to look as far as I could into the ulterior views of those of a different origin who are the majority of the Lower Canadian population—and the result of my observations I must admit to be a greater uncertainty on that point. The Upper Canada Reformers have even ascribed your secession from the ranks of the Canadian leaders, and their views, to personal pique, and the course taken by the Gazette has much confirmed that belief. Perhaps we are all wrong. If I find I am so, none will be more willing and ready to avow it; for I am dependent on no party on earth further than I think that party honest and sincere for what I conceive to be the general interests of all classes of all origins—and the idea of a French Canadian state, province or republic controlling the St. Lawrence, and the Commerce of the great countries situated on its banks is too absurd to be seriously credited. I think that freedom of trade, the free navigation of the St. Lawrence, the gradual abolition of the timber exclusion business, and a better and more responsible system of government in Upper and Lower Canada would prove beneficial to the population, united with general education and the abolition of monopolies; but little good will be effected, if those whose judgment, temper and practical habits of business would best enable them to undertake the arduous task continue estranged from each other. It is only in the belief that their views are manly, statesmanlike and benevolent that I have hitherto clung to Mr. Papineau, and respected and esteemed the opinions of Mr. Viger. We in Upper Canada are getting deeply in debt for objects which yield nothing, and our trade is uncertain, and our population, even the leading men in the government, discontented. Your Constitutional Society, and its prospectus, as understood, were much disliked.

The Commission were to have visited us, but are not to do so now —and I believe the *doubtful uncertain policy* which is so injurious to our interests is to be continued, and the imbecile heads of departments to retain their places, and discontent to increase. I am very sorry for it.

The end must be bad—yet good will surely come out of evil—and better days will be in store for the many kindhearted souls and the many worthy families that are scattered over our territory. Upper Canada never will desire to act unjustly to Lower Canada, neither will we permit our natural rights to be injured by her. I am incapable of moderating the spirit of party—I am hot and fiery and age has not yet tempered as much as I could wish my political conduct and opinions, but you might do much good, by casting oil on the waters, and waiting for the tide in human affairs in Canada in which you could usefully and honourably and kindly come forward as the active friend and advocate of the rights of our common country.

I have written these lines hastily on the boat and a few words to Mr. Neilson Jr. If I had been near Mrs. Mackenzie her warmest and best wishes would have been conveyed to you—she often speaks of you with sentiments of great respect, and whenever it is asserted in her hearing that you are no longer the friend of the people you once was she repels this insinuation. Pardon these few private lines, they were unasked for, unexpected, and I do not imagine that they will be answered. LINDSEY PAPERS.

TORONTO, DEC. 28, 1835

DEAR SIR

I have read your letter with much pleasure, but will candidly acknowledge that the compliment you pay my loyalty sits less easy on my shoulders than it would have done three years ago, when I first met you at Quebec. If the English government had done *its best* to ensure to this colony the advantages contemplated by the Act 31st. Geo. 3rd. ch. 31, I should have remained a contented plodding private individual, loyal from inclination *as well as duty*, "and sincerely desirous of maintaining our connexion with the mother countries." As to my private dealings, my neighbours of all parties certainly shew me confidence enough, and I was not aware that their correctness had been called in question elsewhere until I read your letter. Until my return from England in the *fall of 1833*, I used what little influence I possessed with the yeomanry to persuade them that by petitioning England, a remedy would be found to every wrong of which they had just reason to complain. In an inclement season of the year 1831, I travelled from Toronto [to] Quebec to take your advice on this subject, and you had so much confidence in the honour and integrity of purpose of the English Government, that I was strengthened greatly in the course I had adopted. But I have been in England—I have seen the usage *Ireland met with*—the treatment *other colonies* received—the promises made today to be broken tomorrow—the instructions (in the case of chartered Banks for instance) promulgated in the spring by one colonial minister to be *retracted* in the fall by another under the threat of a tory assembly here. In short, I have seen enough to convince me that we shall continue to have the very *worst possible government in Upper Canada* until we get rid of *the system* which binds us to the earth. I therefore am *less loyal* than I was, and would be wanting in candour if I did not admit the fact—I like *sincerity* in others and try to practice the virtue myself, although it is attended sometimes with a temporary inconvenience.

I am satisfied that Upper Canada, if it had had an honest government, would at this day number a *million and a half* of souls, in place of 350,000 eaten up with debt, degradation and discontent. Do not imagine that I am deceived into the belief that with such a population as we have here, a legislative council of their election would be the grand panacea for all our political ills. Even in New York State they have found it necessary to guard their system with the *veto* of the most *intelligent* man whom they can select for their chief magistrate, against the acts of the other branches of the legislature altho' chosen in the most popular manner—and to enforce many other checks incompatible with a colonial government, all of which appear to be necessary to guard the community against the corruption incident to popular legislative bodies where the responsibility is divided among many. The reason I seek a Senate like that at Washington is, that it is a *step* to the attainment of the only system by which I can ever hope to see anything like the *semblance of justice administered in the country* which was the choice of my early and inexperienced years. Perhaps it was republican and disloyal in me to read with unmingled satisfaction President Jackson's message where he condemns monopolies—but I did so—here, these monopolies keep the Assembly in constant employment exposing those monstrous abuses, which the legislative acts, and the institutions of the country are so well calculated to generate.

The paper money system paved the way for independence in the United States—it is doing the same here. Banks and branches start up like mushrooms—we have already five banks and a branch in this place, and there is only the check afforded by the prudence of the directors. That that will be ineffectual to preserve public credit in the hour of difficulty, the experience of the past might have shewn. I have rather changed my opinions since I resided three weeks in Lower Canada last November, with respect to the state of parties. How much it were to be wished that yourself and Mr. Papineau could go hand in hand for the general good—as you once did! I am sorry that it is a wish not likely soon to be realized.

As to the friendship of the Canadians of French origin towards the English, Scotch and Irish—perhaps it is less warm than I had supposed—but, be this as it may, it is us who are to blame. England conquered their country—turned their *colleges into a barrack*—kept their people in ignorance—insulted their leading men—neglected their best interests—forgot to conciliate and trust in them—preferred strangers to their language, manners and customs—*appeared to* give them popular institutions forty years ago, and now declares them virtually unfit to enjoy them! The executive council contemplated in 1791, did not turn the governor into a mere machine to execute orders from London, and his council into *dummies* set up for a show.

I am in no great hurry for the introduction of the Elective System —public opinion will bring it to pass to the full as soon here as in Lower Canada—there is a large and numerous body of intelligent men here who see that their interests are suffering by the existing system—Who that has tried the speed and comfort of an English Mail Coach would wish to return to the delays of a cumbrous French one? We want better helmsmen here. A ship may make progress enough on the ocean, but it depends upon the steersman or his guide whether that progress shall be the most direct towards the desired haven. I want freedom and security—they are the end and design of good government—we have them not here, that's clear enough. The trial by jury is in the sheriff's power—the sheriff is in the governor's power—the governor, acting without a legal council, consults the minion of his fancy—and injustice is done. It may be said that I am a proof of the freedom that exists. Far from it; where I have survived hundreds have sunk to rise no more. If public opinion could influence the government why has not Bidwell's bill for the more equal division of intestate estates become a law? We have passed it yearly for nearly a dozen of years, in whig, tory, and radical parliaments (if such cognomens be correct) and by immense majorities often approaching to unanimity. It is one of a class that never pass up stairs. I do think we are as effectually enslaved from an inability to pass good general enactments, as by any direct interference of the English Parliament in our affairs. Look at the post office monopoly—charges excessively high, and a person at Quebec collecting nearly £30,000 a year, into whose accounts, books and proceedings no one can look on this side the sea—and on the other side [*tear in* MS.] knowledge is wanting. Look at the orange system, how the government here fosters it for party purposes—see the vagaries of Bishop McDonell, travelling thro' the colony in a political crusade, with a pension in his pocket and religion in his mouth—note too our provincial debt of £500,000— our district debts—our city debt—a little city not yet two years in existence and in debt of £17,000. Again, there is our land system— you told me in 1831, that the country would get more and more

347

into the hands of the resident proprietors—*but it has not done so*—far from it. The Canada Company is in difficulty—vast numbers of *our best farmers* are leaving the province—Education is kept back by the failure of our numerous bills to promote it—the University languishes amid great endowments, *from the like cause*—our clergy reserve sale bills, with the apparent sanction of England, die in the Council, selected by England—many, many a family in the wilderness, pines in disease, want and poverty—far from good roads—far from a market—oppressed with costly courts of law—their places often the prize of petty attornies and shopkeepers—Come to Toronto and look at our judgment book at the crown-office, if they will let you—and you will there see that our *apparently* richest men are the mere *factors* of others in other countries—When the Hon. T. Clark died worth £100,000 the other day his wealth went to Scotland—When Col. Talbot dies his vast property will go to Ireland—When the Hon. John McGill died, his £50,000 went to Peter McGill of Montreal—You speak of "anarchy"—if we are not in the way to anarchy we are on the road to some change, of that I feel well assured.

The Montreal "Constitutionalists" have greatly weakened their cause here by their 800 rifles, congress, army, pikes and muskets. These are not the days when changes of government are produced in America by violence and brute force—Since I returned from England I have been more sensible of this, and have directed my attention more to the *people*. If ever I sign or send a petition across the Atlantic, for redress of grievances, I'll change my opinion marvellously. I have sent you a couple of *Welland Canals*—and I'll send you a couple more—read them and doubt if you can that *things must change here bye and bye.*—If I had ten thousand relations I never would invite one of them to suffer under such a system as ours. What is it to us if the Colonial Ministers are good men enough? They, their governors, commissioners and so forth, have no part and portion with us—they never sat in our houses of assembly—they never thought of settling among us—but we must endure them because of the timber trade!—The doctrine wont do here. We want free trade, and every man to buy in the cheapest market and sell in the dearest—low taxes on exports and imports—these taxes equalized—and each man to follow the [*torn*] or profession he can live best by. Even now the U.S. [*torn*] best grain market. Look at page 4 No. 2 of "the Welland Canal", and see the courses of the Western Trade. Only a few days ago the *tories*, so called, held a meeting to prepare for taking the trade to New York rather than Montreal, and the Hon. W. Allan took the chair! That was a sign. Personal observation enables me to declare that to me the far larger number of your population in Lower Canada must, from differences of language, feelings, manners and customs, be strangers —I am from home among them—altho' *I was at home* with my wife Isabel at your home in the country and gratefully remember your hospitality and kindness on that occasion. In my family I am as happy as an emperor—had it not been so I should have sunk under the difficulties of the last twelve years. Domestic happiness is a fine thing to one whose public duties are onerous and unpleasant. We have lost two children since I was with Mrs. M. under your roof and the third is spared to us—out of nine we have four alive. Your humble correspondent joins his wife in wishing you and yours many a happy return of this cheerful season, and that we may all live to see the time when more unanimity will exist in Canada. I confess I am in good hope—and altho' the way to govern best, like the way to heaven, is still a matter upon which people are allowed to differ, I trust that these lovely countries have many happy days yet in store for the people, when the bickerings of 1835 shall be forgotten. I have read the address of the Montreal Constitutional Association, and many of their arguments are strong and cogent. But when one looks to the individuals of whom the association consists, it is difficult to remember many of them as having been in the ranks of reform of any description until now. The association in Quebec is of a more moderate character—but what I would like to see is some change which would bring such able men as Messrs. Grey, Stuart and yourself once more into an influential position in the Councils of the Lower Canadians. The Legislative Union of the Canadas would be no good—nor would the annexation of Montreal to U.C. be a right measure, unless the people themselves wished it, which they do not. Excuse, I pray you, the haste in which I write. I have written as I think, and as I would have spoken had I supposed that I would have been a welcome visitor at Carouge. If I am wrong I will try to be set right—I have stated my opinions candidly and the reasons I have for holding them. I judged of your sentiments by the Quebec Gazette, and was in error. I often used too strong language when an editor, and perhaps I do so yet. But I remain

Sincerely and respectfully
Your obedient servant
W. L. MACKENZIE

LINDSEY PAPERS.

ORANGE LODGES

Orange Lodges in this Colony are a dangerous nuisance, of the most strictly exclusive kind, from which Catholics are always kept, and their main object is to oppose and oppress the Catholics. These Lodges in Ireland instruct the youth of that ill-fated country that the Catholics are the natural enemies of the Protestants, and thus keep alive differences which the good sense of the age would otherwise get rid of. It has been clearly proved to the British Parliament, that the Orange Lodges are linked together by secret signs and symbols of a nature as detrimental to the peace of society as they are inconsistent with the law of the land; and that they are in Ireland "productive of public disturbance and had often led to the most lamentable results." The Judges have solemnly denounced Orangeism from the Bench, the King has called upon its factious bands to disperse, the people's representatives have denounced it in the House of Commons, the public authorities have, by royal order, intimated that any civil officer of the government connected with an Orange Society shall be instantly cashiered, and the Commander-in-Chief has announced His Majesty's directions, at the head of every regiment in the service, that any soldier who shall dare to enter an Orange Lodge, will do so on pain of a Court Martial. How, then, comes it that the heads of the government here, trifling with the powers entrusted to them, are cherishing this public pest?

THE CONSTITUTION, 20 July 1836.

LOWER CANADA

We lay before our readers Lord Gosford's Speech to the Assembly of Lower Canada; their reply; the King's Answer to their petition of last year for the redress of Grievances; the Quebec Correspondence of the Vindicator, and a very brief sketch of the debates. Awaiting with deep anxiety the result of their important deliberations, we yield a willing and hearty support to the course they are adopting, and most earnestly pray that their success may be commensurated with the object for which they so nobly contend. The reply from Downing Street is a gross insult, and so they seem to understand it. THE CONSTITUTION, 4 October 1836.

RE-STATEMENT OF PRINCIPLES

Having promised to re-state, with plainness and candour, our political sentiments, as soon as the course taken by the people of Lower Canada should become known, we hasten to redeem our pledge.

We are personally of opinion, that the conduct of the executive towards the people of Upper and Lower Canada has been such as in effect to absolve them from an allegiance, the principle of which is reciprocal obligations not deadly injuries. But this extreme view is perhaps not taken by the majority of the people, nor do we, for the present, see the utility of further considering it.

Allowing, for the sake of argument, that the tie of allegiance remains unbroken, the reasonings of some of our correspondents over real or fictitious signatures, that the prices of grain, flour or other of our staple commodities are higher in the United States market than here, and that the regulations of trade are vexatious, are not proper grounds for urging a dissolution of the Union of the *Crown* of England with these Colonies. Nor would we recommend to Reformers that course of proceeding, although we will not hesitate to publish what can be said in favour of it.

In 1774, the 13 Colonies, now the United States, asserted the great principle that representation must accompany the power of imposing taxes upon them—that they neither were nor could be represented in the Parliament of England—and that to taxation by that Parliament they would not submit. Taxes laid on by their representative Assemblies, agreed to by the King, who as the head of the empire might be expected to guard against the imposition of duties which would prejudice the interests of other portions of his dominions, they were ready to pay. In the assertion of this principle, Lord Chatham and the Whigs fully concurred with them, but the British Legislature expended one hundred and forty millions, sterling, with the view of forcing them to submit to taxation without representation, and then declared them an independent nation.

Instructed in the principles of the Constitution by the example of America, the Irish nation insisted in 1778, for that freedom of Trade which was calculated to render the people happy and prosperous; and in October, 1779, being backed by the Irish Volunteers, a species of citizen soldiers, or national guard, composed almost exclusively of Presbyterians and other Protestants, their House of Commons refused to grant more than a six months' supply to the crown, and unanimously resolved that "nothing but a free trade could save the nation from impending ruin."

In the summer of 1780, at a convention of the Dublin Volunteers, the Duke of Leinster in the Chair, it was resolved:

"That the King, Lords, and Commons of Ireland only are competent to make laws binding upon the subjects of this realm; and we will not obey or give operation to any laws, save only those enacted by the King, Lords and Commons of Ireland, whose rights and privileges, jointly and severally, we are determined to support with our lives and fortunes."

The corrupt influence of England prevented their rotten borough Parliament from responding to these sentiments that year and in 1781. But in 1782, the Volunteers held a convention in which Lord Charlemont, and Flood and Grattan, were the leaders. It resolved:

"Resolved—That a claim of any body of men, other than the King, Lords, and Commons of Ireland, to make laws to bind this Kingdom, is unconstitutional, illegal and *a grievance*."

"Resolved—That the powers exercised by the Privy Council of both Kingdoms, under, or under colour of pretence of the law of Poynings, are unconstitutional, and *a grievance*."

"Resolved—That a mutiny bill, not limited, in point of duration, from Session to Session, is unconstitutional, and *a grievance*."

Bad as the Irish Parliament was, it now sympathized with the nation, and in 1783, American independence was assented to, and a bill passed in the English Legislature, "for removing and preventing all doubts which may have arisen concerning the exclusive rights of the parliament and courts of Ireland in matters of legislation and judicature." Thus was the independence of that nation established. £50,000 were then voted to Grattan for his services, and a period of unprecedented prosperity followed.

We contend, that the independence Ireland gained, we, of Upper Canada, of right, possess, and that it is the fault of the people themselves if they do not maintain that right.

Even Mr. Stephen, the successor of Lord Howick, and Law Counsel of the Colonies of England, admits our premises. In his evidence, given in 1828, before the Canada Committee, he says, "It is in vain to conceal the fact, that the Act of 1791, has established a monarchical government without securing any one means of authority or influence to the monarchical branch of it."—p. 245. And again, p. 246—"The Act of 1791, was, I think, in effect, an Act to create two new Republics upon the continent of North America. It contains no one effectual provision for supporting the monarchical power." And again, p. 244—"If you persevere in the present system, I fear it is but too evident that you are sowing the seeds of separation between the Canadas and this country."

We are of opinion, that the Acts of the Imperial Parliament, imposing excise and customs duties, external and internal taxation, and, in some cases, placing prohibitions on the trade of the Canadas, whether at Quebec, Toronto, or elsewhere, are illegal, unconstitutional, and ought to be resisted in our courts of law, and the questions they involve discussed, brought before juries, and the arguments laid before the people, to whose welfare they are of such vital importance.

We solemnly declare our conviction that the Act of the English Parliament, establishing and regulating the Canada Company, and empowering Justices of the Peace to fine and imprison without the appeal to a jury, is an unlawful usurpation of the rights of the people of Upper Canada, entirely illegal and unconstitutional, and that questions on it ought to be raised in our courts of law, the ablest counsel of the colony retained, and the whole arguments laid before the people.

We entertain the same sentiments relative to the Post Office Monopoly, and would advise an organized system of peaceful agitation, and the adoption of legal proceedings to obtain our rights. This course has never been tried, but, if persevered in, it would be abundantly successful.

The Irish Convention that declared a mutiny bill, not limited from session to session, unconstitutional and a grievance, were right, and the attempt to keep bands of armed men in this "republic," or "monarchy," as Mr. Stephen calls it, under the control of the King's Viceroy, and independent of the annual votes of the Legislature of the Province, we hold to be a grievance of the first magnitude and a fit subject for agitation. THE CONSTITUTION, 12 October 1836.

REBELLION

What means this word! The illustrious William Wallace, Scotland's bravest son, was executed as a traitor to the King of England. The noble Marquis of Argyle bled on the scaffold, in Edinburgh, having been condemned for high treason. The virtuous Lord William Russell, third son of the first Duke of Bedford, had his head severed from his body in Lincoln's Inn Fields in 1683—having been condemned as a traitor. Yet these distinguished men were neither traitors nor rebels. Their memories are held in grateful remembrance by the wise and the good in all countries. They resisted oppression to the death, because they loved their countrymen more than the honours which tyrants can bestow; and the youth of Britain as they read of their sufferings become more and more steeled against arbitrary power. The poet glows and gladdens at the recollection of the noble deeds of the patriots of other years; and the Caledonian's blood rises in his veins at the well known sounds of the lyre—

Scots wha hae wi' Wallace bled!

Look into Ireland—into the darkest pages of her interesting history—read the speech of Robert Emmet [*printed by W. L. M. in the same issue*], the warm-hearted defender of his country's rights. He, too, died the death of a traitor. Mark his words. "Oh, my country! had it been *personal* ambition that influenced me—had *it* been the soul of my actions, could I not, by my education and fortune, by the rank and consideration of my family, have placed myself amongst the proudest of your *oppressors*?"

Where do you think we found Emmet's dying words? In Kirkham's Elocution. The youth of America, in their ten thousand schools, are taught, by the crimes tyranny has perpetrated in Ireland, to beware of the John Beverley Robinsons and Lord Norburys whom arbitrary power hath honoured, and to cherish freedom as their country's proudest boast. THE CONSTITUTION, 19 October 1836.

JOHN ROLPH

Dr. Rolph is an extraordinary *public* man. His English connexions are of the tory and aristocratic order—he was educated at Cambridge—is an English Barrister, and holds his medical degree from the London College. Many years ago he returned to Canada, was returned to parliament, advocated the liberal cause for six sessions with unwearied zeal and unequalled ability—retired for a time into private life—and now, in difficult and troublesome times, again comes forward the same eloquent and consistent advocate of civil and religious liberty as when we first heard him address the electors of Middlesex in the brightest days of his friend Captain Mathews, now no more. His speech on the Clergy Reserve question occupies several columns of this paper, and contains a powerful argument against a temporal union of Church and State. Since we first embarked in political life many of the most promising public men of the Colony have veered about for worldly advantage to every point of the compass. Not so Dr. Rolph and Mr. Bidwell. They are as true to the best interests of the country as they were eloquent and zealous on its behalf, at their first entrance into life many years ago. Why should a good example have less influence than a bad one? THE CONSTITUTION, 28 December 1836.

TOWARDS AN EDUCATED DEMOCRACY

When I came before the people many years ago, in the capacity of a public Journalist, I began my career by recommending economy in the public expenditure. When you did me the honour, for the first and for the sixth time, to propose to your brother freeholders that I should represent their feelings, wishes and interests in successive Houses of Assembly, my first pledge was, *never to vote one farthing of supplies to the support of any Governor or Government who refused to acknowledge the authority of the legislature to extend over the whole public revenue raised from the industry of the people for the general welfare.* . . .

Had Earl Dalhousie and his employers taken my view of the question the financial affairs of the Canadas would not now be in a state of irremediable confusion. . . .

When the Irish and Canadian Patriot, Mr. Justice Thorpe was about to be crushed by the little York oligarchy, you stood bravely forward in his defence. Twenty-eight years have elapsed since yourself and the venerable Alexander Montgomery presided at the meeting of the Yonge Street farmers—and still "the family compact" sways the province. But the Dagon totters to its fall, and I hope you and I will be spared to see Freedom triumph.

Surely the present system cannot outlast the year we have now commenced! It is driving thousands of our most wealthy and intelligent inhabitants out of the country, and is ruinous to nineteen out of every twenty of the population. A close observation of its workings adds to my love of an educated democracy—to that we must come; and I rejoice that I am able to say and that truly that I owe no governor or government, British or Colonial, a single personal favour—I never asked for pension or for place—but from the period when I came before the public as a teacher of others, spoke as I thought, and always as free and independent as I do at

355

this day. (*From a letter to Joseph Shepard, Farmer, Yonge Street.*)
THE CONSTITUTION, 4 January 1837.

CRISIS IN LOWER CANADA

[*On 8 March the English House of Commons assented to resolutions reaffirming the responsibility of the colonial executive to the King and Parliament of Britain. Hume's speech on March 6 against this policy is reported at length in this same issue of* The Constitution. *The Resolutions may be read in* Lindsey, *vol. II, p. 9.*]

The secret is told at last.—The screens and councils and constitutions, the pledges and kingly declarations, the proclamations and acts of parliament and ministerial statements, to which the judge on the bench, the representative in the legislature, and the loyalist in his family circle referred as proofs that colonists were freemen are swept away in one instant by an almost unanimous resolution of the House of Commons of England, agreeing to rob, plunder, steal and defraud the people of Lower Canada of their money, the produce of taxation, to apply that money to purposes the people by their representatives would not consent to apply it, and to refuse them all substantial redress of the grievances under which they have so long and so patiently laboured. First, the parliament of England imposes taxes on the Canadians without their consent and in opposition to their solemn remonstrances; next, Lord Glenelg, keeps in authority a Council in Canada which taunts the people with their ignorance at the very time it tramples on their bills to provide for public education, and refuses their bills of supply because these bills provide that while the Chief Justice gets £1500 of their money as Chief, he should not get another £1000 as Speaker of the Council, and check other monstrous pluralities; and thirdly, the parliament of England resolves that the Chief of the Colonial Office may empower the governor of Canada to put his hand in the Treasury of Canada, rob it of its contents, and without consulting the colonial legislature, pay it in thousands and tens of thousands to the host of placemen, pluralists and sinecurists who have been impeached by the country as unworthy of trust, and are protected and upheld only by the Bayonets of the Garrison of Quebec and the terrors of civil war with a cruel and unsympathizing European power.

The resolves of the House of Commons may be opposed by the

people of England before they become a law, but they shew nevertheless the true character of the plausible villains who were enabled to ride into power by offering England a reform bill, who were kicked out of it again for offering to gag and coerce Ireland, and who screamed against Negro slavery in the West India Colonies while they were forging the fetter for the bondsman with a white skin in "conquered Canada." We thank God that he has given us the sense and feeling to despise and abhor the mercenary immoral wretches who, whether their names were Lord John Russell, Thomas Spring Rice, or Henry Labouchere, could degrade the legislature of our native land, and expose its rottenness and corruption, by proposing for its adoption, resolutions more suitable for the Meridian of Russia in its dealings with Poland, resolutions to barter the honour and good name of the United Kingdom for the purpose of giving temporary repose to the Whig government at the expense of British justice, resolutions to degrade and destroy the legislature of Lower Canada because a majority of its members (unlike those of Upper Canada) had refused to sell their brethren for a place or a sum of money!

We do firmly trust that that power who implanted in our minds a hatred of oppression and cruelty, who warmed the heart of Wallace to the deadly struggle for freedom, and upheld the noble Emmet when he offered life and its enjoyments as an illustrious sacrifice for the rights of his brethren, will turn the counsels of the unprincipled, wicked and deceitful men, who surround the King of England's throne, into foolishness; and we feel assured that the attempt now making to degrade and humble the Canadians, by those who were bound by every tie of honour and gratitude to have stood forward as the defenders of their rights, will, by the favour and good providence of that God who seeth the heart, redound to the advantage of the oppressed, and to the injury of those who pervert judgment. THE CONSTITUTION, 19 April 1837.

THE SITUATION IN LOWER CANADA

Will the Canadians declare Independence
and shoulder their Muskets?

This question is of deep interest to our readers, they are therefore entitled to our views upon it, and we now frankly submit them:

In our late numbers we have directed the public attention to the resolutions and proceedings of vast masses of the people, headed by their favourite leaders. These resolutions and proceedings had the sanction of many thousands of freeholders, were in general proposed by militia officers or other official persons, and proceeded from a population as gentle as lambs but as brave as lions.

That they have thrown Sir John Colborne and Lord Gosford into great alarm is evident from the royal proclamation of the 15th ult., by which the world is informed, that "certain of His Majesty's subjects in different parts of this Province, have recently held public meetings, and thereat adopted resolutions having for their object the resistance of the lawful authority of the King and Parliament, and the subversion of the laws"—that "at such meetings, evil disposed and designing men, the instigators thereof endeavoured to persuade His Majesty's subjects that they are absolved from their allegiance, that they can no longer depend on the parent state for justice and protection, and that they must seek for the same, when a convenient opportunity offers, by other means"—and that "representations have knowingly been made, for the purpose of inducing His Majesty's subjects to swerve from their allegiance, and of producing a belief that the Parliament of the United Kingdom has violated or intends to violate the just rights and privileges of His Majesty's subjects in this Province, and is about to adopt oppressive measures towards them."

The instructions lately given to the officers in command at Montreal and Quebec, are evidently in accordance with the spirit of terror and dismay, which dictated the proclamation. But these are minor signs.

The following paragraph is far more clear to our understanding. It is from the pen of the member for Yamaska, Editor of the Vindicator, an active, warm-hearted Irishman, whose journal is the English official organ of the feelings and wishes of the Canadians; and in these words:

"It gives us great pleasure to learn that the Hon. Mr. Papineau experienced the most cordial reception on his arrival to attend the meeting of the Counties of Bellechasse and L'Islet, about 25 miles below Quebec. The people turned out in large numbers, not with colours nor flags, but with something more significant—*with muskets*. We are happy to learn that the people are thus exhibiting a proper sense of their situation. From England they have nothing to expect but insult and robbery."

Two or three thousand Canadians meeting within 25 miles of the fortress of Quebec, in defiance of the proclamation we have quoted, with *muskets* on their shoulders, and the Speaker of the House of Commons at their head, to pass resolutions declaratory of their abhorrence of British Colonial Tyranny, and their determination to resist and throw it off, is a sign not easily misunderstood. THE CONSTITUTION, 5 July 1837.

THOMAS PAINE'S "COMMON SENSE"

We have commenced the publication of an edition of twelve hundred copies of the far famed political publication, "Common Sense," a pamphlet which has received more praise and more abuse than almost any other similar work in our language. It has passed through upwards of two hundred editions in Europe alone; it has been condemned by kings, courts, parliaments, judges and juries; it has been praised by peers and peasants—Fox, Sheridan, Erskine, Mackintosh, Lord Grey in his youth, Pitt before he took office, Horne Tooke, Major Cartwright, The Duke of Richmond, the celebrated Muir, Lord Jeffrey, La Fayette, and many other distinguished men in Europe, greatly admired it—its effect in America is recorded in the annals of the world.

Unlike other political works of its day, it studiously avoids personalities, adhering closely to principle throughout. The author, although afterwards led away by the example of French Philosophy, expresses himself throughout with the most reverential deference for the scriptures of truth, and the revelations of Christianity, and the Editor of this Journal respectfully recommends to those of his readers who have the means to spare, to purchase "Common Sense" by the score or dozen and circulate copies in their several localities, as an antidote to the high church doctrines of the pensioned clergy of the Church of England, and as a ground-work for the contemplations of the people on the question of government and a written constitution.

We have departed from our original design so far as to use a large type, which increases the expense. The price will be one dollar per dozen, or 7½d for a single copy. Copious extracts will be given in this newspaper [*see issues of 19 and 26 July, 2 and 9 Aug.*]; and it is hoped that in this day of unexampled difficulty, calm appeals to the "Common Sense" of the farmers, merchants, and labourers of

Upper Canada will not be without beneficial effects. [*It seems probable that* Common Sense *was not published by Mackenzie in pamphlet form.*] THE CONSTITUTION, 19 July 1837.

POLITICAL UNIONS

The Corresponding Secretary acknowledges the receipt of several lists and certificates, in duplicate, of the formation of auxiliary unions, in most cases filled up with the complement of 40 members, while in others the lists are to be completed after seed time. The Caledon list has been ten days in our possession, and the Whitchurch list was accompanied by several resolutions this day published. The Whitchurch example is an excellent one. Let the associations meet and express public opinion in their respective neighbourhoods; let them investigate matters of general interest, and consider what ought to be done for their prosperity. The Whitchurch union has advanced in knowledge so far as to conclude that it would be better for the country if our fellow citizens could manufacture carriages for our governors. Perhaps they will take one step more, and open their eyes to the important truth that Upper Canada will never prosper till the people can manufacture their governors, without having to borrow them from the other end of the world, and send them off again as well loaded with wealth as Sinbad the Sailor was when the bird mistook him for a piece of meat and flew off with him out of the valley of diamonds.

As to manufacturing coats for Assemblymen, the writer of this article wears a dress, the coat, vest, and trousers of which were made in Toronto from cloth spun, dyed and wove by Mr. Eli Gorham at his cloth factory in Newmarket, and if Mr. Gorham would select a store in this city, and advertise his home made cloth to be sold there, he would not want for cash customers. Even "the hard stoney hearts" of some of the Orange or Cromwellian Irish are beginning to warm to the country of their adoption. America has been a home to millions of their countrymen, and we meet, even among them, some steady friends of home made cloth and Canada Manufactures. Perhaps the time is at hand when the others will see their true interests better—now that the Catholic Bishop of Kingston and more than half the Catholic Clergy of Lower Canada, Bishops and all, are vehement anti-reformers, and loudly bawling with one voice that it is to put down popery (or their snug pensions) that the reformers are working! Unfortunate Reformers! like the quakers of old, they are persecuted for their principles, by orange priests on one side, while the catholic bishop of Kingston takes £600 a year for crying "mad dog" on the other.

One of the letters with Union lists requests the names of the 40 members to be published. This might be injudicious.—The members may publish their names themselves, but we will not do so, for in many cases it would expose good and true reformers to the malicious shafts of the worst of the tories, especially the tory lawyers, merchants, justices, and requests commissioners, who have the power to act very vindictively, and often feel disposed to use that power improperly.

These Unions of 12 to 40 are of immense value to the cause of reform—they may enable the reformers to *find each other* when wanted—they may enable them to act together for a common purpose if required. There were seven orange lodges assembled at Churchville, all organized to do the devil's work—the Unions, when they become general, will oblige all such violent bodies to be peaceable.

The cry hath hitherto been—"Get a good House of Assembly." It is a false cry. You may vote in fifty reform parliaments as you please, but until the great body of the people have considered and decided, in their Unions and town meetings, what measures ought to be carried to insure the promotion of the general welfare, and until they have determined that these measures shall be carried, what can a House of Assembly do, even if it be a reform one? When Dr. Rolph, Mr. Peter Robinson, Mr. Wells, Mr. Markland, Mr. Dunn, and Mr. Baldwin, were the executive council, chosen out of respect to public opinion, Sir F. Head insulted them so far as to act entirely without their advice, and when they remonstrated, he (like the orange duke of Cumberland, now the tyrant of Hanover) upset the constitution so called, declared that his mere will should select and keep in, or turn out of office any councillors he pleased, and that he would be controlled by no one in Canada. The Assembly of that day took part with the six Executive Councillors—Sir Francis pretended that the country would be ruined for want of Supplies, because a few useless pensions and double salaries were not voted, made out about 5000 new deeds, greased the wheels of the priesthood, both catholic and protestant, and sounded the tocsin far and near about invasion! "come if ye dare!", "my reforms", and "the supplies." He succeeded. But if the people had had a hundred political societies of 10 to 30 or 40, *acting in unison*, like the Irish

Volunteers of 1784, he would have been obliged to knock under, and the placemen and magistrates would have been compelled to account for their stewardship to those who pay them, through the medium of a responsible executive.

Agitation! agitation! agitation! then, ought to be your watch-word; and when the great questions on which the prosperity of the country rests are temperately discussed and fully understood out of doors, there will be no difficulty in making any Governor or any Assembly respect the public will truly and solemnly expressed.

It cannot be too often repeated, that Britain has no power here if opinion be concentrated against the measures of her agents. We are far from the Sea—for five months our shores are ice-bound; the great republic is on one side of us; the Lower Canadians on another; Michigan, and the wilderness, and lakes, are to the west and north of us. The whole *physical* power of the government, the mud garrison, red-coats and all, is not equal to that of the young men of one of our largest townships. But so long as opinion is on its side, or wavering, the government wields indeed a gigantic power, the nature and extent of which will form the groundwork of another article. Our object is to oblige all who wield the power of the people, to do so for the common good of the country. THE CONSTITUTION, 13 September 1837.

SLAUGHTER OF NEGROES AT NIAGARA

We have been informed that the town of Niagara was much disturbed on Friday last, in consequence of an order having arrived there from His Excellency the Lieut. Governor to the Sheriff, to give up a coloured man of the name of Moseby to the authorities from the State of Kentucky, who, it is said, effected his escape from thence in April last; and as they could not claim him as a slave, they procured an order from the authorities of that state to Sir Francis Head to surrender him as a horse-thief.

The Deputy Sheriff, accompanied by a number of constables and soldiers, proceeded to carry the peremptory orders of His Excellency into effect, and to deliver the unfortunate man up to the authorities, when a numerous body of coloured people appeared apparently to prevent the execution of the order.

As soon as Moseby was taken outside the gaol gate, we are informed he disengaged himself from his irons, and jumping from the waggon in which he was placed, escaped, when the deputy Sheriff ordered the soldiers and constables to fire, and the result was that two coloured men were shot dead and several wounded. THE CONSTITUTION, 20 September 1837.

.   .   .

Moseby was doomed by law to perpetual slavery in Kentucky—his master might buy and sell and torture him, not because he was a criminal, but because his complexion was dark! Moseby sighed after liberty, and they say he mounted his tyrant's horse, and sought a home and freedom in Upper Canada. This is his crime with Sir Francis!

Moseby's master sought him here, applied to a kindred spirit in Sir F. B. Head, for authority to take him back. The benevolent people of Niagara prayed that he might not be sent back to meet, no doubt, a terrible fate, as an example to others, the sons of African misery. Sir Francis received both applications, ordered the slave back to Kentucky. . . . The Niagara Sheriff got the inhuman order, did his utmost to fulfil it, but the citizens would not assist him; they were horror-struck.

.   .   .

Sir Francis . . . has decided that for a slave whose forefathers were dragged from Africa, put in irons, placed under the cruel lash of the Negro drivers, and perhaps whipped or worked to death—that for this slave to mount a horse and seek his liberty in Canada is a dreadful crime! That the brave young slave is a felon! a guilty felon! and that he must be sent back to Kentucky, a place where those of his colour are looked on as being on a level with the beasts of burden. If this be guilt, then would we be guilty of a like offence, if under the circumstances Moseby was placed in. [*The two men killed while helping Moseby to escape were Herbert Holmes and Jacob Green. See the report of the Coroner's Inquest in the* Constitution, *4 October 1837.*] THE CONSTITUTION, 27 September 1837.

THE LAST CHANCE

We see by the last *Patriot* that the government apprehend that an attempt will be made "by the rebelliously disposed," to take the city of Toronto. Only a few months ago the governor assured the British authorities that his system was very popular—now he thinks of martial law, arrests, captures, and violence, and speaks of putting down the disaffected. He clings to arbitrary power as a safeguard; and, guided by the fearful and spiteful renegade Sullivan, plans and schemes many foolish things. One course yet he might take, and thereby avert much evil—he might dissolve the Assembly, call a free parliament, omit his inflammatory addresses of last year, and simply tell the freeholders that if it should be their wish through their representatives he would agree to regulate our local affairs, dismissals, and appointments, by and with the advice of an executive council possessed of the public confidence. Moderate men would see in this, the fulfilment of Simcoe's promise to give us the British Constitution, as far as a colony can have it, and he would neither need to act the tyrant nor the coward—his government of force would be changed for a government resting on opinion. Such a course all parties would advise, if they dared, but we have no hope of Sir Francis. He has roused the minds of the people in every district in the colony, and in two short years become more generally disliked than all the governors who were before him. THE CONSTITUTION, 8 November 1837.

PROVINCIAL CONVENTION

The Convention appointed to meet this winter for the purpose of taking into consideration the state of the country, will hold its first sitting in Toronto City at Ten o'clock in the forenoon of Thursday the 21st of December next.

W. L. MACKENZIE

Corresponding Sec. Central Union.

THE CONSTITUTION, 29 November 1837.

BIOGRAPHICAL NOTES

Baldwin, Robert, 1804-58

Son of Dr. W. W. Baldwin (see below). Born and educated at York, Upper Canada. Called to the bar 1825. August 1828 served on the committee to protest the dismissal of Willis (see below). Member of Assembly 1829-30. February 1836 appointed by Head to the Executive Council. Resigned with the whole Council in March of the same year to protest Head's high-handed failure to consult it. Went to England with a memorandum to the Colonial Office on responsible government. Refused an audience by Glenelg. December 1837 attempted, without success, to mediate between Head and the rebel forces. In 1838 was chief counsel for the defence in many treason trials. Continued to work for responsible government. In 1840 became Solicitor-General. In 1842, with Lafontaine, headed the administration, and in the second Baldwin-Lafontaine government of 1848 was instrumental in achieving responsible government.

Baldwin, W. W., 1775-1844

Came from Scotland to York, Upper Canada, 1798, and practised both law and medicine. Member of the Law Society 1801; a governor of the same 1807, and Treasurer 1811-1814, 1824-1829 and 1832. In 1802 established a small school for boys in York. Member of the Medical Board of Upper Canada 1821, and Vice-President for life 1832. (The Medical Board was founded in 1818. Its main functions were to examine candidates for certificates to practise in the Province, and to decide on military pensions.) Member of Assembly 1824. President of the newly-founded Mechanics' Institute of York 1831; Magistrate in the town of York 1833. An active member of the Alliance Society 1836, and President of the Toronto Political Union. A leader in organizing the Reform movement, in the defence of Willis and in the voicing of popular grievances through petitions. In 1837 withdrew from active participation; his name is no longer found on appeals and declarations.

Bidwell, Marshall Spring, 1799-1872

Came to Upper Canada from Massachusetts as a boy. Practised law at Kingston. Member of Assembly 1825-1836, and twice, with strong support of Mackenzie, elected Speaker. In 1836, after the resignation of the Executive Council (see under Baldwin, Robert), signed an address to the King from the House, charging Head with tyranny and deceit. December 1837 asked by Head to act as mediator with the rebels, but refused. After the collapse of the rebellion was "advised" by Head to leave the country. Returned to the United States and possibly joined Mackenzie in Navy Island. Later helped in pleas for pardon of the rebels banished to Van Diemen's Land.

Boulton, Henry John, 1790-1870

Came to Upper Canada from England as a child. Returned to England for his education. 1816 began to practise law at York, Upper Canada. Solicitor-General 1818. Attorney-General 1829. Member of Assembly 1830, 1841-4, 1848-51. Connected by marriage with the Jones, Robinson, and Sherwood families. In the session of 1830-1 opposed Mackenzie on questions of chaplain to the House, publication of Bank reports, distribution of House Journals, power of the Executive. From 1830 to 1833 led attacks on Mackenzie and pressed for his expulsion from the House. His criticism of the Colonial Office for listening to Mackenzie led to his dismissal and transfer to Newfoundland in 1833. Dismissed from office there and returned to Toronto 1838.

Buell, A. N.

Of Brockville. Probably related to a William Buell of the same district, elected Member of Assembly for Leeds County 1830. William was a regular supporter of the Reformers with his votes in the House. (See Lindsey, vol. i, pp. 185, 213, 217, etc.)

Gourlay, Robert, 1778-1863

A Scot who came to Upper Canada 1817 to study conditions in the Province. Issued a questionnaire to landowners, suggesting that they consult with others in their townships before filling in their answers. Township meetings followed and representatives were sent to a Provincial Convention at York. Published a second address to landowners in the Niagara *Spectator*. Arrested for seditious libel and acquitted; re-arrested and ordered to leave the country, which he refused to do; re-arrested and jailed at Niagara, and finally banished in 1820. Continued to keep in touch with Canadian affairs and corresponded with Mackenzie, who printed many news items about him, and letters and speeches by him. His *Statistical Account of Upper Canada* was published in Scotland 1822.

Jones, Charles

Of Brockville. Merchant and landowner. Mentioned by Mackenzie in his *Almanack* 1834 as one of the Family Compact. Brother of Judge Jonas Jones who presided over many of the treason trials in 1838. Connected by marriage with the Robinsons. Member of Assembly for Leeds County 1821-9. Listed by Mackenzie in his *Sketches* 1833 (p. 406) as member for life of the Legislative Council and Justice of the Peace in twenty-seven counties. The family gave its name to Jones Falls on the Rideau.

Ketchum, Jesse, 1782-1867

After a childhood of hardship in New York State, ran away and came by foot and by boat to York, via Oswego and Kingston. One of a United Empire Loyalist family, some of whom had preceded him. Joined his brother, a farmer near York Mills. On his marriage in 1804 moved to a house near what was until recently Jesse Ketchum Avenue. In 1812, bought a tannery in York, which was wrecked by American troops while Jesse was serving in the York militia. In 1817, one of three Trustees of the first Common School at York. Fought on behalf of Thomas Appleton, headmaster, against Archdeacon Strachan, who turned the school into a National Church of England school. Began the practice of visiting the school regularly. In 1828 entered the Legislative Assembly, after his energetic work on the Central Committee against the establishment of the Church of England and against the Aliens Act. Active in founding the Mechanics' Institute in York. In 1834 was largely responsible for the formation of the Canadian Alliance Society, and collected much evidence for the *Seventh Report on Grievances*. Led the opposition to Head on the question of responsible government. In 1845 moved his business to Buffalo, joining his son who had escaped arrest after the rebellion. Continued his close contacts with school children, visiting every classroom each year. Acted on a relief committee during the cholera epidemic of 1849, and on a committee for helping the families of enlisted men during the Civil War. Was for his day a model employer in his tannery. Kept up relations with Toronto, and in 1856 gave the site for the school and park on Davenport Road which bear his name.

BIOGRAPHICAL NOTES

McNab, Allan N., 1798-1862

Born at Niagara, Upper Canada. Practised law at Hamilton. Member of Assembly 1830, 1841-57. Proposed, seconded or spoke in favour of all motions for the expulsion of Mackenzie from the House. Opposed Mackenzie's motion for investigation into alleged malpractices during Streetsville election of 1836. Was one of committee of five to defend Head against Duncombe's charges of interference in election. At the time of the rebellion was in command of a militia unit in defence of Toronto. In 1838 put down resistance of the rebels along the shore of Lake Erie. In command of militia at Chippewa opposite Navy Island. Responsible for burning of the *Caroline*, for which he was knighted. Led the conservative opposition in the House 1841-57.

Morrison, T. D., 1796-1856

Born at Quebec, Lower Canada. In 1817 on Board of Trustees (with Ketchum) of the first Common School at York. In 1824 licensed to practise medicine. In 1827 secretary at meeting opposing Strachan's efforts to establish Church of England. Permanent secretary of the Central Committee. Fought Aliens Bill which would declare anyone who had lived at any time in the United States since 1783 an alien. Member of Assembly 1834. On the central board of the Canadian Alliance 1834. Alderman 1834; Mayor of Toronto 1836. Active member of Toronto Board of Health 1835; President 1836. Arrested December 1837 and charged with high treason. Acquitted June 1838. Went to the United States, and returned to Toronto 1843. Resumed his practice and lectured in Toronto School of Medicine.

Neilson, John, 1776-1848

Came to Lower Canada from Scotland as a young man. Worked as a printer, and became publisher and editor of the Quebec *Gazette* in 1793. Handed it over to his son Samuel in 1822, and took it over again on his son's death in 1832. (From 1822 there were two *Gazettes* in Quebec: the Old, or independent, edited by the Neilsons, and the New, or authorized, edited by John Charlton Fisher.) For years worked closely with Papineau in the Provincial Assembly, of which he was a Member 1818-34, and through his newspaper. In 1822 went to London with Papineau to oppose the suggested union of the two Provinces. In 1828 was again in England, with Viger and Cuvillier, with a petition on grievances from Lower Canada. Before the end of 1833 had come to differ from Papineau. Believed in the possibility of reform within the existing constitutional framework. On this issue was defeated in the 1834 election. Withdrew from the Reform movement and in 1837 was appointed to the Legislative Council of Lower Canada.

Robinson, John Beverley, 1791-1863

Born in Lower Canada; educated at Kingston and Cornwall under John Strachan (see below). Brother of Peter who was Commissioner of Crown Lands 1827-36. Related by marriage to the Jones, Boulton, and Sherwood families. Solicitor-General 1814, Attorney-General 1818. Member of Assembly 1821-9. Chief Justice 1829. Saw the danger in Gourlay's encouragement of popular discontent and took action to arrest him on charge of seditious libel. Was consistent supporter of government by the executive and opposer of all demands for redress of grievances. After the rebellion, retired from politics. Presided over many of the treason trials of 1838.

Rolph, John, 1793-1870

Came to Upper Canada from England in 1812. Returned to England where he graduated in both law and medicine. School trustee 1823. Member of Assembly 1824-30, 1836-7. Practised medicine and lectured to students at York, and attempted, with Charles Duncombe, to establish a medical school at St. Thomas. In 1831 Vice-President of Mechanics' Institute. In 1832 member of the Medical Board of Upper Canada. Consistent supporter of Reform movement. In 1836 appointed by Head to Executive Council, but resigned with all the others in protest against Head's autocratic actions. In 1838 indicted for high treason for his part in the rebellion. Escaped to Rochester, where he practised medicine until his return to Toronto in 1843. Continued to practise and to teach, and founded "Rolph's School," which became the Toronto School of Medicine in 1848, and the Medical Department of Victoria University in 1870. In 1851 member of the Hincks government. Resigned from Deanship of Medical Department shortly before his death in 1870.

Shepard, Joseph, ?-1837

Farmer and landowner at the corner of Yonge Street and what is now Sheppard Avenue. One of Mackenzie's closest friends who died a few months before the rebellion. Gave the site for York

Mills Church. His sons took a prominent part in the rebellion. Four yeomen of his name were arrested; two, transported for life, escaped from Fort Henry; two others were held in jail for six months. Member of the Central Committee in 1827, and of the committee organizing the petition to London in 1831.

Strachan, Archdeacon John, 1776-1867

Came to Kingston from Scotland 1799. Opened the Cornwall grammar school 1803. Ordained priest in the Church of England 1804. Head of the York grammar school 1812. On the Executive Council 1818-36. On the Legislative Council 1820-41. Archdeacon of York 1825. Bishop of Toronto 1839. A consistent upholder of Church and State, and champion of the right and duty of the Church of England to be sole disposer of the clergy reserves, and to control education. Opposed immigration from the United States because of the danger of republican influence. Opposed Gourlay's investigations in 1818. In his Chart of 1825 claimed undisputed supremacy of Church of England. His statistics in the Chart on relative strength of the churches disproved by the Central Committee, who were later upheld by Durham. In the founding of King's College, and later Trinity University, did all he could to keep higher education closely linked with the Church of England.

Thorpe, Robert

An Irishman appointed Puisne Judge of the Court of King's Bench in Upper Canada 1805. Quickly came to understand and sympathize with the grievances of the farmers and was elected Member of Assembly in 1807. Took a stand against the executive in favour of greater powers for the elected Assembly. In 1807 dismissed from the Bench by Lieutenant-Governor Gore and sent to Sierra Leone as Chief Justice, from which post he was dismissed for his popular sympathies.

Willis, John Walpole, 1793-1877

An Englishman, appointed Judge in Equity of the Court of King's Bench in Upper Canada 1827. Dismissed June 1828 on a technical point. Was a supporter of the Reform movement and his dismissal was protested by a large meeting at York addressed by prominent Reformers, including Mackenzie. In 1850 author of *On the Government of the British Colonies*.

BIOGRAPHICAL NOTES

Randal Wixon (or Wixson)
Described variously by Lindsey as yeoman, schoolmaster and Baptist minister. (A picture of him is to be found in Lindsey's *Life*, vol. ii, p. 252, the sixth in the group.) Became deputy-editor of the *Colonial Advocate* when Mackenzie went to England in 1832. Arrested after the rebellion and possibly saved from execution by the efforts of Mrs. Wait on behalf of her husband. With others, sentenced to exile in Van Diemen's Land. During months in prison at Kingston and Fort Henry he and his friends kept up the spirits of the group by study and entertainment. They were held for months in England until their release in July 1839, when they returned to Canada. Six others of the name of Wixon were arrested after the rebellion. Two of them, Asa and Joel, were banished.

For further information readers are referred to *The Lives and Times of the Patriots* by E. C. Guillet; *Movements of Political Protest in Canada* by S. D. Clark; *The Medical Profession in Upper Canada* by William Canniff; *Jesse Ketchum and His Times* by E. J. Hathaway; *The Firebrand* by William Kilbourn; and *The Life and Times of William Lyon Mackenzie* by Charles Lindsey.

INDEX

INDEX

poses imprisonment for debt, 156, president of Bank of the People, 212, contacts with Lower Canada Reformers, 280, 284, 290, refuses nomination for Assembly, 305, 309, 317, his character, 354-5, on Executive Council for one month, 361, biography, 369
Rolph, Miss, 46
Romilly, Sir Samuel, 91
Rotten boroughs, 206, 312-14, 338, 352
Rousseau, J. J., 74
Russell, Peter, 32, 106, 272
Russell, Lord John, 357
Russell, Lord William, 353
Russia, 104, 154, 183
Ryerson, Edway, 46
Ryerson, Egerton, 12, 62, 340
Ryerson, George, 169, 199, 280, 307, 309, 321

Ste. Anne de la Pocatière, 97
St. Hyacinthe, 97
St. John, New Brunswick, 116, 121
St. Lawrence, 15, 196, improved navigation needed, 44, 49, 165, 179, 276, 300, 328, 344
St. Thomas, 20-8
Salt, 28, 198
Sandwich, 26, 63
Sawyer, Joseph, 45, 48
Scarboro' Township, 49, 57, 231-2, 246
Schoolmasters, 29, 83, 87, 216
Schools, 25, 28, 32-3, 37, 46-7, 64-6, 83-4, 94-100, 103, 277
Science: study and teaching of, 46, 66, 92-3, 95, 97, 105, 127-8, books and magazines dealing with, 92-3, 111-12, 119, 121, 131, progress of, 89, 90, of agriculture, 108-9, 127, of medicine, 129-30, of horticulture, 109, 127
Scientific societies, 92-3, 127-8
Scotland, 19, 41, 91, 128, 153-4, 170-2, 238, 264
Scotsman, 67, 135, 146, 162
Scott, Sir Walter, 107, 120, 175, 264-5
Servility, 80, 84, 242, 288-9, 298
Settlers, 22, 55, 59, poverty of, 19, 242, character of, 49, 328, life of, 124, appeals to, 175-205, 210-25,

petitions of, 230-46, 255-60, 318-23, reading for, 92-3, 127-8, 210-13, 275-7, and the banks, 53, 211-13
Shakespeare, 24
Shepard, Joseph, 225, 245, 355-6, biography, 369-70
Sheridan, Richard, 91, 359
Sherwood, Levius Peters, 151, 289
Shipping, 28 (see also Canals, Erie, Ontario, St. Lawrence)
Silver Creek, 26
Simcoe, John Graves, 241, 301, 364
Simcoe County, 56-7, 219, 231
Simcoe, Lake, 58
Sinecures, 179, 272, 288, 315, 356
Sissons, C. B., 12
Sketches of Canada and the United States, 11, 106
Slavery, 17, 33-4, 148, 163, 173, 291, 357, 362-3
Smith, Adam, 68, 234
Smuggling, 16-18, 28
Soil, 30, 59
South America, 192
Southey, Robert, 107
Spain, 164, 176, 183, 192
Stage coaches, 105, 233, 238, 309
Stanhope, Colonel, 161
Stanley, Edward, 143-4, 165-6, 282, 325, 326-30
Statistics of Upper Canada, 15, 190
Statute labour, 49, 230-9, 243
Statutes of Upper Canada, 210-11, 248-55
Stayner, Thomas Allen, 108, 143-4, 284, 326-30
Steam engine, 89, 90
Steamboats, 42-4, 55, 60, 105
Stevens, Mr., 54
Stewart, Dugald, 68, 89
Stewart, Rev. Dr., 25
Stormount County, 57-8
Strachan, Ven. John, 60, 65, 91, 93-4, 99, 101, 111, 151, 154, 168, 199, 250, 280, 281, 289, 316, 322, biography, 370
Streets of London, 158, 169
Streets of New York, 156
Streets of York, 35-6
Streetsville, 49
Stuart, James, 250, 316, 325
Suicide of apprentice, 122
Surveyors, 45, 53, 239
Sutherland, Daniel, 28, 114, 143
Sweden, 238